Antonio Rosmini Serbati

The origin of ideas

Antonio Rosmini Serbati

The origin of ideas

ISBN/EAN: 9783742861405

Manufactured in Europe, USA, Canada, Australia, Japa

Cover: Foto ©Thomas Meinert / pixelio.de

Manufactured and distributed by brebook publishing software (www.brebook.com)

Antonio Rosmini Serbati

The origin of ideas

THE

ORIGIN OF IDEAS

VOL. II.

THE

ORIGIN OF IDEAS

BY

ANTONIO ROSMINI SERBATI

TRANSLATED FROM THE FIFTH ITALIAN EDITION OF THE

NUOVO SAGGIO

SULL' ORIGINE DELLE IDEE

VOL. II.

LONDON

KEGAN PAUL, TRENCH, & CO., 1 PATERNOSTER SQUARE

1883

CONTENTS

CHAPTER III.

ORIGIN OF THE IDEA OF BEING.

PART II.

ORIGIN OF ALL IDEAS GENERALLY BY MEANS OF THE IDEA OF BEING.

CHAPTER I.

GIVEN THE IDEA OF BEING, THE ORIGIN OF THE OTHER IDEAS IS EXPLAINED BY ANALYSING THE ELEMENTS OF WHICH THEY ARE COMPOSED.

CHAPTER II.

ANOTHER WAY OF EXPLAINING THE ORIGIN OF ACQUIRED IDEAS, THAT IS, BY MEANS OF THE FORMATION OF HUMAN REASON.

CHAPTER III.

*A THIRD WAY OF EXPLAINING THE ORIGIN OF AC-
QUIRED IDEAS IN GENERAL, THAT IS, BY MEANS
OF THE FACULTIES WHICH PRODUCE THEM.*

CHAPTER IV.

*A FOURTH WAY OF EXPLAINING THE ORIGIN OF AC-
QUIRED IDEAS GENERALLY, THAT IS, BY MEANS OF
A SUMMARY CLASSIFICATION OF THEM.*

CHAPTER V.

THE INNATE IDEA OF BEING SOLVES THE GENERAL DIFFICULTY PRESENTED BY THE PROBLEM OF THE ORIGIN OF IDEAS.

PART III.

ORIGIN OF THE FIRST PRINCIPLES OF REASONING.

CHAPTER I.

CHAPTER II.

CHAPTER III.

CHAPTER IV.

PART IV.

ORIGIN OF PURE IDEAS, THAT IS TO SAY, OF THOSE IDEAS WHICH TAKE NOTHING FROM THE SENSE.

CHAPTER I.

*ORIGIN OF THE ELEMENTARY IDEAS, OR CONCEPTS OF
IDEAL BEING, WHICH ARE ASSUMED IN HUMAN
REASONINGS.*

CHAPTER II.

ORIGIN OF THE IDEA OF SUBSTANCE.

CHAPTER III.

*A FURTHER ELUCIDATION REGARDING THE IDEA
OF SUBSTANCE.*

CONTENTS OF THE SECOND VOLUME. xiii

CHAPTER IV.

ORIGIN OF THE IDEAS OF CAUSE AND EFFECT.

CHAPTER V.

A HINT ON THE ORIGIN OF THE IDEAS OF TRUTH, OF JUSTICE, AND OF BEAUTY . . . 212

PART V.

ORIGIN OF NON-PURE IDEAS, THAT IS, OF THOSE WHICH, FOR THEIR FORMATION, TAKE SOMETHING FROM THE SENSE.

CHAPTER I.

ORIGIN OF THE DISTINCTION BETWEEN THE IDEAS OF CORPOREAL AND SPIRITUAL SUBSTANCE.

CHAPTER IV.

ORIGIN OF THE IDEA OF OUR BODY BY MEANS OF THE MODIFICATIONS OF THE FUNDAMENTAL FEELING.

CHAPTER V.

CRITERION OF THE EXISTENCE OF BODIES.

CHAPTER VI.

ORIGIN OF THE IDEA OF TIME.

CHAPTER VII.

ORIGIN OF THE IDEA OF MOTION.

CHAPTER VIII.

ORIGIN OF THE IDEA OF SPACE.

CHAPTER IX.

 *ORIGIN OF THE IDEA OF BODIES BY MEANS OF THE
EXTRASUBJECTIVE PERCEPTION OF THE TOUCH.*

a 2

CHAPTER X.

THE PARTICULAR CRITERION OF THE EXISTENCE OF EXTERNAL BODIES.

CHAPTER XI.

DISTINCTION BETWEEN WHAT IS SUBJECTIVE AND WHAT IS EXTRASUBJECTIVE IN EXTERNAL SENSATIONS.

CHAPTER XVI.

*ON THE NATURAL DIFFERENCES BETWEEN SENSI-
TIVELY PERCEIVING OUR BODY AS CO-SENTIENT
WITH OURSELVES, AND SENSITIVELY PERCEIVING
IT AS A FORCE ACTING EXTERNALLY ON US.*

PART VI.

CONCLUSION.

CHAPTER I.

CHAPTER II.

CHAPTER III.

SECTION V.

THEORY ON THE ORIGIN OF IDEAS.

Objectum intellectus est ens vel verum commune.—*S. Thom. S.* I. lv. 1.

385. So far, we have passed in review the principal systems on the Origin of Ideas, seeking for one which might give a satisfactory explanation of the matter, but in vain ; for we have found some faulty by defect, *i.e.* because they assume too little (Sec. III.), and others by excess, *i.e.* because they assume a great deal too much (Sec. IV.), of the innate in the human mind. We must, therefore, try to go deeper into this thorny question, and see if we can hit upon the golden mean ; admitting nothing innate of which the necessity is not proven, yet not allowing any prejudice against a harmless word to deter us from conceding that *minimum* of the *innate* which can be demonstrably shown to be an indispensable condition of the existence of our ideas (25–28).

But that we may know how much yet remains to be done, and in what way we must set about it, let us begin by taking a brief survey of the ground we have traversed.

I began, then, by pointing out as clearly and as completely as I could where lay precisely the knot of the difficulty presented by this question, in the following words : 'Those who say that all our ideas are acquired, must admit a certain order in the operations necessary for their formation. In this order, either *judgments* precede *ideas*, or ideas precede judgments; here there can be no middle course. But both these alternatives are equally impossible ; therefore it cannot be allowed that all our ideas are acquired' (41–45).

386. The Sensists and, in general, all those who pretend that all ideas without exception are of our own formation,

have never perceived the true nature of this difficulty ; and this is why they hold with such confidence to their opinion.

For just in proportion as the force of this difficulty is well seen and felt, are we compelled to give up the belief that all our ideas are acquired. The divergencies of philosophical schools as to the origin of human cognitions, arise solely from their not having seen, or not seen clearly, the said difficulty.

Yet even those who did not see the difficulty clearly and, so to say, full in the face, have at times caught glimpses of it, obscurely, and as it were sideways ; or if they did not see it at all, those of their readers who have eyes to see, detect it none the less in their reasonings, and, together with this, the fact that it is left there wholly unanswered.

Of this Locke is an instance. When describing the development of the sensitive faculty, he continually brings in judgments, unawares to himself, and therefore without thinking it at all necessary to explain whence they proceed, and how they are possible (112). So also in another place we find him laying it down that ideas are certainly anterior to judgments, without however examining or even suspecting the fact that the operation by which we form ideas is a judgment, and that this function of judgment must precede the ideas as cause goes before effect (68, 69).

But if Locke shows plainly in these passages that he had not in the least perceived the difficulty ; in other places a slight ray of light seems to have dawned upon him, as for instance where he observes that we can have no *knowledge* without a *judgment* (113, 114) ; and still more where he comes upon the idea of *substance*, and finds it such a stumbling-block that he is forced to confess that in his system it is inexplicable. Nevertheless his imperfect and partial view of the difficulty prevents him from feeling its importance ; so that after having said that all knowledge is preceded by a judgment, he does not draw out any of the consequences which flow from this ; and as for the troublesome idea of *substance*, he gets rid of it by declaring that it has no existence (48-62).

387. Sometimes philosophers have noticed this difficulty

(always under some particular form) in the reasonings of others, but not in their own. Condillac, for example, justly finds fault with Locke, because in explaining the operations of the sensitive faculty he introduces judgments without accounting for them (68, 69). But then Condillac himself, in order not to be harassed with this faculty of judgment, attributes it also to the senses; thus monstrously confounding together the principle that *feels*, with the principle that *judges* of the thing felt (70, 71).

On the other hand, Condillac does not observe the other error into which Locke had fallen, by supposing that we form ideas in the first instance without *judgments*. He therefore begins also with ideas, not perceiving that he is introducing judgments into their formation. Nor does his system explain in any way the origin of the *universality* of ideas; although this is an essential property of all ideas, and it would be impossible, without it, to form any judgment whatever (86–96).

388. Reid saw farther than Condillac. He saw quite plainly that Locke was maintaining an impossibility when declaring that ideas are formed first, and then, with their help, judgments; for we can form no idea without an act of judgment. He therefore laid it down that the first operation of our mind is, not an idea, but a judgment (115–117).— But how is it conceivable that we can form judgments without having ideas?—Reid answers that we make these judgments *instinctively*. But, in the first place, this is only an hypothesis, or rather a gratuitous assertion; and next, it in no way solves the difficulty. In fact, instinct cannot impel us to do the impossible, as it would be to form judgments while not having any ideas; for ideas are necessarily the means and elements of judgments. Instinct may explain well enough why I set myself to make use of my faculty of judgment, instead of allowing it to remain inoperative, but it can never explain the origin of the faculty itself. It cannot constitute in me this faculty; it can only set it in motion; and the faculty of judgment cannot be set in motion without

something on which to exercise itself, and without a rule to go by, in other words, without ideas (121–129).

Reid and his disciple Dugald Stewart, pushed hard by the difficulty which they saw, however imperfectly, went still further. The instinctive judgments, with whatever virtue they may be credited, can never produce ideas truly universal. What did these philosophers therefore do ? They took the short but desperate course of denying the existence of ideas altogether (104, 108, 160). This kind of Turkish justice inflicted on the unfortunate ideas, whose only guilt was that they did not reveal the secret of their origin, had been learned from Locke, who, as we have seen, had decreed that the idea of substance should no longer exist because it did not fit into his system.

None of these Ideologists, then, were so far shaken by the difficulty, as to persuade themselves that it was simply impossible to account for the production of all ideas through mere operations of our own mind ; and the reason of this was because they either did not see the difficulty or saw it only partially and obscurely.

389. But there were others possessed of greater penetration, who clearly perceived that ideas could not be formed simply by sensation and reflection, or more generally, by the operations of our own mind ; for they understood that these very operations could not be done without ideas. Amongst such we placed three rare and lofty intellects, Plato, Leibnitz and Kant (Sect. IV.).

All these great men were unanimous in holding 'That unless the human soul be admitted to have, as congenite and connatural with it, some intellectual element distinct from a bare and simple faculty, it could never begin to think, nor, consequently, form ideas.' Here is an opinion constantly and most firmly held by the most learned and deepest thinkers known.[1]

---

[1] France, which until lately knew only the philosophy of Condillac, was the country also of Des Cartes and of Malebranche, and to-day she looks with favour on the doctrines of the Alexandrian School. Germany, so laborious and so thoughtful, has agreed in acknowledging that it is impossible for all our ideas to be, in all their elements, factitious. And what shall we

390. But if we find a perfect agreement amongst the most acute thinkers on the negative side of this question, that is to say, on the impossibility of all our ideas being entirely of our own forming, when we come to the positive side, namely, to defining what is this necessary element which, being joined with our soul by nature, makes it capable of intellectual operations, we see those thinkers much divided in opinion.

Their differences arose from this, that some considered more of the innate element to be necessary than others. No doubt all those able men were well aware, that ' In explaining the facts of the human soul one must not assume more than is necessary to account for them.' But the difficulty was, how to find that *minimum* which, while on the one hand sufficient for explaining our ideas, had on the other nothing superfluous in it ; and philosophy advanced towards the right solution of the problem in proportion as it came nearer and nearer to this discovery, according to the indubitable principle we have laid down, that ' Of all complete explanations of the facts of the human soul, that which is simplest and requires fewest suppositions, is to be preferred ' (26–28).

In fact, among those philosophers who believed in the necessity of admitting an innate element in the soul in order to account for the formation of ideas, we noticed a progress ; the later ones seeking to remove the superfluous part allowed by their predecessors, and at the same time showing that, even with the ' innate ' so diminished, ideas could be produced (361, 362).

391. To come to particulars, Plato adopted the supposition that all ideas exist in us from the beginning, although in a dormant state, because he was unable to see any other way of explaining why a child, on being questioned, gives a true reply on many things which have never been taught him, and which

say of Italy? We must remember, that even before other nations began to lisp in philosophy, she was laying down the immovable basis of that doctrine which is called from her *Italic*—a doctrine wholly directed to explain the lofty and recondite nature of ideas, by demonstrating their infinite superiority to the senses and to man himself, and hence the impossibility of their proceeding either from the senses or from man. And in no period has this, our ancestral inheritance, been entirely forgotten, and let us hope that it never will be.

he nevertheless seems to know quite well. That child (argued the great Athenian) must always have had those ideas in his mind; only he was not giving them his attention, and by the interrogations now put to him, without however telling him how matters are, he is stimulated to attend to those truths which he knows unawares to himself, and therefore finds them without having learnt them from any one.

392. But Leibnitz perceived that this was too large an admission, and considered that the gradual formation of our ideas could be sufficiently explained if, instead of supposing them to be in us entire from the first, one said that we carried with us some very faint traces of them; even as a block of marble might be said to contain a statue if it had in it coloured veins in such a form as to exhibit, however slightly, the outlines of the statue (278, 279).

393. Kant, who came next, made a more accurate and searching analysis of our cognitions, and noticed that they are composed of two elements, the one supplied to us by means of the senses, and the other impossible to be so supplied. To the first he appropriately gave the name of *matter* of cognition; to the second the name of *form*. The first, he said, need not be supposed innate in us; but the second can only originate from within our own selves. Thus he did not make our ideas innate, either in themselves, as had been done by Plato, nor in their traces, as was done by Leibnitz. He only made one part of them innate, the *formal* part; so that according to him all our ideas are factitious, but not wholly so. This was a great step forward in philosophical science (324, 325).

394. But the process of simplification required to be carried still further; it remained to reduce to the *minimum* possible this *formal part* of our cognitions, which, as had been long known, must come, not from ourselves, but from nature—must be the germ planted in our souls by the Creator, that from it should be developed the vast tree of human knowledge.

Now, our fathers (*in Italy.* TR.) had seen that this element, essential to the existence of the intellective soul, could be but a very small thing, and they had said with as much elegance as truth of diction, that 'God in the act of creating our souls allows them to have a fugitive glimpse, so to speak, of the immense treasure of His eternal Wisdom.'[1]

395. The problem of philosophy which still remains after the efforts made by Kant consists, therefore, 'In determining the nature of that *minimum* of knowledge, or that *light* which renders the soul intelligent, and hence capable of intellectual operations.' Truly, this *minimum* is so slight that we could hardly compare it even to a little spark stolen from the sun in the heavens, it is only so much of truth as can be snatched by means of, as it were, a furtive and instantaneous glance.

Kant missed this *minimum* altogether. He made the formal part of our cognitions much more than it really is. Instead of starting from a principle perfectly one and simple, he tore up the formal part into many independent forms, two of which he gave, as we have seen, to the internal and external sense, four (each of them subdivided into three modes) to the understanding, and three to the reason (357, 358). He did not perceive that the sense, as such, has in it nothing appertaining to formal knowledge, and that all the forms attributed by him to the understanding and the reason are reducible to the one most simple form of *possibility*, or (which is the same thing) of *ideality*, and that from this, as from a little seed, all the others easily germinate, so that anything more would be superfluous. For, given this one form, it readily produces the

---

[1] This passage occurs in a classic work and one truly Italian, and may be read in the *Saggi di Naturali Esperienze fatte nell' Accademia del Cimento sotto la protezione del Serenissimo Principe Leopoldo di Toscana, e descritto dal Segretario di essa Accademia.—Firenze, nella nuova stamperia di Giovanni Filippo Cecchi*, 1691. And that we may the better understand how those men thought who were the teachers of Europe in the experimental art, and who so greatly aided the progress of physical science, I will quote the passage in full: 'Non è però, che la sovrana beneficenza di Dio, nell' atto ch' egli crea le nostre anime, per avventura non lasci loro così a un tratto dare un' occhiata, per così dire, all' immenso tesoro della sua eterna sapienza, ador-nandole, come di preziose gemme, de' primi lumi della verità : e ch' è sia 'l vero. noi lo veggiamo dalle notizie serbate in loro, che, non potendole aver apprese di quà, forz' è per dire ch' elle ce l' abbiano arrecate d' altronde' (*Proemio*). In which words of the Secretary of the Accademia of Cimento, if we leave aside the Platonic imagery, introduced simply for the sake of elegance of diction, and looking to the spirit of the doctrine, we see, (1) that our fathers were aware that there was a certain part of knowledge which could in no way be of our own forming, and must therefore have been given us by nature ; (2) that this could be only a most minute particle, such as might be obtained through a rapid glance, as it were, at the Eternal Wisdom.

rest, not indeed equal, but posterior and subordinate to it
(363–380).

From not having seen his way to this great simplification,
the philosopher of Königsburg suffered most grievously, for
he was thereby disabled from understanding the nature of the
one true form which is *objective*, transcendently high, independent of the soul itself, exempt from all modes, and
therefore from all danger of being counterfeited ; since that
which is not susceptible of a variety of modes cannot be
counterfeited.   Hence Kant was unable to give a solid basis
to science, to truth, and to human certainty (327–329, 379).

396. This I believe I have demonstrated. And it was my
duty to do so ; for, having engaged to take up the work of
previous philosophers from where they had left it, I was bound
in the first place to make the two truths established by them
my own, viz.:

1st. That the *formal part* of our cognitions must be distinguished from the *material part.*

2nd. That it is the formal part only that is given us by
nature.

With this valuable inheritance in my possession, the next
thing I had to do was, to inquire diligently into the nature of
this second part (the *formal*) which they had not succeeded
in discovering—so that I might determine it, and this so
accurately that nothing belonging to the first part (the *material*)
should be left mixed up with it ; and, moreover, in such a
manner that it should be made to stand out in its simplest
and primal character, and not in any of those modes which
it assumes through its various applications. This inquiry I
have endeavoured to make, and as a result I have found that
the formal part of our cognitions, in its primal and original
state, consists in one thing only, that is, in a natural and
abiding intuition of *possible being* [1] (363–380, 52–54, 115–120).

---

[1] *Possible being, Indeterminate being, Ideal being, Being* or *Existence
in general, Initia: being*, &c., are all one
and the same thing (the intelligible
Essence of being), but considered under
different aspects or relations.   See
Preface to first volume, n. 10–12 : also
n. 543 in this volume, where the Author
begins to analyse the idea of *possibility*
better than he had done before.—
TRANSLATORS.

397. Such then is the task which I have attempted in the first volume of this work. I have now to indicate briefly the object of the present volume :—

I propose to draw out in regular order that which I believe to be the true theory on the origin of ideas, beginning with the examination of the intuition of *possible being*. From what I have said, this intuition appears to be the most necessary, as well as the most important of all ideas, nay the only one deserving the name of idea ; and in it centres at last the whole difficulty which I have set before the reader in so many different ways.

None of the philosophers of the Sensist School have ever been able to explain satisfactorily the origin of this idea. It has always been the unlucky rock on which they foundered ; for all our intellectual operations (by which these philosophers pretend that all ideas without exception are produced) require this idea as a *sine qua non*, while on the other hand, given this idea, the mind can start on its work and prosecute it without impediment.

I could not, therefore, begin otherwise than by this singular idea. For so long as it remains unexplained, the others cannot be explained. Some intellectual act is necessary for their formation ; and every intellectual act supposes, as I have said, this very idea, and puts it continually in requisition.

If, then, I can succeed in giving a proper account of this idea, I shall have shown, as a matter of course, where we must look for the origin of all the principles of human cognitions, and of all other ideas or rather concepts, for by means of it they are all easily generated.

I shall therefore, in the first place, demonstrate that *being* is the light shining to our mind by nature: then I shall trace out the *first principles of reasoning*, which, as a diligent analysis will show, are only so many modes of applying the self-same idea of *being*, which immovably adheres to us. I shall thus have explained how it is that we are able to reason ; for the principle of cognition, the principle of contradiction, and the other first principles, are the instruments without which our mind cannot make a single step forward.

Having seen what it is that makes us *intelligent* and reasoning beings, it will not be difficult to show how we become the authors of our many conceptions, since these may readily be formed by the use of reasoning.

Amongst these, however, there are some which stand nearest to the fountain-head, namely, the *pure conceptions*, which contain nothing whatever of the sensible element, but flow direct from the primal and innate idea alone ; and they will come first.

Next I shall proceed to deduce the *non-pure* or *mixed conceptions*, which take more or less of *material* element from the senses.   Here I shall show in the first place, how the concepts of the two species of *substance*—the corporeal and the spiritual—are formed.

I shall then have occasion to unfold the origin of the concept of *body* : and as this presents itself to us in two modes, *i.e.* as *body animated* by our own soul and as *inanimate body*, so I shall begin by analysing the concept of our own body ; nor will it be possible to go on to the concept of *body* as external to ours, without stopping a little on the way to investigate the difficult concepts of *time, motion,* and *space,* which are necessary in order to formulate completely the concept of this kind of body, the analysis of which therefore will come in the last place.   Thus the whole of the present section will be divided as follows :—

Part I. Origin of the idea of being.

II. Origin of all conceptions generally by means of the idea of being.

III. Origin of the first principles of reasoning.

IV. Origin of *pure conceptions—i.e.* of those which contain nothing of the *sensible* element.

V. Origin of *non-pure* or *mixed* conceptions—*i.e.* of those which require for their formation something supplied by the sense.

VI. Conclusion.

PART I.

ORIGIN OF THE IDEA OF BEING.

CHAPTER I.

IT IS A FACT THAT WE THINK OF BEING IN GENERAL.

398. I start from a most obvious fact, the study of which, nevertheless, forms the whole of the theory I am about to expound.

This fact is, that we think of *being* in a general way. However we may explain it, the fact itself cannot be called in question.

To think of being in a general way is nothing but to think of that quality which is common to all things, without minding any of their other qualities, whether generic, specific, or proper. I can, if I wish, give my attention to one element of a thing rather than to another: now when I give my attention exclusively to that quality which is *common* to all things, namely, to *being*, it is then said that I think of *being in general.*

To deny that we can, if we wish, fix our attention on the being common to things, without noticing, or, to say better, by abstracting from, all their other qualities, would be to gainsay what is attested by the simplest observation on our interior operations, to contradict the common sense of mankind, to abjure language.

In fact, when we say in ordinary discourse: '*Reason* is proper to man ; he *feels* in common with the animals ; he *vegetates* in common with the plants ; but he has *being* in common with all things,' we consider the *common being* apart from all the rest. If we had not the power of considering *being* separately from everything else, a discourse of this kind would be impossible.

The fact to which I refer is so evident that to debate on it would seem a sheer loss of time, and the bare mention of it would be enough, were it not that the men of our times have striven to throw doubt on everything. Now this most evident and most simple fact is the basis on which the whole theory of the origin of ideas rests.

399. To think of being in general is equivalent to 'Having the notion or *idea* of being in general;' or at least the first supposes the second, since we could not think of *being* without having 'the idea of it.'

We must, then, trace out the origin of this idea. But that we may do so more easily, we will first investigate its nature and character.

CHAPTER II.

NATURE OF THE IDEA OF BEING.

ARTICLE I.

The pure idea of being is not any sensible image.

400. In order as far as possible to keep clear of all equivocal language, I wish to remark at the outset, that when I say that we can have the *idea of being*, by itself, and divested of all other ideas (394, 395), I do not mean to say that we can form a *sensible image* of *being*. It must be borne in mind that a sensible image cannot be formed except of a thing which is, 1st. determinate and individualized ; 2nd. corporeal and perceived by the senses.

401. Some modern writers have denied the existence of abstract or indeterminate ideas, for no other reason than because one cannot have sensible images of them.

This is a materialistic way of reasoning, and unknown to true philosophers. We must observe nature as it is, and loyally admit whatever we find there, although it may not be what our fancy supposes it ought to be. The nature of things is not a matter to be decided on arbitrary *a priori* laws. Had the writers of whom I speak observed the human mind with simplicity and without preconceived views, they would easily have seen that there are in it three distinct series of thoughts.

(1) Thoughts in the form of *indeterminate ideas*, *i.e.* regarding objects which cannot be represented under sensible images, nor really exist by themselves alone, though they can be *conceived* by themselves alone.

(2) Thoughts relating to spiritual beings which, although

possessed of all that is necessary for *subsisting*, yet cannot be represented under sensible images.

(3) Thoughts of bodies or of qualities of bodies which alone can be represented under sensible images.

The existence of these three classes of thoughts is a fact, and one which is independent of all philosophical systems : and those even who deny the real existence of *spiritual beings* are obliged to admit that we think of them ; for the question of the *real existence* of these beings is quite different from that of the concepts or *ideas* we have of them.

Therefore, arbitrarily to lay down the principle that 'What we cannot sensibly imagine cannot be an object of our thought ;' and thence to draw the consequence, that 'Therefore universal and abstract ideas have no existence,' is to follow a false method—to start from a prejudice, and pretend that facts shall bend to it—to dictate laws to nature, instead of listening to her depositions and interpreting them with wisdom.

ARTICLE II.

The idea of a thing must be distinguished from the judgment on its subsistence.

402. We must also distinguish the *idea* of a thing from the *judgment* on the *subsistence* of that thing. This distinction is of paramount importance in Ideology.

In order to be convinced that the simple *idea* is totally different from the judgment we make on the subsistence of a being, it suffices to observe that we may have in our mind the *idea* or *concept* perfect in every respect—*i.e.* such as will comprise in it all the qualities, essential as well as accidental, of that being—without at the same time *judging* or affirming that the being itself really exists.

Take, for instance, the idea or concept of a horse. I may have the idea not merely of a horse in general, but of one furnished with all those particulars which are necessary for its real existence—the jet coat, the short ears, the long mane, the delicately formed head, the arching neck, the eye of fire, the mouth white with foam, the shapely back, the well knit loins, the taper legs, in fact everything that belongs to the individual horse ; so that, had I creative power, I could call my mental horse into a real existence corresponding at all points with that which is in my idea as in its exemplar or type.

If, on the other hand, I had the power and the will to create a horse, but my concept was not as complete in all details as the horse I wished externally to produce, I should, as I go on with my work, have to stop and think of the parts which are still wanting in the concept ; for I could certainly express nothing externally, unless I had it first in my mind. Thus I should be improving my concept of the animal simultaneously with the external execution.

Suppose now that the horse, being at last perfect in design, were outwardly produced in full accordance with that design ; is it not true that this horse would be simply a copy of the one I have inwardly conceived and imagined ? Beyond all doubt, then, the real horse has had a dependance on my thought or concept.

403. Such being the case, I ask again : has my complete concept of the horse received anything from its real subsistence ? Certainly not ; for the concept must have been already perfect in every particular before the real horse could be produced ; otherwise it could not have served me as a pattern or exemplar in the operation.

404. This is clear to evidence, and from it we may get some light as to the nature of ideas. Ideas are independent (as regards their nature) of the actual subsistence of individuals ; so that they can be perfect before the individuals begin to subsist, nor does the subsistence of these make our idea or concept of them any better than it was before.

405. By considering this independence of ideas (so far as their nature is concerned ; for I do not as yet speak of their *origin*) we can understand that between having the *idea* or *concept* of a thing, and *judging* that the thing really exists, there is a wide difference.

Whether the thing subsists or not, whether or not we pass judgment in either sense, or pass no judgment at all, our idea, as I have said, is equally perfect and entire.

The *judgment*, therefore, on the subsistence of a thing supposes indeed the *idea*, but is not the *idea*, nor adds anything thereto. It simply creates in us a *persuasion* that the thing which we affirm to subsist, subsists. Now a *persuasion* is nothing but an *assent*—an operation altogether *sui generis*, and by no means to be confounded with an *idea*, which belongs to the order of *intuition*.

ARTICLE III.

The idea of a thing never includes the subsistence of that thing.

406. By the *subsistence* of a thing I mean its real and actual existence.

407. The proposition here enunciated is a corollary of the preceding article, in which it was laid down that the idea is essentially distinct from the judgment on the subsistence of things.

For, if the idea of a thing is perfect and complete, independently of the actual subsistence of that thing (399, 400), it follows that ideas are of no use for causing us to know that the things *subsist*; they only present those things to us as *possible*. The subsistence of things becomes known to us through another operation of our mind essentially different from the intuition of ideas. This operation is called *judgment*.[1]

ARTICLE IV.

In the idea of being we see nothing but simple possibility.

408. Wherefore by saying *idea of being* I do not mean the thought of some subsistent thing of which we do not know, or

---

[1] I shall have occasion to analyse the operation of judgment when I come to explain the origin of our idea of *body*. However, the observation I have made above on the distinction to be drawn between the *idea* of a thing and the *persuasion* of its subsistence, confirms what I have said (177) regarding the erroneousness of the doctrine of certain writers who maintain that ideas *lay hold* of and *involve* the subsistent things themselves, whereas the truth is that ideas shew us nothing but simple possibilities of things.

These writers confuse together two distinct truths. We really have a faculty which lays holds of and involves, so to speak, the subsistence of things, but this is not the *faculty of ideas*; it is the faculty of sense combined with the rational operation of *judgment*, which must be kept entirely distinct from the faculty of the intuition of ideas.

from which we abstract all the qualities save the one of actual subsistence, as would be the case with the quantities *x. y. z.* in Algebra.   Neither do I mean the judgment, or the persuasion of the subsistence of a being, although indeterminate.   I mean, purely and simply, a *possibility* seen by the mind.   This is, again, a corollary of the preceding article.

Potentiality is that which remains after we have made the last abstraction we can make on any being we think of. If we think of a subsistent being without knowing its qualities, we may still abstract something from it, namely, the *persuasion* of its subsistence, and there will yet remain the thought of that being in a potential state.

409. The most universal idea of all, which is, therefore, also the last of all abstractions, is *possible being*—expressed simply by the phrase *idea of being*.

ARTICLE V.

We can think of nothing without the idea of being. Demonstration of this.

410. Any one who considers this proposition ever so little must find it self-evident : nevertheless very few have given it the attention it deserves.

Modern philosophers, as I have before observed (50–57, 278–282), have contented themselves with analysing the *faculties* of the soul, and paid but little attention to the analysis of their *product, i.e.* the *human cognitions.* The latter analysis ought, on the contrary, to precede the former, because the faculties are known only by the effects they produce.

The inversion of this method is perhaps the principal cause of the errors of Locke, of Condillac, and in general of all that school which begins straightway by discoursing on the faculties, and from these descends to the cognitions.

To avoid the like errors, I have adopted an opposite course, endeavouring as best I could to ascend from the effect to the cause, from the cognitions to the faculties.

411. Now the analysis of our cognitions gives invariably

as its result, the proposition placed at the head of this article, namely, ' That we cannot think of anything whatever without the idea of being.' This idea is necessarily mixed up with every cognition, every thought.

Of all the common qualities of things, *being* (existence) is the most common and universal.

Take any object you please ; abstract from it in thought all the qualities that are proper to it ; then do the same with the common qualities, beginning with the less common and going on gradually until you arrive at the most common of all, namely, that beyond which nothing is left to be abstracted. You will find that this last quality is no other than *being* or *existence* ; and that, so long as this remains, your mind has still an object before it. It is true that you no longer think of the *mode* in which that object exists—of any of the determinations which distinguish it from other objects —nevertheless you still think of a something that exists or can exist, and therefore has all the qualities necessary to make it exist, although you do not know those qualities, or, at any rate, you do not think of them : and this, although wholly indeterminate, is still an idea.

If, on the contrary, after abstracting from a being all its other qualities, proper as well as common, you also take away the most universal of all, *i.e. beingness*, there remains nothing whatever before your mind, thought is simply extinguished, and you can no longer have any idea of that being. Let us take as an example the concrete idea of our friend Maurice. Let us remove from it every thing that is proper to his individual self ; we have no longer the idea of Maurice as our friend ; the part that was dearest to us is gone, and nothing is left but the common idea of a man. Let us proceed to abstract all the qualities proper to a man, and the object we have before our mind is not a man at all ; reason and free will—the characteristics of a *man*—are no longer there ; a more general idea has remained, the idea of an *animal.* Then, still going on, let us abstract the qualities proper to an animal, and there remains a body without sensitivity and with vegetative force only. After this, let us set aside all organization and vegetative force, and fix our mind only on that which this body has in common with the minerals, and we arrive at the idea of a body in general : but it is yet an idea. Let us, in the last place, abstract all that constitutes *body*, and all we now have is the idea of a being without any determinations. In all these abstractions, our mind has always been occupied with something. It has always thought, always had an object present to it, though seen in a form more and more universal, until it came to the most universal of all, *i.e.* that of a *being* pure and simple. To conceive this object as a being because it has *beingness*, is the last thing we can do. Beyond this it is impossible for abstraction to go without our losing all object of thought, or in other words, ceasing to think.

Therefore, the idea of being is the most universal of all ideas. It is what remains after the last abstraction possible ; and its removal puts an end to all thought and makes every other idea impossible.

ARTICLE VI.

For the intuition of the idea of being no other idea is required.

412. This proposition is the converse of the preceding ones, and follows naturally from what we have said thus far (406).

We have seen that if we take the idea of any thing whatever, and proceed as it were to anatomize it, we can remove those parts which are more special, and afterwards those which are less so ; then such as are more general ; and when we have taken away, so to speak, all the flesh, the last thing left, and, as I would almost say, the backbone of all those qualities which have been removed, is *being*, which must therefore be set down as the most abstract of all ideas, so that if this also is put aside, no other idea or thought can be had ; whereas, by itself alone, such as we have found it in virtue of the above abstractions, it suffices to form an object of thought. Therefore the idea of *being* has no need of any other in order to be known : it is knowable through itself.

This consequence is of the highest importance.

CHAPTER III.

ORIGIN OF THE IDEA OF BEING.

413. Having established the existence of the idea of being and learned its nature, let us see how it comes to be in our mind, or in other words what is its origin.

I shall first say whence it does *not* come, and then whence it *does* come.

ARTICLE I.

The idea of being does not come from corporeal sensations.

414. Thoroughly to grasp the truth of this proposition, it is necessary to consider the characteristics proper to the idea of being, and which are far removed from all that corporeal sensations can give us.

The fact of every one of these characteristics being inexplicable on the supposition that the idea of *being* comes from sensations, is proof unanswerable that it is not derived from them.

§ I.

FIRST DEMONSTRATION,

Drawn from the first element of the idea of being, and which constitutes its first characteristic—i.e. OBJECTIVITY.

415. When we think a being, whether particularised or not, we consider that being *in itself, i.e.* as it is.

Into such consideration there does not enter any relation whatever which that being has with us,[1] or with anything else : the consideration is absolute.

---

[1] Even though this our mode of conceiving things were only apparent, that is to say, even though what we consider as *existent in itself*, existed only relatively to us, the reasoning here made would not have less force. The

This way of perceiving things as they are in themselves, entirely apart from everything to which they might be related, is common to all that is conceivable by our mind. By this perception, we look at them, so to speak, impartially, as they are, with those degrees of entity which they possess. The thought we thus come to have of them may be expressed by the following formula : ' Such or such a thing (which I conceive) has such or such a degree or mode of being. *Being* is the one thing in which our concept terminates ; and this term to which the agent felt by our senses is related, is common alike to all things perceived, for we perceive and conceive them all as beings, as having such grade or mode of being as is indicated, for instance, by our senses.

416. Now I say, that none of our sensations can give us an *objective* perception such as here described. *Objectivity* belongs exclusively to the *intellectual* perception.

In truth, our sensations are nothing but so many modifications, or passions of our own composite nature ; even the thing felt by our senses does not, *as such*, exist, except relatively to us.

All, therefore, that our sensations cause us to feel can only be a relation which external things (supposing that they really exist, which is a point I do not as yet wish to discuss) have with us—a power they possess of modifying us. But the *suppositum* of this power could never be perceived by us as it is in itself, if we had nothing but sensations to draw upon : for, existence considered in itself does not fall under our senses. The two expressions, ' to exist in itself' and ' to be felt by us,' signify two opposite concepts, the *absolute* and the *relative*, each of which directly excludes the other.

question in that case would be as to how to account for this appearance. In a word, whether our perception be true or only apparent, the fact that we perceive things *objectively* must be explained. On the other hand, as I now speak only of the manner in which we perceive things, the distinction between the true and the apparent has no place here. About the manner of our conceiving, there can be no deception ; for, to say, I conceive the object in this way, is neither more nor less than to say I conceive as I conceive : *idem per idem*. Whether the external thing correspond to our conceptions of it or not, is a question I shall have to discuss later on. So much for any objection which might be raised against my present argument by the followers of Transcendental Idealism.

In fact, the mere existence of a thing in itself does not import or imply any sensation produced in another thing; while, on the other hand, the word *sensation* does not convey to the mind any concept or idea of a thing *existent in itself*, but only that of a passion of our own, and of the term of that passion.

Sensation, then, cannot cause us to perceive a thing as it is in itself, but only in relation to us. *Sensation* simply means a modification suffered by us ; *Idea* means *concept of a thing which exists* independently of any modification or passion of another thing.

Therefore the *idea of being* is in no way derived from sensations.

OBSERVATIONS.

On the differences between sensation, sense-perception, idea, and intellect-ual perception.

417. In order to prevent confusion in the use of terms, I shall here define *sensation, sense-perception, idea* and *intellectual perception.*

(1) *Sensation* is a modification of the sentient subject.

(2) *Sense-perception* is the sensation itself and, more generally, any kind of feeling considered in so far as united to a real term.

(3) *Idea* is being, indeterminate or determinate, considered in its possibility, or as an object of mental intuition.[1]

(4) *Intellectual perception* is the act by which our mind apprehends a particular *reality* (a 'sensible') as an object ; that is to say, sees it in the idea.

---

[1] In the work entitled *Il Rinnova-mento della Filosofia in Italia,* &c., which may be described as a commentary on the present work, Rosmini writes as follows : ' The word *Idea* is taken by writers in three significations: (1) to indicate the *intuitive act* of the spirit, terminating in a possible being ; (2) to indicate the *possible being itself* of which the spirit has intuition ; (3) to indicate both these things together. I often use it in the second of these meanings, where the context suffices to make it unambiguously understood ; but never in the first ' (L. II. c. iv. in the note). It will be seen by the context that in this place, besides a great many others throughout the present volume, the term *Idea* is taken in the *second* of the above meanings, *i.e.* as expressing the *object* of the intuitive act—the *intelligible essence* contemplated by the mind. The posthumous work, *La Teosofia,* contains a treatise on *possible* or *ideal being,* which the author has inscribed simply *The Idea* (L'IDEA). It will be well for the reader to take particular note of this.—TRANSLATORS.

The sensation therefore is *subjective*, the sense-perception is *extrasubjective*, the idea is *object*, and the intellectual perception is *objective*.

418. What makes it difficult for us to distinguish the *sensitive* from the *intellectual perception*, is the habit we, as rational beings, have of making the latter follow quickly upon the former ; so that owing to this their natural conjunction in us they seem to us to be one and the same thing, and in order to see that they are two we require the keenest attention.

419. Another reason of the extreme difficulty of distinguishing *sensations* from *ideas*, and forming an exact conception of the first without mixing up with it something belonging to the second, is this :—Whatever we know and reason about, must always be made known to us, through an intellectual perception, or an idea.   Consequently, respecting that of which we have no idea, we know nothing, and cannot therefore discourse on it either in our mind, or by external words.

Hence it is seen, that even as regards *sensation* itself, in order that we may be able to say that we know it—that we may bestow on it our consideration, and express by language the reflections which occur to us concerning it—we must have the idea, or the intellectual perception of it.   Wherefore sensation, taken by itself alone, apart from any idea, remains unintelligible, cannot be an object of our thoughts or of our reasonings.   Whenever therefore we wish to turn our attention on our sensations, so that we may reason about them, we must necessarily join to them an idea.

From this necessity of our thinking the sensations through an idea, arises the extreme difficulty of realizing to ourselves the need there is of separating from them the idea itself, in order that they may remain perfectly isolated, and that we may thus be able to understand what they really are by themselves alone.

420. So arduous an operation is particularly repugnant to our nature, because when we have isolated the sensation in this way, and separated from it the very idea through which we thought it, we find that it is no longer intelligible.

The same difficulty, though hardly ever noticed by any one, is met with as regards our cognition of material things, and of all those which—not being themselves *ideas*, and therefore, of themselves, dark, that is to say, unknown—have a mode of existence impossible to be cognised unless we join it with an idea.

421. Besides this disadvantage under which we labour in forming a genuine concept of bodies, and which is common to the concept of sensations also, there exists a particular drawback in respect of the latter concept.   It is as follows :—

When we have separated from the sensations the idea by which we conceive them, they totally disappear, as I have said, from our mental vision.   Now it is extremely difficult for us to think that the sensations taken by themselves alone are not objects of cognition ; for it seems to us that, being modifications of ourselves, always accompanied by pleasure or pain, and always essentially felt by us, they cannot belong to the region of the unknown.   This difficulty arises from that habit to which I have referred above ; I mean the habit which we, because endowed with intellect and reason, have of intellectually perceiving our sensations the very instant that we receive them.

Observe, moreover, that even if there were in us such a thing as a sensation wholly unaccompanied by any idea, as seems to us to be the case when we feel something but do not advert to it by reason of our mind being otherwise engaged, the fact could in no way help us to form an exact concept of that sensation, because, in reference to our mind, the sensation would be the same as if it did not exist, and therefore we could neither think of nor reason upon it.

422. Hence the concept of a sensation unaccompanied by any idea cannot be formed by us except in an indirect manner, thus : (1) A certain sensation, *e.gr.* that of crimson, has been intellectually perceived by us.   (2) In this perception, the idea and the sensation have been intimately conjoined—the idea as a thing *known through its own self*, and the sensation as a thing *made known* through the idea. (3) By analysing this our perception, or rather this *idea of*

the sensation of crimson, we separate the *idea* which has caused us to know the *sensation*, from the *sensation* cognised through it. (4) Hence we conclude that the *sensation* considered apart from the *idea* can only be a *something unknown*; because we find that, by taking away the idea, we have lost that which made the sensation visible to our mind, in other words, we have taken away the *form* of that cognition, and nothing but the *matter* of it is left. (5) Lastly, by bringing our attention to bear on this *matter*, we see that it is *sensation—i.e.* a *modification* of ourselves, in contradistinction to external bodies, which, in so far as external to us, are not only *not known*, but even *not felt*.

§ 2.

SECOND DEMONSTRATION,

Drawn from the second element of the idea of being, which constitutes its second characteristic, i.e. POSSIBILITY *or* IDEALITY.

423. The simple idea of being is not the perception of any thing *subsistent* (406–409); it is purely the *intuition* of the possible, the possibility of things.

Now our sensations give us only modifications produced in us by subsistent things : I say *subsistent* things, for things merely possible have no force to act on our organs and to produce sensations in us. Therefore, sensations have nothing whatever to do with our idea of being, and can in no way supply it to us.

For the same reason we have seen that this idea cannot be represented by any sensible *image* (400).

OBSERVATIONS.

On the connexion between the two general proofs above given of the incapacity of sensations to furnish to us the idea of being.

424. The idea of being contains, or at least implies two elements so united together that, if one of them is taken away, the idea itself is gone. These elements are, 1st, *possibility*, 2nd an indeterminate *something* to which the possibility refers.

We cannot think of *possibility* by itself alone ; it must be the possibility of *something*; even as we cannot think of a *something* which is not logically *possible.*

The idea of being, therefore, although in itself perfectly simple and indivisible, involves nevertheless or imports two *mental* elements, that is to say, two elements which the mind alone can distinguish.

425. The examination of the nature of the one of these two elements (an indeterminate something existent in itself) has supplied us with the first demonstration ; and the examination of the nature of the other (possibility) has supplied us with the second.

The first element—any thing whatever in so far as *existent in itself*—cannot be perceived by the sense, for the sense does not perceive things in so far as they *exist in themselves*, but only in so far as they *act upon it.* The second element, *i.e. possibility*, cannot be perceived by the sense because that which does not yet actually exist, but is only possible, is incapable of acting upon the sense.

§ 3.

THIRD DEMONSTRATION,

Drawn from the third characteristic of possible being, i.e. SIMPLICITY.

426. Let us now contrast *possible being* with *sensation.*

Every organic sensation has some extension, since it is felt in an organ that has extension ; on the contrary, a *possible* contemplated by the mind, not having any corporeal parts, is perfectly *simple.*

This characteristic of *simplicity*—consisting in the absence of every thing material or in any way resembling matter, of every thing extended or in any way like extension—is the direct opposite to the nature of a real sensation. Therefore that most simple light of our mind, the idea of being, cannot be given us by sensation.

§ 4.

FOURTH DEMONSTRATION,

Drawn from the fourth characteristic of possible being, i.e. its UNITY
or IDENTITY.

427. We will continue our comparison between possible
being and concrete sensations.

Each sensation is in one place only, and divided from, as
well as incommunicable to, other sensations. For instance, the
pain I feel in my finger has no connexion with a like pain felt
by another man, because the limitations of place and of real
subsistence keep the two sensations separate.

Ideal being, on the contrary, or any being which the mind
sees in a state of pure possibility, is not in one place more
than in another; and may be realized in many places, if it be
such as to occupy space when realized, and may be multiplied
indefinitely, even if it be not by its nature subject to the
limitation of place.

Let the mind contemplate the human body in its mere
possibility: this possible body is always the self-same in
however many places it may come to subsist by being
realized, and however many times the realization may be
repeated. The *real bodies* are multiplied; but the *concept* or
idea of *body* remains identically one, and not to one mind
only, but to as many minds as happen to think of any
number of human bodies as subsistent.

The nature therefore of the real beings to which the
sensations belong is the very opposite of that of a simple
idea. Consequently, the latter can neither be found in nor
produced by sensations.

§ 5.

FIFTH AND SIXTH DEMONSTRATIONS,

Drawn from the fifth and sixth characteristics of possible being, i.e.
UNIVERSALITY *and* NECESSITY.

428. Every being, when considered in its logical possibility,
is characterised by *universality* and *necessity*.

In fact, there is nothing logically repugnant in the subsistence of any number of real beings, all corresponding to
one and the same idea. Therefore every idea is a light
by which we are enabled to cognise as many beings as do or
may ever come to subsist in correspondence with it. The
idea is therefore universal and (in this sense) *infinite.*

Each sensation, on the contrary, is particular. All that I
feel in a sensation is strictly limited to it. The *universal*
therefore can neither be found in sensation, nor be extracted
therefrom.

429. The same must be said of the characteristic of
necessity. That which I contemplate as *possible*, I well
understand to be *necessary* ; for that which is, by its nature,
possible can under no circumstances be conceived as impossible.

The real sensation, on the other hand, may or may
not be ; it is accidental, contingent. There is therefore nothing in it that can suggest to the thought an absolute *necessity.* Therefore the idea of possible being cannot be drawn
from sensations.

Observation I.

The idea of being is the source of a priori *knowledge.*

430. Hence the two characteristics of *universality* and
necessity laid down by Kant, and before him by the ancient
philosophers, as the criteria of *a priori* knowledge (304–309,
324–326), *i.e.* of that knowledge which cannot be derived
from the senses, are not the ultimate criteria of this knowledge, but are merely partial criteria, derived through an
exact analysis of the *idea of being*—the one only *form* of
knowledge and the source of all *a priori* cognitions.

Observation II.

The above characteristics, and especially those of UNIVERSALITY *and*
NECESSITY, *are contained not only in the idea of being in general,
but also in all other ideas without exception.*

431. This proposition, which is excellently calculated to

reveal to us the nature of ideas, is only a corollary of the preceding ones.

In fact, I have shown that what we think in a pure idea is the *possibility* and not the *subsistence* of a thing, and that to affirm this *subsistence* belongs to another faculty of our spirit, quite distinct from that of ideas (402, 403). I have also shown that the possibility of a thing extends to the unlimited repetition of that thing, and cannot be conceived as *non-possibility*. This is as much as to say that *possibility* contains the characters of *universality* and *necessity* (428, 429).

Every idea, therefore, is *universal* and *necessary*.

Indeed, it is always from the idea of being, clothed, that is to say, with determinating qualities supplied by sensible experience, that we form a variety of ideas or *concepts* more or less determinate, but representing entities, not yet as subsistent, but only as possible to subsist.

For example, generic and specific ideas—the concepts of *man, animal, tree, stone*, and the like, which do not indicate subsistent individuals—are only the *idea* of *possible being* clothed with the determinations and qualities common to men, animals, trees, stones, &c., as furnished to us by experience. And even if an idea, say that of a tree, were clothed with every one of the qualities requisite for subsistence, down to the most minute details, there would still be no *subsistence* comprised in it, but only a tree in the state of possibility.

It is obvious from this, that all determinate ideas partake of the characteristics of *possible being*—*i.e. universality* and *necessity*.

In fact, every idea is *universal, i.e.* extending alike to all the countless individuals, which may be formed after it as their model ; and it is *necessary, i.e.* none of the individuals belonging to the class determined by a given idea could exist without that which the idea represents ; for it would be an absurdity to imagine an individual as comprised in a certain class, and at the same time not to attribute to it the qualities constitutive of that class.

OBSERVATION III.

Origin of the Platonic system of innate ideas.

432. From the above, we may see more clearly how the Platonic system of innate ideas originated.

Plato had observed that the ideas we have of things are characterised by *necessity* and *universality*. Hence, he concluded that they must be innate in us, because neither of these characteristics could be furnished to us by sensation.

The conclusion was, however, too hastily drawn, owing, doubtless, to the fact that the art of decomposing ideas, and separating in them the *formal* from the *material* part, had not yet been discovered. This decomposition would have shown him that all our determinate ideas have indeed the two characteristics of *necessity* and *universality*, but only by participation.

Then, going further in this investigation, he would have seen that the participation I speak of, flowed from one idea only, which stands high above all others, and has in it those two marvellous characteristics, not by participation but by its own essence. He would likewise have seen that this is the idea of *possible being*, while all generic and specific ideas are only this same idea clothed with various determinations supplied by the experience of our sense, internal or external. He would thus have found :—

(1) That determinate ideas are composed of two elements, viz.: (*a*) an *invariable* one, common to all of them, *i.e.* the *idea of being*; and (*b*) a *variable* one, *i.e.* the determinations added to that idea ;

(2) That what could not be supplied to us by the experience of the senses, was only the first or invariable element, and hence that in order fully to explain the origin of all our ideas, it would be enough to assume the innateness of one idea alone ;

(3) That the variable element [1] could be occasioned by the

---

[1] Whether, from the idea of *being* alone, in case it were perfectly comprehended, there should not necessarily emanate all the possible modes and determinations of beings, is a great question, which belongs, not to the Ideological, but to the Ontological science.

senses, and consequently there was no need to suppose this part also to be innate, as he seems to have done.

I say *seems* to have done, because in some passages of his writings, he approaches the doctrine stated here.

Wherefore, the remark I have now ventured to offer on Plato's system, will either serve to shew what is exaggerated and erroneous in it, or at least (if the reader thinks I am right) furnish a clue for a more correct interpretation of the mind of this great Philosopher than has appeared hitherto.

§ 6.

SEVENTH AND EIGHTH DEMONSTRATIONS,

Drawn from the seventh and eighth characteristics of possible being, i.e. IMMUTABILITY *and* ETERNITY.

433. Again, such is the nature of *possible being*, considered either in all its universality or in any of its determinations, that we cannot conceive it to be other than as it presents itself to our intuition. We can indeed transfer our attention from one determinate form of it to another; but whatever that form may be in each case, we see it as absolutely exempt in itself from change. In other words, *possible being* always stands before our mind as essentially *immutable*.[1]

From this fact there follows another, namely, that the mind cannot think of any time when a possible being was not what it now is and always will be.

This impossibity of the mind conceiving a change or a limitation of time in a possible being, is what is called the *immutability* and the *eternity* of *possible being*.

Nothing of this is found in sensations, which are all mutable and transitory. Sensations therefore cannot in any way suggest to the mind the thought of these characteristics of possible being.

---

[1] For example, the *idea* or (which comes to the same) the *intelligible essence* of the determinate forms of being called *Triangle, Animal, Man,* &c., have ever been and ever will be precisely what they are now. *Triangle* is always *triangle, animal* is always *animal,* &c. —TRANSLATORS.

§ 7.

NINTH DEMONSTRATION,

Drawn from the third element of possible being universally considered, which constitutes its ninth characteristic, i.e. INDETERMINATENESS.

434. So far I have demonstrated that the idea of being in general cannot come from the senses. This I have done by analysing and decomposing it into two of the notional elements included in it: (1) the notion of a *something* ; (2) the notion of the relation of *possibility* (415–422).

The analysis of these two elements has revealed the characteristics of *simplicity, identity, universality, necessity, immutability* and *eternity,* as belonging to the idea of being ; and the consideration of each of these characteristics has proved to evidence the impossibility of its being furnished by sensations (426–431).

Now the same impossibility can be shown from the third element belonging to this same idea, *i.e.* its absolute *indeterminateness.*

Indeed, the arguments hitherto adduced hold equally good for all ideas ; they serve to demonstrate that no idea whatever, considered purely *as idea,* can come from sensations ; since every idea consists in the intuition of a being in its essence or possibility, wholly apart from subsistence (402–407), and is therefore endowed with all the characteristics I have indicated and distinguished (430, 431).

But as regards the idea of being in general there is, further, the proof arising from its *indeterminateness.*

435. In fact, although it is true that all other ideas abstract from real subsistence, they have nevertheless in them the determinations constitutive of genera or of species ; and, in the case of species, those determinations may be such as to come down even to the most minute particulars requisite in order that an individual being may really subsist (402, 403).

On the contrary, the idea of *being in general* excludes, not only *subsistence,* but also all the differences and determinations of *species* and of *genus,* so that if the other ideas are universal because applicable to an infinite number of possible individuals similar to one another, this one idea is more universal still, inasmuch as, not being limited by any determinations, it extends to all possible genera and species.

Now is there, or can there be, anything in our real sensations which has the most distant resemblance to such an idea? Nay, is it not evident that their nature is the very opposite to it, since they are all perfectly *determinate?*

Since they are caused by real beings, these, together with their effects, must possess all those determinations and particular qualities whereby alone they can really and actually subsist. Hence between *being in general* and the sensations as well as the agents which produce them—between that which is essentially *indeterminate* and a pure possibility, and that which is essentially *determinate* and individually subsisting—there is a true contrariety.

For example, a stone cannot really exist unless it has a certain determinate size, form, weight, colour, taste, the power of making a certain noise when struck, and of producing, under given circumstances, certain determinate effects, either on us or on the things on which it acts. On the contrary, when I think of possible being in general, I entirely abstract from all the qualities either essential or accidental, of which any particular being, such as this stone, must needs be possessed. The being I think of is not particular, but universal in the very widest sense : in a word, it is nothing but the possibility of the various beings, the possibility of the countless modes and degrees in which existence may be actually realized. These beings, these modes and degrees I do not in any way distinguish. I simply think of the possibility of all *in globo.* Nay, I think of *existence* without giving any thought to its *modes* or *degrees* ; it being enough for me to know in general that, whichever of these modes or degrees may be necessary in each case, such will they be found in the beings whenever these come into real existence.

436. Nor can it be said that, if from the agent individualized by its particular qualities, and perceived by my senses alone, I abstract the determinations which individualize it,

the residuum will be *indeterminate being*, or *being in general*; for, as I have often observed, by the sensations we perceive the particular only, that which is most strictly proper, without any *relations* and therefore without the *common* as such.

Hence the sensations alone do not cause us to know the 'sensibles' as *beings*, that is, as existent in themselves, as possessed of such or such a degree of entity; they do not cause us to see them in relation to that common existence of which all beings partake. What falls under our sense-perception is merely the *action* which beings exercise on us, their sensible qualities, the effect left by them in our sensorium, where not only is each particular agent separate from the others, but even each action of one and the same agent stands by itself ·alone, separated from every other action. The sense does not refer this action to anything, because it has no experience except of that action, and cannot go beyond it. Supposing therefore, that of the sensible things which act upon us we had the sense-preception only, and not the intellectual also ; and that we then wished to abstract whatever was particular in those sense-perceptions, we should find the remainder to be, not *indeterminate being*, but absolutely *nil*. The sensations, as well as the agents which have produced them, would have disappeared without leaving anything behind. This fact must be well grasped and reflected on, if we would form a correct notion of the human mind and of the manner in which it operates.

But this, for the reason I have stated before, is extremely difficult for us to do. Sense-perception is never in us alone (417–420), but always joined with the intellectual, through which our ideas of bodies are formed. Hence when coming in due course to analyse—not indeed the sense-perceptions, but our *ideas* of bodies—we by abstraction discover in those ideas the *beingness*, the possibility, the indeterminateness, &c., of being, and suppose that all these things are contained in the pure *sense-perceptions* ; whereas they are contained in the *ideas*, having been placed there by ourselves, although we are not conscious of the fact. For it must never be forgotten, that our understanding perceives sensible things, and all other things, as *beings*, that is, it sees them in relation to *being*, of which they all participate—a mode of perception wholly beyond the sphere of sense.   But as this point is the most important of all in connexion with the matter in hand, I shall return to it later on.[1]

§ 8.

A Recapitulation of the foregoing proofs, and some other particular proofs suggested of the impossibility of deriving a priori knowledge from sensations.

437. To sum up our analysis of the idea of being : we have seen that this idea contains three elements which cannot be separated, but are connected together so intimately, that one is involved in the other ; nor can we think of one without thinking by implication of the other two, namely, (1) *a something* (a being) ; (2) the *possibility* of this *something* (this being) ; (3) *Indeterminateness.*

We have also seen that none of these elementary concepts, or elements of one and the same idea can be supplied to us by sensations, because they are essentially different in nature from sensation, even as sensation is essentially different in nature from them, so that the one by logical necessity excludes the other.   Whence we have drawn three fundamental demonstrations of the proposition : 'The idea of being cannot be derived from sensations' (414–424 ; 433·437).

Then analysing still more diligently the two first elements, and especially that of *possibility*, we have found that it contains divers other characteristics, all equally impossible to derive from sensations (426–433).

Now, were we to go on yet further with the analysis of *possible being*, we would detect in it many other things incompatible with sensation, and would thus have many other proofs that this idea cannot be found in and therefore obtained from sensation.

We should, in that case, be confronted with all those

---

[1] I will merely make here this passing observation, that *inde crminateness* is not a thing inherent to *being itself*, but arises out of the imperfection of our mental vision.

particular difficulties against which the various philosophers who sought to explain the origin of ideas have stumbled, and which I have expounded in the two preceding Sections, when giving the history of this question—that is to say, the difficulties of explaining the ideas of substance, of cause, of relation, &c.—all which ideas, when duly examined and analysed, are seen at last to present no other difficulty than is met with in accounting for the idea of being, whence they all originate as from their source.[1]

But as all these ideas which have so much exercised the minds of philosophers will have to be discussed later on, when it will be my duty to describe how they originate in the idea of being combined with sensible experience, I shall not stop to detail here those further proofs which would confirm the truth of the above proposition.

ARTICLE II.

The idea of being does not come from the feeling of our own existence.

§ 1.

This proposition is a consequence of the doctrines above expounded.

438. If the *idea of being* and, by consequence, any other idea,[2] cannot come from external *sensations*, it follows that neither can it come from the *feeling* of our own existence; since this feeling is nothing else but a permanent internal sensation, endowed with certain particular qualities; and hence is of such a nature that the same reasoning by which I have hitherto proved that the *idea of being* cannot come from corporeal sensations, is equally applicable to it.[3]

---

[1] This derivation is made by means of the diverse applications and the diverse uses of which the idea of being is susceptible. (See Sec. iii. C. i. art. v. ; C. ii. art. ix.-xi. ; C. iii. art. iii. iv. ; C. iv. art. i. xiii. xx. xxi.—Sec. iv. C. i. art. iii. xiii. ; C. ii. art. i.-iii. ; C. iii. art. xix.—Sec. v. Introd.).

[2] Art. i.

[3] D'Alembert in France, and Falletti in Italy, believed that the idea of being in general could be derived from the feeling of the *Ego, i.e.* the feeling of one's own existence. 'The abstract notion of existence,' says D'Alembert, 'is formed very soon in us by means of the feeling of the *Ego,* which is the result of our sensations and thoughts combined ; subsequently we come to regard this feeling as *possible* to be separated from the subject in which it is found without this subject being annihilated, and by this means we acquire the abstract idea

§ 2.

Distinction between the feeling and the idea of the Ego.

439. The internal feeling of *self*, must therefore be distinguished from the idea or intellectual perception of *self*.

The feeling of *self* is simple ; the idea of *self* on the contrary is a compound of, (1) the feeling, which is the *matter* of the cognition ; (2) the idea of *being*, the *form* to which the

of existence, which we afterwards apply to the external beings that seem to us to be the causes of our sensations.' (*Mélanges, éclaircissemens sur les élémens de philosophie,* § 11). It would be almost impossible to enumerate in a note the inaccuracies contained in this passage. I will briefly touch on the principal ones : (1) It confounds the *feeling of the* EGO with the *idea of the* EGO—two things absolutely different, as I shall show in the following paragraph. (2) It says that the feeling of the EGO is acquired by means of our sensations and thoughts. If this were true, the EGO would only begin to exist when it begins to be modified by sensations. (3) It says that the subject possessed of the feeling of the EGO, is something distinct from the EGO itself, and can be separated from it ; whereas the truth is that the *Ego* and the *subject* are one and the same thing. (4) After making this (imaginary) distinction between the EGO and the *subject,* it advances the astounding assertion, that the *subject* taken by itself is the same as the *idea of being in general!* (5) It supposes that to be possible which in truth is a contradiction in terms, namely, that from a *particular being* (for such is the EGO) we can draw *the idea of being in general* ; whereas a *particular* is the very opposite of an universal, and the actually subsistent, considered as such, excludes the purely potential.

The Italian philosopher, although he also tried to derive the idea of *being in general* from the feeling of the EGO, did it nevertheless with a little more caution and sagacity than d'Alembert. He saw that the EGO, as our fundamental feeling, must be in us essentially from the first moment of our existence, since *We* can never exist

without Ourselves. He saw likewise, that 'the idea of *being in general* must always be' (I use his own words) 'most present to our soul' (*Saggio sopra l' origine delle umane cognizioni dell' Abate Condillac, tradotto—colle osservazioni critiche di Tommaso Vincenzo Falletti.* Roma, 1784. Vol. i. p. 4). Hence he supposed that the soul draws this idea from its own self by means of a primitive and natural act. Now although this be an untenable view, because the soul, being a mere *particular,* cannot draw from itself the idea of *being* which is *universal,* nevertheless one can see how near Falletti came to the truth which I have endeavoured to set forth throughout this work.

Amongst living Italian philosophers (1829), Galluppi is of the same opinion as the two I have named ; but his penetration makes him sometimes feel a repugnance thereto ; and throw a doubt on the doctrine he professes to follow, as when he says : 'Our spirit, although it begins its operations with the perception of *individual existences,* cannot say, *I exist,* until it has acquired the most universal idea of existence ; even as, when it perceives a fig-tree or an orange-tree, it does not say : this is a *tree,* until after it has acquired the general idea of *tree* ; UNLESS INDEED WE WISH TO SAY THAT THE IDEA OF EXISTENCE IS INNATE IN US ; but even in this hypothesis the soul, in order to be able to say, *I exist,* requires that reflex consciousness of which I have spoken before' (*Saggio sulla critica della Conoscenza.* Napoli, 1819. T. i. p. 51).

In this passage, the acute Calabrian touches the true system ; all he wants is the courage to lay hold of it.

mind refers that feeling, that self, and thus cognises it, *i.e.* considers it objectively, as a *being*, as existing *in se.*

Self is the subject, a pure *particular* ; it has no relation except to itself, a determinate and real being.

To know this subject, to have the idea of it, I must, as I have just said, conceive it objectively, like everything which has nothing to do with me ; in short, I must conceive it in relation to *being*, as I conceive in relation to *being* every other particular ' sensible.'

Being, therefore, may fitly be called the common standard of reference ; when I have applied this standard to what I feel, I then not only *feel*, but also *know* what I feel.

§ 3.

The feeling of the Ego contains nothing but our own particular existence.[1]

440. The feeling of *Ourselves*, then, gives us the sensation of our own existence, but not the idea of existence or being in general : moreover, this feeling is our existence itself ; but it is not on that account the intellectual perception of our existence.

The intellectual perception of our existence arises indeed in us at a very early period ; but it arises by virtue of an act in which we consider the feeling of *Ourselves* as a *being* : we consider it impartially like everything else ; and by placing ourselves in the class of beings, we see ourselves as belonging to that class, and we distinguish ourselves from other beings through the same *feeling* which individualises us, and to which, by a judgment, we apply the idea of existence.

§ 4.

The feeling of our own existence is innate; the intellectual perception of the same is acquired.

441. It follows from the above, that even as the substantial feeling which we express by the word *Ego, myself*, is innate

---

[1] I here speak of the EGO as the proper and substantial feeling of ourselves, but not as including all that has been added to it by reflection up to the moment when we pronounce the word *Myself.*

(because I must be innate to myself), so the *intellectual perception* of this feeling is acquired, and the two must not therefore be confused together.

§ 5.

The idea of being precedes the idea of the Ego.

442. The idea of the *Ego* in general is formed by an abstraction exercised on the intellectual perception of our own *selves*, while this perception is formed by means of the idea of being in general (436).

In the order therefore of ideas, the idea of being precedes that of the *Ego*, because the first is necessary for the formation of the second.

This corollary flows directly from what we have already established, namely, that in every object whatever the first thing which our understanding apprehends is *being*.[1]

---

[1] The whole of this doctrine is found in the store of knowledge which has come down to us from antiquity. S. Thomas, in his work *Contra Gentiles*, teaches that our soul, in order to know itself as well as all other things, requires an *intelligible species*; and by this *intelligible species* nothing else can be understood, as I shall have occasion to show further down, than an *universal* under which the soul (a particular being) falls as under its genus, or, to speak more accurately, as the subject of a judgment under its major predicate. The soul, therefore, does not know itself in a manner different from that in which it knows any other thing, *i.e.* not otherwise than through that light of the *intellectus agens* (the *idea of being*) by means of which all other things are known. Thus does S. Thomas come to distinguish, here also, between the *matter* and the *form* of our cognition. The soul by the feeling it has of itself furnishes the *matter* of cognition, but nothing more; it is only by means of an innate light that this *matter* becomes *informed* so as to be in the true sense of the word cognition. I will quote the words of S. Thomas: 'That is natural knowledge which is formed through something implanted in us by nature (*quæ fit per aliquid naturaliter nobis inditum*); and such are the indemonstrable principles, which we know by the light of the *intellectus agens*. If therefore we knew what the soul is through the soul itself (*per ipsam animam*), this would be natural knowledge. But in those things which are naturally known no one can err; for in the knowledge of the indemonstrable principles no one errs. No one therefore would err in regard to what the soul is, if this were known through the soul itself; which is manifestly false.' Then he adds: 'That which is known through itself must be known before all those things which are known through something other than themselves, and is the principle of their cognisableness. Such are the primary propositions in respect of their conclusions. If, then, the soul knew its own nature through itself (*per seipsam*), it would be known *per se* and, by consequence, would be the first thing known (*primo notum*) and the principle by which other things are known. But this is evidently false; for in scientific disquisitions the nature of the soul is not assumed as known, but

§ 6.

Error of Malebranche, who held that we have the intellectual perception of ourselves immediately, i.e. without the medium of an idea.

443. Those therefore who make the idea of the *Ego* anterior to the idea of *being in general* seem to have fallen into this error in consequence of confounding the intellectual perception of the *Ego*, from which the idea of the *Ego* in general is subsequently drawn, with the *feeling* found in the *Ego*.

This feeling is anterior to all acquired ideas, but the *idea of being* is still more and necessarily so.

Malebranche, then, is mistaken when he asserts that our soul knows itself, not through an *idea*, but solely through *feeling*.

He is right enough when distinguishing a feeling from an idea : but then he does not perceive that feeling does not, by itself alone, constitute a cognition and therefore an intellectual perception ; and that it only supplies the matter of a cognition which is *informed* by the *idea* of being in general (*Recherche de la Vérité*, L. iii.).

If we had nothing but the feeling of ourselves we could not reason about our soul at all, nor consider it as a *being*, as an object of our thought.

is proposed as a subject to be inquired into, and to be deduced from other sources ' (*Contra Gent.*, L. iii., C. xlvi.)

In these passages we see how the Angelic Doctor held, (1) that the knowledge of the first principles is anterior in us to the particular knowledge of our own soul ; (2) that the latter knowledge can only come from the former ; (3) that the first principles are known at first sight and immediately by means of the light innate in us, which, as shewn all throughout this work, can be nothing else but the *idea of being*; (4) that our soul being known through the same principles by which we know other things, is not itself the *first thing known* (*primo notum*) and the *principle of the cognisableness of other things*, and therefore that the knowledge of our soul cannot be the source whence we derive ideas and universal principles, as was maintained by Des Cartes, and other philosophers after him ; but must be itself derived from the universal principles

Aristotle saw this same truth, when he said that the 'possible intellect' understands itself in the same way that it understands other things (*De Anima*, L. iii., 15).

ARTICLE III.

The idea of being cannot come from Locke's Reflection.

§ 1.

DEFINITION.

444. By Locke's *Reflection* I mean that faculty by which our mind can fix its attention on the external sensations, or on the internal feeling (and in this are included also all the intellectual *operations* of which we have the feeling), that is to say, either on the whole or on any part of the sensation or the internal feeling, without however adding anything to them, and hence without forming to itself any new object.

445. That this is the right interpretation of Locke's *Reflection* seems to me clear from comparing what he says about it, with his teaching on innate ideas ; thus explaining Locke by means of himself.

In fact, if we take his definition of reflection by itself alone, viz. 'The perception of the operations of the mind upon the ideas received from the senses,'[1] we can make no meaning out of it. It is too equivocal to express any system. For if reflection be only the perception of the operations of our spirit on the ideas which have come from the senses, then the ideas are supposed as already formed ; and since there can be no idea of anything unless the idea of *being* is included in it, this much dreaded *idea* is simply assumed, and thus the whole knot of our question receives as little attention as if it had no existence. Well might this *reflection*, therefore, proceed securely, since it began its journey on the smooth level ground, having left all the rugged passes behind it. We will, however, pause a moment to glance at those difficulties which our philosopher treated so lightly. *Ideas*, he tells us, were first formed by *sensation*. But *how* did sensation form them? This is just what he does not state, much less think of explaining. He considers it quite enough to inform us that 'Our senses do convey into the mind

---

[1] *Essay on the Human Understanding*, Book II. ch. i. § 4.

several distinct perceptions of things,' and all the explanation he has to give us is this : ' When I say the senses convey
into the mind, I mean, they, from external objects, convey
into the mind what produces there those perceptions.'[1]

I leave the reader to judge if this be a satisfactory explanation ; why, it is not even a sufficient description of the fact
of sensation.   The explaining, therefore, how sense can cause
in the soul the act by which the latter perceives, first *sensibly*
and then *intellectually*, is not what Locke proposes to himself.   It is the same as if he said : ' The sense produces the
act by which our soul feels, and it also produces the act by
which our soul understands and forms ideas : I do not care to
show you the difference between *sensation* and *understanding*,
or to seek what may be required for the first of these acts to
take place, and for the second to follow upon it.   Whatever
that difference or this requisite may be, I start from the
principle that all ideas come from sensation and reflection !'
—This principle is as it were the fundamental postulate of
Locke's whole philosophy.   He seems to say : ' I beg leave
to use the two words *sensation* and *reflection*, without being
bound to give an accurate definition of them, so however that
they shall be understood as including in their meaning (about
which you must ask me no questions) whatever is necessary
for expressing the causes of all our ideas.   Now starting
from this postulate, let us make out a list of all the ideas man
possesses, and see how they can all be traced to *sensation* and
reflection as their sources.

This enumeration of ideas forms in reality the main pur-
port of Locke's *Essay* : and here we have in a few words the
genuine analysis of the whole of that work which has made
so much noise in the world.

446. Now from this analysis we may see, that the question
of the origin of ideas has been, as I said, eliminated by the
English philosopher : and so should one have judged of his
intention, had he not, by an addition quite superfluous and irrelevant to his subject, employed the whole of the first book
in impugning the existence of any innate idea or principle.

[1] *Ibid.* § 3.

It is this opinion, propounded at such length in the first Book, which authorises us to fix the sense of his definition of *reflection*—a definition so ambiguous, when taken by itself, that we could not, from it alone, conclude anything to our purpose.

In fact, if there be no idea or principle innate in us, it is obvious that *reflection* can add nothing to our *sensations*, but simply fixes itself on them to find what they already contain : and such is the function which Locke assigns to the faculty of reflection in the above definition.

§ 2.

FIRST DEMONSTRATION.

447. What I have said above proves to evidence, that the idea of being does not come from reflection as understood by Locke.

For I have demonstrated, (1) that the idea of being is in no way contained in our external sensations (414-436) ; (2) that it is not contained in the feeling we have of ourselves (437-443) ; (3) that Locke's reflection is a faculty which observes and discovers what there is in the sensations or in the internal feeling without adding anything to either (444-446).

From these three propositions it follows that, since Locke's reflection cannot find in these two things what they do not contain, it cannot find the *idea of being* in them, and therefore this idea must come from some other source.

§ 3.

SECOND DEMONSTRATION.

448. It will be demonstrated that the *idea of being* cannot be furnished to us by Locke's *Reflection*, if I can shew that this reflection is itself an impossibility.

Now, that it is an impossibility we shall easily see if we recall to mind its definition (440).

We have seen that Locke's reflection is ' That faculty by which our mind fixes its attention on the external or internal sensations, taken either in their whole or in any of their parts, without however adding anything thereto, and consequently without creating any new object to itself.'

Now our attention may be determined to stop here or there by the pleasure which is found in the sensations or in a certain aggregate of them, or in their parts ; and, in such case, it is not Locke's reflection. This has for its end, not the resting in pleasure, or the more easy receiving of it, but the acquiring of ideas ; and if it turns and fixes itself on these or those parts of the sensations and their aggregates, it is only in order that it may obtain new ideas.

But is it possible for our mind to reflect in this way upon the internal or external sensations, unless it be already possessed of the very ideas which it seeks—namely, universal ideas ?

The business of this reflection, which has for its object to analyse the sensations and draw ideas from them, is, to divide and to compare, to find in them the parts that are similar and those that are dissimilar ; in a word, to classify. Now every classification necessarily presupposes the general idea whereon the class is founded ; for without that abstract idea to which two individuals correspond, we could not compare them together and see their points of similarity or dissimilarity. We should perceive with our senses the two similar individuals, for example two pieces of red cloth, without our mind being at all aware that they are similar. The two sensations of red would thus remain perfectly divided, even as all sensations are, at least by time or place, so that the existence of the one would neither be known to, nor have anything in common with the other (180–187). Locke's reflection, therefore, that is to say, the reflection bestowed on the sensations with the object of drawing ideas from them, while we are supposed to be as yet without any idea whatever, is a sheer impossibility. On the contrary, it is by ideas that our mind is guided in its acts of reflection, and has the power of uniting or decomposing the sensations and freely transferring its attention from one to another.

449. Our spirit devoid of ideas and furnished with sensations alone can indeed, by the force of *instinct*, rest leisurely

on this or that sensation, to enjoy more intensely the pleasure which it affords. But this is not, properly speaking, *reflection*. It is only an increase of attention. I say attention, not of the mind, but of the sense ; to speak still more accurately, rather than *attention*, it should be called an *application of the instinctive force of the animal*, naturally attracted and held fast by the pleasurable sensation. Here I have not time to describe this fact at greater length : it is enough for me to indicate it, in order that it may not be confused with *intellectual attention*, from which alone reflection springs. I shall only add in passing, that that *sensible attention* is in no way different from the faculty of feeling. Indeed, we may, if we wish, call it a natural actuation of this faculty. And from this may have arisen the error of Condillac, who attempted to reduce *attention* to *sensation* (73, 74).

This writer does not seem to have noticed that, in this sense, there are two kinds of attention, the one sensitive (that is, instinctive), the other intellectual (that is, voluntary) ; and as a consequence of this oversight, he imagined that all attention could be regarded as a mode of sensation.

450. Therefore a reflection which, on the one hand, is directed to the formation of ideas, and, on the other, begins its operations before it has any idea to direct and regulate it, is an inconceivable thing, because made up of two contradictory elements, *i.e.* having to form ideas, and not having any idea to begin with.

If then Locke's reflection is impossible and absurd, surely we cannot get from it either the idea of being or any other idea (for all other ideas require the idea of being for their formation) : and this is what I had to demonstrate.

ARTICLE IV.

The idea of being does not begin to exist in our mind with the act of Perception.

§ 1.

FIRST DEMONSTRATION OF THIS,

Drawn from the observation of the fact.

451. Corporeal sensations do not contain the idea of being (409–433) : therefore this idea cannot be discovered in them by reflection ; for reflection adds nothing to sensation, but only takes note of what is therein contained (444–450).

It remains to be seen whether perhaps in the act of our feeling a sensation, or in the act by which we think of that sensation, the idea of *being* suddenly presents itself of its own accord to our mind, and is thus conceived or acquired by us.

452. And first of all, putting aside the question as to the possibility of so singular a phenomenon, we must take all due care to ascertain whether it actually does take place or not.

Reid, who protests that it is not his intention to explain the fact of human cognition, but only to describe it accurately by distinguishing its different parts and detailing all its circumstances, seems to have no doubt that this fact, as regards the existence of bodies, consists of three parts wholly unconnected with one another : (1) The *impression* made on our bodily organs ; (2) the *sensation* ; (3) the *perception* of the existence of bodies (109, &c.). He also thinks he has discovered, that these three things follow one another according to a fixed law ; so that, given the first, the second makes at once its appearance, and, immediately after this, the third ; but at the same time the three are perfectly dissimilar in nature, nor is there between any of them the least connection as cause and effect. Having thus described the fact, he tells you that it is inexplicable and, in all its parts, a mystery. Willingly do I acknowledge that this description of the perception of bodies shews in its author an intention and an effort worthy of a philosopher ; but the question is, has he

succeeded in making the description accurate and complete?
I doubt it ; however, let us see.

453. That the three things above indicated should be
distinguished [1] the one from the other, and that one follows

[1] In my opinion, these three things must be distinguished ; but as regards the second (*sensation*) it does not seem to me to have been sufficiently described by Reid ; for he considers sensation to be nothing more than a modification of the soul, so simple as to convey no other notion than that of a relation of the soul with its own self, or, speaking more accurately, as to be merely an altered state of the soul.

The analysis I have endeavoured to make of sensation gives me another result. Sensation is a *passion*, and the analysis of passion always reveals three elements ; (1) that which *suffers* the passion ; (2) that which *causes* the passion ; and (3) the *passion* itself. Now I would observe in the first place, that what we call *passion* is the very same thing as what we call *action*; only that it is *passion* relatively to the patient, and *action* relatively to the agent. Owing to this diversity of *relation*, the thing which is one in itself becomes two to the mind, according to the two aspects under which the mind looks at it ; and it becomes two in reality as regards the terms to which it is referred, so that for the patient it is something entirely different from and contrary to what it is for the agent.

It will be seen from this, that *sensation* as such, because passive, does not cause the said one thing to be perceived by the sentient subject (the patient), in its own self and apart from all relations, but solely in so far as it affects the percipient subject, *i.e.* solely as *passion*. Farther than this the sentient subject cannot go. But this does not prevent our being able, by reflecting on this *passion*, to see that, although felt by the sentient subject, it is not caused by it, but by something else. Thus, in that thing which is one and indivisible in itself, our mind descries two relations : (1) a relation with the sentient subject ; in other words, the sentient subject in so far as it feels ; (2) a relation terminating, not in the sentient subject, but in some being different from it.

I have reserved the word *sensation* for designating exclusively the corporeal *feeling* experienced by the sentient subject ; and to designate the same sensation in so far as it is a *passion*, and therefore necessarily related to something extraneous to and different from the sentient subject, I have adopted the phrase *sensitive perception of bodies*.

Hence two kinds of perception of bodies : the *sensitive*, and the *intellectual* (417, 418).

Now, in the *sensitive perception*, that takes place which I have often said, namely, that our soul *takes hold of* and *involves* the bodies themselves ; whilst the intellectual perception does not do so except in so far as it supposes the sensitive, which serves as its matter.

If this manner of speaking be retained, the error of Reid will be seen to consist in having distinguished in the fact of the intellectual perception of bodies three things only, when he should have distinguished four ; *i.e.* (1) the *mechanical impression* made on our bodily organs ; (2) the *sensation* (considered solely in its relation to us, the sentient subjects) ; (3) the *sensitive perception* (*i.e.* the receiving in ourselves of a *passion*, caused by something outside of us) ; (4) the *intellectual perception* (*i.e.* the cognising of agents which act in a given mode upon us).

By this want of precision in his distinction, Reid was led to confound the *sensitive* perception of bodies with the *intellectual*, and to say of the former what he ought to have said of the latter.

As a result of this confusion he denied *ideas*; for in the sensitive perception he found, not ideas, but *perception of bodies*. Hence his contention, that for the perception of bodies no ideas were required.

That the *sensitive perception of bodies* has no need of ideas, I fully admit ; but that the *intellectual perception of bodies* can take place without, at least, the idea of *existence*, I utterly deny.

Our philosopher would not have fallen into such a mistake, if he had formed to himself a clear notion of the

the other, seems to me true, and the Scottish philosopher has done it with a clearness which leaves nothing to be desired.

I likewise admit that these three things have no true similarity to one another, and that one cannot be as it were a reproduction or copy of the other. Certainly, the mechanical *impression* made on the bodily organs is of a nature essentially different from sensation; nor has *sensation* any the least resemblance with the *perception of a being* [1] as formed by our understanding. It is therefore absurd to suppose that one of these things causes the other by, so to speak, imprinting itself upon it.

sensitive perception of bodies; for he would then have seen that this did not suffice for *cognition*, inasmuch as there was nothing intellectual in it. No doubt, it is extremely difficult to grasp well the nature of the *sensitive perception of bodies*, because in it we perceive the bodies not in themselves, but only in and with us. We perceive them not as *agents* (*i.e.* as causes of our sensations), but as terms of our *passion* and nothing more. Hence even the expression *sensitive perception of bodies* does not seem to me strictly accurate; for in this expression the word *body* indicates a thing already perceived intellectually, and it would therefore be better, if it did not look a little strange, to say *sensitive corporeal perception*.

[1] The *intellectual perception of bodies*, has no resemblance to *sensation*. But has the *sensitive corporeal perception* any resemblance to the intellectual? I reply, that between these two kinds of perception there is a very close relation, but not one of resemblance.

In fact, in the *sensitive corporeal perception* we do not, properly speaking, perceive the body itself, but only a *passion* which terminates in the extraneous agent. In the *intellectual perception of bodies*, on the contrary, we perceive the *body itself* as an object acting on us. These two *perceptions*, therefore, are the opposite of each other, even as *passion* and *action* are.

But *passion* and *action*, although, as such, the opposite of each other, are nevertheless one and the same thing when considered apart from the particular and contrary relations they have with the patient and with the agent: and this mode of considering them belongs to the understanding—a faculty which, in virtue of its nature, perceives things, not as limited to any particular relation, but in themselves.

When the understanding has so perceived the one thing of which I speak (the change produced in our sensitivity), it then finds also the relations of *passion* and *action*, for it has perceived the link of communication between them, *i.e.* the thing susceptible of those contrary relations. Such is the nature of the relation existing between *sensitive corporeal perception* and the *intellectual perception of bodies*.

The *sensitive corporeal perception* is an element (the *matter*) which forms part of the *intellectual perception*.

The *intellectual perception*, therefore, composed of *matter* and *form*, cannot be said to resemble the *sensitive perception*, because the latter is not co-ordinate with, but *sub*-ordinate to the former; it is, as I have said, an element and not a copy of it. Thus we do not say that a man's mouth resembles another man's head because the latter has also a mouth; or that a square figure resembles the substance of a given body because that body happens to be square.

Nevertheless, so intimate is the relation between these two kinds of *perception*, that by the one as well as by the other we perceive the self-same thing, though not in the same manner. By the intellectual perception we see in an universal mode that which the sensitive perception has given us purely as particular. In other words, to the effect felt by the sense the understanding adds *being*, *i.e.* the cause.

But are we therefore to conclude that the fact itself, in all the said three parts, is wholly inexplicable, involved in absolute darkness ? [1]

454. Reid says: given the sensation, we have the *perception of bodies as existent*, although the two things are entirely

[1] Sometimes philosophy removes us from mysteries, and sometimes it leads us to them. What does this mean? Is philosophy, then, opposed not to all, but only to some mysteries? Here I request the reader to take notice that I speak solely of the tendency exhibited by a certain species of philosophy—a tendency which in great part is independent of the individuals professing it. If I, for example, happen to attach myself to a particular school, or to a particular method of philosophising, I imbibe its spirit without being myself clearly aware of the nature of it ; I walk along a road of which I do not myself know the issue, though I hope that it may be favourable. I deem it proper to make this declaration, lest any one should think that, in describing a certain philosophy as characterised by a tendency to abhor some mysteries whilst cherishing and proposing others, I intend to cast injurious reflections at any particular persons. Do you, then, wish to know which mysteries are of the first, and which of the second class? You will find, that the philosophy I refer to abhors those mysteries which assume the existence of something *spiritual*. Suppose that this philosophy has proceeded with its reasonings up to a point beyond which it cannot advance without admitting some spiritual being; it will suddenly stop and tell you gravely : here is a thing incomprehensible to human reason, it is impossible to know anything about it ; and so it creates a *mystery*.

Then the philosopher takes advantage of the occasion for applauding (not very modestly I must say) his own modesty, and for dilating on the presumption of those who are not satisfied with his method of disposing of troublesome questions. Whence all this ? From the secret prejudice, that ' *matter* must be all that exists, and that therefore what we call *spirit* may well be relegated to the world of dreams ! When one starts from a proposition not proven, supposing it true, and is so firmly attached to it that he will have it absolutely to be true, and its contrary excluded, what happens? So long as it is thought that the reasoning may be carried on without having recourse to elevated notions, well and good ; but no sooner does this cease to be the case, than the philosopher is seen to assume the garb of humility, and, in the name of philosophical sober-mindedness, to protest against the temerity of attempting to tread upon ground which he is pleased to declare forbidden to human thought.

This arbitrary limit put to the freedom of philosophical reasoning, this self-imposed humiliation, this blind belief in the incomprehensibility of that which is not to one's taste, in the first place, restricts unduly the circle of human knowledge and tyrannises over the human family by forbidding it the free use of the highest of its faculties, the reason ; then, in due course, it ends in the destruction of all philosophy, of all science, by making knowledge itself impossible. Indeed, the more we consider the matter, the more clearly do we see that all human knowledge is annihilated or made an absurdity if *spirit* be excluded from the universe, and things divine from the ken of man's intelligence, which, together with all human things, receives its being from God. The Scepticism, Indifferentism, Egotism, Epicureanism of our times is the fruit of the philosophy here alluded to. And yet the Sceptic reasons, the Indifferentist feels, the Egotist loves, the Epicure raises himself from his mire by the very act of proclaiming himself in favour of his system ! Thus man, by a perpetual self-contradiction, essentially condemns himself ; for it is impossible for him to annihilate his own nature, and that truth which is necessarily blended with it.

different. In this manner of stating the fact there is an inaccuracy.

That *existence in general* is different from, nay the very opposite of *sensation*, is a fact to which I also have called attention (402–429).

But that the *intellectual perception* of existent bodies differs entirely from *sensation*,[1] will be seen to be incorrect by recalling to mind the analysis I have made of this perception (411–417).

I shall not now speak about the way in which sensation arises in us on occasion of the external impression on our bodily organism : this is irrelevant to my present purpose. I shall only dwell on the last part of the fact in discussion, that is to say, on the way in which, given the *sensation*, the *perception of bodies*, as existent arises in our soul. I say that this last part was declared inexplicable by Reid because he did not sufficiently analyse it ; and this is what we must try to do.

The intellectual perception, when carefully analysed, is found to be, not simple like sensation, but resulting from several distinct parts. If it were simple, certainly one could not understand how it came into our soul except by an inexplicable apparition. It would be a creation suddenly operated in the soul on occasion of the sensation. But if it consists of several parts, before pronouncing it inexplicable, we ought to go further ; and in the first place we ought to distinguish between those parts, then examine what relation they have the one to the other, whether they are contemporaneous or following in succession, and how they are connected together so as to result in the perception of bodies.

I. It will be remembered that we have found the intellectual perception to consist of three parts : viz. (1) *Sensation*, in which the sensible qualities—not indeed in a universal and abstract form, but purely in the form of particulars—are the terms felt by our sensorium : and it is these sensible qualities so felt, that attract the attention of our mind ; (2) the *idea of*

---

[1] In *sensation* I include here what I have called *sensitive corporeal perception* (417, and note to 453).

existence in general; since to conceive a body as existent is to place it in the class of existing things, and this presupposes in us the idea of existence in general which constitutes, so to speak, that class ; (3) the *relation* affirmed by us *between the sensation and the idea of existence,* or the *judgment* whereby we attribute the existence known in the idea (the predicate) to the *force acting* in the sensations—which attributing is the link which joins these two things together into a being, and in it lies precisely the act of the *intellectual perception of bodies.* We have also seen that our spirit performs this act in virtue of its perfect oneness, that is to say, in virtue of its being a subject at once sentient and intelligent. I mean to say, that the same principle which receives the sense-perceptions, also perceives a being in them ; and that it has the energy, by turning on itself, to regard those perceptions, in relation to the agents which have caused them, and whereof it affirms the existence. Thus it is that it sees things in themselves, *objectively.*

455. II. If we now inquire whether the said parts are of their own nature contemporaneous, or successive, we.shall discover that their order, both as to nature and time, must be the following : First, the *idea of existence* ; next, the *sensation* (including the *corporeal sensitive perception*, TR.) ; thirdly, the *judgment*, which joins the two together, and thus generates the perception of the existence of bodies ; this perception being nothing but the application of *existence*, (as predicate) to the corporeal agents, which in that very act become *objects.*

In fact, that a judgment cannot be closed unless its two terms (predicate and subject) go before it, seems self-evident.

Again, that the idea of existence must, in us, precede the sensation, will be easily seen by attentively considering the two terms of the judgment.

In the first place, be it noted that this idea enters equally into all our ideas, and consequently into all our judgments (405, 417). Given, then, that we have formed a judgment or acquired an idea, it is obvious that we have made use of the idea of existence, and that therefore we had it previously.

456. The same thing may be made still clearer by another

consideration.   The doubt 'Whether or not the idea of existence precedes in us the sensations' can only refer to the first
of the judgments we make after being born.   To be convinced
of it, we have only to bear in mind the laws *essential* to all
judgments ; for if these laws are essential, they must hold
good also in reference to the first of all judgments.   Now in
every judgment which we make when anything strikes our
sensitivity, we think of a particular 'sensible' as existent.
This is a constituent law of judgment.   But what is it to think
of a particular 'sensible' as existent?   Certainly not to receive the idea of existence, but to make use of it ; and the
use presupposes the idea, for we cannot use that which we
have not.

457. Again, let any one who takes observation as a sure
guide for ascertaining the facts of nature, reflect on the way
in which he comes to use the notion he has of existence or
being in general.   He is certainly not conscious of receiving
it on a sudden, or of any intermediate step between not having
it and having it.   The only thing of which he feels conscious
is, that he makes use of it as of a thing which is already in his
mind, and which, on occasion of the sensations, he draws forth
as it were from a repository, and uses.   He is in no way sur-
prised at his knowing already what existence is.   He uses this
knowledge in the most off-hand and natural manner.   *Existence* stands before him as a thing with which he is and always
has been perfectly well acquainted, and which goes therefore
without saying.   Such is the result of a diligent observation
on ourselves as regards the act by which we affirm the existence of external beings.[1]   In this affirmation, that *existence*
which we join to the corporeal force acting on our senses, is a
thing so familiar to us that it does not detain our attention at
all ; and this is what makes it so difficult for us to observe.

To say therefore that the intellectual *perception of bodies*
follows upon the sensation in a mysterious and inexplicable

---

[1] This observation did not escape the notice of the ancients.   An author of great penetration, speaking of the first principles of reason, remarks, that 'the mind feels obliged to assent to them, not as though it perceived any-thing new, but as recognising in them something innate and perfectly familiar' (*Itin. mentis*, c. iii.).

manner, seems to me a modesty savouring somewhat of rashness. You pretend that the limits of the explicable should be no wider than those of your own observing. Is it not possible that the observation of others may be pushed a step further than yours? We must not, therefore, always believe philosophers when they tell us on their own authority that philosophical investigation can go no further merely because they themselves have not been able to go further. That there is a mystery in our intellectual perceptions, I verily believe, but not where Reid has placed it.

458. The intellectual perception of bodies is only the applying of an idea or a knowledge which precedes in us the corporeal sensations. This is confirmed by the very words in which we express it, and which Condillac [1] calls an 'analysis of our thoughts.' Does not the phrase 'Perception of the existence of bodies' comprise and express the *idea of existence* as applied to *bodies?* The perception therefore of the existence of bodies is generated by the idea of *existence* which we have in us beforehand, and which we apply on occasion of the sensations, the result of this application being that object to which we give the name of *body.*

459. To conclude: The idea of existence does not begin to be in our mind in the act of *intellectual perception*; for the observation of our own interior gives us no consciousness, either of this idea suddenly manifesting itself to us on that

---

[1] Condillac defines languages as *analytical methods*, that is, methods for decomposing ideas. Certainly, they may be so called; but what has escaped the notice of Condillac is, that as every *analysis* presupposes a *synthesis*, so also languages must be, first, *synthetical* and afterwards *analytical*, that is to say, first they must unite and then decompose. When I pronounce a noun substantive, *e.g.* the word *body*, I join together several ideas, all signified by the one term. If I enunciate a proposition, *e.g. body is possible*, I decompose the idea of *body*. In the word *body*, I, in fact, express an essence possible to be realized; but by saying *body is possible*, I divide *possibility* from *body*; and thus I have the idea of possible existence united in the word *body* and separated in the word *possible*. The word *body* is a *synthesis*; the proposition *body is possible* is an *analysis*. All substantives are so many *syntheses*, and the propositions into which these substantives enter are *analyses*. Now, just as the single words precede the propositions which are composed of them, so *synthesis* precedes *analysis*, and this is true as well of mental as of vocal enunciations. It may therefore be said that languages are the faithful exponents of thoughts (as also to a great extent aids to them); and that therefore they are not merely analytical methods, but 'synthetico-analytical.' This designation embraces all and avoids the partial and the arbitrary.

occasion, or of the immense leap which our mind would make, from not having it to having it, in the event of its receiving it then for the first time. We have no memory of a period when we had it not, or of a moment when we began to have it. On the contrary, we are intimately conscious that we have always put this idea into continual requisition ; that from time immemorial, so to speak, we have considered it as our property. Now, without consciousness of it, or some other proof, we have no right to affirm so singular a fact as would be that of the instantaneous creation within us of an idea which has nothing to do with external and corporeal things.

§ 2.

DEMONSTRATION II,

By the argument called REDUCTIO AD ABSURDUM.

460. We will now suppose that the idea of existence or being in general comes into our mind simultaneously with or immediately after our experiencing a sensation, and that, having thus suddenly received it, we make use of it for perceiving the existence of bodies, by applying it to the corporeal force which we feel in that sensation.

In the first place, this would be a veritable prodigy ; for the sudden apparition in our mind of an idea which has nothing in common with sensations, would be a creation, or certainly an event isolated from everything else, and out of all keeping with the usual working of nature. This ought to be enough to make us exclude such an hypothesis, seeing that it is unnecessary, and that there is a much simpler way of explaining the origin of our ideas.

461. Besides, this instantaneous creation of the idea of existence could only have one or other of two causes, that is to say, a being external to us, God, Who on occasion of the sensations produces it in our mind ; or the nature of our own soul which by a physical and necessary law creates and emits it from itself.

The first of these hypotheses coincides with the system of

the Arabians which I have refuted before ; the second is the system of Kant.

In fact, the Arabian School maintained that the *intellectus ugens* of Aristotle was a something separate from ourselves—was God. Now we have seen that the *intellectus agens* of Aristotle or that principle by which the ideas of things are formed in our mind, is nothing but that which presents to us *existence*. To say, therefore, that what causes us to see existence in sensible things (viz. the *intellectus agens*) is God, is the same as to say that it is God Who causes the being to appear before our mental vision on occasion of the sensible phantasms.

In like manner, although Kant overlooked the consideration of existence in general, occupying himself rather with existence as already clothed with certain forms ; yet the whole tendency of his philosophy is to educe whatever we perceive, and therefore also existence, from the depths of our own soul, much in the same way that the root, the trunk, the branches, boughs and leaves, the flowers and fruit of a tree spring from its seed.

462. To suppose with the Arabian School that we have not in us the faculty of thought complete, but that, to make us capable of thinking, God Himself must, by an act dependent on the contingency of the sensations, create in our mind the idea of existence, is an hypothesis so extravagant and so badly supported by proof, that it is not likely to gain many followers, especially at the present day.

463. But is there more truth in the Kantian principle that ' The soul has an intrinsic virtue whereby, on occasion of the sensations, it emits the idea of existence from itself ? ' So singular a phenomenon would be either an emanation or a creation, and each of these suppositions is as inexplicable as it is gratuitous.

Again : if the idea of existence or being were an emanation, it would be supposed as already present in the depth of our soul, and so it would be innate. There would be question only of a kind of revelation which the soul would make to itself on occasion of the sensations : the soul would not then

begin to possess that idea, but would have possessed it previously, though in a hidden state.   I do not just now wish to
examine the question as to the possible ways of such an
emanation.   I only say, either the idea emanating from the
soul pre-existed in it, and then we fall into what I hold to be
the true theory ; or the idea is really a production of the soul
itself ; and this hypothesis, wholly unsupported by the testimony of observation, bristles with absurdities.

If the idea of existence is of a nature entirely different
from that of sensation, how can it arise in us on occasion of
a sensation ?

We should be obliged to fall back on the system of *pre-
established harmony*, or on that of *occasional causes* ; both of
which systems have recourse to an agent outside of nature—
a thing repugnant to the Kantian philosophy.

Granting however that sensation, although unable of
itself to supply the *idea of existence*, can give to the perceiving
subject such an impulse as will bring it, conformably to the
laws of its nature, to an immediate intuition of this idea ;
would our consciousness tell us nothing about such an
operation ?

464. But what more than everything else shows the untenableness of this hypothesis, is the following reflection.

Given that the *idea of existence* did not pre-exist in the
perceiving subject, this subject could never produce it from
itself ; for the subject has nothing in it which bears the least
resemblance to that idea.   The subject is particular, just as
are the bodies and the sensations caused by them ; but the
idea of existence is universal.   The subject is contingent, but
the idea is necessary.   The subject is real, *i.e.* subsistent, but
the idea is the opposite because it only contains the possible.
Lastly, the one is *subject* ; but the other is, again, exactly the
opposite, *i.e. object* (415, 416).

465. Let us pause a moment on this last circumstance.
The *Ego* (*subject*) has the intuition of *existence* or *being* (*object*).
Observation tells us this, and nothing more.

Now what is *intuition ?*   It is simply to *see*, but not by
any means to *produce* that which is seen.

When we produce something, we are conscious of the effort made by us in that production ; but when we simply *see*, we know very well that we do nothing as *producers*, and that the object before us is altogether independent of our eyes ; so much so that even the bare fact of its having been brought within sight is not due to the eyes themselves, but to an entirely different source. In like manner, *existence* or *being* stands before our intellectual eye as a thing to be looked at, and not to be formed or created. Its essence is as independent of the mind which contemplates it, as a star in the heavens is independent of the eye that gazes thereon.

466. Lastly, remembering the analysis I have made of the idea of being (414–433), and in which I have given an enumeration of its sublime characteristics, it would not be difficult to demonstrate that its production would be a task transcending the sphere, not merely of human, but of all finite power. But as what I have already said in proof of the proposition laid down at the head of this article seems to me sufficient, I will reserve this new demonstration, more intrinsic and cogent than the others, for another place.

ARTICLE V.

The idea of being is innate in us.

§ 1.

DEMONSTRATION.

467. This proposition is a consequence of the preceding ones ; for

(1) If the idea of being is so necessary that it enters essentially into the formation of all our ideas, so that we cannot think except by making use of it (410–411);

(2) If this idea is not contained in sensations (414–439);

(3) If it cannot be drawn from sensations, external or internal, through reflection (438–447);

(4) If it is not created in us by God in the act of intellectual perception (461, 462);

(5) Lastly, if it would be absurd to say that it emanates from within ourselves (463, 464);

It remains that it is innate in us; in other words, that possible being is present to and contemplated by us from the very first moment of our existence, although we do not advert to it until much later.[1]

---

[1] It might be asked of what kind is this union of the idea of being with our soul. From some passages of S. Thomas, he would seem to have been of opinion that this union is similar to that of ideas which lie deposited in our memory without being actually thought of, and which form what he calls *habitual knowledge* (*De Verit.* Q. x., A. viii., ix.). In the same way, the innate principles, both speculative and practical, of which S. Thomas speaks, are inserted in us as *habits* (*habitus principiorum*), and then on occasion of the sensations (*phantasmata*) they are instantly reduced to actual thought by the *intellectus agens*, and, so to speak, remembered.

But we must observe, that according to the Doctor of Aquin, besides these conceptions innate in *habit* and not in *act*, there is an *intellectus agens* which is truly in *act*, and by its *light* illumines all things, *i.e.* renders them actual objects of our thought. Now I believe that this principle of knowledge belonging to the *intellectus agens* – which S. Thomas expresses under the metaphor of *light*, and from which the ancient writers never, or certainly very seldom, and only in a fugitive manner take off the metaphorical veil—is precisely the *idea of being*. Such is undoubtedly the opinion of S. Bonaventure. There is, however, a passage in S. Thomas which at first sight might make one doubt as to whether this were also his view, or whether he herein differed in some degree from his intimate friend the great Franciscan. But it seems to me that it is possible to reconcile these two master minds by giving a discreet interpretation to the words of the Angelical. The following is the passage to which I refer : 'The same must be said as regards the acquisition of knowledge ; certain seeds of the sciences pre-exist in us, that is to say, the primary intellectual conceptions which are at once known by the light of the acting intellect (*intellectus agens*) through the species abstracted from sensations (*phantasmata*), be such conceptions complex, as the axioms, or be they simple, as the notion of being (*ratio entis*), of oneness, and such like, all of which are at once apprehended by the intellect. From these universal principles, as from so many seminal reasons, all the other principles are derived' (*De Verit.*, Q. xi., a. i). 'Similiter etiam dicendum est de scientiæ acquisitione, quod præexistunt in nobis quædam scientiarum semina, scilicet primæ conceptiones intellectus, quæ statim lumine intellectus agentis cognoscuntur per species a sensibilibus abstractas, sive sint complexa, ut dignitates, sive incomplexa, sicut ratio entis, et unius, et hujusmodi, quæ statim intellectus apprehendit. Ex istis autem principiis universalibus omnia principia sequuntur, sicut ex quibusdam rationibus seminalibus.'

Now the doubt which this passage suggests as to the meaning of S. Thomas, is as follows. He places the *notion of being* amongst those things which the *intellectus agens* sees immediately, but on occasion of the phantasms. Therefore, to him, *being* is not that which, as I conjecture, is the constitutive *form* of the *intellectus agens* itself. The interpretation I would propose is, that, according to this manner of speaking, it is one thing to have the *notion of being* (*ratio entis*) and another to have *being*, and nothing more, present to the mind. For us to have the notion of being, would mean that we understand the force of it, *i.e.* understand that it is susceptible of being applied, and thus producing in us, by the virtue intrinsic to it, diverse cognitions. That we cannot know the force, the fecundity of the idea of being, its aptitude to be applied, until on occasion of the sensations (*phantasmata*) we actually do apply it, is what I also say. In that case, this idea remains no longer solitary or inoperative, it becomes active ; we then consider it attentively and with a new

468. This demonstration *per exclusionem* will be unanswerable if I can show that the enumeration of the alternatives possible in the case is complete.

Now, that it is complete, may be seen in the following manner :—

We have the idea of *being in general* : this is the fact to be explained.

If we have this idea, either it was given to us when we received our nature, or it was produced in us later ; there is no middle term here.

If it was produced later, it must have been produced either by our own selves or by some other being ; here also there is no middle term.

By our own selves it was, most certainly, not produced (463, 464) : if then it was produced by some cause different from us, this cause must be either something *sensible* (the action of bodies) or something *non-sensible* (an intelligent being other than ourselves, God, &c.). Again there is no middle term here.

purpose, and discover its true import or intimate nature (*ratio entis*). Be this as it may, it is necessary to admit that the idea of being adheres to our mind either actually or habitually ; for if we possess this idea, we shall be able to deduce from it all principles, both speculative and practical, and thus to explain the existence of human cognitions ; whereas if we do not possess it, it must either be revealed to us by God, or created by ourselves in the act of our experiencing a sensation— two suppositions equally inadmissible. Lastly, I observe that S. Thomas himself makes use of the very same expressions which I have adopted, and therefore sanctions their correctness ; *e.g.* where he says that the light of the *intellectus agens* is *formally* inherent in our mind (*formaliter inhæret intellectui*) (*S. I. Q. xxix., iv*) ; and speaking of the habitual knowledge which our soul has of itself, he says that 'its essence itself is present to our intellect '—*ipsa ejus essentia intellectui nostro est præsens* —and that ' the soul sees itself by means of its own essence :' '*Anima per essentiam suam se videt*' (*De Verit.*, Q. x., A. viii.);

although, according to him, this vision is not an actual, but an habitual knowledge. If I could here find time to establish a truth which would require a long discussion in order to be made intelligible to the many, but which must seem clear enough to those who have been thoroughly accustomed to observe and reflect upon their own interior —viz. : that ' Every act of our mind is essentially unknown to itself'—I am convinced that every difficulty presented by the statement that ' We *always* have an actual intuition of indeterminate being,' and even in those first moments of which we have retained no recollection, would vanish entirely. The light of this truth would cause us to accept the statement, not without a certain wonder, I confess, yet with readiness and without our feeling any need of having recourse to an *habitual* or dormant knowledge. But since the question as to the mode in which we conceive the union of the idea of being with ourselves is of little consequence, provided this union be admitted, I will not add anything more on the subject.

But both these alternatives have also been excluded.

Therefore, the enumeration of possible cases is complete, because reduced to such an issue that any middle term would be an absurdity. If then the idea of being in general can in no case be supposed to arise in us posteriorly to our coming into this world, it only remains to say that this idea is innate ; which was the thing to be demonstrated.

§ 2.

Why we find it difficult to advert to the idea of being always present to us.

469. Here those who have not properly habituated themselves to reflect on their own interior will be apt to raise the usual objection : ' How is it possible that we should have this intuition of *being* without having consciousness of it, without knowing or being able distinctly to say that we have it ? '

Leibnitz answered this objection very conclusively on occasion of his remarks on the book of Locke, who thought it the *Achilles* of the arguments against innate ideas. I quoted that answer in the Chapter on the Leibnitzian system (288–292).

I will, however, add here a few observations.

In the first place, I would ask the objector, whether when his thoughts are wholly engrossed with any particular subject, he takes time to reflect on and actually to advert to all the other cognitions he has acquired in the course of his life, and which lie deposited in his memory ? I believe his reply will be, that while he is thinking of one thing he cannot think of another ; while he is dealing with one subject he cannot attend to so many others. And yet he has in him all that while a large store of knowledge ready to be brought out whenever a fitting opportunity should arise. This is a fact, and from it we can see two things :—

(1) That it is possible for many ideas to be in our mind without our giving actual advertence to them, so that practically, for the time being, it is much the same as if we knew nothing of them.

(2) That, in order to reflect on an idea different from the one actually before our attention, we must by fresh act of our mental energy transfer the attention from the second to the first idea, which was indeed in our mind, but lay there neglected as it were and unnoticed.

I need not stop here to investigate how these two things can be, or what is the state of cognitions lying dormant and unheeded in our memory. This would be superfluous to my present purpose. The simplest observation assures us that these things are exactly as I have stated ; and this is all I require.

Since, then, a fresh act of attention on our ideas is necessary in order that we may become conscious of having them, and able to put them into words ; it follows that so long as our attention is not moved by some stimulus to reflect on a given idea, that idea must remain in our mind unobserved.

It is therefore neither absurd nor strange that the idea of being also should, in the first moments of our existence, lie in our soul without any advertence, and consequently without our being able to speak of it. On the contrary, this must necessarily be so ; for when we come into the world, what reflection do we give to the things that are within us ? The *idea of being* therefore will remain unnoticed until such time as reflection be aroused in us by some adequate agency. Thus aroused, it will turn towards that idea, and so find and contemplate it, and at last, having obtained a sufficiently distinct view of it, enable us to express it in words, and to reason upon it with all security.

470. And this is precisely what takes place.

In our earliest infancy there is nothing to excite and direct our attention to our inner selves. We have no interest in doing so, no stimulus of a nature to make us feel the need of it. On the contrary, everything which affects us from all around tends continually to divert the application of our mental activity from ourselves, and draw it to sensible objects. Our senses are struck on all sides by innumerable impressions new to us ; the eyes are dazzled and enchanted by the light : the palate and the nerves of the stomach incite us towards the sweet aliment of the maternal breast ; the soul is nothing to us. How far, then, are we as yet from knowing what kind of thoughts we have, and which is the better part of our being ? The infant does not begin so soon to philosophise, or to search into the depths of his own heart and intellect. He is ignorant of a great many things regarding even his body, although he has an intellect and a heart as well as a body.

But when the infant has grown into an adult, and some cause leads him to reflect on himself, then philosophy begins in him ; for philosophy is reflection upon oneself. And, leaving other considerations aside, is not the difficulty which the philosophical student experiences when trying to discover what passes within himself, proof sufficient of the truth of what I have said, namely, that in our heart and mind there are affections and cognitions to which we do not advert, and hence cannot speak about them to others ?

In fact, for us to be conscious of an idea existing in our mind, it is necessary, not only that our attention should turn to and catch sight of it, but also that it should be stimulated by some want, some curiosity ; and even when so stimulated, it does not succeed in compassing its object immediately, nor without labour, nor always. If all that is in our mind and that takes place within us were always actually noticed by us, the study of the philosophy of man would be useless : indeed every man would be a born philosopher, or rather would know everything about his inner self without so many meditations and philosophical observations as we now find to be necessary in order to discover and accurately distinguish what is in our interior. No philosopher would ever know less than another, or have to correct the observations of another, or say that he sees within himself what is not there, or contrariwise. In short, however singular the fact may appear, it is none the less true, and attested by observations too numerous and too certain to be gainsaid, namely, that it is one thing for an idea to exist in our mind, and quite another thing for us to advert to it, to be actually conscious of it, and to be able to say to ourselves and to others that we possess it.

Wherefore the above objection need not deter anyone from admitting the idea of being as innate ; it being certain that, at the beginning of our existence and for a long time after, we are unable to observe it in us, (1) because our attention has no motive or stimulus to concentrate and fix itself on what passes within our interior ; on the contrary, it is continually drawn outwards by the impressions of sensible objects ; (2) because even when, having attained to a riper age, we, either from curiosity or from some other excitement, seek to ascertain what exists or takes place within ourselves, even then I say, it is by no means easy to discover this idea of pure being ; for if we wish to see it immediately in its own self, there is nothing to direct our attention to it ; and if we search for it in the ideas we have already acquired, as for instance those of corporeal things, and try to distinguish in them *pure being* from the other elements, an exceedingly difficult mental process must be gone through, that is to say, we must go on step by step from one abstraction to another until we arrive at the last of all abstractions, whereby from the object on which this function is exercised, we remove completely every accident, every form, every mode of being (408–411).

To acquire the art of doing all this, a long exercise, to say the least, is necessary ; but very few are endowed with the requisite parts for it, and, even with them, full success can only be the fruit of long-continued application. Hence the greatest number grow faint in the inquiry, and stop on the road which would certainly end in their discovering that recondite idea, provided they persevered long enough.[1]

---

[1] These difficulties did not escape the observation of Plato. With that loftiness of mind which raised him so far above the common herd, he remarks (and his own experience had so taught him), that to speak of the things which are found within the human soul to those who have not yet arrived at a reflex knowledge of them, is only to incur ridicule and pass for a visionary. Hence the *esoteric* or secret doctrine, both of Plato himself and of others before him, which was communicated only to the initiated few, lest, if exposed before the multitude, it should be made the target for irreverent sneers. The idea of *being*, the purest of all ideas, is also the last and most difficult to be adverted to ; and from some passages of Plato I am induced to think that he saw this idea, but spoke of it disguisedly, as a thing too difficult for the many, or presented it under images and only in a fugitive way, according to the words of Dante :—

. . . . . . ' Ever to that truth
Which but the semblance of falsehood wears,
A man, if possible, should bar his lip ;

Even such a man as Kant, one of the most experienced in abstraction, stopped half way, *i.e.* in the forms of space and

Since, although blameless, he incurs reproach.' — *Inferno*, *Canto* xvi. (Cary's translation).

'Sempre a quel ver ch' ha faccia di menzogna,
De' l' uom chiuder le labbra quant' ei puote ;
Però che senza colpa fa vergogna.'

Addressing as I do, a Christian world, I have a right to presume well of men, and to speak to them openly on these difficult topics. But that what I have said of Plato may not remain unsupported by proofs, I will quote in confirmation some passages from his works. In many places, this great thinker compares the human mind to the eye, which sees only by means of the rays of the sun. Now what, in the opinion of Plato, is this light which enlightens the mind and which the senses do not possess? It is the idea of being or, to use his own word, of THE BEING (ENS) ; and I say the *idea of being*, because although Plato says that this light comes from God (THE ENS) : nevertheless he tells us clearly, that it is not God Himself (*De Repub.* vi.) ; a distinction which has been abused by the Platonists. Plato says : 'The Sun, in so far as seen, is not the Sun himself,' and he proceeds to argue the matter thus : --

'*Socrates.* When the eyes turn to those things whose colour is illumined and manifested by the full light of day, they see ; but when they turn to the things involved in the obscurity of night, they grow dim and suffer hallucination, and seem almost as blind as if the faculty of vision were not in them.

'*Glaucus.* Just so.

'*Socrates.* And when the eyes look at things illumined by the sun, then it becomes apparent that they have the power of sight in them.

'*Glaucus.* Such is the case.

'*Socrates.* I say the very same of the mind. When the mind applies itself to that in which truth and BEING itself shine (*i.e.* to *intelligible* things), it then understands and knows, and shows that it has discernment. But when it is drawn to that which is

mixed up with darkness, is subject to generation and corruption (so Plato was wont to characterise *sensible* things), its acuteness is blunted, it is distracted between different opinions and seems devoid of understanding.'

Then Plato, in the next Dialogue (vii. *De Repub.*), undertakes to shew by a simile, how difficult it is for men to withdraw their attention from *sensible* things, and rise to the vision of intelligible things and to *being*. He supposes a cavern, deep but perfectly straight, into which a great lighted torch, placed afar off, but in a direct line with it, sends its rays, illuminating it down to the very end. In it dwell men, but so bound that they can never turn their backs or heads to see the opening and the torchlight, but must gaze only at the opposite wall. Meanwhile, at the mouth of the cavern there are carried past, vases of different sorts, and statues of men and animals, which throw their fleeting shadows on the said wall. The unhappy men inside, seeing only shadows, would suppose that nothing existed but shadows ; and if they should hear any voices, they would very likely imagine that it was the shadows that spoke. Now, he continues, let us suppose that a number of them were set loose and taken outside. They would at first complain of the new light which dazzled their eyes ; but after they had got accustomed to it, they would perceive how much better their new condition was, both on account of the better light, and of their seeing the objects as they truly are ; and they would have no wish to bury themselves in that dungeon. But if any one of them, much to his discomfort, were to be sent back into it, and then (even before he had time to recover from the blindness consequent upon that sudden return to darkness) 'he were to address his former companions who had never been loosed from their chains, and try to convince them of the illusion under which they had been labouring all through, would he not make himself their laughingstock ? Would not every one taunt him as one who, as a penalty for his temporary escape, had lost the right use of his eyes? And would they not all

time, in the twelve categories, and in the Schemata ; all which are, as we have seen (Sec. iv., c. iv., art. ii.), only more or less general determinations and modes of the *idea of being*, which stands yet further beyond them, and is perfectly exempt from all determinations whatever.

§ 3.

The theory propounded above was known to the Fathers of the Church.

471. If, then, the theory on being in general has been discovered and brought out to view only very late in the history of the world, this arises from the nature of the thing.

Although we make use of the idea of being in all our thoughts, yet we do not advert to it; and to do so—to set this idea before our intellectual gaze by its own pure self and divested of everything extraneous thereto, and to observe the intimate relation it has with all other ideas—is extremely difficult for us ; because those ideas originate from and by

agree that in future no one should be allowed to leave the cavern ; and that any such attempt should be punished at once with death?'

Such, says Plato, is the lot of those sages who lay open to men truths which are beyond their ken. Whence he concludes : ' Whoever has good sense and reflects on the matter, will see, that the sight may be injuriously affected in two ways and from two causes, namely, by descending from light to darkness, and by returning from darkness to light : and so when he finds the mind of his fellows disturbed and incapable of discerning, he will perceive that this is due to similar reasons. Therefore, he will not too lightly laugh at others, but will first inquire carefully whether those to whom he speaks may not perchance, from a state of greater intellectual light, have passed into one of darkness, or whether in consequence of emerging from supine ignorance into effulgent light, they are not overpowered by the dazzling brightness. And he will applaud the condition of the latter and esteem their life blessed ; but will commiserate the former. Or if he will

laugh at either, it will be rather at the first than at the second.' After this, Plato concludes with a passage very much to my purpose : ' As the eye cannot turn round from a dark to a bright object unless the whole body turn round as well ; even so we must turn the whole power of our mind from things generated (sensible things) to that which is called BEING, in order that we may with our investigation rise even to that which is most luminous.' *Being* therefore, according to Plato, is the light which illumines other things.

Now I leave the reader to judge if the ' cavern ' of Plato can be compared to the ' *camera obscura* ' of Locke, as has been done by Reid and Stewart (*Elements of Philosophy*, Vol. i., C. i., Sec. 1). Locke introduces his ' *camera obscura* ' to explain ideas which he confounds with sensations. Plato introduces his ' cavern ' to mark the difference between shadows and realities, sensations and ideas. To confound the ' *camera obscura* ' of Locke with the ' cavern ' of Plato, is the same as to take a wooden head for a living one for the reason that the shape of both is round.

means of this one ; nay, as I have already pointed out, they are in truth nothing but this same idea brought into relation with the passions we experience in our senses (internal and external), and, speaking generally, with some determinations more or less extensive, down to the narrowest of all, which, in the case of bodies, are the sensible qualities.

Nevertheless, this primal and innate idea, this *form* of all other ideas, which shines to every mind, was noticed very clearly by the loftiest intellects of antiquity; but more particularly have the doctrines relating to it been in the possession of Christian society, and are contained in the books of her sages.

472. In proof of this I will only quote a passage from a work attributed to S. Bonaventure, in which the author lays great stress on the distinction between *seeing* an idea with the intellect, and *considering* it, that is, directing our attention to it so as to be aware that we see it. And he applies this distinction precisely to the theory of the *idea of being*, as that parent idea with which we form all the rest, and yet notice last of all and with the greatest difficulty. Here are his words : ' Wonderful, then, is the blindness of our mind,[1] which *considers* not that which it *sees* first, and without which it can know nothing. But as the eye, intent on the various differences of colours, sees not the light by which it sees all other things,[2] or, if it sees it, does not advert to it, even so

[1] Our mind requires to reflect upon itself in order to advert to what it sees. This arises from its natural limitation. But the deterioration which befell our nature has had the effect of rendering us inert and slow to reflect on ourselves, as well as uncertain in our reflections. This defect is appropriately called *blindness*.

[2] In expounding the doctrine of Aristotle, I have shown that the Stagirite had gone so far as to see that the human mind, although it did not carry with itself any particular *cognitions*, must nevertheless have an innate *light*, which enabled it to illumine sensible things, and so to *cognise* them. Now if any one had wished to follow out Aristotle's line of thought, and push his reasoning further, all that remained for him to do was, to explain clearly in what that mysterious *innate light* consisted. This inquiry I have taken in hand, from the point at which Aristotle stopped, and, as a result, I am convinced that that light can be nothing else but the *idea of being in general*, which I have proved to be the true light of the mind, and that whereby the things falling under our senses are illumined, *i.e.* perceived and known (262–275). Now all this was taught six hundred years ago, and held as a thing past questioning (*a*).

(*a*) For a great number of proofs that S. Thomas of Aquin held the idea of being in general (*ens commune, ens universale*) to be the *primo notum* or the constitutive form of the human intellect, see Rosmini's *A'innovamento*, &c., Lib. iii. Cap. liv. lv. lvi.—TRANSLATORS.

the eye of our mind, intent on these beings, particular and universal,[1] does not advert to *that being which stands outside every genus*, although it is that which occurs first to the mind, while all other things occur through it. Thus do we see in very deed, that as the eye of a bat is in respect of the light, so is the eye of our mind in respect of the most manifest things of nature'[2] (*Itin. mentis in Deum*, C. v).

---

[1] *Universal—i.e. genera and species.* The idea of being, on the contrary, is *most universal*; and it is most properly said to be *outside all genera*, because there are in it absolutely none of those differences and determinations which are necessary to constitute some particular *genus*.

[2] 'Mira igitur est cæcitas intellectus, qui non considerat illud quod prius VIDET et sine quo nihil potest cognoscere. Sed sicut oculus intentus in varias colorum differentias lumen, per quod videt cætera, non videt, et si videt, non tamen advertit : sic oculus mentis nostræ intentus in ista entia particularia et universalia, IPSUM ESSE EXTRA OMNE GENUS, licet primo occurrat menti, et per ipsum alia, tamen non advertit. Unde verissime apparet, quod sicut oculus vespertilionis se habet ad lucem, ita se habet oculus mentis nostræ ad manifestissima naturæ' (*Itin. mentis*, C. v).

PART II.

ORIGIN OF ALL IDEAS GENERALLY BY MEANS OF THE IDEA OF BEING.

CHAPTER I.

GIVEN THE IDEA OF BEING, THE ORIGIN OF THE OTHER IDEAS IS EXPLAINED BY ANALYSING THE ELEMENTS OF WHICH THEY ARE COMPOSED.

ARTICLE I.

Connection of the Doctrine I have expounded above with that which is to follow.

473. In now starting from the idea of being, not as acquired but as innate, in order to explain the origin of acquired ideas, I do not proceed upon a vain hypothesis; for I have heretofore established the existence of this idea.[1]

It only remains for me to show how all other ideas are derived from this one, so that, given it alone, the difficulty of explaining the rest vanishes.

To be convinced of the truth of such derivation, it might

---

[1] Newton observes that we must not propose any hypothesis in order to explain facts, except on the two following conditions :—

(1) That the thing which we assume as the cause of the facts to be explained be not itself hypothetical, but really existing.

(2) That it be capable of producing those facts.

My explanation of the origin of ideas not only possesses these two characteristics, but a third also, which removes it from the hypothetical class, and places in the class, as it seems to me, of well established theories.

This third characteristic consists in this, that I prove, not merely that the idea of being, of which I have first of all demonstrated the existence, is *capable* of generating from itself all other ideas, but that it actually does generate them; because by duly analysing any other idea, we find that whatever is *formal* in it is nothing but the idea of being. While therefore I trace all ideas to this one as to their (*formal*) *cause*, I also demonstrate that such cause is a *fact*. Thus the theory of the origin of ideas may fairly claim a place among the sciences strictly so called.

be enough to consider that the idea of being is the simplest of all ideas, and that it would be impossible to assume less of the innate than is therein contained (368, &c.).

ARTICLE II.

Analysis of all acquired ideas.

474. A diligent analysis of our ideas has given us the following results :—

(1) All ideas have in them, essentially, the conception of *possible being* (408, 409); which conception constitutes the *a priori* part and the *form* of our cognitions (304–309, 325–327).

(2) If there be in an idea something over and above the pure conception of being, this something is merely *a mode of being*; so that we may say with truth that every idea is nothing else but either *being* conceived without any mode, or being more or less determined by its modes: and these determinations form the *a posteriori* knowledge, or the matter of cognition.

ARTICLE III.

Since all acquired ideas are a compound of two elements, form and matter, a twofold cause is required for their expldnation.

475. In undertaking, then, to explain the origin of ideas, two things had to be accounted for: (1) the conception of being ; (2) the different determinations of which being is susceptible.

ARTICLE IV.

The twofold cause of acquired ideas is the Idea of being and Sensation.

476. Now, having already shown that the conception of being is innate in the human soul,[1] we have no difficulty

---

[1] Part I.—Let us hear S. Thomas on this matter also. 'Remanet igitur ipsa anima intellectiva in potentia ad DETERMINATAS similitudines rerum cognoscibilium a nobis (quæ sunt naturæ rerum sensibilium) : et has quidem determinatas naturas rerum sensibilium *præsentant nobis* PHANTASMATA' (*Cont. Gent.* II. lxxvii.).

I am accustomed to attribute to the *sensations* the suggesting of the determinations of things present : and to the *imagination* those of things not present : the word *phantasmata*, as understood by S. Thomas, includes the one and the other.

remaining, since all the various determinations of being are manifestly suggested to us by the senses. For instance : Let us suppose we have to explain how we came to acquire the idea of a corporeal being of a given size, form and colour, say a ball of ivory.

In the idea of a ball of ivory I think two things: (1) a something possible to exist ; because an impossibility cannot be an object of thought ; and (2) this something conceived as being of a certain size, a certain weight—spherical, smooth, white, &c.

Now assuming that the idea of possible being is in my mind, what more is wanted to explain how I came to think of the ivory ball ?

Nothing except to show how I came to determine to myself that possible being by the qualities of weight, form, size, colour, &c.

But this is easy enough, since all these determinations of the being are suggested to my mind by that which my exterior senses perceive of it, and of which I retain the memory.

ARTICLE V.

Doctrine of S. Thomas on the cause of our ideas.

477. S. Thomas is very far from saying that *sense* is the sole cause of human cognitions.

He also distinguishes between the *material* and the *formal* cause of ideas ; and credits the senses with being the *matter of the cause* (*material cause*), while reserving to the intellect the quality of being their *formal cause.* 'It cannot be said,' he writes, 'that the sensible cognition is the *total and perfect cause* of the intellectual cognition ; but it is rather in a certain way the *matter of the cause.*'[1]

[1] 'Non potest dici quod sensibilis cognitio sit totalis et perfecta causa intellectualis cognitionis ; sed magis quodammodo est MATERIA CAUSÆ' (*S. I.* lxxxiv. iv.). Hence in the system of S. Thomas the sense is not the principal agent in the formation of ideas, but only a secondary agent. Let us hear himself : 'In receptione qua in- tellectus possibilis species rerum' (*i.e.* the ideas) 'accipit a phantasmatibus, se habent phantasmata ut agens in- strumentale et SECUNDARIUM ; intel- lectus vero agens, ut agens PRINCI- PALE ET PRIMUM' (*De Verit.*, Q. x., art. vi. ad 7). The author of the *Itinerarium mentis in Deum* agrees with S. Thomas in recognising a two-

ARTICLE VI.

The true interpretation of the Scholastic dictum : 'There is nothing in the mind, which has not been first in the sense.'

478. Since, then, according to S. Thomas (477), the senses furnish only one element of our cognitions, *i.e.* the *matter*, while the other element, *i.e.* the *form*, can be furnished by the mind only, it follows that the Scholastic dictum, 'There is nothing in the mind which has not been first in the sense,' is wrongly understood by modern Sensists, who imagine that by it the Schoolmen meant to declare the sense as the only source of our cognitions.

The true meaning of that celebrated dictum, as it must have been understood by the greatest among the Schoolmen, could only be this, that 'All that belongs to the *matter* of our cognitions is suggested by the sense.'[1]

What is to be understood by 'All that belongs to the matter of our cognitions,' I have already explained (474).

I have said, that in all our ideas we think (1) *being*, and

---

fold cause of our ideas, and these two causes he lucidly distinguishes in the following passage : 'Non solum habet [MEMORIA] ab exteriori formari per phantasmata, verum etiam a superiori suscipiendo et in se habendo simplices formas quæ non possunt introire per portas sensuum et sensibilium phantasias' (*Itiner. mentis,* &c., iii).

[1] Nevertheless, the word *sense* in this place is still an incomplete expression, if by it we mean only the *external sense* (the five sensorial organs), and do not include also the *interior feeling* which the soul has of itself. In fact, how could we form the ideas of an intelligent being and of his operations, unless by means of the *feeling of ourselves* ? S. Thomas teaches this expressly in his work *Contra Gentiles* :— ' Neither by demonstration nor by faith could we know that the separate substances are intellectual substances, unless the soul first knew from itself what an intellectual being is. Wherefore we must start, as from a principle, from the experimental knowledge of what

our own soul is, in order that we may arrive at all that we know of separate substances.'—' Cum enim de substantiis separatis hoc quod sint intellectuales quædam substantiæ cognoscamus vel per demonstrationem vel per fidem, neutro modo hanc cognitionem accipere possemus, nisi hoc ipsum quod est intellectuale anima nostra ex seipsâ cognosceret : unde et scientia de intellectu animæ oportet uti ut principio ad omnia quæ de substantiis separatis cognoscimus' (L. iii., C. xlvi). According therefore to S. Thomas the sources from which we draw the *matter* of our cognitions in this life, are (1) the external senses ; (2) the internal feeling of ourselves.

In the opinion of the Angelic Doctor *sensation* and *reflection* are not the sources of cognition itself, as Locke maintains, but only the sources of the *matter* of our cognitions : and the doctrine of S. Thomas is derived from S. Augustine (see S. Thomas, *Ibid.*), so that this is an old doctrine sanctioned by a long and venerable tradition.

this is their *formal* part ; (2) a *determinate mode of being* ; and this is their *material* part.

The meaning, then, of the above Scholastic dictum comes to this : ' The mind cannot think of any determinate *mode* of being except this be furnished to it by the sense.'

479. Now so long as we think indeterminate being only, we think nothing subsistent, nothing therefore which can lay claim to the title of *real thing* ; therefore every cognition of a real thing is furnished by the senses, inasmuch as *subsistence* is that which determines a being in such a manner as to entitle it to the name of *real thing*.

CHAPTER II.

ANOTHER WAY OF EXPLAINING THE ORIGIN OF ACQUIRED
IDEAS, THAT IS, BY MEANS OF THE FORMATION OF
HUMAN REASON.

ARTICLE I.

*The idea of being, present to our spirit by nature, is that which consti-
tutes the two faculties of Intellect and Reason.*

480. We receive the *matter* of our cognitions from sensation (476).

The *matter* of our cognitions, taken by itself alone, is not
cognition.

It becomes cognition when the *form,* that is to say, *being,*
is added to it, or which comes to the same, when our soul—at
once *sensitive* and *intelligent*—considers that which it feels by
means of the sense, in relation with the *being* which it sees
with the intellect, and finds in the thing felt a something (a
being) acting upon it.

481. I have defined the intellect as 'the faculty of the
intuition of indeterminate being.'

Reason, on the contrary, I have defined as 'the faculty of
reasoning,' and consequently, in the first place, of the application of being to the sensations—of seeing being determined
to a *mode* presented by the sensations,—in a word, of uniting
the *form* to the *matter* of the cognitions.

Now, if *being* is the essential object of the intellect and of
the reason, it follows that these two faculties exist in us only
because we are endowed with the permanent intuition of
being.

482. It is *being* therefore which, as object, draws our soul
into that essential act which we call *intellect,* and which gives

the soul the aptitude to see afterwards this same being in relation with the particular modes furnished by the sensations —an aptitude which is called *reason*. In short, the idea of being united to our soul is that which forms our *intellect* and our *reason* : it is that which constitutes us intelligent beings and rational animals.

ARTICLE II.

Doctrine of S. Thomas and S. Bonaventure on the formation of the Intellect and the Reason.

483. The doctrines of S. Thomas and S. Bonaventure, derived from the tradition of antiquity, seem to me to be in accordance with what I have thus far laid down.

S. Thomas appears to me to have clearly known that the intellect was nothing but the faculty of the intuition of *being* ; which is the same as to have known that the intuition of being is what constitutes the *form* of our intellect.

He says expressly, that ' The proper object of the intellect is *common being* or *truth.*' ' Objectum intellectus est ens vel verum commune.' [1]

Now S. Thomas teaches that the nature of a faculty is determined by its object ; to him therefore, *being* contemplated by us, was that which made the intellectual faculty what it is.

Again, we must observe that S. Thomas did not by any means neglect the analysis of ideas ; and it was this analysis which led him to see that the first thing we apprehend in any idea is *being*, so that he calls *being* the first knowable (*primum intelligibile*).

484. And here mark well my argument, which is entirely based on the teaching of the great Doctor of Aquin.

He describes the *form* of a thing as that element in virtue of which the thing first presents itself to our mind as in act.[2]

---

[1] (*S.* I. lv. I.) S. Thomas uses the substantive word *ens* ; when I say simply *being*, or *being in general*, I take the word in the infinitive sense (*to be, esse*). I do not think it necessary now to point out the difference between these two terms   it is enough for me to observe that the ancients often used them indifferently one for the other.

[2] The Scholastic definition of *form* is : ' quod in unaquaque re primo agit.'

If then *being* is what our mind apprehends in all its intellections ; we must admit that, before we see in a thing a being, we have no intellection of that thing. On the other hand, so soon as we have apprehended a being, the intellection exists ; for we have some knowledge. *Being* therefore is the form of intellectual cognition, because it is that which from its first moment causes it to be in act, to exist.

Now, if the mind or intellect is the faculty of contributing the *form* of our cognitions, and if this *form*, according to S. Thomas, can be nothing else but *being*—the first thing our intellect sees, the first thing that makes it to be in act—we are forced to conclude that, in the opinion of the holy Doctor, the idea of being is the *informing* principle of the human intelligence.[1]

485. The author of the *Itinerarium* saw the same truth. Hence he says : '*Being* is that which first presents itself to the intellect, I mean that being which is pure act,'[2] so that it constitutes in act or *informs* the intellect itself.

And because *being*, present to the intellect, is *truth*, he says with S. Augustine, that 'the intellect is formed by truth.'[3]

ARTICLE III.

Corollary : All acquired ideas proceed from the innate idea of being.

486. All philosophers agree in this, that ideas belong to the faculty of cognition.

[1] Aristotle calls the intellect *species specierum*. His commentators, anxious to keep the minds of his readers far aloof from any suspicion that he admitted anything innate in the human soul, are always ready to interpret this expression as referring to that intellect which the Stagirite calls *habitus principiorum* and looks upon as acquired. I do not care to enter on a philological discussion with these able interpreters. I content myself with observing that the denomination of *species specierum* would be perfectly suitable to the idea of *being in general*, that most universal idea which in its one self represents to us all other ideas.

[2] '*Esse* igitur est quod primo cadit in intellectum, et illud esse est quod est purus actus :' and the reason he adduces from this is the manifest fact : ' Si non ens ' (he says), ' non potest intelligi nisi per ENS ' (*Itin. ment. in Deum*, C. v).

[3] ' Cum ipsa mens nostra immediate ab ipsa veritate formetur,' &c. (*Itiner. mentis*, &c., C. v.). This doctrine is repeated almost word for word by all Christian antiquity. S. Augustine, treating of the human mind, writes : ' Nulla substantia interposita, ab IPSA FORMATUR VERITATE.' (*Book of the LXXXIII Questions*, q. lxi).

I will show still more clearly in the Sixth Section of this work, that the *idea of being in general* is precisely that which all men call *truth*, and by union with which the human intellect is made to exist.

But the faculty of cognition exists in virtue of the union of the idea of being with our spirit (470-485).[1]

Therefore the idea of being, which is the informing principle of this faculty, is also the informing principle of all the ideas which the same faculty is capable of acquiring : and this is what I had to prove.

[1] We shall gain some light as to the mode in which the idea of being in general adheres to the human spirit, from what will be said later on (534, 535).

CHAPTER III.

A THIRD WAY OF EXPLAINING THE ORIGIN OF ACQUIRED IDEAS GENERALLY, *i.e.* BY MEANS OF THE FACULTIES WHICH PRODUCE THEM.

ARTICLE I.

Faculty of Reflection.

487. I have already distinguished such *reflection* as may be capable of producing ideas in us, from that sensitive instinct which we find also in the brute, and the force of which causes it to adjust its sentient power to the sensations, and, when these are pleasurable, to remain intently fixed on them, so as to enjoy them to the fullest extent (448–450).

The *reflection* which may be capable of producing ideas in us, is a function of the *reason*.

The difference between simple *perception*,[1] and *reflection*, is as follows :—

Perception is limited to the *object perceived*; it does not go beyond. In so far as I *perceive* a certain thing, I know of nothing outside that one thing. *Reflection*, on the contrary, is the turning anew of my attention on the things I have *perceived*. Hence it is not limited to the object of a single perception only, but may extend to several perceptions at once, and, of many objects perceived, together with their relations, make to itself one sole object.

Reflection therefore, considered in respect to *perception*, is *general*, because it has for its object as many perceptions as it chooses ; while *perception* considered in respect to the *reflec-*

---

[1] *Perception*, according to me, is of two kinds, namely, *sensitive* and *intellectual*. See notes to No. 453.

tion corresponding to it, is *particular.* Thus *reflection* may be called a *general perception,* that is to say, a *perception of many perceptions.* Consequently, in so far as I *reflect,* I find myself placed in a sphere higher than that of my perceptions; and from this point, as from an eminence, I observe the objects beneath, contemplate my various perceptions, confront them with one another, unite them or separate them at pleasure, and form such combinations, natural or even abnormal, as I like best.[1]

When I survey the state of my own mind, and pass in review the ideas which are in it, when I say to myself, ' I have such and such cognitions,' when by means of reasoning I arrange these my cognitions in a certain order, deduce one from another, &c. ; then it is that I *reflect.*

488. If I should fix my attention on one of my ideas only, would this be an act of *reflection ?*

We must distinguish : Have I an end in thus fixing my mind on this one idea, and do I fix my mind upon it because I am bent on attaining that end ? If so, this fixing of my mind would be an *act of reflection* ; but let it be noted, that the case is against our hypothesis, which assumes that ' I fix my mind on one idea only ;' for it is no longer true that I fix my mind on one idea only, if I think of it for an end, for then I think, and therefore have the idea of this end also : I do not consider the idea on which I fixed my mind by itself alone, but in so far as it is *related* to the end I have proposed to myself.

On the contrary : do I fix my mind on that idea without any further aim ? Is my attention kept to it by a pleasurable impression made on me by its light, in the same way that a pleasurable sensation ravishes and holds to itself instinctively my sensitive activity ? In such case, this fixing of my thought is not *reflection,* but merely direct *attention,* which is drawn

---

[1] The whole of this doctrine may be said to be contained in the following passage of S. Thomas of Aquin : ' Intellectus enim UNICA VIRTUTE cognoscit omnia quæ pars sensitiva diversis potentiis apprehendit ' (perceives), ' et etiam ALIA MULTA ; intellectus etiam quanto fuerit altior ' (*i.e.* the higher it rises in the order of its reflections), ' tanto ALIQUO UNO plura cognoscere potest, ad quæ cognoscenda intellectus inferior ' (a lower order of reflection) ' non pertingit nisi per multa ' (*C. Gent.* LI. xxxi).

into a more intense act, and naturally kept in it. Now this *intensifying* of activity must be carefully distinguished from *reflection*.

Reflection, then, is 'a *voluntary attention* given to our conceptions'—an attention governed by an end ; and this supposes an intelligent being capable of knowing such end, so that he may propose it to himself (73, 74).

489. By *reflection* therefore we form the *ideas of relation* ; we group ideas together (synthesis), or we divide them (analysis).

And when we make use of *reflection* in order to analyse an idea, and separate what is *common* in it from what is *proper*, we then perform the operation called *abstraction*.

All these are functions of reflection.

ARTICLE II.

Universalisation and Abstraction.

490. *Abstraction* must be distinguished from *universalisation* ; and the confounding of the one with the other has been the cause of many errors.

By *abstraction* we take away something from a cognition (*e. gr.* the notes proper to the thing known) ; by *universalisation* we add,[1] enlarge, in short universalise. Subtraction and addition are contrary operations.

---

[1] The doctrine of S. Thomas appears to me to agree with this. But then one must be well acquainted with his manner of speaking. He teaches, (1) that the *sensible phantasms* are nothing but similitudes of things ; (2) that the understanding perceives the things themselves in their essence or quiddity : 'quidditas rei est proprium objectum intellectus' (*S.* I. lxxxv. 5).

If then the understanding finds in the phantasms nothing but similitudes of things, and if, according to S. Thomas, it nevertheless *perceives*, not the *similitudes* but the things themselves, how can it do this unless by supplying on its own part the *things*, *i.e.* the beings? The understanding therefore supplies *being*, whilst the sense furnishes only the similitude of being. Let any one read attentively the following passage of the Angelical, and then say if the interpretation I have given is not the right one :—'Inasmuch as the phantasms are SIMILITUDES of the individuals . . . they have not that mode of being which belongs to the human intellect, . . . and therefore they cannot by their virtue alone impress anything on the possible intellect.'

The phantasms therefore cannot, by themselves alone, communicate anything to the understanding. How then do they come to be capable of doing this ? S. Thomas continues as follows : 'But by virtue of the *acting intellect* there results a certain similitude in the *possible intellect*, through the *acting intellect* turning itself upon the phantasms (*ex conversione intellectus agentis super*

491. What do we add by *universalisation* ?—' Universality' (the *intentio universalitatis* of the School); and universality, as I have already shown, is nothing but the *possibility* of a thing (418, 419). To put this briefly: (1) I receive a sensation ; (2) I join with it the idea of a being, the cause of

phantasmata), which similitude is representative OF THOSE THINGS OF WHICH THEY ARE PHANTASMS, only as regards the nature of the species.'

The *species* (idea) which is produced by the acting intellect does not, then, represent the phantasms, the similitudes, or effects of things ; it represents the *things themselves.* If therefore the phantasms do not contain the things themselves, how does the acting intellect form the pure ideas of those things on occasion of the phantasms? By its own virtue (*virtute intellectus*), through the innate light, in a word, because the intellect sees the *being* (the nature) of the thing where the phantasms are, and thus sees the thing. What then is the meaning of the expression ' the understanding turns itself upon the phantasms' (*converti supra phantasmata*)? It can only mean that to the *phantasms* received by the soul from the senses, the understanding adds *being.* Man becomes affected by sensations ; conscious of them, he immediately says to himself : ' here there is a being which has produced in me these sensations.' Thus does the soul turn itself to the phantasms and thereby form the similitude, the *species*, not of the phantasms, but of the being that has caused the phantasms.

Here it may be objected, that according to S. Thomas it is the acting intellect, and not the soul, that turns itself to the phantasms. I answer, that this manner of speaking originates in the fact that it is the acting intellect which furnishes *being*, and that it is therefore through its agency that the *species* (ideas) of things are formed ; but to speak more accurately, this operation should be attributed to the soul itself. S. Thomas, with whom propriety of language was always a great point, tells us this in express terms, saying : ' Properly speaking, the act of understanding is not done by the intellect but by the soul through the intellect. ' Intelligere,

proprie loquendo, non est intellectus, sed animæ per intellectum ' (*De Verit.*, Q. x. ix. ad 3 in contrar.). And this beautiful observation holds good in general for all the operations of the several powers of the soul. It will therefore be better to say that it is our soul which turns itself to the phantasms received in it and, where they are, sees a *being* (supplied by the *acting intellect*), and thus forms the *species* or idea of the thing ; and this is the first step of the *reason* (the primitive synthesis). Now be it observed, that this turning of the acting intellect to the phantasms, is synonymous with the other phrase of S. Thomas, 'to illumine the phantasms' (*illuminare phantasmata*), which means ' to shed upon them the *light* of the acting intellect,' *i.e. being.* But I will explain this more fully in Note 2, § 515. Meanwhile, let us hear how S. Thomas concludes to our purpose the passage above quoted : ' Et per hunc modum dicitur abstrahi species intelligibilis a phantasmatibus, non quod aliqua eadem numero forma quæ prius fuit in phantasmatibus, postmodum fiat in intellectu possibili, ad modum quo corpus accipitur ab uno loco et transfertur ad alterum.'— 'And thus the intelligible species is said to be abstracted from the phantasms, not as though a given form that was first in the phantasms were—its very self, that is, in its numerical identity, transferred into the possible intellect, in the same manner as a body is transferred from one place to another' (*S. I.* lxxxvi. ad 3).

According, then, to S. Thomas, from the phantasms nothing is transferred into the understanding. What really does take place is this : the understanding, on occasion of the phantasms, forms the *species* (ideas), that is to say, by means of the light of *being* which shines before it, sees the beings by whose action the phantasms are produced.

that sensation (*intellectual perception*) ; (3) I consider this being simply as possible (*pure idea*).   The being is *universalised*.

Suppose this being is a bird, for instance, a dove.   By having universalised a dove which falls under my senses, have I taken away anything from my representation of it ?   Nothing whatever.   I can even have the corporeal image of the dove vividly before me—its silvery wings, the changeful hues of its neck, its eyes, its feet, its form, its movements—and yet I can have, united to all this, the thought of the possibility of other real doves, corresponding in every detail to the same representation.   In this case my representation, although now universalised, remains fully as complete as it was before being so, *i.e.* furnished not only with the features essential to this kind of bird, but also with all the accidental ones, less alone the reality or subsistence.

492. But if, on the other hand, from my representation of the dove in question I should take away the colour, form, particular movements, in short all the accidents, and should restrict my thought exclusively to that which constitutes the essentials of the genus dove, I should then be also performing an *abstraction* ; since my representation of that bird would no longer be intact and complete as heretofore, but deficient in a part.   I could no longer have the corporeal image of a dove, but only the thought of a dove in the abstract.

493. Keeping in mind this distinction between *universalisation* and *abstraction*, we may say that all ideas are *universal*, but not all are *abstract*.   It will be well to preserve strictly this manner of speaking, as an effectual means for keeping separate two kinds of ideas, which, owing to their affinity, may easily be confused together.

OBSERVATION I.

Why the faculty of abstraction has been confused with that of universalisation.

494. The reason of this confusion was this : In every case of *universalisation* our mind has before it the representation of a thing wholly apart from the judgment on its *subsistence* ; and this resembles *abstraction*.

495. To me however it seems more appropriate not to use the term *abstraction* in this sense; for by *universalising*, we do not take anything from the representation itself. But I must bring this out more clearly.

The reader will have already grasped the difference between the *idea* of a thing, and the *judgment* on its subsistence (402–407). I may have the complete idea of a thing, without at all judging that it actually subsists.

But when I judge a thing as subsistent, I have at one and the same time the *idea* of the thing, and the *judgment* on its subsistence.

The *idea* of the thing accompanied by this judgment is what I have termed *the intellectual perception* of the thing (417).[1]

The *intellectual perception,* therefore, not only includes the *idea* of a thing, but also at the same time determines and fixes that idea to an individual which actually falls under our senses: that idea applied to this individual is what *illumines* it,[2] what makes us perceive in it a being, which we afterwards denominate *body*.

---

[1] The distinction between these two operations of the mind, *idea* and *judgment*, was very well seen by the Angelic Doctor. In the following passage, where he distinguishes them, he uses the terms *cognition* for what I call *perception*, and *apprehension* for what I call *idea*. ' Ad cognitionem quo concurrere oportet, scilicet APPREHENSIONEM et JUDICIUM de re apprehensa' (*De Veritate*, Q. x. a. viii.). I am glad to quote passages of this description from S. Thomas and other ancient writers whenever I can, because I wish it to be clearly seen, that in the present work I have very often nothing to do but to translate into modern phraseology the language of antiquity. As regards, however, the *judgment* of which S. Thomas speaks, it does not refer to subsistent things only, but to every thing which, after having had perception of it, we affirm to be such or such. This extension of meaning belongs also to the *Verbum* of the mind ; and the reason is, that every thing which is affirmed, is considered as a *being*, in virtue, as we have seen, of a constituent law of our mind.

[2] The two phrases, *illustrari phantasmata* and *abstrahere phantasmata*, are often used by S. Thomas to indicate two different operations of the *intellectus agens* (see *S.* I. lxxix. 4, and lxxxv. 1, ad 4). Now what does the metaphorical expression *illustrari phantasmata* properly mean? I think I am not wrong in taking it, as I have already said, as corresponding with what I call *universalisation* or the operation by which, on occasion of the phantasms, ideas are formed and sensible things understood. It is certain, that the addition which our mind makes of the idea of *being* to a thing which falls under our senses, and by means of which addition that thing becomes to us a *being*, may very legitimately be called an *illustration* or *illumination* of this thing, since it is thus only that the thing is made cognisable, *i.e.* visible to the mind. Nevertheless some passages in the writings of the Aristotelian philosophers might suggest

Now if the *idea* (one of the elements of the *perception*) is considered alone, it is *universal*. This *universality* exists in it even when regarded as an element of the *perception*. But in the act itself of the perception that *universality* is not attended to, because the idea is considered only in its relation with the individual thing perceived by the senses.

When therefore I happen to detach the *idea* from the concrete perception in order to consider it separately, it seems that I have abstracted it, because I have taken away the bond which united it to the phantasm or thing perceived by the senses. I have dismissed from it the *subsistence* of the

a doubt as to whether they always attached a precise and fixed meaning to those two expressions, or rather did not often use the word *abstraction* to signify *universalisation*. But if we attentively consider their teaching, I believe that those passages may be reconciled with the sense I have given. See, for example, how S. Thomas describes the two operations of *illumination* and *abstraction* : 'The phantasms are *illumined* by the acting intellect, and then again by the virtue of the acting intellect the intelligible species are *abstracted* from them. I say they are *illumined*; because as the sensitive part through its conjunction with the intellect acquires a greater virtue, so the phantasms are, by the virtue of the acting intellect, rendered capable of having the intelligible species abstracted from them. Now the acting intellect *abstracts* the intelligible species from the phantasms, inasmuch as we can, through the virtue of this intellect, fix our consideration on the *natures* of the various species apart from the individual conditions, according to whose similitudes the possible intellect is informed.—'Phantasmata illuminantur ab intellectu agente, et iterum ab eis per virtutem intellectus agentis species intelligibiles abstrahuntur. Illuminantur quidem, quia sicut pars sensitiva ex conjunctione ad intellectum efficitur virtuosior, ita phantasmata ex virtute intellectus agentis redduntur habilia ut ab eis intentiones intelligibiles abstrahantur. Abstrahit autem intellectus agens species intelligibiles a phantasmatibus, in quantum per virtutem intellectus agentis accipere pos-

sumus in nostra consideratione naturas specierum sine individualibus conditionibus secundum quarum similitudines intellectus possibilis informatur' (*S.* I. lxxxv. 1, ad 4). Now what can be meant by saying that 'the sensitive part acquires a greater virtue (*efficitur virtuosior*) through its conjunction with the acting intellect? That 'it acquires the virtue by which the phantasms are capable of undergoing an abstraction resulting in the intelligible species of the things, or in the ideas'? It will be easy to see what this virtue is, when we understand how it comes to pass that we are able to abstract the specific *natures* of things (*the ideas*). Now, I think I have already shown clearly that this takes place in the following manner. The sensations or corporeal images (*phantasmata*) are united by us with the *idea of being*, and with the *judgment* on the subsistence of the thing. This gives the *intellectual perception* of the individual objects, that is to say, determines it precisely to them by means of the sensations (*phantasmata*). Now it is from this intellectual perception that the specific ideas of things, or universal ideas pure and isolated, can be drawn by the two species of abstraction above referred to, *i.e.* (1) that which simply sets aside the judgment on the actual subsistence of the object ; (2) that which abstracts also from the *individual conditions* of the object. It seems therefore evident that the *illumined phantasms* of S. Thomas correspond perfectly with those which I call *intellectual perceptions*.

thing. I say it '*seems as if*' in this operation I have made a kind of abstraction, to denote which we might call it *abstraction from the subsistence* or from the judgment.

It must nevertheless be observed, that when in an *intellectual perception* I separate the judgment on the subsistence of the thing, and retain the idea only, I thereby take away nothing from the essence of the idea itself; I only divide the idea from that which, although adhering to it, is no constitutive part of its nature; since the persuasion of the subsistence of the thing represented to me by the idea, is not the idea, nor anything appertaining to it. Wherefore the idea itself has undergone no abstraction, no change whatever: it remains perfectly the same as when it was united with that persuasion.

There has been no *abstraction* therefore in the proper sense of the word. The separation has fallen entirely on the *intellectual perception*, and not on the *idea*, which is only an element of it. If then we wish to retain the term *abstraction* in this case, we ought to declare that the idea is obtained by an abstraction exercised on the perception.

496. Again : if the idea is an element of the intellectual perception, and this element by being considered separately by itself alone has undergone no abstraction, no change in its nature ; we are bound to admit, that since the idea is universal when contemplated apart from the perception, it was universal also while united with it, and universality did not come to it from abstraction, but was in it *ab initio*, by virtue of the act itself of intellectual perception (90–97).

497. In describing therefore the process of this operation, improperly termed *abstraction*, which is exercised on the *perception* and not on the *idea*, we must take note of the three following stages :

(1) Corporeal *sensation*, phantasm, sense-perception.

(2) Union of what falls under the senses with the idea of being in general, which union takes place in the unity of the thinking subject (intellectual perception).

In the intellectual perception therefore there is, simultaneously and in virtue of the self-same operation, (*a*) a *judg-*

ment on the subsistence of the thing, (*b*) the intuition of the particular being (*idea* of the thing).

(3) *Abstraction* or separation of the *judgment* from *the idea*. By it we obtain the idea pure and alone ; which, although it was universal from its first existence in the perception, nevertheless was till now considered in union with the subsistent individual ; but now, being disengaged from that bond, it is seen alone, in its universality.

498. *Universalisation* therefore is, properly speaking, the function which produces ideas,[1] while *abstraction* is the function which changes their form and mode of being.

OBSERVATION II.

Universalisation produces the species, *abstraction the* genera.

499. All antiquity has distinguished things into two classes, namely, *genera* and *species.*

So universal a consent induces the belief that this mode of classification is not arbitrary, but founded in the very nature of the faculties of the human soul.

And such is really the case ; for on careful reflection we find that the *species* and the *genera* answer, respectively, to the two faculties of *universalisation* and *abstraction.*

The faculty of *universalisation,* or of forming *ideas* gives us the *species* (hence the *species* are also called *ideas*[2]). To form *genera,* on the contrary, we require furthermore the faculty of *abstraction.*

---

[1] It is worth while to observe, how all the greatest philosophers of antiquity were aware that to *know* is simply to apprehend the *universal.* Not only Plato, but Aristotle himself says this expressly in many places. Let the following passage from the *Metaphysics* suffice (Lib. III., lect. ix.) : 'Quatenus universale quid est, eatenus omnia cognoscimus.' On which passage S. Thomas comments as follows : ' Thus therefore the knowledge of particular things is not had except in so far as universals are known by us.'—' Sic igitur scientia de rebus singularibus non habetur nisi in quantum sciuntur universalia.' We must therefore have some universal present to our mind in order that we may know particular things ; and thus it is, I may fairly say, with the unanimous consent of antiquity, that I place in the faculty of *universalisation* the fount of human cognitions.

[2] The term *species* originally signified *aspect, thing seen, representation, idea,* &c. How then did it come to be applied to express certain classes of things? I answer, because every idea, being universal, is the foundation of a class.

OBSERVATION III.

Doctrine of Plato concerning genera *and* species.

500. The truth last enunciated gives us a clue to understand an important doctrine of Plato concerning *ideas*.

The *Ideas* which Plato considered to be substances separate from real things, and subsisting by themselves, were (be it well noted) the *species*, not the *genera*.[1]

[1] It is nevertheless certain that Plato in many places speaks doubtfully of his ideas, so that it seems as if they were of the abstract kind, namely, ideas of the things divested of their accidents. But this manner of speaking (for which however there is a reason which I shall mention later) does not prevent one from seeing the main drift of his thought. S. Thomas expounding this platonic thought, uses words which coincide with my interpretation, as for instance where he says, that Plato's species were *substances of the individual things* (In *Metaph.* Arist. Lib. viii. Lect. xxi.) Accordingly, to each individual thing which in some way differs from others (all these things, however, being considered as perfect) there corresponds an idea, an exemplar whence the maker of the thing copied and formed it; and whence he can always copy and form new ones, provided they be reducible to the one type. The correctness of this interpretation seems to be borne out by all that Aristotle says (Lib. viii. *Metaph.* Lect. xvi.) about the way in which Plato came to adopt his doctrine. That I am probably right in the view I attribute to Plato seems to be further confirmed by a statement made by himself on the subject of *species* and *genera*. He tells us that when something 'common' is predicated of many beings, but in such a manner that it belongs to one before it belongs to another (the ancient phrase was, *secundum prius et posterius*), this 'common' cannot be a thing existing by itself and apart from the beings to which it is attributed; and this is the case as regards *genera*. On the other hand, this 'common' exists by itself outside of the beings to which it is attributed, when it is predicated equally of many beings; and this is true as

regards *species*. The individuals of a *species* then, according to Plato, must be such as to have no difference either in the qualities or the degrees of their being, but must be perfectly equal, at least in all that they have of positive. I conclude therefore that the *species* as understood by Plato were ideas, not *abstract*, but *universal* only, into which there enters indeed all that is intellectually perceived in an individual, but not the real individual itself, the matter of the perception or, more generally, the *subsistence*, which, as I have shown above, never enters into ideas (401–403).

If the Platonic *species* are understood in this way, some of the objections which Aristotle brings against his master's doctrine would seem to fall to the ground. Thus, for example, in the place where he endeavours to prove against Plato that *matter* must enter into the formation of the *species* of things (*Metaph.* L. viii.), there seems to me to be nothing but an ambiguity of expression, a misconception. Doubtless, when I think of a corporeal thing, I think also of the matter of which the thing must be composed; but this my idea of the matter is not the matter itself. Now if by *species* we understand the *idea*, *matter* does not enter into the *species*. Hence S. Thomas, in order to remove the ambiguity, and to defend in some way the Philosopher so venerated in his time, said that the *matter* which entered into the formation of the *species*, was not the identical matter which constitutes the *proper principle of the individual*—' non hæc materia quæ est proprium principium individui,'—but *matter considered in general*; which is the same as saying the *idea of matter*: —' *Into the notion of the species man*, flesh and bones enter, but not this

This leads me to think that the Athenian philosopher had some inkling of the distinction between the functions of *universalisation* and *abstraction*.

In fact, amongst Plato's *ideas* there were the *exemplars* of particular things. Now the exemplar according to which the artificer works must be complete in all its parts (398–401), and must be furnished, not merely with what is essential to the thing, but also with all those accidents which are suitable to it : and though the accidents may vary, it is nevertheless necessary that the thing should have some of them ; so that if the artificer had only a notion of the thing in the abstract and could conceive nothing further of it, he would never be able to produce it outwardly.

501. But this would not yet suffice to make us understand well what the *ideas* of Plato were, or form a true concept of the nature of *species*. It is, moreover, necessary to know what follows.

Plato had observed that every being in this world is susceptive of greater or less perfection.

I can therefore, he said to himself, push my concept of any being further and further until I arrive at its complete and ultimate perfection ; or at any rate this involves no absurdity. For every being therefore there is such a concept as represents it in all the perfection of which its nature is capable, and without any defect whatever.

Plato held that this absolute and complete concept of any being could be but one ; that is to say, that a being could not be conceived as furnished with its ultimate perfection, except in one mode only : and indeed this kind of intellectual *optimism* seems probable. But leaving aside this question which belongs to Ontology, I argue thus : If a being can be naturally perfect in two modes, it has two *primitive concepts*,

flesh and these bones which are the individuating principles of Socrates and of Plato '—' De ratione speciei hominis sunt carnes et ossa, non autem hæ carnes et hæc ossa quæ sunt principia Socratis et Platonis ' (*Contra Gent*. II. xcii.) It would appear, however, as I have already observed, that Aristotle also, in other places, saw that the principle whence the *species* arise is the *universalisation* of an individual, and not *abstraction*. Thus in the eighth Book of the *Metaphysics* he compares *species* to *numbers*, and says, that every unit added to a number causes in it *ipso facto* a change of species.

two exemplars, two ideas ; and these constitute two species of things.   Viewing therefore the matter in this light, it would be true that the individual of a species can be naturally perfect only in one mode : for if it could be perfect in two, it would constitute or belong to two *species.*

From this it follows, that to the one idea, which represents the being in its typical perfectibility, are reduced the other ideas which represent the same being as defective in some part.   All of them are that same idea, less only the element whose absence makes it imperfect.

502. Wherefore, if an artist had in his mind the perfect idea of a thing, he could by means of it execute a perfect work, and still more easily all the imperfect ones, which are reduced to it as the imperfect to the perfect.

503. We can thus see whence the *species* of things arises. The *species* is constituted by that most perfect idea which, although it contains all the accidents of the thing (because, being the perfect exemplar, it requires these also, and determines them by receiving from among them such as are necessary to its perfection), has nevertheless an indefinite number of other ideas subordinate to itself, *i.e.* representing the thing in its various states of imperfection, and therefore not constituting a new species, since they are not truly different *ideas,* but that selfsame most perfect idea, curtailed indeed of some part or quality, but not changed into another.

ARTICLE III.

Synthesis of ideas.

504. Besides the faculties above enumerated, we have also the power of giving our attention to many ideas simultaneously, and of reducing them to unity through the relation seen to exist between them.

This is the same as saying that we have the power of forming *complex ideas.*

CHAPTER IV.

A FOURTH WAY OF EXPLAINING THE ORIGIN OF ACQUIRED IDEAS GENERALLY; *i.e.* BY MEANS OF A SUMMARY CLASSIFICATION OF THEM.

ARTICLE I.

Classification of our intellections.

505. By *intellection* I mean every act of the mind having for its term an idea, either alone or conjoined with something else, or the mode of an idea.

506. Hence all our intellections are reduced to the three following classes:—

1st class: *Intellectual perceptions.*

2nd class: *Ideas* properly so called.

3rd class: *Modes of ideas.*[1]

Intellectual perception, as I have said (495), is the judgment we make of a thing as subsisting, and which causes in us the persuasion of that subsistence. It is the compound result of two elements, the *judgment* on the subsistence and the *idea* of the thing.

507. It would be well to distinguish the *modes of ideas* from the *ideas* themselves, reserving the term *idea*, as Plato does (501),[2] for the *full species*, and using the phrase *modes of ideas* to signify *abstractions*, and groups of ideas.

[1] Of all these *intellections* we have also the *memory*, if we had them in the past, and the *imagination* if we frame them on the model of others which we have had. But, not to make the argument too complicated, I refrain from dwelling on these powers here.

[2] In order to confirm the explanation I have given of the Platonic ideas, and throw some light on an important point in the history of Ancient Philosophy, I beg leave to add a remark. It has been much disputed by modern philosophers whether the *numbers* of Pythagoras were the same as the *ideas* of Plato. For me it is enough to observe that *numbers* are *abstract ideas*, while the Platonic *ideas* which are to serve as exemplars cannot certainly be other than *specific* ideas. Of them

508. But it is usual to give the name of ideas to these modes also, calling them *abstract ideas*, and *complex ideas*.

According to this nomenclature there would be three classes of ideas: (1) Ideas properly so called ; (2) abstract ideas; (3) complex ideas.

The sources of these three classes of ideas are the three above-named intellectual functions—*i.e. universalisation*, which produces *ideas* properly so called (one of which is the *perfect* idea) (503) ; *abstraction*, which produces *abstract ideas* ; and *synthesis of ideas*, which produces *complex ideas*.

509. But, as I have said (507), *abtract ideas* and *complex ideas* do not contain anything beyond the *full ideas*. These three kinds of ideas are distinguished solely by the different way in which our mind considers them. If it considers them as they are when first produced, they are *full ideas*.[1] If it considers them in some of their parts, leaving aside the rest (abstraction, analysis), they take the name of *abstract ideas*. If it considers them in union with other ideas (synthesis), they take the name of *complex ideas*. These terms indicate therefore three *modes* of our intellectual attention, and conse-quently three *modes* of the ideas, which are the object of it ; but not, strictly speaking, three classes of *ideas*.

Cicero writes : ' Nos recte *speciem* pos-sumus dicere ' (*Academ.* Lib. i.) Pure *numbers* can never be exemplars of things ; just as a pure abstraction cannot be used by an artist as the *exemplar* by which to execute a statue or any other work. Plato therefore by substituting *ideas* for *numbers* perfected the doctrine of which Pythagoras had an inkling— at least his way of speaking admits of this construction. Towards this im-provement it seems that the Pytha-goreans themselves had already made some advance, as we may gather from certain passages in the *Timæus* of Plato. It is remarkable that modern writers (Brücker especially) have not perceived this difference, though it is very clearly indicated by Plato himself. The Platonic doctrine on this point is thus stated by the eminent Tuscan philosopher Marsilius Ficinus : ' Ac-cording to Plato there is a first and a second *intelligible* ; in the former are contained the *ideas*, that is, the species and notions of the Divine Mind, as also other minds, and souls : in the latter are contained *numbers* and figures.' ' Vult enim (Plato) esse intelligibile primum et secundum : in eo ideas, i.e. Divinæ mentis species, notionesque, et mentes alias, et animas contineri ; in hoc numeros et figuras ' (in *Theætet.* —See also Dial. vi. *De Repub.*, in fin.) Here then we have the *exemplar-ideas* separated from and placed before *numbers*, because these latter are drawn from the former by means of abstraction, and are a part of them as all abstractions are parts of *ideas*.

[1] It should be noted, that when first produced, the ideas of things are *full species*, that is, they have all the constitutives of the things represented by them, the accidental ones included ; but they are not *perfect species*, since the things that produce them are not perfect. To make them perfect, another intellectual operation is required, which I call *integration*.

ARTICLE II.

Where lies the difficulty of explaining the three classes of ideas just enumerated.

510. Our mind performs three successive operations: (1) it perceives intellectually; (2) it separates the idea from the perception; (3) it draws from the idea the abstracts, which are also the links whereby ideas are joined together and complex ideas formed.[1]

The first of these three operations is performed through *universalisation*; the second through an *abstraction exercised on the perceptions*; the third through an *abstraction exercised on the ideas already formed.*

511. *Universalisation* has no need of the faculty of *reflection.*[2] It takes place by a direct and natural action of our

---

[1] Complex ideas are formed subsequently to the *abstract* by reflection. When *reflection* and *abstract* ideas are explained, it is no longer difficult to understand the formation of *complex* ideas : hence I do not think it necessary to dwell on these.

[2] If by reflection is meant *that capacity which the intellectual faculty has of turning itself upon the products of its own operations*, universalisation has no need of reflection. On the one hand there is the *sensation* which is a direct act of our soul, and on the other there is the intuition of *being*—also a direct act ; and in the midst of these there is the unity of the subject, possessed at once of the sensation and of the idea. The *consciousness* of feeling the one while having intuition of the other, is universalisation almost completed.

But if by reflection we mean a *capacity of the* SPIRIT *to turn itself upon its own operations*, it might be said that there is a partial *reflection* in the primitive synthesis as well as in the universalisation which is therein contained. For the subject—which by reason of the unity of the feeling of its own self connects the sensations and the idea of being—turns itself upon its sensations, although it does this by another kind of operation, which is in itself *direct*. We might therefore distinguish two reflections, the one on *sensations* and the other on *ideas*. Reflection on sensations is a *direct* act in respect of the *intellectual faculty*, to which alone it belongs ; and it is a *reflex* act in respect of the *spirit*, to which that act and the sensations on which it turns equally belong. I make this observation in order to prevent all ambiguity. Nevertheless, as a general rule, I use the word *reflection* to indicate a reflection, not of the spirit, but of the intellectual faculty. The *reflection* spoken of by Scholastic writers, when they tell us that ' The understanding knows particulars by a certain reflection ' (*per quandam reflexionem*), must be understood in the other sense, (See note to 252).

The whole defect in this their manner of expressing themselves consisted in saying *understanding* instead of *spirit* ; for it is the *spirit* which perceives (through the sensitive faculty) the *particular* sensations, and (through the intellectual faculty) the *universals* ; and which, by uniting together these two elements, produces to itself one sole *perception* ; wherein it is said to know both the *particulars* (the things felt) by reflecting on them, and the *universals* by that direct act whereby it sees being. S. Thomas puts us on the way to this interpretation of the above scholastic spirit, which, leaving aside the judgment affirmative of the subsistence inherent in the perception, retains the *determinate idea* alone.   By *determinate idea* I mean that union between the thing felt and the idea of being, which is effected in virtue of the unity of the human subject, at once sentient and possessed of the intuition of being ; so that these two elements —*i.e. being*, as determinable, and the thing felt, as *determinant* —come of themselves to be found together in the same subject, and are conjoined, by the *identity*, so to speak, of the place in which they meet.

512. *Abstraction*, on the contrary, is an operation of the faculty of *reflection* ; for I cannot abstract anything either from my perceptions or from my ideas unless by turning my reflection on them.

513. Now the *primitive synthesis*, wherein *universalisation* is already contained—although as yet bound up with an extraneous element—is not a deliberate act ; it is formed, or at least aided, by nature, which has placed in man a vigilant mind like, so to speak, an eye wide open to see all that comes before it—a mind essentially possessed of the intuition of being.

Consequently it is not difficult to understand how, given the sensations, the operation of primitive synthesis is performed by the soul spontaneously, since in respect of this operation, the soul is already in a state of activity and in motion by virtue of its nature.

As regards *universalisation*, therefore, there is no need for me to explain how the soul moves from the state of quiescence, even as many words are not needed to explain how the sun illuminates an object presented to it, when once it is known that the sun is continually in the act of darting forth its rays all around.   But what remains for me to do, is to describe accurately how this operation takes place, and to analyse it in all its parts.

With *abstraction* the case is different.   Since this function

---

saying where he remarks that sometimes by an impropriety of speech we attribute to the *understanding* what should, properly speaking, be attributed to the *spirit* (*De Verit.* Q. x. Art. ix. ad 3).

belongs to reflection, which is a *voluntary* faculty, and not moving by itself, of its own nature, it must needs proceed always from an act of man's own will. Here therefore it is necessary to assign a *sufficient reason* why the will decides on setting reflection to work on the perceptions and the ideas, and from the former to abstract the latter, and again from these the ideas which are called *abstract.*

Unless this be done, we can never say that we have explained the acts of the faculties in question, and shown the origin of *abstract ideas,* and of the *complex* ones, which are derived from them.

Let us then take this matter in hand, assuming the perceptions as already formed, and we shall return to these afterwards, and describe how they can be formed by means of the primitive synthesis.

ARTICLE III.

Necessity of language for moving our understanding to form abstract ideas.

514. Our faculty of reasoning has not a self-moving activity independently of external stimuli.

This is a truth proved by experience, and by the nature of the human understanding.

Were we left entirely to ourselves, and to the internal forces which constitute our nature, and were not brought into contact with, or affected by, any of the forces outside of us, our understanding could never begin to move, or make the least act of any kind, although Omnipotence should preserve us for thousands of years in this state of isolation from other beings. All would remain perfectly quiescent in us, and necessarily so ; for there would be nothing to set our understanding in motion, and no term for it to be directed to. Ours would be an existence resembling non-existence—a state which affords matter for deep philosophical meditation, and furnishes a key to the most marvellous secrets of the study of man (*Teodicea*, n. 90).

Let us therefore see what kind of stimulus is required

(1) for the act of perception, (2) for universalisation, (3) for the formation of abstract ideas; and how our intellectual faculty is moved to each of these operations.

§ I.

Our soul is drawn to the act of perception by sensible things.

515. In order that we may perceive a thing, it is necessary that it be presented to our perceptive faculty.[1]

Unless therefore some term be presented to the act of this faculty, we can neither have a sensation nor a thought; our soul remains in that motionless state which I have just described, and which constitutes one of the limitations of the human understanding.

Hence it follows, that the action of our spirit is limited by its term.

If then the term is what draws forth our intelligent spirit into its proper act, wherein its action rests, we must concede that the presence of the term accounts only for that special activity which has reference to and terminates in it.

Consequently, the term cannot explain an activity different in nature or higher in degree, than that which ends in the term itself.

516. Now, according to these principles, it is clear that the corporeal things falling under our senses cannot move our spirit to abstraction, or to any other act except *perception.*

In fact, the sensations present to our spirit sensible things, and these account for a new activity besides the innate one of the intuition of being.

But again, 'the terms limit and terminate in themselves the activity of our spirit.'

Therefore that activity of our spirit which is set in motion by the sensible things acting on us cannot go beyond, but is bounded by them. These, therefore, cannot account for that activity by which the spirit forms abstract ideas; for abstract ideas are not sensible objects.

[1] Not as bodies stand in the presence of one another, but as the terms of the acts are present to the spirit that performs those acts.

When, therefore, the senses present to us anything corporeal, I understand well enough how our intelligence can be attracted and moved by it, and perceive the corporeal being. This faculty being naturally active and always with its eyes, so to speak, wide open, a term has only to present itself, in order to be at once caught sight of and cognised.

What then is this presenting of a term to our intelligence so as to be seen by it? Whence does such presenting arise? Originally, it does not, and cannot arise, except from the sense. We, as sensitive, receive in us, by means of our external organs, the action of corporeal agents. Hence the agent, being in us by its action, is placed where our mind can see it; for it is not difficult to understand how that which is in ourselves can be seen by us. I repeat, we have by nature a mind which always sees, and is always on the alert to see everything which affects, and the manner in which it affects, our sensitivity (*Teodicea*, n. 153).

Such being the case, it is obvious that sensible things can attract to them the attention of our spirit; therefore, they can also be cognised by us without anything else being needed; since we have here all that is requisite for this mental operation, namely, on the one hand, the *faculty* (the intelligence), and on the other, the terms capable of drawing this faculty into its act, that act which terminates in them.

Given therefore the sensations, we can see at once that nothing else is wanted to enable the intelligence to form perceptions of individual corporeal things,[1] or in other words, that these things perceived by us sensibly can *ipso facto* be perceived intellectually.

517. Now, seeing that we do not always take the coporeal images of the things seen by us, for the subsistent things themselves; and that we can notice a difference between the first and the second (whatever that difference may be); it is, at least, probable that we can be moved by these *images* to form *pure ideas*, *i.e.* divested of the *persuasion* of the actual presence and subsistence of beings. Hence, as the *sensations*

---

[1] I speak here of external sensations; the same doctrine may be applied to the internal sentiment.

give occasion to the *intellectual perceptions*, so the more attenuated *images* give occasion to the ideas of corporeal things separated from the persuasion and the judgment affirmative of their subsistence.   Therefore that kind of *abstraction* which consists in detaching *ideas* from *perceptions*, seems to have a sufficient cause in the *phantasms*, or *corporeal images*, just as the *perceptions* of bodies have a sufficient cause in the *sensations*.

OBSERVATIONS.

*On the limits of the intellectual development attainable by human beings
    cut off from all society, and whose intelligence therefore would have
    no other stimuli than sensations and corporeal images.*

518. The *sensations* and *phantasms*, then, are followed by *intellective perceptions* and by full specific *ideas*.

Hence, supposing that a human being is acted upon by *sensible* things, this will sufficiently account for three activities : (1) that which he puts forth by the act of *sensation* and of the forming of *corporeal images* ; (2) that which is exhibited in him in virtue of the laws of the *animal instinct* corresponding to these two activities ; (3) that by which he forms the perceptions and, together with them, the *full specific ideas* of corporeal things.

Let us now consider the nature and the limits of this third species of activity.

Such is the nature of our *intellective perceptions* and *full specific ideas* of corporeal things, that they follow upon, and are inseparably conjoined with what is either *felt* by us, or *imagined*.   By the *intellectual perception* we indeed judge that the thing which acts sensibly in us subsists, but we do not go any further ; all terminates in the particular thing felt.   Thus the *intellectual perception* consists of an *idea* tied with a *sense-perception*, *plus* the judgment affirmative of *subsistence*.   Now, owing to this tie of the *idea* with the *sense-perception*, it comes to pass that the first is bound to act in unison with the second, in the same way that our right eye cannot help acting in unison with the left ; or, to say better, the *idea* is like to a generous steed which, if yoked with a much slower and heavier animal than himself, has his speed restrained and must accommodate it to the sluggish pace of his fellow.

The *idea* so tied with *sense-perception* cannot, therefore, go one hair's breadth beyond it. Consequently, a human being with only this kind of ideas could not, in his movements and actions, exceed the sphere of the movements and actions possible to the beasts, which are led by sense and instinct alone. Hence, whenever human beings were found in some wild forest where they had been lost from their infancy, and had remained bereft of all chance of communing with other human beings, as well as of the aid of language, and with no other stimuli to act upon them than the sensations natural in that state, they never exhibited any indications of intellectual development, but showed evidently that they had not been able to rise ever so little above the level of sensible things, and to follow other than a brute-like life. Guided merely by instinct (for the faculty of reason, although existing in them, did not lead the instinct but simply followed in its track), they never attained to that stage of existence which is, in the full sense of the word, entitled to the name of *human*, and which is seen in those born and educated in the bosom of society. The same may, in due proportion, be said of the deaf and dumb who have received no special training.

All this is simply a consequence of the law we have laid down, namely, that 'The action of the human spirit is limited by its term.'

So long, then, as the term of that action consists only of corporeal things (and here we suppose that these things do not as yet perform the office of *signs*), our spirit cannot put forth any other activity than that which terminates and obtains its end in them. Therefore the spirit, in that condition, is unable to think except *corporeal* and *individual* things. The ideas, then, of which I have spoken are always closely con-joined with the sensations or the images and cannot be separated from either of them.

Our spirit, therefore, by means of these ideas, cannot get much beyond the point to which the sensations and the instincts alone would lead it.

§ 2.

The corporeal images sufficiently account for that activity by which our spirit forms ideas separated from perceptions.

519. *Abstraction* is performed on that which is already in our mind, and it is of two species: the first, less properly called abstraction, is exercised on the *perceptions*, from which *ideas* are separated; the second is exercised on *ideas*, the result being what I have called *abstract ideas* (494–498).

The first *may* proceed from *reflection*; but the second *must*.

The abstraction which is exercised on the *perceptions*, consists in fixing one's attention on the simple *apprehension* of the thing (the idea), leaving aside the judgment on its subsistence.

The abstraction which is exercised on *ideas*, consists in *reflecting* upon them and fixing the attention on a part of an idea, be this part something essential or something accidental to the being which is thought in that idea.

In the first kind of abstraction, the idea of the thing remains entire, it represents an object as yet with all its parts; there is nothing wanting except the persuasion of the subsistence of the object.

520. Now this *persuasion* of the subsistence may be detached, not merely by means of reflection, but also naturally, as we have indicated already, by means of the corporeal *images* which remain in us and are quickened up in our interior sensitivity according to certain laws of the animal nature; for these images are not at all times so vivid, so complete, so coherent and firm, that we cannot know them as a thing distinct from the realities present to us, and actually impressing our external sensories.

§ 3.

Language is sufficient to account for that activity whereby we form abstract ideas.

521. But how is our reason moved to form abstract ideas? If the *sensations* and the *images* cannot move it to this opera-

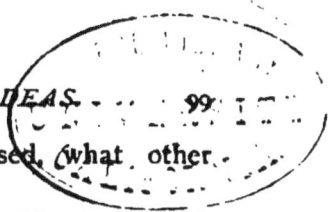

tion, whereby its development is increased, what other stimulus will be required?

In the first place, in order to remove any objections which might be raised, I must observe that the natural act by which our spirit has the intuition of *being* cannot in any way set the mind in motion, and impel it to occupy itself with the work of abstraction.

It is true that *being in general* is always present to our spirit, and keeps it in a primal act which constitutes the intellectual faculty itself. But since the activity of our spirit terminates and rests in its object, and in that only (515); it follows that *being in general* (the object now spoken of) does not account for any other activity than that which terminates and rests in it.

The primal activity of our spirit, then, is an immanent act, which does not move accidentally; it is a steady, uniform, constant vision of *being*, and nothing more. This immovable and direct act, therefore, gives us no explanation of that activity by which the spirit turns its attention to particular beings, or to the (abstract) modes of them.

How then, I ask again, shall our reason be moved to abstraction?

By means of signs. Let us see this.

An *abstract idea* is merely a *part of an idea*.

In order, then, to explain that activity by which we form *abstract ideas*, it is necessary to indicate a cause of such a nature as will make us suspend our attention from the idea as a whole, and limit it to and concentrate it upon a part only, to the entire exclusion of the rest.

Let us take as an instance the abstract idea of *humanity*. *Sense* furnishes to the mind the matter of the perception of *real men*; but *humanity* in the abstract, or divested of all the accidents of individual men, does not fall under the senses, nor is there anything sensible in it.

The *images* of these men really perceived, either owing to casual sensations of a nature akin to those we have experienced, or else by some internal movement of our nervous system, will be revived in us with more or less vividness. By these images our mind will again be stimulated, and, in consequence, form the *full idea* of one or more kinds of men.

But how to get at the idea of *humanity?* This idea is quite a different thing from all that I have described. It is not a sensation, not a corporeal image, not an object of perception, not an idea separated from perception. How then can we think of it?

The law which we discovered and laid down respecting the motors of our attention was this: 'Our spirit is not drawn to the act of perception otherwise than by the terms that are presented to it' (515). Now, can *humanity* be presented to us *in propria persona*, when there is no such thing to be had anywhere?

Here we must obviously and necessarily have recourse to a *vicarious sign*. *Humanity* has no existence outside of the mind; it cannot therefore attract our attention, unless in some sensible *sign* which, being external to the mind, holds the place of that idea, thus giving it, as it were, subsistence. It is impossible, then, for the mind to conceive *abstract ideas*, that have no realities corresponding to them, unless it be moved thereto by sensible signs which may take the place of those realities and represent, or, to speak more accurately, raise them before it. Let us see how *signs* can fulfil so important an office.

Signs, whether *natural* or *conventional*, and principally *words*, express whatever meaning a tacit or expressed *consensus* has attached to them. They are therefore equally adapted to signify a subsistent thing, a sensation, an image, a complete idea, or even a part of an idea, *i.e.* a single quality common to many objects, but isolated from them; although this quality, thus isolated, does not subsist outside the mind, being simply a notional object. Now if words are capable of all this, as we see they are in fact, it is evident, that even as they draw our attention to subsistent things when they denote and express these, so will they have power to draw it to everything else signified by them; and therefore to abstract ideas, and draw it in such a manner that it will limit itself to and be concentrated on them exclusively; for he that hears has naturally a wish to understand what is meant by the word, and nothing more.

522. Be it noted, that it is not my intention here to enter into the question of fact as to whether language be of divine or human origin, nor into the philosophical question about the possibility of its having been invented by man.[1] I take language as we find it in the society in which we were born and from which we learn it; and starting from this fact, I maintain that it is a fit and proper means for exciting the attention of the child—whose ears are from his earliest infancy struck by the sounds of the voice of his parents and others around him—to find out the meaning of all that is said, and, amongst the rest, also the ideas of qualities separated from the individual things, or of relations; all which are continually named and expressed by those sounds.

Neither is it my intention to describe minutely the fact I am speaking of, or to explain how it happens that the *natural language* is the first key to the child's development, and the medium, so to speak, by which it comes to understand the meaning of *artificial* and *conventional language.* It is enough for me to appeal to daily experience which shows manifestly that children first understand the words expressive of subsistent and real things and relating to their own wants, instincts and affections, and then come to understand the

---

[1] It is impossible for any man to invent language before he has acquired abstract ideas; for no one can appoint a *sign* for ideas which he does not possess. Hence the saying of Rousseau that 'Language could not have been invented without language,' applies only to that part of language which has reference to abstract ideas. From missing this distinction, Rousseau, although he caught a glimpse of the truth, was unable to demonstrate it; and I am not aware that anyone after him, not excluding Mons. de Bonald, has given a rigorous demonstration of the same. If therefore Rousseau's proposition be restricted to abstract ideas and terms, there is in it a substratum of truth. In the first place, it would be impossible for language to be invented by any man who is completely cut off from society, because in that state, no occasion or possibility would exist of an inter-communication of wants and thoughts. But supposing a human individual placed in the midst of other men who are devoid of language, two questions may then arise. The first is, ' Whether these men could invent a language before having formed some abstract ideas, or form these abstract ideas *before* having invented some sort of language or some signs;' and to this I answer, no. The second is : 'Could they do these two things *simultaneously, i.e.* could they invent words or signs with the same act by which they form abstract ideas?' And this I think would not be impossible (*Psicologia,* 1456–1473).

whole language perfectly, and also to speak it.   This proves beyond all doubt, that language is suitable for directing man's attention to abstract ideas, which is the same thing as forming them ; because in every language, in every reasoning as well as in every judgment, the noblest and most important part consists of abstract ideas.

If, then, language can do this, and if neither the sensations, nor the images, nor the idea of being taken by itself, are able to do it, we must needs admit that the intellectual development by which the child arrives at abstract ideas is due entirely to the aid of language.   That this could not be otherwise, is proved, as I have said, by the cases of children lost in the woods, and found as grown up men, without language, walking on all fours, and never giving the least indication either of having conceived abstract ideas, or of having risen a single hair's breadth above the perception of material and individual objects.   The same must be said of the uneducated deaf and dumb.

OBSERVATION I.

Of an objection that might be raised against what we have said, on the score of human free-will.

523. It will perhaps be objected, that there is in man a free activity by which he is master of his own powers, and can, if he pleases, direct his attention either to a whole idea, or only to a part of it, *i.e.* to a single common quality separately from the rest ; and that by means of this interior activity so exercised he can form abstract ideas without being obliged to have recourse to *signs* intended to divide that part or quality from the whole, and fix it by itself before the mind.

524. This objection will be dispelled by an attentive consideration of the laws or conditions according to which our free activity goes to work.

In the first place it is certain that the human activity can be made to move in two ways—the one *instinctive*, the other *deliberate*.

The *instinctive* is that of which we have spoken thus far.

In it the act is elicited, I would almost say, physically by its term ; that is, the mechanical *impression* made by the external agent draws the sensitive faculty to sensation, and sensation sets the imaginative faculty in motion : here we have *sensitive instinct.* Besides this, there is a *rational instinct,*[1] which is naturally drawn, by sensation to the intellectual *perception* of the corporeal agent, and, by the *image* or *phantasm*, to the *idea*, which is the object conceived by the mind apart from the persuasion of its subsistence. I am also willing to admit that an instinct prompts the human being to express externally, by movements, gestures, and also by the voice, what he feels with his senses and perceives with his understanding ; and so this instinct, in as far as it is sensitive, breaks forth into inarticulate sounds and interjections—expressions of the sense—and in as far as it is rational, it will express itself in some articulate sounds or *words*—signs of intellectual perceptions and of ideas. But none of these instincts will ever cause a human being to express that of which he has as yet no notion, such as are the abstract ideas now in question. To this length, then, the sensitive and rational instincts can go, but not any further. Now the question arises, is the *free-will* able to continue the work of the instincts by itself alone, without those stimuli and helps which man receives from communing with his fellow-men ? I answer :—

The *free-will* is conditioned by this law, that for every one of its acts it must have an end in view, as the reason why it operates.

Therefore the intelligent and free activity called *free-will* cannot make the least act or movement except by proposing to itself the attainment of an object. Without this, it must remain inoperative, motionless.

Now what object can I have in resolving to restrict my attention to some part of a concrete idea, to some quality common to many objects, exclusively of all the rest ?

---

[1] To the faculty receptive of ideal being (the intellect) corresponds the active faculty of *rational instinct*. The word *spontaneity* signifies, properly speaking, the mode in which every instinct, whether sensitive, rational, or moral, operates.

Undoubtedly, none other than that I may, by this means, form to myself *abstract ideas.*

But can I propose to myself the forming of *abstract ideas,* if I have not as yet any such ideas at all, and therefore do not know of what use or value they may be to me ? No ; for nobody can propose to himself an object of which he has no knowledge, and of which he sees neither the advantage nor the need.

The *condition,* therefore, upon which alone the *free-will* can move towards the discovery of abstract ideas, is wanting. There is no knowledge of the *end* to be secured (the sufficient reason for taking action) ; nor of a *good* possible to be derived from the attainment of that end, without the knowledge of which good, however, this faculty can have no interest, no incitement to induce it to decide on the course of which we are speaking.

Thus the free-will cannot move and direct the mind to abstract ideas unless it be already in possession of some of these ideas.

It cannot *move* the mind to abstract ideas, because it does not know any of them ; according to the axiom : 'Voluntas non fertur in incognitum.' It has therefore no *motor* ; and cannot *direct* it, because it has no conception of the object which it proposes to itself, and therefore no guiding principle.

If therefore the free-will, in order to form abstract ideas, requires to have some of these ideas already formed, it clearly follows that it is impossible to explain their formation by means of our free activity alone, without the aid of language.

OBSERVATION II.

On the intellectual development attained by men through social inter-
course and language, and on the necessity of this development in
order that we may gain the free use of our powers.

525. Not only is our free-will unable to move itself towards the formation of abstract ideas without the aid of signs ;

but *abstract ideas* are also invariably necessary to enable it deliberately to move the other powers.

In fact, the will does not deliberately set in motion the powers subordinate to it—the *attention* for instance—except for the sake of a *good* it knows.

Now, to move these powers in view of a good supposes some abstraction, that is to say, it supposes the knowledge of the *relation* of the means to the end, which relation is of its nature an abstract idea.

526. Moreover, how is it possible for me deliberately to transfer my attention from one idea to another unless by means of a *relation*, which (in some way or other) links these ideas together? But every *relation* conceived between two things or ideas is an abstraction ; for it is neither the one nor the other of those things or ideas, but a *link* by which they are connected in the mind that thinks of them. Every *relation*, therefore, is an *abstraction*.

Suppose for example, that upon reflection I make up my mind to go on a journey to a place noted for certain mineral springs whose waters are likely to benefit my health. In this decision, I think of the *aptitude* of those waters to do me good ; I think of the *means* requisite for the journey, &c. This *aptitude* and these *means*, &c., present to my mind, are all abstract ideas.

Again, suppose I occupy myself with reviewing *seriatim* all the new cognitions I have gained by conversing with a learned man. How are all those cognitions linked together in my mind? How do they form a distinct series to themselves? How is it that I can distinguish them from all my other cognitions, and regard them as a class apart ? Through an abstract idea—*i.e.* through seeing them in a common *relation*, which is that they were all equally derived from one and the same source—my conversations with that learned person. This common relation or quality it is which enables me to pass with my thought from one of those cognitions to the other, and to stop when I find that the series is exhausted.

Again, if after deliberating as to which subject I had

better select for study among the many that I might choose from at this present, I decide in favour of this or that one, why do I do so? For an end, for a reason, in short for an idea linked in my mind with that subject; and this *link* is an abstract idea.

Without abstract ideas, therefore, we could not freely dispose of our intellectual powers; we could not turn our attention at pleasure to one subject rather than to another. By means of them, our several ideas are connected together, and the passage is opened from one to the others; whereas, apart from them, these ideas would for ever remain a mere heap of loose units, with no possibility of our reflecting on them, or contemplating them collectively by a single *coup d'œil*, or making any reasoning. All the action of our understanding would terminate exactly where that of the senses terminates, *i.e.* at particulars only. Such and so great is the importance of abstract ideas!

527. But we have seen that abstract ideas are formed by the aid of language as received from social intercommunication.

The proposition, therefore, which I undertook to demonstrate, namely, that 'Language is necessary to us for acquiring the free use of our powers,' is incontrovertibly true, and, as a consequence, it is to this immense benefit, derived from society, that the whole of that marvellous progress which mankind is continually making must be ascribed.

ARTICLE IV.

The Intellectual Perception is explained.

§ I.

We have no other intellectual perception than that of ourselves and of bodies.

528. In our present natural state we have no other intellectual perception than that of ourselves and of bodies.

In fact, we cannot *perceive* [1] *the subsistence* of any being

---

[1] We may indeed have the belief or persuasion of the subsistence of other beings; but this must not be confounded with *perception*, which is produced immediately by means of the external and internal senses.

unless that being acts on us, and acts in such a manner as to make us feel its action.

Feeling is therefore necessary for our intellectual perception of a subsistent thing.

Now, we have only (1) the *feeling* of ourselves, (2) the *feeling* of bodies.

Therefore we can only have intellectual perception of ourselves [1] and of bodies.

---

[1] There are some passages in S. Thomas from which it might appear that the *matter* of our cognitions is furnished by the external senses only, and not also by the internal feeling of our own selves. But by putting together all the passages in which the Angelical speaks of this subject, it seems to me quite clear that he really looked upon the matter of our cognitions as proceeding from two sources, viz. the external sensations, and the internal feeling of the soul itself. That the soul has a feeling, or rather that the soul itself is this substantial *feeling*, and hence that it furnishes to the mind a *matter* of cognition which the corporeal sensories can in no way furnish, is clearly taught by S. Augustine when he says' 'Mens . . . . . . semetipsam per seipsam novit, quoniam est incorporea' (*De Trin.* Lib. ix. c. iii). Against this doctrine, however, there stood a saying of Aristotle, whom the Schoolmen had chosen for their guiding star (whenever his teaching was not opposed to the Christian faith), namely, that 'The mind knows nothing without a corporeal phantasm' (Lib. iii. *De anima*, xxx). To the most acute mind of S. Thomas it seemed that both these two doctrines—that of the great Bishop of Hippo, and that of Aristotle—were true, though not in the same sense ; and he endeavoured to reconcile them together in the following manner :—

In the first place, he laid it down that from the phantasms no species could be drawn which was a similitude of the soul, and that therefore from corporeal phantasms we could not abstract any idea of our soul, whose nature is entirely different from the corporeal. 'Anima non cognoscitur per speciem a sensibus abstractam, quasi intelligatur species illa esse animæ similitudo' (*De Verit.* Q. x. vii. ad I).

Then he reflected that there could be no better way to arrive at a knowledge of the nature of the soul than to examine how philosophers had reasoned concerning its diverse properties. Those philosophers, he observed, who meditated on the nature of the soul, began by examining its acts, and principally the *ideas*. Let us hear him : ' Ex hoc enim quod anima humana universales rerum naturas cognoscit, intellexerunt quod percipit quod species qua intelligimus est immaterialis. . . . Ex hoc autem quod species intelligibilis est immaterialis, intellexerunt quod intellectus est res quædam independens a materia ; et ex hoc ad alias proprietates intellectivæ potentiæ cognoscendas processerunt' (*Ibid. in corp.*). — ' Considering that the human soul knows the universal natures of things, they saw that the *species* (idea) by which we understand, is immaterial. . . . But from the fact of the intelligible *species* being immaterial, they argued that the intellect must be something independent of matter ; and thence they proceeded to investigate the other properties of the intellectual faculty.'

Hence the holy Doctor concludes, that the *species* (ideas) abstracted from material things were necessary to enable philosophers to know the nature of the soul, not indeed because such species did or could furnish a similitude of the soul, 'Sed quia naturam speciei considerando, quæ a sensibilibus abstrahitur, invenitur natura animæ in qua hujusmodi species recipitur' (*Ibid.*). ' But, because by considering the nature of the *species* which is abstracted from sensible things, we discover the nature of the soul in which that species is received.' It was not, then, the

§ 2.

What is required to explain intellectual perception.

529. When I shall have explained one of the above two kinds of perception, a similar process of reasoning will explain the other.

sensible phantasms themselves that gave us the knowledge of the soul, but the species formed in us, as we have seen, by the *intellectus agens.* The species, whose nature is entirely different from that of the phantasms, supplied a principle, by starting from which, the nature of the soul could be discovered.

Moreover, this was the scientific knowledge of the soul, which could be reduced to a definition. But, besides this, there is a knowledge of the soul which is natural to us. Is not every one of us conscious of having a *feeling proper to himself* and incommunicable (which he expresses by the monosyllables I, ME), or rather of being himself this feeling, and of perceiving it ? A feeling of which not the slightest trace can be found in the corporeal qualities of extension, &c., which are all *extra-subjective,* whilst the I, ME is the *subject itself?* This species of cognition did not, I think, escape the notice of S. Thomas ; but in order fully to understand his thought, we must keep before us the expressions he uses for signifying the two kinds of cognition of which I speak, namely, the *scientific* and the *vulgar—*the first founded on elaborate reasonings, the last consisting of an immediate perception.

S. Thomas, then, observes that we cannot be said to know the nature of a thing, unless we know its specific or generic *differentia,* by means of which we may formulate a definition of it ('cum res speciali aut generali cognitione definitur '). It is therefore the scientific knowledge alone that makes known to us the nature of the soul.

But the knowledge which I would call *vulgar* or natural, is, according to S. Thomas, 'That whereby the soul knows itself individually ' (*i.e.* 'quantum ad id quod est ei proprium '). This species of knowledge corresponds exactly to what I term the *percep-*

tion of our own soul ; since this perception is formed the first time that we say interiorly, I EXIST. It is composed (1) of the feeling of *self* (*matter*), (2) of the idea of existence or being in general (*form*), without anything else, that is to say, without our knowing expressly any of the differences existing between the soul and other beings, or instituting any comparison of it with other objects. Now by this kind of knowledge we do not, according to S. Thomas, understand the *essence* of the soul, but know only that the soul *exists* ('per hanc cognitionem cognoscitur an est anima ;— per aliam vero scitur quid est anima' (*Ibid. in corp.*)

Before going further, I would make an observation on this way of defining *perception—i.e.* 'Cognitio qua cognoscitur an est anima.' S. Thomas himself makes the following objection : 'Non potest sciri de aliquo ipsum esse, nisi quid ipsum sit cognoscatur ' (Quæst. x. *De Verit.* art. 12, obj. 4)—' We cannot know concerning anything whether it exist, unless we first know what that thing is.' To this objection he replies : 'Ad hoc quod cognoscatur aliquid esse, non oportet quod sciatur de eo quid sit per definitionem, sed quid significetur per nomen. '—' To know that a thing is, we do not require to know what it is by way of *definition* (that is, there is no need to have a scientific knowledge of it), but only to know what is signified by its name ; ' which is the same as to say that it is necessary to have that kind of knowledge which the vulgar have of things when they call them by their names : and I maintain that this knowledge is reduced in our case to a perception of the thing *in globo,* without our having compared it with other things, or adverted to the differences necessary for formulating a perfect definition. My object in this observation is to invite the reader to reflect

Taking, then, the perception of bodies, let us first of all resume the description of the fact. It consists of three parts. (1) We are affected by *sensations*. (2) Immediately upon this, we say to ourselves, 'A something exists' (*judgment*).

that the knowledge mentioned by S. Thomas, 'whereby something is known to exist' ('qua cognoscitur aliquid esse'), does not express the pure *being* of the thing; for it could not be had without some other knowledge which singles the thing out from among all the others with which it has being in common.

With this preliminary remark, I will proceed to state what are the doctrines of S. Thomas regarding that *knowledge*, which I call *perceptive*, or *natural* and vulgar, and by which, as he says, 'We know that the soul exists' ('qua cognoscitur an est anima'); and the reader will see how well my views accord with those of the Holy Doctor.

Following S. Augustine, he lays it down that 'The essence of the soul is always present to our understanding' ('ipsa ejus essentia intellectui nostro est præsens'). What then is required in order that our understanding may perceive the soul? Nothing more than that it should make the act necessary for this perception: hence he concludes, that 'Anima per essentiam suam se videt, id est, ex hoc ipso quod essentia sua est sibi præsens, est *potens* exire in actum cognitionis sui ipsius' (*De Ver.* X. viii. *in corp.*)—' The soul sees itself by means of its essence; that is, in consequence of its essence being present to itself, it has the power to come forth into the act by which it knows itself.' And he compares this knowledge with the cognitions we preserve in our memory: 'Sicut aliquis ex hoc quod habet alicujus scientiæ habitum, ex ipsa præsentia habitus est potens percipere illa quæ subsunt illi habitui' (*Ibid.*)—'As he who has the habit of a certain science is able, by virtue of that habit, to perceive those things which fall under it.' This is why the knowledge which the soul has of itself immediately, without phantasms, is called by him *habitual*.

But (he continues) in order that the understanding may arrive at an actual knowledge of the soul, there must be some adequate cause; and this cause can only be furnished by the acts of the soul itself:—' Quantum igitur ad actualem cognitionem, qua aliquis considerat se in actu animam habere; sic dico, quod anima cognoscitur per actus suos. In hoc enim aliquis percipit se animam habere, et vivere, et esse, quod percipit se sentire et intelligere, et alia hujusmodi vitæ opera exercere.'— 'With respect, then, to that actual knowledge by which a man perceives that he actually has a soul, I say that the soul is not known except by its acts. For, a man perceives that he has a soul and that he lives and exists, by this that he is aware of feeling and understanding and performing such like acts which proceed from life' (*Ibid.*). No exception of any kind can be taken to this.

I will conclude with another observation. Let us put out of our thought all the reflex knowledge we have of ourselves, and remember that the question here is solely about the direct and immediate knowledge, in a word, about the perception of SELF; since our soul is, after all, nothing but the *feeling* proper to this SELF. Now, it is evident that we cannot intellectually perceive ourselves except by our acts. But there are in us acts which are essential to our nature, namely (1) the feeling of ourselves, (2) the act of the *intellectus agens* (by which we have the intuition of being in general), an act which is admitted also by S. Thomas and by Aristotle. These acts, because essential to our nature, can never fail in us. It would not, therefore, be impossible for us to have the actual intellective perception of ourselves even in the first moments of our existence, provided there were something to direct our attention to ourselves; but so long as that stimulus is wanting, we have nothing more than the *power* of forming this perception— *est potens* [*anima*] *exire in actum cognitionis sui ipsius*.

(3) This something is determined by the nature of the affection produced in us (*idea of bodies*).

There is no question of explaining the first part of this fact—*sensation.* I start from sensation as from a simple and primitive fact.

Nor is there question of explaining the nature of the *idea* of bodies (the third part), *i.e.* the *mode* in which that something which we judge to exist is limited and determined by the sensation. This I shall be called upon to do in another chapter where I shall examine the idea, such as we have, of bodies.

What I have now to do, is simply to give a satisfactory explanation of that *judgment* by which, in consequence of the sensations, we say 'There exists a something that is not myself;' this being the judgment which generates in us the intellectual *perception* of bodies ; *i.e.* the persuasion of their actual and particular existence (subsistence).

§ 3.

Explanation of the judgment which generates in us the perception of bodies.

530. The idea of being, which is in our mind, does not of itself alone cause us to know any one being in particular ; it only shows us the possibility of beings generally.

By saying *being*, I express a something, an actuality ; for the concept of being is nothing else than the concept of a *first act* (350–352).[1] It is therefore impossible to conceive

---

[1] *Ideal* or *possible being* may be considered from two aspects : (1) in so far as it is an essence or quiddity seen by the mind, and having all that is requisite to make it such an essence or quiddity ; (2) in so far as, by being seen, it *illuminates* the mind, makes it an intelligence.

Considered from the second aspect, it is the 'first intelligible,' the *means of knowing* or the *intelligibility* of all things that present themselves to our mental vision, through the sensations.

Considered from the first aspect, it is a true *something*, because an *essence* or *quiddity* is something. In this sense the author calls it an *actuality*, a *first act*, the *act of being.* Indeed, *being*, or *existence*, is the *first act* in everything, whether we speak of principles of reason, or of ideas, generic or specific, or of subsistent realities. None of these things would be thinkable, or have any property or relation, unless it *was*, had the *act of being.* They are all modes or forms or terms in which *being* presents itself, and therefore presuppose it, at least logically (TRANSLATORS).

being without conceiving an *act of being*, since the two expressions mean exactly the same thing.

But this *act of being* can be conceived by us in two ways : (1) as not applied to a real thing, and (2) as so applied.

If we conceive it in the first way, we conceive the possibility of beings, and nothing more ; and this is the idea which is innate in us.

If we conceive it in the second way, we think what I usually term *subsistence* or real being ; and this is precisely the *judgment* which produces in us the *intellectual perception*, and which I have to explain here.

Now when we make this judgment, we add nothing to the idea of being (402–407) ; we merely see the being of which we have the notion as applied to a real thing. How then do we perform this operation ? In the following manner :—

We have by nature the idea of being in general : to have this idea is, to conceive a *first act*.

The sensations are *actions* produced in us, of which we are not the authors.

Being *actions*, they suppose a *first act*, a something actually existing, a being.[1]

They are also actions of a determinate nature ; therefore they suppose a first act, a something actually existing, a being of *a determinate nature* : and this is the same as to say a being existing in a determinate mode.

Comparing, therefore, that of which we experience, *i.e.* *suffer*, the sensible action with the *being* or *act of being* whereof we have the notion, we find that the former is only a particular case of the latter. With our original intuition, we saw indeed an *act*, but only in the general ; we were not determining that act in any particular way, nor affirming it as realised here or there. In the sensation, on the contrary, or rather in the thing felt therein, we see that act in a determinate form, that form which gives us the particular kind of thing called *body*.[2]

---

[1] An agent which produces those actions, because *ex nihilo nihil fit*, 'from nothing, nothing comes' (TRANSLATORS).

[2] Hence to the child it is extremely easy to pass from the sensations to the forming of the judgment affirmative of subsistent beings ; for this judgment

In other words, knowing by nature what the *act of being*
is, when we come to *feel* a something acting on us, we find
the *first act* limited to what the sensation indicates ; and we
recognise it as the same kind of thing that we were acquainted
with before : and so we say to ourselves : ' Here is one of
those acts (that is to say, a grade or mode of act) which were
virtually comprised in what I already knew.'

This noting of the particular case, this recognising in the
thing felt by us, a being, a something belonging to the same
order as that which we were already thinking in the general,
is what constitutes the intellectual perception of a real thing
—the judgment of which we are speaking.

In this judgment the mind—which, before then, for want
of a particular point whereon to fix its attention, gazed on
nothing but being, pure, indeterminate, uniform—concentrates
itself, so to speak, on the particular and limited being, wherein
it finds existence realised, and perceives that of which it has
already the notion, and for which it was, as it were, on the
look-out (513).

Thus is explained how a certain comparison and judgment
takes place in us, between the thing felt in the sensation, and
the *idea of being*; and how the first becomes the *subject*,
inasmuch as it is seen contained in the second, which is the
predicate.

If we only bear in mind, that what we know by the idea
of being in general, and what we compare with that idea
when experiencing a sensation, are alike *acts*—one *without*,
and the other *with*, particular conditions and determinations—
all the difficulty of understanding this matter will be got over.
In fact, what wonder if, the occasion being given me, I perceive and recognise a *particular act*, when I already know
what *act in general* is ?

After this it is not difficult, from the *action* to ascend to
the *being*, since, as we have said, this is nothing else than the

is only an intellectual perception to
which the nature itself of intelligence
carries it. In so many other systems,
the judgments on the existence of substances and of causes, which children
make in their earliest infancy, are inexplicable.

first act: now if there is a *second act* there must be a *first*;[1] to say the contrary would be an absurdity.[2]

OBSERVATION I.

Doctrine of the ancients on the Word of the Mind.

531. From the description we have given of the *intellectual perception*, it seems to me that we may gain some light to understand what that *Word* (*verbum*) of the mind is of which the ancients speak.

So long as I have only the idea of a thing, I do not as yet know if that thing *subsists*.[3]

Now suppose that I make the *judgment*, by which I affirm to myself the thing as subsistent: this act is the *word* of the mind.[4]

[1] *I.e.* if there is an action, there must be an agent (TRANSLATORS).

[2] It is a universally known fact, that on occasion of experiencing certain sensations, we say that a thing *exists*, and exists as *such or such*. Looking up to the heavens, we see a countless number of luminous bodies which we affirm to exist, and to be of such a size, such a splendour, such a motion. We say that the bodies around us exist, because we hear them, taste them, smell them; and we say that they exist in a certain mode, *i.e.* coloured in this or that way, large or small, savoury, sonorous.

The act by which we pronounce interiorly that some thing which falls under our senses exists, is called *intellectual perception, affirmation, primitive judgment*. But in order to say that that which falls under our senses exists, we must know what *existence* is; and in order to say that it exists in a given mode, we must know what that *mode* is. Therefore, before pronouncing these judgments, we must know something, and know it in a way different from that by which we know it in the judgment, by a different act, which is called act of *intuition* (see *Esposizione ragionata della filosofia di Antonio Rosmini*, &c. By Calza and Perez. Intra, 1878. Vol. i. p. 157-8). Now, the intuition of *existence* is in us by nature, and the intuition of the *modes* in which the

various beings exist, is determined for us by our various sensations (TRANSLATORS).

[3] By saying the *idea* of a *thing*, it seems that I speak of two different elements, (1) the idea, (2) the thing; but it is not so. In the concept of a possible thing, there is but one object, but with two relations. If I consider the object of my thought *in se*, I call it, *thing conceived*, or *essence*; if I consider it in its relation to my mind I call it, *idea*. The simple *idea* therefore (*species*) does not contain *the word*, which is the *thing subsistent*, in so far as *pronounced* or affirmed as such. The thing conceived can be considered *in se*, not indeed because it exists independently of a mind, but because it serves as an *exemplar*, according to which the intelligent being imagines or also produces it. Therefore the *idea* of a thing means simply *possible thing, exemplar*, according to which the intelligent being thinks and acts.

[4] That there may be the word of the mind, it suffices that I fix my thought on a subsistent thing, giving my assent to the fact of its subsistence. Hence I can think, (1) of a thing actually subsistent (*intellectual perception*); (2) of a thing which was formerly subsistent and perceived by me (*memory of the perception*); (3) of a thing which I do not perceive as subsistent, but believe on the authority of others (*faith re-*

532. The *Word* of the mind therefore is produced through an energy of the will, which fixes and determines the thing seen in idea, assenting to the belief of its subsistence.

The *word* of the mind is not therefore a simple *idea* or *species* ; but an affirmation of the subsistence of a determinate thing corresponding to an idea as its type or exemplar.[1]

533. If we had *pure ideas* or *species* only, we should see nothing but possibility, we should affirm nothing, *pronounce* nothing.

The external language, as also the interior one of the mind, begins only when the mind becomes aware of some subsistent being : until that takes place, the mind utters no word ; it looks on in perfect silence, it is as yet mute. Nor does it stir from this stillness to assent to any *subsistence*, except by the impulse of sensations internal or external. From these, therefore, all *words* of the mind take their beginning.[2]

---

specting the subsistence). In all these three mental operations, whether I am deceived or not, I always form a *word* of the *mind*, that is, I affirm a *thing* as *subsistent* ; (4) besides this, I emit a *word* also when I consider as subsistent that which is not so in itself, either by an *error*, or by a trick of the *imagination*, or in consequence of having based my reasoning on *suppositions*.

[1] S. Thomas writes :—'Licet utrumque sit accidens, species scilicet et verbum ex specie genitum, quia utrumque est in anima ut in subjecto ; verbum tamen magis transit in similitudinem substantiæ quam species ipsa. Quia enim intellectus nititur in quidditatem rei venire, ideo in specie prædicta est virtus quidditatis substantiæ spiritualiter, per quam quidditas spiritualiter recte formatur : . . . unde verbum quod est ultimum quod potest fieri intra per speciem, magis accedit ad ipsam rem repræsentandam, quam nuda species rei ' (Opusc. xiii. *De Natura Verbi Intellectus*)—'Although the *species* and the *word*(*verbum*) generated by the *species*, are both in the soul as in a subject, nevertheless the *word* takes more of the similitude of the substance, than the *species* itself ' (so it must be, for the word is the assent given to the determinate subsistence). ' For the intellect endeavours to arrive

at the quiddity of the thing, and therefore in the *species* there is virtually in a spiritual manner' (that is as *possible*) 'the *quiddity* of the substance (the *subsistence* of the thing) ; and this quiddity being virtually in the *species* can rightly be formed spiritually ' (*i.e.* in thought ; the subsistence can be affirmed by a judgment) :—' hence it is that the *word*, which is the last thing that can be interiorly formed by means of the species, approaches more to the representing of the thing' (subsistent) ' than the simple species of the same.' And certainly, it is only by means of the *species* or idea of a thing that the *word of the mind* can be formed ; for it is possible to *imagine* a thing corresponding to that idea as individually present. Thus the statuary imagines the statue in the block of marble which he has before him : so that even the *human imagination* has in some way, its *word*, and this is all that the sensitive faculties have of creative power.

[2] S. Thomas, following S. Augustine, defines the *word* ' A certain emanation of the understanding'—'Quædam emanatio intellectus ' (*S.* I. xxxiv. 2) : and elsewhere : 'Properly speaking, the *word* is that which the thinker forms by the act of understanding '—' Verbum proprie dicitur quod intelligens intelli-

OBSERVATION II.

Relation between an idea and the word of the mind.

534. By the *word* we affirm as subsistent that thing, which by the idea we conceived as only possible.[1]

Therefore the thing contemplated in *idea* stands to the thing subsistent, affirmed by the *word*, as a *faculty* stands to its *act*.

This is why I said, that the object seen in the idea, and the reality acting on our sense, are reduced to one and the same nature (530). The subsistent being is that *first act* which we already conceived (by the idea), but could not affirm as existing in the *real world*,[2] until we felt its action on ourselves.

ARTICLE V.

Necessity of the intellectual perception.

535. It may be asked : Are we, immediately on receiving sensations, necessitated to form the intellectual perception of some being ?

This question of fact does not belong to my present scope. The necessity of which I intend to speak in this article is of

gendo format' (Opusc. xiii.) : which is the *definition* of or any *enunciation* whatever about something.

[1] The scientific language of the Schools expressed this observation as follows : ' Cognitione universali magis cognoscitur res in potentia quam in actu ' —' By the universal concept' (that is by the *species*, which is always universal) ' the thing is known in *potentia* rather than in act' (*Cont. Gent.* I. l.) By ' knowing the thing *in potentia* ' it was simply meant to say that the thing is conceived in a state of possibility. Thus it happens that many expressions of the Schoolmen, which at this day present a certain obscurity, and even sound like unmeaning and clumsy verbiage, when divested of that antiquated form, are found to contain plain and admirable truths.

[2] Whoever attends to this distinction between the *idea* and the *word* will, I think, understand the distinction drawn by Plato between a *true opinion* and

knowledge. The latter consisted of ideas, of ' possibles ;' the former referred to particular subsistent beings (affirmed by the *word*); for it is by affirming a thing that we speak truth or falsehood : and these are the attributes of *opinion*, and not of *knowledge*, which, according to Plato and S. Augustine (*De Trinit.* lxv.), is always true. In *Timæus* Plato distinguishes *knowledge* from a *true opinion* by saying that ' the first comes into us through a *doctrine* ; the second through a *persuasion* which we form to ourselves.' In fact, by judging that a thing subsists, we do not acquire a new *doctrine* ; for by our idea we already know the thing ; but we acquire a new *persuasion* of its *subsistence* by giving our assent to it. Nevertheless an exception must be made as regards the BEING necessarily subsistent, the BEING by essence, in the perception of WHOM the *word* and the *idea* are one and the same thing.

another kind. What I say is, that if we cognise anything, we must do it in the way I have described, that is to say, by means of a primitive judgment, whereby the being which we already know in general, subsists in that particular mode to which it is determined and limited by our sensations.

What I have thus far said proves this necessity; for I have shown that the cognising of particular things consists in nothing else than forming that judgment of which I speak.

In fact, granted that we have the idea of being in general always and necessarily before us; granted that this idea is the informing principle of our intellect and our reason (480–485), and consequently that our intelligence is constituted by the intuition of being, it follows that our intelligence 'can conceive nothing except as a being, as a something.'[1]

536. But this law of the intelligence is not *subjective* or arbitrary; it is necessary, so that it is impossible even to think the contrary.

In truth, would it not be a contradiction in terms to say that our mind knows the things which are presented to it, without conceiving a something? and is not the conceiving of a something the same as the conceiving of a being?

Therefore the general formula which expresses the intrinsic nature of the intellectual perception is this: 'A judgment, affirmation, persuasion that a being, furnished with its determinations, subsists.'

To make the thing clearer, let us suppose that we received sensations from bodies, but had not within us the power to see that a *being* produces them, and therefore could not consider those sensations in relation with being. In this case our spirit would have been modified by corporeal sensations; but these would not appear to us as determinations of being; consequently we should not perceive a determinate being, a subsistent thing, a body; for to

---

[1] With this doctrine agrees the celebrated dictum of the Schools; 'Intellectus habet operationem circa ens in universali'—'The operation of the intellect regards being in general' (See S. Thomas, *S. I.* lxxix. 9); and that other of S. Thomas: 'Intellectus respicit rationem entis '—'The intellect sees every thing under the aspect of being' (*Ibid.* ix.) Hence also the Scholastic teaching, that 'Quod non est, non intelligitur nisi per id quod est'—'That which is not, is not understood except by that which is.'

perceive a body is to perceive a determinate being. The sensations would in no way be perceived by the understanding, but would remain in the sense only: hence we should not cognise anything. In order that, besides having the sense-perception of that *body* (and this word *body* has been itself invented in consequence of the intellectual perception), we may also cognise it, there must be in us the power of seeing, where the sensation is, a determinate being.

It is therefore through the idea of being, natural to us, and through it only, that we have cognitive power; and to *cognise* is nothing but to conceive a *determination* of *possible* or *common being*—a determination which has the effect of making it a 'proper' being.

OBSERVATION I.

On the question, 'Is the human soul always thinking?'

537. The theory we have till now expounded enables us to solve the question proposed by Des Cartes, 'Whether our soul be always thinking.'

Our soul is intelligent because it has always the vision of being in general (535).

Hence our intelligence is a faculty essentially active [1] and

---

[1] S. Thomas, in agreement with Aristotle, gives the same solution of this question. He applies, as I have observed, to our intelligence the celebrated principle: 'Nihil agit, nisi secundum quod est actu' (*S. I.* lxxvi. 1); and from it he deduces the necessity that this faculty should be essentially *in act*; for otherwise ours would not be an intelligent nature. And I do not see why we should not understand as referring to the 'acting intellect' (*intellectus agens*), rather than to the acquired intellect (*intellectus adeptus*), the saying of Aristotle, that 'The accident of sometimes understanding and sometimes not understanding (*aliquando quidem intelligit, aliquando non*), cannot be predicated of that intellect;' meaning thereby that it always understands (*De Anima,* L. iii). S. Thomas does not deny that this may be applied to the *acting intellect*, for he says: 'In omni enim actu quo homo intelligit, concurrit operatio intellectus agentis et intellectus possibilis. . . . Unde quantum ad id quod requiritur ad nostram considerationem ex parte intellectus agentis, non deest quin semper intelligamus; sed quantum ad id quod requiritur ex parte intellectus possibilis, quod nunquam impletur nisi per species intelligibiles a sensibus abstractas.' ('In every act by which man understands, there is the concurrent operation of the *acting intellect* and of the *possible intellect*. Now, as regards our present consideration, there is nothing to prevent us from admitting that the *acting intellect* always understands; but the same cannot be said of the *possible intellect*, inasmuch as this is never filled except by means of the intelligible species abstracted from the phantasms') (*De Verit.* Q. x. art. 8). And the reason why the holy Doctor allows to the *acting intellect* the property of 'always

thinking ; and this, not because it has all ideas present to it,
but simply because it has the first idea, viz. that of being in
general.   By means of this, which is its light,[1] it sees and
distinguishes that which is presented to it by the senses, in
the way I have explained, and understands what is said by
other rational beings.

The reason why this idea, although inseparably conjoined
with us from the very first instant of our existence, is not
adverted to until a much later period, has been already
stated (469–470).

OBSERVATION II.

In what sense the intellect is a tabula rasa.

538. Here it will also be seen why I have elsewhere made
use of the old simile of the *tabula rasa*[2] to describe the state
of our intellect in the first beginning of our existence.

This simile is well adapted to its purpose, when understood in the following way.

The *tabula rasa* is 'indeterminate being,' of which we
always have intuition.   This being, not having any determinations, is like a perfectly uniform tablet, without as yet
any characters traced or written on it.

It receives therefore any mark or impression that may
be made on it ; that is to say, ideal being—wholly indeterminate—is determined and applied alike to anything felt, to
any form or mode which may be presented to us through the
external or internal senses.   Hence what we saw at the
beginning was like a sheet of white paper where nothing was
written, and consequently there was nothing to read.   But

understanding,' is, that this intellect
'receives nothing from without'—
'Non recipit aliquid ab extrinseco'
(*Ibid.*), but draws all from itself,
namely *the formal part* of cognition,
ens commune.

[1] Norris, an English writer who has
developed the system of Malebranche
in his *Essay towards the Theory of the
Ideal or Intelligible World* (Part ii.
ch. vi. 7), amongst other theses, proposes the following : ' If material

things were perceived by themselves,
they would be a true light to our
minds, as being the intelligible form of
our understandings, and that whereby
they become actually intelligent, and
consequently would be truly perfective
of them, and indeed superior to them ;'
a proposition which he justly finds
erroneous and absurd.

[2] Aristotle has made this simile
famous by using it in his III. Book
De Anima.

the sheet was ready to receive any writing whatever, that is, the idea could admit of every one of the determinations of particular existences.[1]

[1] I conjecture that this is the true interpretation of the *tabula rasa* of the ancients; and I believe that the moderns in their extreme inclination to scoff at all antiquity have not understood its meaning. The reasons of this my opinion are as follows: (1) The simile of *tabula rasa* conveys indeed the notion that there are no particular characters to be seen there, but at the same time it admits the *tabula* itself on which anything may be written. What then is this *tabula* perfectly *plain and smooth*, innate in our soul? I maintain that it is *indeterminate being*, capable of receiving any determinations whatever. (2) This simile can be explained by the other which Aristotle introduces, namely, of the *light* and the *colours*. There are, he says, no *colours*, but there is an *innate light*, which is *per se* uniform (behold the smoothness of the tablet), and fit to make us see equally all the colours of things. (3) By so interpreting the *tabula rasa*, we are enabled to reconcile many passages of Aristotle which would otherwise be irreconcilable. (4) Among those Schoolmen who adopted the simile we find some who say expressly that we have the idea of *being* innate in us. Suffice it for all to mention S. Bonaventure, or whoever be the author of the *Compendium Theologicæ Veritatis* from which I am quoting. In ch. xlvi. of Book ii. he makes use of the Aristotelian simile; and in ch. xlv. he says that all cognitions come from the senses. Nevertheless it seems certain that this writer admits as innate in man the idea of the *ens actualissimum* (*Itin. Ment. in Deum*); that is he admits more than I do, for I admit only the idea of *being perfectly indeterminate*. What then are we to say? That the ancients did not understand the simile in question in that wretched sense which is attributed to it by the moderns.

CHAPTER V.

THE INNATE IDEA OF BEING SOLVES THE GENERAL DIFFICULTY PRESENTED BY THE PROBLEM OF THE ORIGIN OF IDEAS.

ARTICLE I.

Solution of the difficulty.

539. The difficulty involved in the problem of the origin of ideas, has been reduced by me to this simple question : ' How is our first judgment possible ? ' (41–45).

On Locke's hypothesis, that all our ideas come from the senses, the difficulty was insuperable.

By my admission, of which I have given the reasons, that the most universal of all ideas is in us by nature antecedently to all our sensations, the difficulty of understanding how we form the *first judgment* is entirely removed.

ARTICLE II.

Objections and replies.

§ I.

First objection.

540. But there are objections which we must examine ; and the first is this :—The judgment which I have said to be necessary for the formation of ideas, was described as coming to the same thing as the conceiving of an idea ; so that *judgment* is the only means through which ideas are conceived.

If this be true, it is of no avail to say that the most universal of all ideas is innate in us ; it is an idea ; and that is enough to prove that, in order to be conceived, it stands in need of a judgment, like all other ideas.

The fact of its being innate does not exclude its having to be conceived by the mind ; it only imports that its conception takes place from the very first moment of our existence, through a virtue or power natural to us.

If, then, ideas are conceived only by means of a judgment the difficulty which I wished to avoid, returns, and the question arises, ' How is that judgment possible by which we conceive the most universal of all ideas ? '

Answer to first objection.

541. This objection is based entirely on a false supposition, viz. that a judgment is necessary for the conception of *all* ideas.

The truth on the contrary is, that a judgment is necessary for ideas of *our own formation, i.e.* those which unite in themselves a predicate and a subject, and are therefore composed of two elements, one of which must be a universal, as, for instance, the ideas of bodies. But if there be an idea which does not consist of these two elements, and is one of them only, there is no need of a judgment in order that we may have and conceive it. A judgment is always an intellectual operation by which two terms are joined together ; hence, supposing there are not two terms, but one only, no judgment of any sort will be necessary, nay, possible ; there will simply be an immediate *intuition*, not preceded by any judgment.

Now, by examining all the ideas possessed by the human mind, we discover that there is one, and one only (the idea of existence or being in general), which has this singular property, that it is perfectly simple, and not composed of a predicate and a subject ; consequently, unlike all other ideas, it demands no judgment for its conception.

Therefore this idea, on the one hand, cannot be *formed* by any operation of our own, but can only be seen by direct *intuition*; while on the other hand, we could not have intuition of it, unless it were present to our mind : and this is a fresh and evident proof that we have it presented to us by nature.

§ 2.

The first objection is urged with greater force.

542. Nevertheless I feel bound to acknowledge, that it is no easy matter to understand how we can have the intuition here spoken of, without some sort of judgment being mixed up with it.

Nay it seems at first sight, that the idea of being may be expressed by the proposition, 'A something is possible to exist ;' which proposition is a judgment. If, then, we conceive that proposition, we judge that 'a something is possible.' And that this judgment is included in the idea of being, could be further demonstrated from the analysis I have made of the said idea (423, 424). By that analysis I found it to consist of three elements, two of which are, (1) *the notion of a something*, and (2) the *possibility of this something*. Here, it will be urged that we have a predicate and a subject, both expressed in the proposition 'a something is possible ;' *possibility* being the predicate, and the indeterminate *something* the subject. This is a difficulty which deserves to be carefully considered.

Continuation of answer to first objection.

543. The difficulty arises from the uncertainty presented by the concept of *possibility*. Let us make a more accurate analysis of this concept.

In the first place, it should be observed that here we speak of *logical possibility*, which must not be confounded with *probability*, the two being totally different from each other. What, then, is *logical possibility ?*

By a possible entity is meant an entity which *can* subsist, can be conceived as subsistent.

Whatever does not involve contradiction, is called *possible*. We can always think it existent, we can imagine it such as often as we please.

In order that a thing may be pronounced *impossible*, the mind must see a necessary reason, with which the existence of that thing is incompatible ; so that either the reason must be false, or the thing cannot exist. From the moment that the reason has been recognised as necessarily true, it can no longer be pronounced false ; therefore the thing is pronounced impossible.

The contrary of *impossibility* is *possibility*. As, then, in order to declare a thing impossible we must have a necessary reason incompatible with that thing ; so for the *possibility* of that thing nothing is required save the absence of such concept as would make it an absurdity, a contradiction in terms ; for in every case in which no such concept exists, a thing is possible.

The reason why the term *possibility* happens to have a positive sense attached to it, lies in the nature of our mind and of language. Language expresses positive as well as negative entities by a word, *i.e.* by a positive sign. Hence the facility to confound them together. Thus, when we use the term *nothing*, we simply mean to exclude all existence, and yet we seem to be speaking of something, because we designate nothingness by a word.

What I say of *possibility* cannot be applied to *probability*. If *possibility* signifies the absence of contradiction, *probability* imports some positive reason over and above the concept of the thing, on the strength of which reason we say: ' It is probable that this thing I am thinking of exists or will happen '—whether that reason consist in a number of cases in which the thing has been seen to take place, or in the knowledge we have of the existence of some special power fit to produce it.

Hence it will be seen that I take *possibility* in a logical and absolute sense, and not in that approximative sense in which this word is often used in common discourse.

We say, ' It is impossible that this tree could be here in the garden, if there had been no seed for it to spring from.' This is a case of *physical impossibility*, or of repugnance to the physical law that ' Every plant comes from a seed.'

Again, we say, ' It is impossible that, exposing yourself as you do to so many dangers, you should not, at one time or other, meet with some serious mishap.' This impossibility amounts only to *improbability,* that is to say, it means that safety under such circumstances is not in accordance with the common order of events. The impossibility here is not a repugnance to physical laws, or to the ordinary course of things, or even to moral laws. It is a repugnance to the laws of *thought,* so that, one of the terms of the proposition being admitted, the other cannot be conceived as co-existent with it. Whatever does not involve this latter kind of contradiction, I call *possible.*[1]

544. The *possibility* of a thing is, therefore, nothing positive in itself, and outside the thing. To use a common

[1] Sometimes there is in certain things a logical impossibility which is hidden from us, and requires a good deal of thinking before we can discover it. This is because the idea we have of those things is imperfect; has too great an extension; does not descend to the thing in itself, but takes it in only as forming part of a genus or a species, without our troubling to penetrate so to speak into its individual character. Hence, before we can make sure that the thing is possible, it is necessary that we should bestow our attention, not merely on its common qualities, but also on its own self and on its properties. Let us take an example from Mathematics. Let it be asked : ' What is the square root of 2, expressed in a finite series of numbers?' This problem, before mathematicians had tried it, might have seemed possible enough of solution. But, when tried, it was found to be quite the other way ; so much so that a rigorous demonstration has been produced of the impossibility of expressing in a finite series of numbers, whole or fractional, the square root of 2, or of any other of those numbers which are called *incommensurable.* Here a demonstration of the *impossibility* of the problem became necessary ; precisely because this *impossibility* was hidden, and did not at once present itself to the mind of the thinker.

The reason of this imperfection of our mind, which does not see at a glance the impossibility of certain things, and therefore cannot be sure of their *possibility,* is found in what we have said above concerning the *indeter-*minateness of ideal being. This being is a tablet not yet inscribed with any particular characters, *i.e.* it is only *in potentia* as regards all determinate beings. Hence the mind cannot judge of them, nor of their possibility, without (1) thinking of their determinations, (2) confronting them with the idea of being as the supreme rule. The rule for judging of the possibility of things is, then, innate in us ; not so the *judgment* nor its subject-matter. Hence that judgment must be sought for, and sometimes with considerable labour.

If Kant had observed that *possibility,* considered by itself alone, is only a negative concept expressing that ' The existence of the thing which happens to form the subject of our discourse is not repugnant to the laws of thought ;' and moreover if he had not confused *possibility,* with the danger in which we sometimes are of judging erroneously of this or that thing, he would not have denied that, in order to be able to judge that a thing is possible, it suffices to demonstrate, that there is no contradiction in it (*i.e.* in its concept), nor would he have required anything more for the notion of possibility, as he has done in his *Critique of Pure Reason,* thus going further and further away from the truth (See Part i. Book ii. C. ii. Sec. iii. § 4). Nevertheless there is a truth in this, that the positive foundation of possibility lies in *ideal being* itself, since whatever is conceived by us has in it this property, that it is conceived as possible, so that to *conceive it* and to *conceive it as possible* are one and the same thing.

expression, it is a mental entity, *i.e.* the result of a reflection whereby the mind, looking at the essence of the thing, does not find in it any intrinsic repugnance. This absence of repugnance in the order of ideas is expressed by the word *possibility*, whence it seems to us as though it were something existing separately from the entity conceived, whereas in point of fact it is not so.

The same may be said of mental entities generally. They are all products of a reflection by which we become aware of the absence of something, or of some relation, or of some quality, &c. For this reason, none of them can have been in our minds separately and in itself from the beginning of our existence ; they are only noticed and set distinctly before the mind when this faculty has become sufficiently developed for that operation.

To conclude : the *possibility* of things, in so far as it is a mental entity capable of being expressed by a word, is not known to us by nature, but observed by an act of our mind ; and in so far as it is a mere absence of logical repugnance, it means nothing more than that in *indeterminate* or *ideal being* we find no such repugnance, and therefore can find none in any of the things which we see in it. *Possibility* therefore is not a thing distinct from *being* itself.

Now the consequence of this is obvious : we have nothing innate in our minds except the most simple idea of *being* ; and *possibility* is a predicate which adds nothing to it, but excludes from it something (*i.e.* logical repugnance), and serves us for simplifying it, *i.e.* for recognising it in its perfect simplicity and oneness.

545. In the light of these principles, we can see that the proposition, 'Something is possible to exist,' if intended to signify what is innate in the human mind, is inexact. That proposition supposes that the *idea of possibility*—a purely mental entity—has been already set apart by our mind from the most simple idea of being ; and that, what is by its nature negative, has been clothed by us with a positive form, *i.e.* a thought and a word ; in short, that we have converted it into a predicate apparently positive.

If, then, we wish to analyse and find precisely what there is of innate expressed in the proposition, 'A something is possible to exist,' we must take away from it all that has apparently been added thereto, in consequence of our manner of conceiving and of expressing ourselves.   For this end the proposition, 'Our mind sees by nature that a something is possible,' should be translated into this other : ' Our mind has by nature the idea of being, and sees no logical repugnance in it ; ' or into the following : 'Our mind has *ab initio* the idea of being, and later on, by reflecting on that idea, it comes to discover that there is no logical repugnance in it.' And since the idea of being is what constitutes, as objective form, our intelligence, our intelligence may be defined as ' The faculty of the intuition of being ; ' which clearly leads to the conclusion, that if this intuition were to cease, our intelligence would cease likewise.

Being, therefore, cannot be taken away, *i.e.* removed from the human mind.   Now to leave *being*, and at the same time to take it away, is what is called *contradiction*.   Therefore our intelligence cannot understand, cannot think except what does not involve contradiction.

546. It is only in course of time, then, that we observe how *being* takes those various determinations which are presented to us in real beings.   Hence we say, that in that essence (being) is contained the possibility of things ; which, as I have observed, simply means, that ' between indeterminate being and its determinations and realisations, we see no repugnance.'   The concept of possibility, then, involves a *relation* with the *determinations* of *being*, which were unknown to us at the first, and are learned only from sensible experience.

Briefly, from observing (when our mind has gained the capacity for that reflection), from observing, I say, that the essence of *being*, present to us by nature has no determinations (which is purely a negation, and not a positive predicate), we conclude that an indefinite quantity of real beings, *i.e.* of determinations and realisations of that essence, are possible and thinkable ; in other words, that the admission of all those determinations and realisations involves no repugnance to it. This evidently shows that the concept of mere possibility is not innate in us, but *acquired*, although its foundation—the ideality and indeterminateness of being—is innate.

Thus the innate idea of *being*, while standing before us entirely without predicate, is itself the most universal of predicates. On the other hand, having in itself none of the determinations and actions belonging to the real world, it admits of being united or applied to these determinations and actions as predicate to subject. This idea therefore does not include any judgment, but constitutes the possibility of all judgments, inasmuch as when anything presents itself to us by its action on our senses, we can, by means of this idea—the common predicate—judge that thing.[1]

§ 3.
Second objection.

547. The objection which I have just endeavoured to answer was drawn from the second of the elements we have assigned to the idea of being, namely *possibility* (423). My answer rested on the fact that this element, in so far as conceived separately from *being*, is negative, and therefore does not take away but rather shows forth the simplicity of that idea.

But the difficulty to admit that we can have the idea of being wholly apart from any judgment, might also, in some minds, arise from the consideration of the first element—the *something*, the essence of being, seen in the said idea.[2] This difficulty would be as follows: 'In the act by which I see *being*, there are two distinct terms—the *Ego* who sees, and the *being* which is seen. In this act therefore my consciousness tells me 'I see *being*;' and this is a judgment. It seems therefore that in every objective conception which is not a

---

[1] That our *cognitions* suppose a *measure*, a *rule*, is taught also by S. Thomas; for he says: 'Intellectus accipit cognitionem de rebus mensurando eas quasi ad sua principia.' 'The mind comes to the knowledge of things through measuring them as it were by their principles (*De Verit.* Q. x. art. 1).

[2] The author has designated this element by the term *objectivity* (see nn. 415, 416) (TRANSLATORS).

mere modification of the thinking subject, there must necessarily be a judgment.'

Answer to the second objection.

548. The answer to this lies in an observation which, notwithstanding its subtlety, may not be omitted here.[1]

The act by which I see *being* is entirely different from the act by which I say to myself, 'I see it.'

Let it be well noted that it is not my object here to examine whether or not this second act follows always or necessarily upon the first: this would be irrelevant to our

---

[1] He would indeed be a bad observer of nature, who should make it a rule to notice only the most obvious and patent facts, and who, whenever coming upon anything which appears singular, or of a recondite or mysterious character, should argue thus: I need not trouble to investigate this, for things of this sort are too difficult to observe, and, when observed, to verify, and the labour thus spent is only repaid by obscure and uncertain results. And were the occupant of a professional chair to act thus, would he not be justly chargeable with playing the fool with nature, as well as with those he pretends to instruct? To pretend to construct a theory and at the same time to dispense with the necessity of basing it on the things which it undertakes to explain? As if it were optional for any one to declare a fact of nature unnecessary to science, solely because of its difficulty and obscurity; or as if man could under any circumstances make the nature of things different from what it is? Yet such is precisely the method of those minute philosophers who have followed in the wake of Locke—the Sensists and Materialists. Even very able men, I regret to find, have allowed themselves to be beguiled by this absurd presumption; and clear evidences of this bad system of reasoning have been exhibited by writers who piqued themselves most on their rigorous adherence to sound method. Thus, for example, Bonnet, a thinker really of great parts, when asking the question, 'Whether there be in us a feeling of our own existence,' dismisses it with the remark that: 'It is not well to admit a feeling of existence of which we cannot form any idea to ourselves: it is undoubtedly better not to accept any but CLEAR THINGS, and on which we can reason' (*Analyse abrégée de l'Essai analytique*, ii.).

Now if we are to accept nothing but what is quite *clear*, our intellectual stock will be very small indeed; since nature is full of obscurity and mystery. If one must seek only that which it is *well* to admit, and not that which is *true*, who will ever know what each philosopher may think it *well* or *best* to admit into his system? The duty of a philosopher is, to observe nature entire as it stands; not to say, 'I will accept only what is clear,' but to strive, by observation and reflection, to make clear that which is *obscure*. Where he meets with something mysterious, the true philosopher will labour all the more assiduously to decipher the enigmatic characters in which nature presents her secrets, and, when he fails, will be lost in admiration of the depths of the wisdom of Him, who has made nature so pregnant with matter for thought, so immense and sublime. Do what you will, therefore, you cannot eliminate certain questions from philosophy. You must rather attack them with courage, with that right kind of daring which always goes hand in hand with modesty. In particular, the *fundamental feeling* is a fact of such importance, that if it be excluded from philosophical observation, or declared impossible to observe, there is an end to all explanation of human cognitions.

present argument. What it is now important to understand is, that *having the intuition of an idea*, and *judging that we have it*, are two different acts of the soul.

By intuition I fix my attention on the idea. If my attention is weak, if it is not fixed, but vacillating, so that its force is as it were scattered over other objects; the nature of the act is not, on that account, changed. Now it is of great consequence to observe, that this act, like its object, is essentially one; and the spreading out of our attention does not take away its character of oneness, but, at the most, it associates with itself other acts entirely different, each of which, taken in itself, is one.

This act, one and simple, and isolated from all the other acts with which it might happen to be mingled, is what we must now examine.

Now it is an essential property of the act by which I fix my attention on an idea, to be restricted to its object, and to terminate therein.

549. That it may be easier for us to consider an act of attention separated from all the others, let us try to find a case in which the whole force of our attention is concentrated on a single point.

Let us imagine that the object of our attention is the same as that which forms the whole object of our affections, and whose surpassing beauty and perfection so enraptures us that we are absorbed by and lost in the contemplation of it. If this interior contemplation should rise to the requisite degree of intensity, a singular phenomenon will take place. Charmed away completely by the excellences of the object, we have no power left for anything else. The entrancing delight of that vision makes us forget ourselves and all surrounding objects, which to us, while in that state, are as if they were not. Our entire activity, both of thinking and of loving, is there fixed and exhausted. This species of alienation is a fact, which I believe there is hardly a man who at some period of his life has not experienced in some degree, and who therefore may not, from what has happened to himself in a lesser measure, be able to form a pretty good idea of that greater intensity

VOL. II.   K

to which a similar mental excess could, under given circumstances, be carried.   I ask : will a man in this condition turn
his attention on himself?   Will he be capable of taking a
survey of the state of his mind ?—Not more than the infant
who, when sucking its mother's milk, is wholly absorbed in
that action.   He cannot make these reflections on himself,
nor on that state of self-oblivion, until he has, so to speak,
come to himself, as one waking from a profound sleep.   Then,
and then only, will he be in a position to bestow upon himself
that attention which had been engrossed by an altogether
different object.

But if the act by which the mind and the affections adhered
to the said object was such as to exhaust in itself the whole
of our interior energies, that act cannot be directly joined
with the state which follows ; there must be a break, a rest
between the two.   Hence the new action will start as totally
unconnected with the previous one ; whose intensity was so
overwhelming as to cause even the memory of it to be lost
—a remarkable fact described by Dante in the following
lines :—

> ' Perchè appressando sè al suo desire
>   Nostro intelletto si profonda tanto,
>   Che retro la memoria non può ire.'   (*Parad.* i.)

> ' For that so near approaching its desire
>   Our intellect is to such depths absorbed,
>   That memory cannot follow.'   (*Cary's Translation*)

550. All these observations help us to understand, that to
reflect on the operations of our soul is an act entirely different
from the operations themselves.

Hence it follows, that I can think an object, for instance
being, without *reflecting* on myself and becoming aware that I
am thus thinking.

Now, I cannot pronounce the judgment, 'I see being,'
except in consequence of a reflection I make on myself, *i.e.*
on the state of my mind, which thus becomes the object of
my attention.   But the *state of my mind*, is an object widely
different from *being*.   Therefore I contemplate *being* by an

act different from that by which I contemplate my own state. By the first act I see what is purely and essentially *object*; by the second I see myself, the subject who has that vision. The first act is an *intuition*; the second is, a *perception* relatively to myself, and a *reflection* relatively to being. The first act is simple, primary, spontaneous; the second is composite (a judgment), and posterior to the first. The first may be innate in me; not so the second, although there is nothing to prevent this from following more or less closely upon the first. The first is intrinsic, and therefore necessary, to my nature; the second may be purely acquired and voluntary.

551. In distinguishing these two acts, I have introduced the state of a man wholly absorbed in a single object, not as a proof of that distinction, but as a means to assist the reader in comprehending it. In the state of mental concentration, all the forces of our attention are directed to one single point;[1] hence it is seen how an act may exist unaccompanied by those other acts which usually go along with it. For the purpose of my argument, however, there is no need to show that one act of attention is distinct even as to time from all the others. It is enough to have made it clear that one act is not the other; because this proves that one may be innate and the other not.

But how much stronger would my position be if I were here to dwell on a truth which was well known to the ancients, namely that our mind can perform but one act at a time? And that *being* (in general anything conceived by the mind), and the *Ego* who sees it are two separate objects and

---

[1] The fact of a man absorbed in the contemplation of a given object, affords me the opportunity of making an observation which brings to light an erroneous way of judging, of very common occurrence. When a thing is but faintly remembered, or when a sensation has been accompanied by little or no advertence, one is very apt to say that the impression produced by that thing, or the sensation, must have been extremely feeble. Now the truth may be quite the other way. The sensation may have been very strong, and yet one may not have adverted to it at all; and the same applies to mental concentration. Nay, I think that when a sensation, or the concentration of the mind on a particular object, has reached the highest point of intensity, we have no knowledge of it, no advertence, no recollection; we are left without any power of thinking of ourselves. The importance of this remark for properly understanding the operations of the human spirit, will be best comprehended by those who have dived deepest into these matters, and are in the habit of meditating on them.

consequently require, in order to their apprehension, two mental acts. Then indeed the absurdity of supposing, that to apprehend an object and to know that we apprehend it, are one and the same thing, would be apparent. And still more, if I were to demonstrate, if indeed a demonstration can be necessary of a thing which seems self-evident, namely that the second of these acts cannot begin to exist until the first, which is to be its object, has been fully completed? and that therefore it would be a contradiction in terms to say that the two acts—knowing and knowing that we know—are simultaneous?

COROLLARY I.

There is an idea which precedes all judgments.

552. As a necessary consequence of the above there is a primitive intuition natural to us and anterior to all our judgments : and this it is which constitutes our nature intelligent, and forms our cognitive faculty. The object of this intuition is *ideal being*, or, more briefly, the *idea*.

COROLLARY II.

There is in man an intellectual sense.

553. Our spirit, then, sees *being* by an immediate intuition, just as our sense receives immediately the impression of sensible things. This vision of being creates in us what may not be inappropriately termed an *intellectual sense.*

Our intellect therefore, inasmuch as it has the intuition of *being*, may be called *a sense* (different of course from the corporeal) ; but in so far as our spirit forms judgments, *i.e.* descries the relations between the things felt by the corporeal sense, and *being in general*, it performs an operation entirely different from that of the sense ; it does not receive sensations, but pronounces, synthesises, and thus produces cognitions and persuasions.[1]

[1] By this we can understand that saying of S. Thomas, ' Intellectus est vis passiva respectu totius entis universalis.' 'The intellectual faculty is passive' (properly speaking *receptive*) ' in respect of the whole universal *being* ' (*S.* I. lxxix. 2). And so also it seems to me that we may apply to the *innate idea* of being—which makes us know all things and itself also—that

OBSERVATION I.

Difference between the corporeal sense and the intellectual.

554. The difference between the *corporeal sense* and the *intellectual* consists in the difference of their terms. The terms of the corporeal sense are corporeal, determinate, and real ;[1] the term of the intellectual sense is purely spiritual and perfectly indeterminate.

From this difference between the terms of the two senses there springs another, which is as follows :—

Although the nature of *sense*[2] imports an action produced in, or a modification received by the sentient subject ; yet in the corporeal sense the object does not communicate itself *as object,* but *as a force in action,* as an *agent.* In the intellectual sense, on the contrary, the communication consists in the *manifestation of an object* rather than in the *action of a force* ; since, properly speaking, an object does not *act* on us, but is only *present* or *manifested* to us. Wherefore that which comes first in the case of the intellectual sense is, not the act by which the intellect feels its own self, but the act by which it understands being. From this act there naturally arises a pleasurable feeling in the intellect itself ; and on this account we may say with truth that the intellectual sense is subsequent to the act of understanding.

Hence we see that being in general is *idea* ;[3] but from this idea, the subject who has intuition of it, *produces to himself* what we may term intellectual sensations.[4]

---

sentence of Aristotle, ' In all which is separated from matter ' (*i.e.* which is purely *form*, like *ideal being*) ' that which we understand and that by which we understand are one and the same ' (*De Anima*, Lib. iii).

[1] *I.e.* subsistent (TRANSLATORS).

[2] Whether corporeal or intellectual (TRANSLATORS).

[3] *I.e.* essentially belongs to the order of *knowledge*, and therefore the act by which we see it is a *cognitive* act. See next note by the Author (TRANSLATORS).

[4] Should any one demur to applying the term *knowledge* to that one idea

which has been placed in us by nature, and of which we have immediate intuition without any act of judgment, I would not care to quarrel with him about words. Indeed this seems to have been the opinion of S. Thomas, whose doctrine I will endeavour to expound, hoping thus to throw some light upon it. The Holy Doctor teaches that our mind does not understand and know anything except by means of phantasms. It is very important to see what this doctrine meant according to this great master. He observes, then, that it is the property of the human mind to know *the things themselves*

OBSERVATION II.

The Nature of IDEAL BEING.

555. Whoever has perfectly understood all I have said thus far, must be convinced, that besides that mode of being which belongs to subsistent things, and which I have called REAL, there is an entirely different one, which I have called IDEAL, and constitutes the foundation of their possibility.

Indeed, IDEAL BEING is an entity of a nature wholly peculiar, not to be confounded either with our own spirit, or with bodies, or with anything pertaining to REAL BEING.

556. Hence it would be a most grievous error to suppose that, because IDEAL BEING or the IDEA, does not belong to the order of things which enter by their action into our feeling, therefore it is nothing.

On the contrary, *ideal being*, the *idea*, is a most true and most noble entity; and we have seen how sublime are the

('quidditas rei est objectum intellectus'). But by what means does the mind know the things themselves? By the *idea* or *species* of them. Consequently, that which the mind knows is not the idea or species but the real thing. The idea is only the means by which it knows ('Non quod cognoscit sed quo cognoscit'). Hence the dictum: 'Ad cognitionem duo concurrere oportet, scilicet apprehensionem' (the idea) 'et judicium;' which judgment (*the word of the mind*) terminates in the real thing. If, then, we had in us the simple apprehension or pure idea only and no reality, that is, nothing felt by the senses, we could not, in this sense, say that our mind *knows*, but only that it has the *means* of knowing. Such precisely is the condition of the human mind so long as it has the innate idea of *being* alone, and, as yet, no phantasms received from the senses. We could not say that it knows or understands anything, but only that it has the *power* of knowing or understanding. I will quote a passage where the Saint himself enuntiates this doctrine.— 'Nulla potentia potest aliquid cognoscere non convertendo se ad objectum suum, ut visus nihil cognoscit nisi convertendo se ad colorem. Unde, cum phantasmata se habeant hoc modo ad intellectum possibilem, sicut sensibilia ad sensum; quantumcumque aliquam speciem intelligibilem apud se habeat, nunquam tamen actu aliquid considerat secundum illam speciem nisi convertendo se ad phantasmata. Et ideo . . . intellectus noster secundum statum viæ indiget phantasmatibus ad actu considerandum.'—'No faculty can know anything unless by turning itself to its object, as for instance, the sight knows nothing except by looking at colour. Since, therefore, the phantasms stand to the possible intellect as sensible things stand to the sense; it follows that the intellect, however it may have in itself some intelligible species, never can actually consider anything according to that species except by turning itself to the phantasms. Consequently our intellect, in this our present state, stands in need of the phantasms in order actually to consider' (*De Verit.* Q. x. art. xi. ad 7). S. Thomas therefore admits, that the mind can have some *idea* or species, anteriorly to all the phantasms, and that it nevertheless requires them for *knowing*, in the restricted sense of the term.

characteristics with which it is endowed. It is true that we cannot give a definition of it, but we can analyse it, and declare, by what we experience from it, that it is the LIGHT of our spirit. What can be clearer than light ? Put out this light, and you have nothing but darkness.

557. Lastly, from what has been said, we can form a conception of the way in which *ideal being* adheres to our spirit ; that is, we can know that it does not, in order to be seen, require any assent or dissent on our part, but stands present to us as a simple fact (398).

The reason of this is, that this idea neither affirms nor denies ; it only constitutes the possibility of either affirming or denying (546).

PART III.

ORIGIN OF THE FIRST PRINCIPLES OF REASONING.

558. Hitherto I have shown that the intuition of *ideal being* is proper to the intelligent spirit, and necessary to make it such (Part I.)

I have also shown that, given the intuition of ideal being, it is easy to explain the origin of all determinate ideas by means of *sensation* and *reflection*; and I have likewise indicated this origin, both as regards all such ideas taken in a body, and as regards some of their larger divisions (Part II.)

It now remains for me again to deduce the various ideas and cognitions distributed in another order. This will serve the better to confirm the theory I have expounded, as well as to render its application easier.

To proceed with clearness, I shall begin with those cognitions which lead the way to, and are a necessary condition of the others; I mean,

(1) The *first principles* of reasoning;

(2) Certain *elementary* and most abstract notions, which are always assumed in human reasonings, and without which, these could neither be formed nor understood.

Once furnished with these *first principles* and *elementary* notions, as with so many appliances, the mind is fitted for its noble functions, and can therefore produce to itself new ideas and new cognitions.

Let us, then, in the first place, unfold the genesis of the supreme principles of human reasoning.

CHAPTER I.

FIRST PRINCIPLE—THAT OF COGNITION.
SECOND PRINCIPLE—THAT OF CONTRADICTION.

559. Principles are expressed by propositions.

In order to analyse a proposition, we must reduce it to its most simple expression, after the example of mathematicians, who, having to deal with a certain formula, ask leave to reduce it to the expression best suited for the operation they propose to make ; which, being a fair and reasonable request, is granted to them, provided that by changing the outer garb, they do not alter the value of the formula, or the substance of the equation.

560. A *proposition* expresses a *judgment.*

A *judgment* is the relation between two terms—*predicate* and *subject.*

The *principles* of reasoning, therefore, being so many judgments, are the result of a predicate and a subject.

Hence the simplest and most natural form in which the principles of reasoning can be presented, is that wherein the *predicate* is expressed directly and distinctly by a word (or by a phrase), the subject by another, and, by a third, their mutual relation. I will take as an instance the principle of contradiction.

561. This principle put in the simplest terms is as follows : ' That which is (being) cannot at the same time, not be.'

That which is, is the subject of the judgment ; *not be,* is the predicate ; *cannot,* is the *copula* which expresses the relation between the two terms, namely, the relation of *impossibility.*

We have seen what logical *impossibility* is : it is the

unthinkableness of a thing, in short, it is *nothingness* (543-544).

The principle of contradiction, then, says that '*being* (that which is) cannot be thought together with *non-being*; inasmuch as this would be to affirm and at the same time to deny what is affirmed, and an affirmation uttered simultaneously with a negation leaves *nothing*, no object of thought.

Therefore the principle of contradiction is nothing else than the *possibility of thinking*.

562. If then we take away this principle, no investigation of any kind is possible. No doubt can be entertained about its validity; since the act of doubting, as well as every other species of thought, presupposes that validity. Surely, no one can begin to think, to investigate, to reason, without taking thought, investigation, reasoning, for granted. The principle of contradiction is, therefore, absolutely unassailable ; for in order to assail it, one must think, and in order to think, one must admit that *it is possible* to think, whatever be the opinion to which one may come by thinking ; and the principle of contradiction says nothing more than this. Pray, would you think without thinking ? I trow not. If then you think (no matter what opinion you may form by thinking), you admit the principle of contradiction, which is the enunciation of the following fact: 'Either you think or you do not think: there is no middle term here, for to think without thinking is not possible.'

Thus the principle of contradiction is independent of all human thought and opinion: it precedes all thoughts and all opinions, because it constitutes the possibility of them all.

563. But you may say, 'I deny the possibility of thought.' I could answer that by your denial you think ; for to deny, as well as to affirm something, is to think. But to make the matter plainer, I answer thus: 'You deny the possibility of thought. Well, perhaps you are right and perhaps you are wrong: let this pass. Only tell me: in stating your denial, do you think ? If thought is impossible, I should rather imagine that you do not. But I am quite willing to leave the reply to yourself: do you, then, think or do you

not think? Whether you say yes or no, the principle of contradiction remains untouched, because it does not oblige you to think, but leaves you to do as you please. In order to exclude and annihilate this principle, what ought your reply to be? This and no other: 'I think without thinking,' or, I think, but I do not think.' Now, speaking seriously, would you like anyone to hear you make such a statement?

564. But to return to our analysis of the principle of contradiction; we have said that it is a proposition which expresses the fact that *'Being* cunnot be thought simultaneously with *non-being,'* or, 'There can be no thought unless it has *being* for its object.'

This is the same fact which I have noticed and, as it seems to me, proved beyond the possibility of doubt—the 'idea of being' as the informing and producing principle of our intellectual faculty (473–557); which I therefore define as 'The faculty of the intuition of being' (that which is). The phrase *'To be and at the same time not to be,'* means *nothing*, and *nothing* is the contrary of *something*, of *being*. By demonstrating, therefore, that our intellectual faculty is the faculty of seeing *being*, I have demonstrated the converse of this, viz. that nothingness cannot be an object of mental sight, and this is all that the principle of contradiction affirms.

The principle of contradiction, therefore, originates in the idea of being, the 'form' of our intelligence, or in other words, it is only the *idea* of being considered in its application.

565. Can we say, then, that the principle of contradiction is innate in us? We can say so in a certain sense, as was said by the author of the *Itinerarium* and by S. Thomas,[1]

[1] 'Retinet (memoria) nihilominus scientiarum principia et dignitates, ut sempiternalia et sempiternaliter, quia nunquam potest sic oblivisci eorum (dummodo ratione utatur), quin ea audita approbet, et eis assentiat, non tanquam de novo percipiat, sed tanquam sibi INNATA et familiaria recognoscat.' —' Nevertheless our memory always retains, as eternal and in an eternal mode, the principles and axioms of the sciences; because we can never (provided we have the use of reason) forget them in such a manner, as not to approve of and assent to them when stated to us, not as though we perceived something new, but as recognising in them, things which are INNATE and familiar to us' (*Itin. Mentis*, &c. c. iii). This is to observe the facts of nature keenly, and it is precisely what our modern sensists overlook, though they always make profession of being guided in their reasonings by facts.

namely, in the sense that in the very first use we make of our reason this principle manifests itself from the inmost depth of our soul.   To me, however, it seems more strictly true to say that we have, innate in us, not the principle itself but its foundation ; and I will give my reason for this opinion.

A principle has the form of a *judgment*, and is expressed by a *proposition*.   Sometimes it also supposes a reasoning, that is, if it be not absolutely the first ; and the principle of contradiction is not such.   In fact this principle can be deduced from a previous one, which I call the *principle of cognition*, and express in the following proposition : 'The object of thought is *being*, either indeterminate or determinate.'   Now the process of reasoning by which the principle of contradiction is deduced is this : the object of thought is *being*; but the phrase, *being* and *non-being*, expresses nothing ; and *nothing* is not *being*.   Therefore *being and non-being*, taken simultaneously, is not an object of thought.

Facts, however, albeit neglected by men, remain ; and if some do not observe them, others will, in due time.   Do what we may, it is impossible to dispense with them.

S. Thomas is of the same mind as the Author of the *Itinerarium*.   He says :—' Prima principia QUORUM COGNITIO EST NOBIS INNATA, sunt quædam similitudines increatæ veritatis.'—' The first principles, OF WHICH THE KNOWLEDGE IS INNATE IN US, are certain similitudes of the uncreated truth' (*De Verit.* Q. x. vi. ad 6*m*).   A similar expression of thought is very often met with in S. Thomas, as for instance in the following passage :—' In eo qui docetur, scientia præ-existebat, non quidem in actu completo, sed quasi in rationibus seminalibus secundum quod universales conceptiones, quarum cognitio est NOBIS NATURALITER INSITA, sunt quasi semina quædam omnium sequentium cognitorum.'—' In him who is taught, knowledge pre-existed, not indeed in a complete form, but, so to speak, in the seminal reasons, in as much as the universal conceptions, the knowledge of which is PLACED IN US BY NATURE, are as it were seeds of all the subsequent cognitions' (*De Verit.* Q. xi. i. ad 5*m*).   And that it may be seen that the interpretation I give of

these passages, is correct—namely that the *innate* or *naturaliter insitum* is not to be understood in a rigorous sense as regards the *first principles*, but only in the sense that those principles manifest themselves in us in the first acts performed by our reason, *i.e.* in the first use we make of the *idea of being (ens commune)*, which alone can, rigorously speaking, be called *innate*, and which corresponds to the *light* of the *intellectus agens* of S. Thomas – it will be enough to explain S. Thomas by himself.   Compare for example with the above extracts from the Holy Doctor the following :—

' In lumine intellectus agentis nobis est quodammodo omnis scientia originaliter indita, mediantibus universalibus conceptionibus, quæ statim LUMINE INTELLECTUS AGENTIS cognoscuntur, per quas sicut per universalia principia judicamus de aliis, et ea præcognoscimus in ipsis.'—' In the light of the *intellectus agens* there is placed in us originally, in a certain way, all knowledge, through the universal conceptions, which are at once known IN THE LIGHT OF THE INTELLECTUS AGENS, and by which, as by universal principles, we judge of other things, and know them therein beforehand' (*De Veritate*, Q. x. art. 6).

566. In order therefore that the *idea of being* should take the form of the principle of contradiction, it is necessary for me to have applied it ; to have begun to judge and to reason. I must therefore have formed to myself the mental entity called *nothingness.* I must have acquired an idea of *affirmation* and of *negation*, which are acts of thought ; I must have observed that negation united with *affirmation* is tantamount to *nothing.*

Now, however rapidly all these operations, judgments and reasonings may be performed, however naturally and proximately they may be derived from the idea of *being*, yet are they nothing else but this self-same *idea of being applied*, presented under various forms, accompanied by relations. Our intelligence must in every case move out of that primal state of perfect quietude, where it is lying as it were in wait for an occasion to come forth into action. But whatever is in us in consequence of some action not essential to and innate in our intellectual faculty, is *acquired* ; and such, therefore, in its explicit form of a judgment, is the principle of contradiction.

CHAPTER II.

THIRD PRINCIPLE—THAT OF SUBSTANCE.
FOURTH PRINCIPLE—THAT OF CAUSATION.

567. The *principle of contradiction* depends on the *principle of cognition* (565).

The *principle of cognition*, expressed in the judgment, 'The object of thought is *being*,' is a necessary fact, the principle of all principles, the law of the intelligent nature, the essence of the intelligence (565).

The second *principle*, following immediately from the first, is that of *contradiction* :—'*Being* and *non-being* cannot be thought simultaneously.'

The third is that of *substance* :—'The accident is unthinkable without the substance.'

The fourth is that of *causation* :—' A new entity is unthinkable without a cause.'

568. The *accident* is perceived by us through a sensible action exercised on us. It may also be called by the general name of *event*; and this all the more when we consider, that it is not necessary but supervenient to the substance. The only difference between an *accident* and an *effect*[1] is, that the *accident* is considered as forming one thing with the substance and giving it completion; whereas the *effect* is considered as separated from the cause and belonging to another being. Hence from the manner in which I shall deduce the principle of causation, the reader will be able to deduce by himself the principle of substance (52–54).

569. The principle of causation follows from the *principle*

---

[1] Those readers who do not see at once how the concept of *event* involves that of *effect*, may refer to nn. 350-352 (I. vol.), where the author has demonstrated this (TRANSLATORS).

of contradiction, and consequently from the *principle of cognition,* in this way :—

The principle of causation may be expressed thus : ' Every event (everything that begins) has a producing cause.' We found this formula in another place, and analysed it : here it is necessary to recall to mind that analysis.

The proposition, ' Every event has a producing cause,' is perfectly equivalent to this other : ' It is impossible for our mind to conceive an event, without conceiving a cause that has produced it.'

To demonstrate this proposition, one must show that the concept of ' an event without a cause ' involves contradiction. This will give the principle of causation deduced from that of contradiction.

I demonstrate it as follows :—To say that which does not exist, operates, is a contradiction. But to say ' an event without a cause,' is equivalent to saying that that which does not exist, operates. Therefore, an event without a cause is a contradiction.

The major is proved thus :—To conceive an operation (a change) without a being, is to conceive without conceiving : which is a contradiction. In fact, the principle of cognition says : ' The object of thought is being ; ' therefore, without a being, it is impossible to have a conception. To conceive an operation, therefore, without at the same time conceiving a being which does it, is to conceive without conceiving. Therefore, to say that that which does not exist, operates, is a contradiction in terms : which was the thing to be demonstrated.

The minor is proved thus : An event is an operation (a change [1]). If then this operation has no cause, it is conceived as isolated, as not belonging to any being ; there is, therefore, an operation without a being, or, what comes to the same, that which does not exist, operates. The minor, then, is also proved (350–352).

The principle of causation, therefore, flows from the

---

[1] From non-existence to existence (TRANSLATORS).

principle of contradiction, and both come from the principle of cognition : and this last is nothing but the *idea of being applied*, which, when considered in relation with human reasoning, whereof it is the *formal cause*, becomes a principle and is expressed in a proposition.

CHAPTER III.

WHAT ARE SCIENTIFIC PRINCIPLES IN GENERAL.

570. As we have seen, the above named principles—viz. (1) the principle of cognition, (2) the principle of contradiction, (3) the principle of substance, (4) the principle of causation— are but the self-same *idea of being applied*, or the law which governs its application, expressed in a proposition.

This observation enables us to understand the nature of all the principles of reasoning generally.

These principles are simply ideas which we use for making judgments.

The application of these ideas can always be conceived as a judgment, and put into a proposition.

And since this proposition, this judgment serves as a rule whereby to form a series of other judgments, subordinate to and virtually contained in it, as a particular is in the general ; therefore it is called *principle* in respect of the latter judgments, which are deduced from it ; and their deduction is called *reasoning*.

571. For example, the *idea of justice*, expressed in a proposition, becomes the *principle* of Ethics, when, by reasoning, the aggregate of its applications is reduced to a regular system : the *idea of the beautiful*, likewise expressed in a proposition, becomes the principle of Æsthetics, when we consider it as the rule and guide, or rather as the generator of all our reasonings about things beautiful.

572. Speaking generally, the *essence* of things is the *principle* of the reasonings which are made concerning them.

573. Hence the principle of each science is the *definition* expressive of the essential *idea of the thing* which forms the

subject-matter of the science.   From this arises the art of appropriately dividing the various sciences, and of bringing them all into harmonious unity ; so that they may not be mere collections of detached pieces of information, but well-ordered treatises, where a single principle rules supreme, and generates the particular truths appertaining to each science, as light generates light.

CHAPTER IV.

ORIGIN OF SCIENTIFIC PRINCIPLES IN GENERAL.

574. We have seen that *principles* are nothing else than *applied ideas* (570–573), or ideas which serve as the rule and exemplar whereby to form other more particular judgments.

The origin therefore of principles is reducible to the origin of ideas; hence the explanation of the latter is also the explanation of the former.

PART IV.

ORIGIN OF PURE IDEAS, THAT IS TO SAY, OF THOSE IDEAS WHICH TAKE NOTHING FROM THE SENSE.

CHAPTER I.

ORIGIN OF THE ELEMENTARY IDEAS OR CONCEPTS OF IDEAL BEING, WHICH ARE ASSUMED IN HUMAN REASONINGS.

ARTICLE I.

Enumeration of the elementary concepts contained in ideal being.

575. The elementary concepts assumed in all human reasonings are principally the following : (1) unity, (2) numbers, (3) possibility, (4) universality, (5) necessity, (6) immutability, (7) absoluteness.

ARTICLE II.

Origin of these concepts.

576. All these concepts included in *ideal being* are characteristics or natural qualities of it. They are, therefore, given to our intellect together with ideal being itself ; and all that remains for us to do is, to notice them one by one, to distinguish them in it, and to designate each by a name ; which is done by means of the various uses we make of the idea of being, and by reflection.

577. Hence we see why these concepts are so familiar to and supposed by all in their discourses. And though, when considered in themselves, they are seen to be of a nature the farthest removed from everything material, so that it would appear at first sight that in order to their formation a long and difficult mental process would be requisite, yet such is

not the fact. They are, on the contrary, the most obvious, the most easily understood, and the most universally used of all notions.

OBSERVATION.

578. I will only observe, that each of these abstract concepts, taken singly, is an element rather than an idea of itself : for, by themselves alone, they do not make us know anything. For this reason I call them *elementary concepts* of ideal being ; and, in general, *abstract ideas* may be termed elementary concepts of the idea from which they are respectively abstracted.

ARTICLE III.

Reasonings of S. Augustine on the ideas of unity, of number, and such like, which confirm the theory I have expounded.

§ 1.

579. Seeing that the elementary concepts above named belong to *ideal being*, it is no wonder that they baffle all attempts to explain them by means of sensation.

Nay it has invariably been the case, that when great thinkers happened to have their attention arrested by one or other of these concepts they were struck by the singularity of its nature, and, as such men always do when confronted with a difficult problem, made it a subject of intense meditation, being well aware that it could be no easy matter to account for the possession of a knowledge to which there is nothing similar in the sensible world. Thus the consideration of each such concept has enabled some master mind to soar above the sphere of visible things, to transcend all nature and fix its piercing gaze on the infinite. But, while noticing this fact, I am also bound to confess I have not found many, who by the contemplation I speak of have been led so far as to discover that the seat of all these concepts is in *ideal being*, and who could therefore be in a position to express the great Ideological Problem in its completeness.

It may not be out of place here to quote some example illustrating the way in which powerful intellects, through reflecting on even one only of these elementary concepts, have sometimes been rapt up to the highest regions of thought, and there discovered many of those truths which I have been endeavouring to set forth.   The concept I take is that of unity and numbers.

580. Disputing at Rome with his friend Evodius, S. Augustine, as he tells us in his second book on *Free-Will,* came upon this very question, opening it by calling attention to the difference between the *individuality of our faculties* and the *universality of truth* which shines to all minds alike.

Augustine.—' I will ask you in the first place, whether the feeling I have of my body be the same as yours, or whether mine be mine only, and yours, yours only.'

Evodius.—' I fully allow, that the sensations we experience in seeing, in hearing and in our other sensible operations, are exclusively proper to our several selves, although they are of the same species.'

Augustine.—' And would you not also say the same of that interior feeling of which I have spoken ? '

Evodius.—' Quite the same.'

Augustine.—' And now what about reason itself?   Has not every one of us his own particular reason ?   For it may certainly happen, that I understand something which you do not ; nor can you know whether I understand or not, whereas, if I understand, I do know it.'

Evodius.—' Clearly, each man has his particular mind proper to himself alone.'

Augustine.—' But can you also say, that there is a particular sun, a particular moon, a particular morning-star, &c., for each man who sees these things with his particular eyes ? '

Evodius.—' Certainly not.'

Augustine.—' Therefore many of us can see the same thing simultaneously, although the sense with which we see and therefore feel it, is exclusively proper to each.   My sense is not yours, and yours is not mine ; but the thing present to and seen at the same time by us both, is identically one.'

Evodius.—' Nothing could be clearer.'

Augustine.—' Likewise, one and the same voice can be

heard by many of us, so that, though my sense is different from yours, yet the voice which we hear together is the very same, and my hearing does not receive one part of the sound and your hearing another part, but the same sound is heard, whole and undivided, by each of us.'

Evodius.—' This also is clear enough.' [1]

Augustine.—' Now pay attention : do you think there is anything which all who reason see in common, yet each with his own particular reason—since that which is seen by the eyes is, as we said, present to all, and is not transmuted in the using, like food or drink ; but, whether seen by anyone or not, it remains uncorrupted and entire—or is there nothing of this kind ? '

Evodius.—' Nay, I am sure there are many such things. To give but one example ; the reason and truth of *numbers* is open to all who calculate,[2] so that each calculator endeavours to apprehend it with his own particular mind ; which some can do more easily than others, while some cannot do it at all. Nevertheless that reason and truth offers itself alike to all who are capable of understanding it ; and when understood by anyone, it is not changed, as food is changed into the substance of the eater, neither is it altered ;[3] and if anyone errs in the calculation, it does not itself fail, but remains

---

[1] The analysis of sensation was not carried so far in the days of S. Augustine, as it has been in modern times. Hence it is not to be wondered at, if in this passage there does not seem to be an accurate distinction made between the sun as perceived by the senses, and the sun as perceived in itself by the understanding. The senses do not, properly speaking, perceive the sun itself, but only the particular action of the sun ; and the action which the sun produces in different individuals is numerically different, although similar in kind. Hence we may say that different sensitive organs perceive in a certain manner different suns, but it would be still more accurate to say that the sun is not perceived *as existent in itself*, except by the understanding ; while the corporeal sense perceives only the *agent* in its various and separate *actions*.

[2] See here how carefully S. Augustine distinguishes the *subject* from the *object*, the *faculty of reason* from the *truth* apprehended by it. The differences to which he calls attention are manifest, undeniable. And yet there are people nowadays who insist on confounding knowledge and *truth* with the *mind* of man, and making the former a mere effect or emanation of the latter !

[3] It should be carefully observed, that the subject who understands, is various, mutable, liable to defect ; whilst truth (the *object*) is in no way affected by the various states of the subject who endeavours to contemplate it. With these last words, S. Augustine destroys all those systems which would have us believe that truth is informed by the qualities of the thinking subject —a thing simply impossible, because *truth* is, of its own nature, immutable.

in all its entirety ; whereas the calculator sinks the more deeply into error, the less he sees it.'

Augustine.—' Excellent ! I see that you are no novice in these questions, for you have the correct answer at your fingers' ends. Nevertheless, if anyone were to say that these numbers are impressed on our mind, not through any virtue of their own, but by those things which we perceive with the corporeal sense, as though they were a sort of images of visible things, what would you answer ? Do you believe this to be possible ? '

Evodius.—' I could never believe it ; because even if I were to perceive the numbers [1] with my corporeal sense, I should not be able, with this sense, to perceive the principle which regulates their divisions and combinations. For it is only by the light of this principle shining to my mind that I can correct a sum in addition or subtraction, when I see it going wrong. As regards the things which I perceive with the corporeal sense, for instance the heavens, the earth and all the other bodies which are in them, I do not know how long they will continue ; but that seven and three make ten, I know is true, and always was and always will be.[2] Now this incorruptible truth of numbers is, as I have said, common to me and to everyone else who thinks on the matter.'

Augustine.—' All that you say is perfectly true and certain. But I wish you to observe, that not even the ideas of numbers can be abstracted from the corporeal senses. This you will easily see, if you consider that every number is a compound of units ; for example, if the number contains the unit twice, it is called *two* ; if thrice, it is called *three*; if ten times, it is called *ten* ; in short, the names of numbers vary exactly according to the quantity of units contained in them. Now anyone who thinks accurately of what the *unit* is, finds that it cannot in any way be perceived by the senses of the body. For everything that is perceived by these senses is proved to

---

[1] Here S. Augustine seems to admit the possibility of numbers being perceived by the corporeal sense ; but he very quickly rejects this also as impossible.

[2] We see here the characteristics of immutability, necessity, eternity, observed by S. Augustine in the properties of numbers.

be, not one, but many, because it is a body, and therefore has parts innumerable. But not to speak here of those parts of bodies which are more minute and less distinguishable, I say, that however small a body may be, it certainly has a right and a left, an upper and an under side; or parts of it lie at the extremities and a part at the centre. For it would be useless to deny that these things exist in each of the bodies which present themselves to us, no matter how diminutive its size; and therefore we must concede that none of the bodies we see is truly and simply *one*; although the things I speak of could not be numbered unless we distinguished them through the knowledge we have of the unit. For when I seek for the unit in a body, and know for certain that I cannot find it there, most undoubtedly I know what it is I am seeking, and do not find, and indeed cannot find, because it is not where I am looking for it. Hence my knowing that the *unit* is not a body, supposes in my mind the idea of the unit, since if I did not know what the unit is, I could not number the *many* things which are in the body. But whatever be the source whence I derive my knowledge of the unit, that source, certainly, is not the corporeal sense; for by means of this sense I know nothing but the body, which is never truly and purely *one*.[1] But if the corporeal sense does not give us the knowledge of the unit, neither can it give us the knowledge of numbers, that is to say, of those numbers which we contemplate with our mind.[2] For there is not one of them which is not called by a distinct name corresponding

[1] Even admitting that there is in bodies some kind of *unity*, as would be the case with those which have *continuous extension*, it is always necessary, in order that we may know the unity of a body, to perceive that body, first as a *being*, and then as *one*, *i.e.* to perceive it objectively. Now this cannot be done by the corporeal sense, which receives nothing but the *action* of things and feels that action, and therefore not the things themselves as they are *in se* and outside of it. For the rest, the unity of the 'extended' is not perfect inasmuch as it never excludes the *possibility* of division and multiplicity.

[2] To superficial observers multiplicity seems a very easy thing to conceive. Yes, it is easy *to conceive it*, but difficult to explain *how* it is conceived. These good persons confound the fact of the conception of multiplicity, with the theory of that fact; the facility of the one with the difficulty of the other. Those, on the contrary, who can penetrate into the true nature of this question, will perceive, (1) that we cannot conceive the *many* unless we have beforehand the idea of the *one*, and (2) that we cannot conceive the *one* unless we have already the idea of the *being*.

precisely to the amount of units severally contained in it ; and the unit, as I have said, is not perceived by the corporeal sense.'

Here S. Augustine goes on to speak in a similar strain of the properties and relations of numbers, demonstrating that they are eternal and independent of everything temporal. He says :—

581. 'Moreover, by taking note of the order of numbers, we see that after one comes two, which is twice one, but the double of two does not come next, but number three must be brought in so that four may follow, which is the double of two. And the same holds good by a most certain and immutable law with respect to all other numbers. Whatever be the amount of units contained in a given number, we must count as many more if we wish to double that number. Now, where do we see this property, its evidence, its firmness, its unchangeable, incorruptible validity for all numbers alike ? Not in what we obtain from the senses ; for there is no man who with his corporeal sense perceives or can perceive all possible numbers.[1]   Do we, then, see it in some imagery or phantasm ?   Again I say no : a truth so certain, a law which can be applied, and so unerringly applied to innumerable series of things, is seen only in that *interior light* of which the corporeal sense knows nothing.'

Hence he concludes :

'On these and many such other grounds, those who have received from God a talent for disputation, and whose minds are not darkened by prejudice, are forced to confess that the reason and truth of numbers does not belong to the corporeal senses, but stands inflexible and inviolable, and manifests itself in common to all who make use of their reasoning powers.'[2]

[1] Here we see how S. Augustine perceived that those reasonings which deal with the order of the possible and necessary, transcend all sensible experience.

[2] 'His et talibus multis documentis coguntur fateri, quibus disputantibus Deus donavit ingenium, et pertinacia caliginem non obducit, rationem veritatemque numerorum et ad sensus corporis non pertinere, et invertibilem sinceramque consistere, et omnibus ratiocinantibus ad videndum esse communem' (*De Lib. Arbitrio*, II. viii).

§ 2.

582. S. Augustine applies a similar method of reasoning to all necessary truths whatsoever, and shows that, like those relating to numbers, they lie wholly outside the sphere of sense, and proceed of necessity from a much higher source than the sensible and temporal natures. In illustration of this, I beg leave to subjoin another extract from the same Book, by which the reader will see still more clearly, both, the conclusions deliberately arrived at by so great an authority, and the truth which it is one of the main objects of this work to establish in the fullest manner; namely, that our knowledge in its formal part cannot come from the senses. Let us hear, then, how, passing on from numbers to other truths, he discusses them with Evodius.

Augustine.—'We hold that there is such a thing as Wisdom, and that all men wish to be wise and happy. Now where do we see this? For I have no doubt whatever that you see this and see that it is true. Do you, then, see this truth in the way that you see your own thought, of which, if you do not manifest it to me, I am ignorant? or rather do you see it in such sort that you at the same time know perfectly well that what you see can be seen by me also, though you do not tell me of it?'[1]

Evodius.—'Exactly so; for I am full sure that you can see that truth by yourself even though I should wish you not to see it.'

Augustine.—'Now, if we both see with our individual minds this same truth, is it not a thing common to us both?'

Evodius.—'Evidently.'

Augustine.—'Let us now take another similar proposition: for example, I believe you will not deny that to study and to love wisdom is a duty.'

Evodius.—'On the contrary, I am perfectly convinced of it.'

---

[1] This subtle and very just observation is admirably calculated to mark the distinction between the knowledge of contingent and that of necessary things.

Augustine.—'Can we deny, then, that this truth also is one, and that it is seen in common by all who know it; although each one beholds it, not with my mind, nor with your mind, nor with anyone else's mind, but with his own; and nevertheless that which is seen is present to all alike?'

Evodius.—'This is undeniable.'

Augustine.—'That we ought to live justly, that things of less value must be esteemed less than those which are better, things of equal value esteemed equally, and its due given to every being, will you not admit are most true principles and shining in common before my mind, your mind, and the minds of all beholders?'

Evodius.—'I agree with you entirely.'

Augustine.—'Again, can you deny that the incorruptible is better than the corruptible; the eternal than the temporal, the inviolable than the violable?'

Evodius.—'Who could deny it?'

Augustine.—'Since, then, this truth presents itself to the contemplation of all who are capable of receiving it, and shines with an immutable light, can anyone say that it is exclusively his own?'

Evodius.—'No one can assert that it is his own, it being as much one and common to all, as it is true.'

Augustine.—'Now I will ask no more of these questions, it being enough for my purpose that you see with me, and grant as most certain, that these moral rules and principles are, on the one hand, true and unchangeable, and on the other, whether taken singly or collectively, they offer themselves in common for the intuition of all who have the capacity to see them, each, however, with his own individual reason and mind. Tell me, therefore, do these things seem to you to appertain to wisdom?'

Evodius.—'It would be impossible to think otherwise.'

Augustine.—'Therefore, even as the rules for calculating numbers—the reason and truth of which you have admitted to be shining unchangeably and in common to all who look at them—are true and immutable; so likewise are the rules of

wisdom, concerning some of which you have just now spoken
so rightly.'[1]

Evodius.—' How could I doubt it ? '

Augustine.—' Conclude, then, that you cannot deny there
is an *immutable truth* containing all those things which are
immutably true, and that you cannot say of this truth that it
is yours or mine or any other individual's ; but can only
say that it is seen equally by all who know how to fix the eye
of their mind on the particular immutable truths—like as it
were to a light endowed with the marvellous property of being
at once secret and public.'

Evodius.—' Nothing could be truer or clearer.'

Augustine.—' Now I will ask you one question. In your
opinion, is this *truth* about which we have been speaking so
long, and wherein we see so many things, more excellent than
our mind, or is it equal, or inferior to it ? '

Evodius.—' Perhaps it is inferior.'[2]

Augustine.—' But if it be inferior, we should judge, not
according to, but *of* it, even as we judge of bodies, which are
of an inferior nature to ours, and often say, not only that they
are such or such, but also *what they ought* to be : and you
may say the same of our own interior dispositions, concerning
which we not only know what they are, but also very often
what they *ought* to be. As regards bodies, we pass the
judgment, " This is not so white, or so shapely, &c., as it should
be." And of ourselves we say, " There is much room for
improvement in me ; my temper is too impetuous," or, " I am
wanting in energy of will," &c. All these things we judge
according to those interior rules of truth which are seen by
all of us alike ; but of the rules themselves no one ever
judges ; for if a person is heard to say that things eternal are
of more value than things temporal, or that seven and three
make ten, no one thinks of submitting this to examination ;

---

[1] Thus does S. Augustine prove
that the ethical and metaphysical
sciences have a basis no less firm than
the mathematical.

[2] To aid the reader in better understanding the drift of the above reasoning
of S. Augustine, I have made two
breaks in it, by putting this and the
next observation into the mouth of
Evodius. They, however, do not in
the least affect the substance of the
doctrine propounded by the holy
Doctor.

on the contrary, knowing that it is the truth, instead of discussing, he gladly accepts it.'

Evodius.—'Suppose, then, we say that truth is on an *equality* with the mind.'

Augustine.—'In that case truth would be mutable like the mind itself.[1]

'For our minds see at one time more and at another less—a clear proof of their mutability ; but truth remains always the same, neither increasing by our seeing it more, nor decreasing by our seeing it less. Unchangeable and uncorruptible, now it gladdens with its light those who turn themselves to it, now punishes with blindness such as refuse to accept it. Moreover, is it not a fact, that *by it* we judge of our minds themselves, whereas *of it* we cannot judge at all ? Thus we say, so and so does not understand, or he understands well enough. Indeed, such is the nature of our mind, that it understands only in proportion to the degree in which it can approach and adhere to the immutable truth.

'What are we therefore to conclude ? That truth, being neither *inferior* to, nor on an *equality* with the mind, must needs be *superior* and of a more excellent nature' (*De Lib. Arbitrio*, Lib. II. vii.–xii).

Thus far S. Augustine.

---

[1] All these arguments prove to demonstration, that *truth* is not a subjective production of our own mind, but that it comes to us from an infinitely higher source. It is to be regretted that Galluppi did not see this.

CHAPTER II.

ORIGIN OF THE IDEA OF SUBSTANCE.

583. Hitherto I have demonstrated, that from one primal idea present by nature to our spirit, proceed on occasion of the sensations, (1) all other ideas generally ; (2) the principles of reason, and (3), in particular, those which I have termed *elementary concepts of being*, and on which every use of our reason is conditional.

It was satisfactory to find, that by means of this theory we overcome that difficulty which has been a stumbling-block to so many philosophers, and indeed to all philosophy (539–551), *i.e.* the difficulty of tracing all our various ideas to their true origin.

It will be remembered that I stated this difficulty in a comprehensive and general form. But as it has presented itself under sundry particular aspects to different thinkers according as they attempted to explain the origin of this or that special class of ideas ; I think it may not be without advantage, after having shown that the above theory meets the difficulty in general, to continue my demonstration also in reference to all those partial forms which, Proteus-like, it incessantly takes. This demonstration will be complete if I can succeed in deducing from the fundamental idea of *being* all those special ideas, in the process of explaining which so many philosophers have unfortunately come to grief.

As regards the elementary concepts of being, I have done this already.

Next in order, the ideas of *substance* and of *cause* present themselves to us as being at once the most difficult and the most necessary.

ARTICLE I.

State of the question about the origin of the idea of substance.

584. What renders the difficulty of showing the origin of the idea of substance greater than it would otherwise be, is the inaccurate and confused notion which many philosophers form of this idea.

They confound the idea of substance in general with the idea of specific substances.   They will say, for example, ' We cannot know what the substance of bodies, &c., is ; therefore we have no idea of substance at all.'   But is this sound reasoning ?

Surely, we might have the idea of *substance in general*, without at the same time having an intimate knowledge of the *substances* of particular things.   Thus we might know well enough that a heavy block, which we see hanging from a lofty column, must be fixed to it in some way, in order to be kept suspended therefrom, although we do not know *how* it is fixed—whether by a rod of iron, or a hinge or another kind of fastening.   Of all this we may be ignorant, and nevertheless understand, that there must be something to connect that weight with the top of the column.

In like manner, suppose we could know that in bodies there must be a substance besides the sensible qualities or other accidents ; would it necessarily follow that we must also know what that substance is, and fully understand its nature ? Certainly not.   Conversely, from the fact of our not knowing what the substance of bodies is, it cannot be inferred that we have not the general notion of substance ; for if we had not this notion, how could our minds have seen that bodies must have a substance ?

585. Nay, to demonstrate that we have the notion of substance would be, as a writer now living has observed, a *petitio principii.* [1]

[1] Victor Cousin writes : ' En entrant dans une pareille discussion, je me sens convaincu moi-même de pétition de principe.   Je veux chercher si les notions de substance et de cause se trouvent dans l'esprit humain, et moi, esprit humain, je suppose d'avance ces deux notions ; il y a plus, je les pose, après leur avoir appliqué une définition. Il est clair encore, que je ne puis pas ne m'en pas frapper, parce que, comme l'a si bien dit Pascal, il ne faut jamais vouloir prouver l'évidence ' (*Fragmens philosophiques*, p. 425, ed. Paris, 1826).

I should like to ask those who deny the existence of such a notion, how can they deny it, if they have it not, if they do not know what it is that they deny?[1] As I remarked before, the idea of substance is a fact attested by all mankind, including those, who in words pretend to deny it. For even supposing that all men were deceived in believing themselves possessed of an idea, which they have not, it would still be necessary for them to be under the impression that they have it. Now no one can be under the impression that he has an idea, unless that idea be present to his mind ; hence an apparent idea is as much an idea as any other, and so the matter ends.

ARTICLE II.

Description and analysis of all that we think concerning substances.

§ I.

Where ought the inquiry concerning the ideas of substance to begin ?

586. Since our object here is to explain the cognitions we have of substance, or the different thoughts which our mind entertains concerning it, we must first of all determine exactly what these cognitions or thoughts are.

In the first place, it is a fact that our minds think of substance. It were useless to say, 'This is an illusion, a deception.' Such a remark would be irrelevant to our discussion. Whether true or false, illusory or real, these thoughts about substance *are* in our mind, and we are therefore bound to explain how they came there. The philosopher must assign a cause not only for what our mind does, but also for all that we *believe* it does. When the origin of these thoughts, which we have, or believe we have, has been discovered, it will be easier to judge of their value and of the use to which they may be legitimately applied; for from the nature of the source whence they flow we shall be able to see whether they are true and valid, or else spurious and illusory, if not in

---

[1] The error of the Sceptics consists in supposing that *ideas* are something *external* or mediate ; on the contrary, the *idea* is wholly *internal* and imme- diate, and hence is not a matter of controversy, but a plain, simple fact of observation.

themselves—which can never be the case—at least in their applications.

Let us begin, then, by an analysis of all that the human mind conceives about substance.

Definition of substance.

587. Substance is ‘ That energy by which a being, and all that appertains to it, actually exists,’ or, ‘ That energy in which the actual existence of the being is founded.’ As this definition may not fully indicate the relation of the *substance* with the *accident*, we shall supply the deficiency later.

§ 3.

Analysis of the concept of substance.

588. Let us see, then, in how many ways, the human mind conceives this energy, and in order to this, let us analyse the concept of it.

In this concept we may note two elements : (1) the act of existence, or that *energy* by which a being actually exists ;[1] (2) the being itself which exists (*essence*).

This distinction is only the result of an abstraction, but abstraction is precisely what suits our purpose here, since we are going to speak of that which is in our mind, and not outside of it. That which is in our mind cannot be seen part by part except by means of abstraction ; whilst on the other hand abstraction does not produce any division in the thing subsisting outside of us. Abstraction is a fact, an operation which takes place within the mind alone.

Another fact is, that by means of abstraction one thought is divided into several. Antecedently to the abstraction, our attention turned itself to a thought taken in its entirety, and this by a single act; but through the abstracting process

[1] The two expressions, *The energy which constitutes the actual existence of beings*, and *The energy by which beings exist*, come to one and the same thing. The first is merely an explanation of the second. We must, however, be careful not to make two different things of the energy here spoken of, and of the *actual existence* of beings ; for the *actual existence* is the energy itself.

that same thought is considered in its various parts, and by as many distinct acts as are the parts on which the attention fixes itself. It would be unreasonable to object here, with the modern Sophists, who would be glad of an honest excuse for escaping this knotty question, that I am making an unfair use of the power of abstraction to create imaginary entities. On the contrary, such is the nature of my present argument, that it makes it imperative on me to explain the fact of abstraction itself and of its products. I cannot therefore prescind from abstraction, or omit noticing and describing all the diverse thoughts or concepts which it forms and originates in our mind. Whether there be something corresponding to these thoughts or concepts outside our mind or not, they are ideas none the less ; and I stand pledged to account for all ideas, as the title of this work shows.

§ 4.

Various modes of the idea of substance.

589. Under what forms, then, can the idea of substance be conceived by us ?

Firstly, we can conceive the *energy* by which beings exist (the substance), in an entirely universal manner—*i.e.* without thinking of any one being in particular, but thinking only of a possible being generally, and fixing to it no determination of any kind, although we, implicitly, assume it to have all such determinations as are necessary in order that it may actually exist. This is the idea of *substance in general.*

Secondly, we can conceive the said *energy* in connection with a being furnished with that kind of determination which constitutes a *genus*. This is the *generic* idea of substance.[1]

Thirdly, we can conceive the same *energy* in connection with a being *specifically* determined ; that is to say, we can think the actual existence possible to be had by an individual of a determinate species, assuming in that individual the presence of all the qualities—common as well as proper—

---

[1] The reader must here bear in mind what I have said above on *genera* and *species* (490–503), and in what way we conceive these two modes of classification.

which it requires for actual existence. When our mind has come to conceive the possibility of an individual of this sort actually existing, but without knowing as yet whether it does really exist, we have then the *specific* idea of substance, that is, a typical idea, or such as can be reduced to the typical.[1]

590. Before proceeding further, let us dwell for a few moments on the consideration of these three, more or less abstract, ideas of substance.

I have called them, the *idea of substance in general*, the *generic*, and the *specific*.

Now it must not be supposed that, in all and each of these three concepts, we do not think an individual, that is, a being one and undivided, furnished with all that is necessary to it for existence. We *do* think this in every one of them. The difference lies in the *mode* or *form* under which we conceive the individual, *i.e.* with its determinations or without them.

To make the thing clearer, I would ask this question: when I think of *substance in general*, what is it I think of, what does this my idea include in it?

I think of a being, therefore of an individual, which has in it the energy termed actual existence. I do not then seek to know to what particular class, or genus, or species it belongs, I think only of the act of its existence. True, by this I imply that the being has all the determinations or properties necessary in order that it may exist; but I do not represent to myself any of them in particular, nor trouble myself as to what they are.

In the idea of *substance in general*, therefore, there is (1) the thought of the act of existence; (2) the thought of an individual being of which that act is predicated; (3) the thought, in general, of all the determinations or properties requisite to make that individual being as complete as it must be in order actually to exist: I say *in general*, to indicate that in this thought none of those determinations are distinguished or specified.

In the *generic* idea of substance, we may in like manner

---

[1] As the imperfect to the perfect (TRANSLATORS).

distinguish these three elementary thoughts, namely, (1) of the act of existence ; (2) of an individual being to which that act belongs ; (3) of the determinations, which are required by that being in order that it may actually exist within its *genus.*

The variable part, or the difference between these two ideas, lies in the different mode in which we respectively conceive their third element.

In the idea of *substance in general* we assume that the being has all the determinations or properties necessary to make it capable of actual existence ; but we do this only in the general ; we do not specify any of those things one way or other.

In the *generic* idea of substance, on the contrary, we think also of some determinations of the being—I mean those which mark out a genus. For example, when I think of the spiritual substance, or of the corporeal, I think, not merely of an individual not determinate in any way whatever, but of an individual of a particular genus, that is, of the genus of things corporeal, or of the genus of things spiritual.

Lastly in the *specific* idea of substance, if full, we have the individual being complete in all its determinations as well generic as proper. Thus, if I think the substance of an individual tree, and not of a tree in general, I am obliged to think everything which distinguishes that tree among all others.[1]

Therefore in each of the three ideas of substance, we always think of a thing (which thing I call an *individual*) possessed of all the determinations necessary in order to its existence, and wanting nothing except *subsistence.* If an architect forms in his mind the design of a house, down to its minutest details, including also the kinds of materials requisite

---

[1] From what I shall say in P. V. c. 1, a. v. on genera and species, the reader will see, that it is unnecessary for me in this place to make another class of ideas of substance for individuals of a species which are marred by some imperfection ; for the ideas of these are nothing but the idea itself of the individual in its highest perfection (complete specific idea) less some of the excellences shown in that idea. Moreover, we are not here speaking of the affirmation of individuals as *subsistent* ; for this affirmation is not made by means of *ideas* alone, but by a *judgment.* I shall also speak of this in due course.

for its construction, that house, ideally considered, is perfect. The work of construction adds nothing to that ideal perfection as such : its only effect is, that the same house which till then existed only in the mind of the designer, now exists also externally, in itself, while at the same time preserving, entire and unchanged, the mode of existence it had before.[1]

To recapitulate : an individual being can be conceived in a general or universal manner, as when our thought of it assumes its possession of whatever is necessary to capacitate it for existence, without however specifying anything in particular about that *necessary.*

The individual being can be conceived as possessed of *generic* determinations only, *i.e.* such determinations as are necessary to capacitate it for actual existence within the limits of a given *genus.*

Lastly, the individual being can furthermore be conceived as possessed of that assemblage of determinations which is necessary to capacitate it for actual existence within a distinct *species.*

In the first case we have the idea of substance in general, or taken *universally* ; in the second the *generic,* and in the third the *specific* idea of substance.

All these are ideas of that *energy* which constitutes actual existence, and which can only be predicated of individuals.

§ 5.

Origin of the idea of ' Individual.'

591. I cannot think the actual existence of a being without thinking at the same time that this being has all the determinations which are necessary to it in order to that existence.

The idea therefore of *individual* is intimately connected with, in fact, comprised in the idea of substance ; so that by explaining the latter we also explain the former.

Now whether we speak of ' substance,' or of 'individual,'

---

[1] The reader would do well here to bear in mind what the Author has said, when dealing with the system of Kant, about the two modes of existen (*objective* and *subjective*) belonging to the identical being (TRANSLATORS).

the three kinds of ideas we have already described are the only ones conceivable by the human mind : we must therefore explain the origin of each of them.

§ 6.

Judgments on the subsistence of substances, and how they differ from the ideas of substances.

592. But, besides ideas, we form *judgments* on the real subsistence of substances ; and this kind of thoughts I must also explain.

So long as an individual, *i.e.* a being furnished with all the qualities necessary to it, is seen by us only in an ideal form—as for instance the house as designed in the mind of the architect—that individual, that being, is not yet subsistent for us : even by conceiving it as possible to subsist, we do not yet lay hold of any real subsistence.

But suppose that an individual corresponding to our idea really subsists, and that we can have intellectual perception of it. How does this perception take place ? It takes place, as we have seen, by a judgment. We affirm as subsistent the individual of which we had the concept or idea.

The act therefore, let me repeat, by which we pronounce, 'Such a thing subsists,' is essentially different from that of simple intuition. To the idea of the thing this act adds a *persuasion* or belief that what we were contemplating before in a state of possibility has entered into the world of real things, of subsistences.[1]

Hence it is seen that, even as we have three different ideas of substance, so we may form three different sorts of judgment concerning its subsistence ; that is to say, we may judge, (1) that a substance not specified in any way subsists ; (2) that a substance of a given genus subsists ; (3) that a substance of a given species subsists.

---

[1] Let it not be said that by this we acquire a new idea—the idea of subsistence : this we had already, for, without it, we could not have thought ' that a being *could* subsist.' The *per-* *suasion* therefore of real existence is something entirely distinct from a pure *concept* ; its nature is altogether different from that of ideas.

§ 7.

Recapitulation of all the thoughts the human mind forms about substances.

593. The thoughts, then, which we form about substances consist of *ideas* and *judgments.*

The ideas are of three kinds, and so are the judgments— idea of substance in general ; generic idea ; specific idea: judgment on the subsistence of a substance in general ; of a substance of a given genus ; of a substance of a given species.

We must now describe the origin of all these ideas and judgments, or in other words, show how it is possible for the human mind to form them.

ARTICLE III.

The above three ideas of substance proceed one from the other.

594. To make our task easier, let us see if we can somewhat simplify it by reducing all the inquiries suggested by these several ideas and judgments, to a single question.

Now, beginning with the three ideas, I observe that they are connected together in such a manner that the *specific* generates the other two ; whence it follows that by explaining its origin, we also explain that of the others.

To see this, let us suppose as given the specific idea of substance. In order to obtain the generic idea, and that of substance in general, all we require to do is to abstract them from the specific. In the specific we conceive the possibility of the actual existence of a being fully determinate in all its qualities, common as well as proper. By setting aside, in this idea, whatever is distinctive of the species and of the individual, we obtain the generic idea ; then by setting aside the determinations which remain, we obtain the idea of substance in general. Assuming, therefore, that the specific idea of substance has been already formed, abstraction will do the rest.

The case is parallel to that of the question of the origin of ideas generally (41–44). In that question, the problem resolved itself into this formula : 'Explain how we come to have the one idea of *being*, and all other ideas will be easily explained by means of abstraction.' In the subordinate question relating to substance, the problem is : 'Explain how we form the *specific* idea of substance, and there will no longer be any difficulty in explaining, also by means of abstraction, the other ideas we have of substance.'

ARTICLE IV.

In explaining the judgments we make on the subsistence of substances, there is but one difficulty to overcome.

595. How, then, do we form the specific idea of substance ?

In seeking for the origin of this idea, we find that it is connected with the judgments we make on the subsistence of beings : and this connection narrows still more the field of our inquiries, because when we shall have properly understood it, we shall perceive that one and the same answer does for both these queries, namely, 'What is the origin of the specific idea of substance ?' and, 'What is the origin of the judgments we make on the subsistence of substances ?'

I have said that these judgments are of three kinds : let me now point out how they are connected together, and how the difficulties of explaining them are reduced to one only.

In judging that there subsists (1) an individual being in no way specified as to kind, (2) an individual being of a given genus, or (3) of a given species, we must be moved by a reason.

The reason which determines us to affirm the subsistence of individual beings, is the same as that of our intellectual perception of them. This reason once discovered, the judgments in question will have their explanation, in other words, we shall see how it is possible for us to form them.

Consequently, in determining the origin of all these three species of judgments, there is but one difficulty to overcome, and it consists in showing clearly for what reason we say to ourselves, 'Such an individual subsists.'

ARTICLE V.

The explanation of the specific idea of substance depends on the solution of the difficulty which is found in accounting for the judgments on the subsistence of substances.

596. We must, therefore, answer two questions: (1) How do we form the specific idea of substance? (2) What is the reason which determines us to affirm by a judgment that substances subsist?

To this simple form have we, thus far, reduced the subject of the discussion in which we are now engaged (594, 595).

But it can be simplified still further, by reason of the connection which the two questions have with each other.

Let us suppose as given the reason by which we are induced to affirm the subsistence of an individual.

On the strength of this reason we say to ouselves, 'Such an individual subsists.' Now in our intellectual perception of that individual, the idea of substance is already included. Why? Because we cannot conceive a being as subsistent, without at the same time conceiving the energy, the act, by which it subsists; and this energy, this act, is its substance (587).

The two questions are therefore reduced to this one: 'How can I make a judgment to the effect that a being subsists?' For, if I make this judgment, and thus perceive the being, I also perceive its substance, and hence can easily form, or rather have already formed the idea of that substance.

ARTICLE VI.

Explanation of the intellectual perception of individuals.

597. But how the intellectual perception of individuals takes place, and how our ideas of them are formed by the same act of judgment with which we affirm their subsistence, I have already explained (528–534).

This difficulty, to which the whole question was reduced, being solved, everything is explained. To sum up:—

(1) We form the ideas of individuals by the same act by

which we intellectually perceive, and therefore affirm, the subsistence of those individuals.

(2) From the intellectual perception of individuals we can draw [1] the specific idea of substance ; and from this, by means of abstraction, the generic idea ; and from this again, through a further abstraction, the idea of substance in general.

(3) The intellectual perception of individuals has been already explained.

The difficulty therefore of explaining the origin, as well of the three ideas of substance as of the judgments we make concerning substances, is at an end.

---

[1] Through *universalisation.* See n. 490-498 (TRANSLATORS).

CHAPTER III.

A FURTHER ELUCIDATION REGARDING THE IDEA
OF SUBSTANCE.

ARTICLE I.

Necessity of this elucidation.

598. Some may perhaps have thought within themselves
that on the subject of substance I have already said even more
than was necessary ; but judging by what I know of the time
in which we live, I fear I have not yet said sufficient to
convince everyone—certainly not those who have already
adopted one or other of the various opinions which are current
respecting the origin of the idea of substance, and have
perhaps grown old in it.   These persons will hold by that
opinion with all the greater tenacity, the more ingenious it
seems to be ; and none seems more so than that which, having
sprung from the German School, is spreading every day more
and more through France and Italy ; and should it succeed
in gaining a firm footing in these countries, it might easily
extend throughout the whole civilised world.

I will therefore endeavour to set forth more clearly than I
have done, the above doctrine, which I believe to be the only
true one, and to support it with such good reasons that even
those who are prejudiced against it must feel that it is, if not
absolutely certain, which it would be very difficult to demonstrate, at least thoroughly well founded, and impregnable to
argument.

ARTICLE II.

Enumeration of the various systems on the origin of the idea
of substance.

599. The systems severally proposed by modern philosophers to solve the difficulty about the origin of the idea of

substance, and which have been noticed in the course of this work, are four, viz.

I. Some, unable to find any other solution, have denied the existence of this idea. Their argument amounts to this: 'I am unable to account for the origin of the idea of substance; therefore it does not exist.' Of the value of such reasoning I leave the reader to judge for himself.

II. Others (and, singular to say, they are those who make the greatest pretension of being guided by facts) have attempted to extract it from sensations. Their argument is as follows: 'All ideas *must* come from sensations, for these are the only sources of human cognition which we admit; therefore the idea of substance must come from them like other ideas.' Whether this mode of reasoning be strictly philosophical and based on facts, I also leave the reader to judge.

III. Others again, observing that, on the one hand, we cannot deny the idea of substance, and on the other, cannot draw. it from sensations, have said that it must be innate in us.

IV. Lastly, some, impressed by that most determined opposition which has been shown to the doctrine of innate ideas in our times, were led to consider whether, besides the system which derives the idea of substance from the senses, and that which makes it innate, there could not be a third; and they thought there was: noticing that between the idea of accidents (or accidental qualities) and that of substance, there is a link so close that the two are simply inseparable, they accepted this as a primitive fact. Our mind could not, therefore, conceive the accidents without at the same time conceiving the substance. But why? Because of a *psychological* law intrinsic to our nature. The connection between substance and accidents is indeed called by these philosophers *ontological*, that is, *ex parte sui*, but only in the sense that it *appears* such to us owing to a subjective necessity which we cannot help. When they consider this connection in relation to our spirit itself, by which it is conceived and formed, they, as I have said, call it *psychological*. In other words, 'The idea of substance emanates from ourselves on occasion of our perceiving the accidents ; but it emanates in such a manner as to seem necessary to the accidents.' This necessity, then, is objective, but only *apparently* ; which is the same thing as to say, it is not *objective* but *subjective*. Why we should be obliged to see it as objective, is, say these philosophers, a question impossible to answer, because at this point the powers of human thought are exhausted.

A recent follower of this system (which, however it may be modified, is nothing but that of Kant), speaking of the universal conceptions, amongst which he places the idea of substance, says that 'These conceptions have, not a logical, but a psychological origin ;' that 'Whoever seeks to account for any of these truths, labours in vain ;' and that 'From the moment we conceive them, we conceive them as immutable, eternal, absolute.' Hence he describes them as proceeding from our spirit, without the possibility of any reason being given for this except necessity, the fact of the thing. So constituted is our nature that we draw these conceptions from within ourselves, or, some way or other, behold them on perceiving the sensible qualities. In this mysterious fatality, according to the *Critical Philosophy*, all human investigation ends. To put it in plain honest language, what these writers mean is this: 'The idea of substance in general does not come from the senses, it is not innate, we cannot say it is nothing ; therefore it is an apparition (only that to us it seems a reality) which emanates from the nature of our soul.'[1]

600. This system, disguise or dress it up as you will, is nothing but Idealism and Scepticism in its worst form.

The argument on which it is based comes in ultimate analysis to the following: 'There are only four systems by which one could account for the idea of substance ; but the three first are indefensible ; therefore the last is the true one.'

This reasoning might hold, provided it had been demonstrated that a fifth system would be an absurdity ; but unfortunately the thought of giving this demonstration never occurred to the philosophers of whom we are speaking. It does not therefore seem too much to say that their method of

[1] Even Galluppi, like all Subjectivists, fell into this blunder.

arguing betokens in them a singular presumption ; which is
the more surprising as they are the very men who credit
themselves with having been the first to enter an emphatic
protest against the audacious presumption of philosophy, and
to set to the world an example of philosophic modesty and
caution. Had they been what they professed to be, they
would not have forgotten, when laying down the major of
their syllogism—' There are only four systems by which one
could account for the idea of substance '—to add the little,
but necessary clause, ' So far as is known to us :' and this
addition would have sufficed to make them adopt a course
totally different from the one they followed.

In my opinion, the language of true philosophic modesty
and discreetness would be this : ' So far as I am aware, there
are only four systems by which it would be possible to account for the idea of substance. The three first are open to
the gravest objections ; the fourth leads directly to Idealism
and to Scepticism—two consequences clearly inadmissible
because absolutely repugnant to our rational nature. I am
therefore bound to confess that the way of accounting for the
idea of substance' is more than I can pretend to know.'

ARTICLE III.

Another way for discovering the origin of the idea of substance.

601. But in point of fact there is a fifth system, and we
have already expounded it. This system keeps clear of all
the difficulties of the four already known to and exhausted
by modern philosophy.

It derives the idea of substance from the *form* of all
human cognitions, *i.e.* the idea of being.

In it the idea of substance is neither denied, nor pretended
to be drawn from sensations, nor assumed as innate, nor yet
represented as only apparent and subjective : it is deduced
from the first and most essential of all ideas, the only idea
which is innate, the idea which, as we shall see more clearly
in due course (Sect. VI.), carries its explanation with itself,
because it is truth itself.

Accordingly, the idea of substance is conceived by man so soon as he has the occasion to deduce it from the primal idea; and this occasion is given him by his very first sensations and perceptions.

He does not then conceive it in an abstract state, alone, disengaged from all which is not its pure self;[1] but he conceives it nevertheless.   To have it in an abstract state, pure, belongs to a later period, namely, the period in which he begins to philosophise and to exercise his powers of abstraction on the concepts he has already acquired.

Hence it is manifest that (to use the phraseology of Professor Cousin) the idea of substance has *logical antecedents* and not merely *psychological* ones.   It does not emanate, as though by a blind fatality, from our own soul; it is obtained through deduction: we can assign to it a reason which proves it to be true.

I must now proceed to give a more detailed explanation of this idea.

ARTICLE IV.

First proposition:—' If our mind thinks at all, it thinks of something.'

602. This proposition has been already demonstrated. 'For the mind to conceive without conceiving something,' and 'not to conceive at all,' are perfectly synonymous expressions (564).

But if our mind, in order to think and to act, must have an object, it is necessary to admit that it must (by the principle of cognition) (565), think of *some being*, of *something*, for these words are the most universal of all, and beyond them there is nothing.   Hence we also saw, that the mind is 'the faculty of conceiving being,' that is, a something having an existence of its own (480–482).[2]

---

[1] This refers to the idea of *substance in general*, which is the result of an abstraction on the *generic* idea of substance, itself the result of a previous abstraction on the *specific* idea.   See n. 590 (TRANSLATORS).

[2] The mind is the faculty of conceiving things as having an existence of their own.   This, however, does not mean that it cannot be deceived as to the real existence of things; but even when deceived, it still conceives them as having an existence of their own.

ARTICLE V.

Second proposition :—' Everything can be an object of the mind.'

§ 1.

Demonstration.

603. As a consequence of the above, 'Everything can be an object of the mind,' because everything has an existence of its own.

To say that a thing exists without having any existence, is a contradiction in terms (principle of contradiction).

That which does not exist in itself or in some other thing, is not thinkable, is not an object of the mind, but may at once be said not to exist, since the two phrases 'to have no existence' and 'not to exist,' have the same meaning ; therefore it is nothing.

§ 2.

Objection against the principle of contradiction.

604. Here it is most important that the reader should note the legitimacy of my reasoning.

For I am well aware that the followers of the fourth of the systems above described will be ready to object as follows : 'To prove that the intellect, or as you call it, the faculty of the intuition of *being*, can conceive everything, you have recourse to the principle of contradiction. But how do you prove the validity of this principle ? The ancients indeed said that a demonstration, when carried up to the principle of contradiction, was complete in the fullest possible sense of the word, because they admitted the force of this principle ; but we do not find it of any intrinsic and objective value. On the other hand, the nature of the present argument makes it strictly imperative on you to produce incontrovertible proof of the principle of contradiction. For your object now is to show that we, whom you call Sceptics, are in the wrong, and likewise to demonstrate that the idea of substance is, not merely subjective and apparent, not an emanation issuing by a blind fatality from the human soul, but something objectively true. Now, by basing your reasoning on the principle of contradiction, you assume the existence of objective truth. We, on the contrary, deny the real objectivity of the idea of substance for the reason that we consider the knowledge of any really objective truth as a sheer impossibility. You therefore start by begging the very point which lies at the bottom of the whole question; and thus your proof of the objectivity of the idea of substance, being deduced from this gratuitous assumption, goes for nothing.'

§ 3.

Reply to the above objection; defence of the principle of contradiction.

605. Whoever raises the above objection, has not understood the way in which I have deduced the principle of contradiction from the idea of being, and shown that it is in substance identical with that idea. Neither can he have felt the logical force of the same idea, which essentially carries its justification with itself, and by its light satisfies and dispels all doubts in those who look it direct in the face. Hence, not wishing to repeat what I have said before, nor yet to anticipate what I have intended for the Sixth Section, I will now adopt a simpler plan, but one not less calculated to persuade, if possible, even a Sceptic opponent. And this will serve not a little to confirm the doctrine I am trying to establish; because truth shines forth with all the greater brilliancy, the more diversified the aspects from which we regard it.

All I ask here is to be allowed to postulate 'the use of speech;' for if this is denied me, I am reduced to silence, and thus my adversaries, having all the talk to themselves, will be able to claim an easy victory.

Now if my right of speaking is recognised, I must also have the right of insisting that when I say, 'a thing,' I shall be understood as saying 'a thing;' for were I then to be understood as saying a 'non-thing,' a 'nothing,' my right of speaking would be a mockery.

By all acknowledged rules of language, therefore, what a

man says, he says; for instance, when he says 'bread,' he says
'bread;' when he says 'stone,' he says 'stone,' &c.

Clearly, if I say a word and then immediately retract
or deny it, I make no statement. If with my pencil I
make a mark on a blank sheet of paper, and then rub it
out, what remains? A blank as before. If I were told to
draw the outlines of a person, but on condition that I must
efface every line as soon as drawn, could it be said that
the commission was given me in earnest? Certainly not;
for no serious man could ever imagine that, under such circumstances, the outlines in question could be executed, either
wholly or in any part however small, on the sheet of drawing
paper furnished to me. In the same manner, if I were
allowed the use of speech, but with the condition that I must
unsay every word the instant I have uttered it, would this
be a *bonâ fide* granting of the use of speech? Language is
not a chance medley of mere sounds, but an ordered arrangement of words signifying ideas. Therefore the possibility of
my making use of language necessarily involves an understanding that I shall avoid expressions which give no sense
because self-contradictory; otherwise language would not be
the thing of which I am allowed the use.

To return now to our case; let us take the phrase, 'A
thing which does not exist in any way.' Waiving the question whether or not this phrase be logically correct, I say
that it is not language, because it expresses nothing; and that
to use it is, not to *speak*, but simply to strike the ears with
the noise of unintelligible sounds, just like the man who in
the same breath says and unsays the same thing.

In fact, the word 'thing' conveys the idea of an existence
of some sort: when therefore I say 'thing,' I express the idea
of some kind of existence; but by adding, 'which does not
exist in any way,' I deny the idea I have just expressed, and
thus the word 'thing' is as if it had never been said. My
sentence resembles the Algebraic formula: $a - a$, which is
equivalent to zero.

§ 4.

Conclusion of the demonstration.

606. Such being the case, my proposition that 'every-thing can be an object of the mind,'[1] seems to me evident, take what system we like; for it requires only one postulate, which all who speak are obliged to grant me ; and surely the Sceptics have never shown a disposition to be silent any more than other classes of philosophers.

ARTICLE VI.

Third proposition :—' Our mind cannot perceive the sensible qualities, without perceiving them as existing in a subject.'

607. The reason of this is, that the mind cannot perceive things otherwise than in the existence they have (602).

But sensible qualities do not exist in themselves, but in a subject external to us.

Therefore the mind, which can perceive everything, be-cause everything has an existence of some sort (603–606), when perceiving sensible qualities, must also perceive with them the subject in which they exist : otherwise it would not perceive them ; they would be unperceivable, since they are only perceivable because their subject is perceivable.

Let us suppose on the other hand that the mind perceives these qualities ; by so doing it will have perceived something (602). If it has perceived something, it has already perceived an existence, a thing existent : now to say ' a thing existent,' is the same as to say ' a substance,' for the substance is the act by which a thing exists (587).

ARTICLE VII.

Distinction between the Idealism of Hume and that of Berkeley.

608. The above line of reasoning goes against Idealists of the school of Hume.

[1] I think that even those who deny the objectivity of truth cannot feel any difficulty in admitting the definition I have given of the *mind*, and the pro-position that this faculty can conceive everything ; only that, according to their theory, they must attribute to these two propositions a subjective truth, as they call it, *i.e. appearing* as truth to the thinking subject.

Hume, unlike Berkeley, was not satisfied with proposing the doubt as to whether bodies be nothing but ideas, but asked furthermore whether those ideas might not exist by themselves alone, without a subject, so that the universe would consist simply of an infinite multitude of ideas roaming about by chance, and fluctuating like the waves of a vast and restless ocean, or like atoms in infinite space.

We have therefore two different questions before us : (1) 'Can sensible qualities (be they ideas or otherwise) be conceived without a subject ? ' (2) 'Is the human spirit itself the subject of those qualities, that is, are they merely acts of this spirit, or is their subject something different from it (*i.e.* a body) ? '

Berkeley confined himself to the statement, that sensible qualities—according to him synonymous with sensations—exist only in our spirit, which therefore is their whole and only subject.

This, however, implied the admission of the necessity of a subject, and of the impossibility of sensible qualities existing by themselves alone, and therefore of being conceived except as existing in something else, which is the same as to say in a substance.

But the necessity of a substance which Berkeley had thus recognised, was peremptorily denied by Hume.

I must, therefore, in the first place, confute the Idealism of Hume. For this purpose I shall have to prove, that to say 'The sensible qualities exist, but not in a subject or substance,' is a manifest contradiction in terms.

ARTICLE VIII.

Confutation of the Idealism of Hume.

609. To be convinced of this, let us assume the truth of Hume's opinion, that the sensible qualities can be conceived by themselves alone independently of a subject, and see what follows from it.

I ask, in such an hypothesis, what should we be conceiving with our mind ? Doubtless, something which exists, the sensible qualities themselves.

But on hearing this admission of a follower of the old philosophers, the Humist, believing that his contention is as good as gained, might probably retort as follows : ' It is not true, then, that the sensible qualities require a subject or, as you call it, a substance in order to exist. So indeed thought the ancients, but it was only a prejudice, the work of their imagination. Why cannot the sensible qualities exist by and in themselves alone ? '

The follower of the old philosophers however, nothing daunted, might very properly reply thus :

' I am ready to admit that, having divested yourself, as you are pleased to say, of old-world prejudices, you have succeeded in forming the idea of sensible qualities as existing by themselves and, alone, constituting this entire universe. Permit me, however, to analyse a little this new and interesting idea, so that I also may understand it somewhat better. For, as you will admit, it is by analysing or decomposing our ideas, that we come to know them intimately. Tell me, then, do these sensible qualities, which you conceive apart from any substance, exist or not ? '

Humist.—' Nay, they are the only things that exist in the universe.'

Follower of the old philosophers.—' That is to say, they exist in themselves, since according to you they do not exist in any subject, in any substance.'

Humist.—' Exactly, in themselves ; and this is precisely the discovery made by the new philosophy, the discovery of Hume.'

Follower, &c.—' Now, before going further with the analysis of this idea, I must remind you what it was that the ancients understood by substance. The definition of this entity, a product, as you say, of their untrained imagination, may perhaps be found necessary in the course of our argument. Do you then know this definition ? '

Humist.—' I know that the Schoolmen defined substance as, " That which subsists by itself " [1] (" Ens quod per se

---

[1] The phrase, to *subsist by itself*, must be taken as meaning *to subsist as* a subject. This definition will be more clearly explained later.

subsistit "), that is, not by some other thing, like the accidents which subsist (according to their way of speaking) in and therefore by the substance.'

Follower, &c.—' My good friend, if this is the case, then you admit substance.'

Humist.—' How so ? '

Follower, &c.—' Did you not say just now, that the sensible qualities, from which you profess to banish all substance, subsist in and by themselves ? Now this is precisely the definition of substance. Therefore by your supposition that the sensible qualities exist in and by themselves, *i.e.* independently of everything else, you have in reality changed these qualities into so many substances. I apprehend that you have unwittingly laid for yourself a trap from which you will find it difficult to escape. In fact, you do not deny the sensible qualities ; you recognise their existence ; moreover you say that such existence must be understood as standing by itself alone, for you declare every addition to it arbitrary and illusory. This amounts to saying, " I declare that sensible qualities are substances, because substance is that which exists in and by itself, without the need of our conceiving it in and through any other thing, which is precisely the way in which I suppose them to exist." It is therefore manifestly impossible to admit the existence of anything whatever and at the same time to deny substance. The proposition, " Sensible qualities alone exist, but no substance exists," is simply a contradiction in terms ; for it says, " Sensible qualities are substances, but there is no such thing as substance." Such undoubtedly, when stripped of all that is mere rhetoric, which often has only the effect of hiding the contradictions lurking in the reasonings of philosophers, is the vaunted discovery of Hume. By its adoption, you have been made to say precisely the reverse of what you intended. You began as the avowed enemy of substance—an exploded and unmeaning term, as you thought —and with a determination to set up in its place the sensible qualities, or, as the ancients called them, the accidents. But like those good people who while thinking they were doing one thing, find that, without knowing how, they have done the very opposite, you have ended in transforming every sensible quality into a substance. Your thesis that " Sensible qualities alone exist in the world " has proved itself to mean, " The world contains nothing but substances." This seems a strange blunder, but I think I can see how it has come about. Instead of retaining the simple definition of substance as given by the ancients, you have been fighting against an imperfect notion of substance, imbibed by you in common with the vulgar. You have imagined that " to constitute a substance " more is required than is really the case. By substance you understand something material and solid which lies lurking beneath the accidents. Indeed this kind of notion seems even suggested by the terms *fundamentum, substratum, substantia*; which in their etymology, express something placed under another. But you ought to have known that these are metaphorical expressions, which must, in a matter like this, be understood with great caution ; else, as has happened to yourself, much confusion of mind will ensue.'

ARTICLE IX.

Origin of the idea of accident.

610. I do not know what answer a follower of Hume could make to the above argument ; for it seems to me to prove in the clearest manner, that if anything exists, substance must exist, and that to think of something as existing, is *ipso facto* to think of a substance. Let us therefore assume that the Humist has acknowledged the justice of his adversary's observations ; and that the two disputants finding the prospect of a mutual understanding more hopeful than they had at first anticipated, continue their discussion. I think that they might gradually arrive at a full agreement by proceeding as follows :—

We will designate the Humist by the letter *A* and his opponent by the letter *B*.

A.—'I thank you for what you have said thus far on the philosophy of Hume, and I fully admit its force. Nevertheless I must beg leave to continue, for it seems to me, that we have not yet by a long way got to the bottom of the question. I grant, then, that the existence of substances as we have defined and explained them, is an undeniable fact. What I still demur to is the distinction of substances from the so-called accidents. You have shown that substances cannot be denied, but you have not shown the same as regards accidents. Indeed, what is there to forbid the belief that the accidents are themselves substances ; that between accident and substance there is not the distinction the Schoolmen made, who to the definition of substance, "that which exists by itself," added, " and which sustains the accidents" (" Ens quod per se subsistit, et sustinet accidentia ") ; in a word, that the sensible qualities—call them substances or whatever you like—are the only things that exist, which, after all, is the main point of Hume's philosophy ?'

B.—' Your difficulty will be solved if we go on with the analysis we had begun of your concept of sensible qualities. You imagine these qualities as having an existence independent of everything else, and therefore as substances. Tell me, then, does this apply only to some of them, or to all without exception ?'

A.—' To all, of course ; for if I were to say that only some exist in this manner, I should be admitting between substance and accidents the very distinction I am anxious to eliminate, as an incongruity, from philosophy.'

B.—' But when we say, " The sensible qualities of a body," do we mean that they are so linked together as to form one being only, *i.e.* the body, or that each one stands by itself separately from every other ?'

A.—' Undoubtedly we mean that they exist in a state of union. To divide them is as impossible as it would be to divide a body in such a way that its whiteness should be in one place, its weight in another, its hardness in another, and so on ; for these qualities cannot even be conceived subsistent, except in so far as they are united together.'

B.—' Very well ; from this it follows, that all the sensible qualities which we find in a body have something in common, and this is the energy which causes them to subsist, and to subsist as united together in such a manner that, if we separate them, we can no longer think of them as preserving that energy by which they subsist.'

A.—' This is evident.'

B.—' Therefore I say the energy which causes those qualities to subsist, and is common to them all, is not any single one of them, nor yet all of them together.   Am I not right ? '

A.—' So it would seem.'

B.—' So true is this, that if that energy were any one of those qualities, it would be that which causes all the others to subsist ; and thus it would have them all in itself, which is absurd ; or at least it would certainly have to be distinguished from all the others, because it would be that energy which the others are not.'

A.—' I cannot contradict you.'

B.—' Nor again does that energy consist of all those qualities together, because they are many, but the energy is one, and cannot be more than one if it has to join all the said qualities into a unity.'

A.—' Certainly it cannot.'

B.—' We are agreed, then, that the sensible qualities in question have something in common, which is neither any one of them nor all taken together, but is the energy which causes them to subsist—a something existing in and by itself, in short, the substance.'

A.—' Agreed.'

B.—' And yet, are not these qualities distinguished from one another ? '

A.—' There can be no doubt of it, and what distinguishes them are the features proper to each.'

B.—' I should be glad if you would explain.'

A.—' The colour red, for example, is different from yellow ; sound differs from colour, and so with the other sensible qualities.   These differences are manifest, and we cannot make them more clear than by simply picturing them to ourselves.'

B.—' Nothing could be better said. In the qualities, then, which you had represented as the only things existing in the universe, there is something common and something proper; and the " common " is the energy which unites them together and causes them to subsist.'

A.—' Just so.'

B.—' Thus far, therefore, we have come to a settled understanding : the diverse qualities of colour, sound, taste, &c., all agree in this, that they have in them an energy or force in virtue of which they exist. In fact, whenever we say, " A thing exists," we express an act, an action, a force ; whilst on the contrary the term *non-existence* signifies the absence of all action, of all force of whatever kind. . . .'

A.—'Pardon me for interrupting you, but here I must make an observation. You say truly that the term *existence* expresses, or rather is synonymous with, an energy of some sort. But at the same time I would not wish you to consider the energy and the existence as two distinct things. They are one and the same thing, one and the same act. Please to bear this in mind.'

B.—' This is exactly what I mean, and I therefore argue thus : To say that all the qualities of a body exist by an identical energy, so that whatever distinction there is between them, arises, not from this energy, but only from those diverse features which you have described as being severally proper to each quality, is the same as to say that all these diverse and differentiating features exist alike by that energy which, as you have also admitted, they have in common.'

A.—' Well I see no objection to your putting the thing in this way. But this is only saying that the qualities exist, because they have in them that energy which is called existence; in other words, they exist because they exist. You therefore say nothing new.'

B.—'If I do not say anything new, I say at least what is self-evident; and this is, that having once admitted the principle that the sensible qualities exist, we must not deny it in the progress of our argument ; for were we to act thus, it would be impossible for us to reason ; we should not be carrying on a reasoning, but uttering sounds without meaning; we should be saying and unsaying, building up and pulling down at the same time.   Now if it be true that these qualities exist all united together, it must also be true that they have an energy whereby they thus exist; since, as you have very properly observed, to have this energy, and to exist, are synonymous phrases.   By saying, therefore, that they have the energy called existence, I say nothing more than you have said, viz. that they exist.   I ask you then, can that which is proper be at the same time common, and that which is common be at the same time proper?'

A.—' Assuredly not.'

B.—' Now, could you tell me what the old philosophers meant by *accidents?* '

A.—' As they defined substance to be " that which subsists by itself and sustains the accidents," so they defined accident to be " that which subsists in or by something else " (" quod in alio subsistit tamquam in subjecto ").'

B.—' And have we not seen that the sensible qualities, although in themselves distinguished one from another, exist all together by virtue of one and the same energy? '

A.—' We have.'

B.—' What then prevents our giving the name of *substance* to this energy by which all the several qualities of which we speak subsist; and the name of *accidents* to the qualities themselves in so far as they exhibit features or have each a mode of being different from that of the others? '

A.—' If this be all you mean by the distinction between substance and accident, I see nothing wrong in it. But who understands by this distinction a mere abstraction such as you now indicate? '

B.—' All sound philosophers understand it so, especially the ancients.   I have simply referred you to the old definitions as repeated by yourself, and I think that, adhering strictly to these, I may conclude as follows : In the sensible qualities of a body, which you have imagined as existing by themselves, two things must needs be recognised : (1) a force, by which they exist and which must be one and common to all of them ; (2) the qualities themselves, each having its own distinctive properties. This is neither more nor less than the distinction of *substance* and *accident* as made by the ancients. To be consistent, therefore, you will have to admit, that your disagreement with the old philosophers does not relate to the doctrine itself, but only to the manner of expressing it. Therefore your proposition, "The sensible qualities alone exist," involves of necessity a contradiction ; for by supposing it true as we have done, and then analysing the sensible qualities as you have imagined them, we find that they are necessarily the result of two elements, viz. the energy which causes the qualities to exist, and exists in and by itself (substance), and the qualities themselves which receive that energy, and unitedly exist only in and through it (accidents). Hence that proposition is not less absurd than this other : " The qualities exist, but have no existence."

'Or you may, if you like, take the thing in another way. Language is the expression of ideas. Analyse, then, the wording of your proposition as it stands. When you say the *qualities*, you express a thing concerning which you do not as yet know whether it really exists or not ; but when you say (they) *exist*, you express and attribute to them the energy called *real existence*. These two things are therefore distinguished even verbally ; so much so that you could very well think and name the *qualities* without thinking that they really exist ; in which case you would not as yet have any thought of their *substance*. But when you think of those qualities as existent, either actually or potentially, as furnished with that energy by which alone they do or can exist, then the thought of their substance also is in your mind.

'And now I believe I can also explain to you, how it was, that modern philosophy came to make a confusion so utterly at variance with the nature of things, I mean the confusion of substance with accidents.'

611. *A.*—' Pray do so, even as you did when commenting ·on Hume's attempt to abolish substances.'

B.—' In my opinion this arose from a misconception of the old doctrine. It were idle to deny that, in its latter period, the philosophy of the Schools was taught in a very material way, and men learned in it the terminology, or if you will, the jargon of the old philosophy rather than the science itself. On the other hand, the world felt ill-disposed towards it on other grounds too numerous to mention. Hence the new thinkers, looking upon it simply as a thing to be scoffed at, took no pains to understand it, but whenever any Scholastic phrase or axiom chanced to awake in their mind some stupid or ridiculous meaning, they instantly pounced upon it as a God-send, glad of the opportunity of holding up the decayed old doctrine to scorn, and establishing their new-fangled theories on the ruins of ancient authority. It was a wonderful satisfaction thus to exchange the humble position of learners for the ambitious role of enlighteners of mankind. Apply this general leaning to those who attempted to take away the old distinction between substance and accidents, and you will find that they were combating, not the true distinction, but one of their own inventing. They imagined accident and substance as being two things altogether separate from one another, two real elements entering equally into the composition of a third thing ; two things and therefore two substances, not perceiving that this was directly contrary to the Scholastic definition of those two elements. For when I think a thing as existent, I think a being one and indivisible. I can indeed analyse and decompose the *concept* I have of that thing ; but by so doing I do not in any way decompose the thing itself. To decompose a concept is nothing but to fix one's attention on some part of that concept without heeding the remainder. If I find in it several parts, it does not follow that these parts are also things separable in themselves, or that they have an equality of nature. They may be simply different aspects or relations, internal or external, of the concept itself. Thus the distinction between substance and accident, is only the result of a mental abstraction which considers the thing at one time purely in so far as it is the energy termed existence, and at another in respect of the particular *mode* in which that existence shows itself, apart from the energy through and in which such mode exists.

'In conclusion therefore I say, it is impossible for us to think of an actual being [1] without distinguishing in it, (1) the energy whereby it exists, (2) the mode in which it exists, or the accidents : for to think an actual being imports our having the concept of that being; and in that concept we can always, if we like, distinguish, between the act existence and the *mode* of that act. Thus are formed the two elementary concepts, (1) of substance and (2) of accidents or, more generally, the mode of existence. And this distinction which we make with our mind, being founded in the idea of the thing itself, is a true and real distinction.'

ARTICLE X.

A few words on the invariability of substance.

612. It appears to me that the above reasoning places beyond all controversy the distinction between that which exists in and by itself, and that which exists through and in something else ; which is the same as to say between substance and accidents.

The whole force of that argument lies in a very simple point, namely, in accurately defining the notions of these two elements, and taking care that the imagination does not mystify or confuse them by mixing them up with extraneous matter.

If we consider the ideas of substance and of accident as two abstractions, in which the same thing is thought, but now on the side of that energy which makes it exist, and now only on that of the *mode* in which it exists ; the distinction of which I speak has no longer in it anything difficult, mysterious or absurd.

Yet it is always easy for the imagination, which seems to delight in tampering with the simplicity of our ideas, to distort the primary and genuine notions of substance and of accident by some embellishment of its own, *i.e.* by affixing to them certain properties, which although perhaps consequent upon them, are no essential part of their nature. Two of these properties are the *invariability* of substance and the

---

[1] The discourse here is always about finite beings.

variability of accidents ; to understand which aright, great caution and discernment are necessary. Indeed we do not require for our purpose to think of such properties at all ; nay it would be much better if we did not think of them, since the clearness and simplicity of our ideas are all the more likely to be preserved, the more care we take at the beginning of our reasonings to sever these ideas completely from every element not absolutely necessary to them.

613. Hence if our two disputants should now wish to discuss these, as it were, secondary properties of substance and of accident, I think that their new dialogue ought to proceed as follows :—

A.—' You say that, according to the old doctrine, substance is something invariable and accidents are something variable. Now in Hume's hypothesis that the sensible qualities exist by themselves, there would be nothing variable in them ; for the colour red could not change into yellow, without first being destroyed, and you may say the same of every other quality.   In this hypothesis, therefore, it cannot be said that the sensible qualities are accidents ; since although they might cease to exist, they could never vary.'

B.—' Before replying, I must ask you to repeat the definitions of substance and of accident.'

A.—' " Substance is that which exists by itself ; " " accident is that which exists in and through something other than itself." '

B.—' Now please to take note : the definition says nothing more than this ; do not therefore add to the notions of substance and accident anything which is not expressed in their definition.   We must never forget that the first characteristic of substance—that which constitutes its essence—is, *relatively* to the accidents, "to exist by itself;" which is the same as saying that we conceive it as existing without any subject other than itself, because it is the very act of its existence [1] ; whereas the essence of the accident consists in

---

[1] My definition of substance is this : 'The energy (*l'attività*) by which a being exists,' or else : 'A thing which we can conceive at first without being obliged to think of any thing different from it.'   I say we can *conceive at first*, because when, taking any created substance whatever, we begin to study it

existing in something else as its subject ; which means that
the accident, as such, is an abstract concept whereby we think
the *mode* in which a thing exists, apart from the energy which
makes it exist. Hence it would be impossible for us to think
the accident as really existent, without at the same time
thinking it (this *mode* of existence) conjoined with the said
energy, which is the subject or substance wherein alone it
really exists. Having therefore demonstrated in our previous
discussion that a sensible quality, as imagined by Hume, can
only be a thing in which we think, (1) an energy constituting
actual existence, and (2) a certain mode in which that energy
exists ; I have, by implication, demonstrated that Hume's
notion of a sensible quality is in very deed composed of these
same two elements—a substance and an accident, the energy
called *act of existence,* and the mode or term in which that
energy is seen to manifest itself.

'If various other properties besides this primary and
essential one have been attributed to substance and accident,
it will be necessary to take them separately, and examine
whether they be necessarily implied by it, or not. If we
find that they are, we shall have to admit that they also are
essential to substance and accident ; but if not, we shall have
no authority for setting them down as absolutely necessary
to the concept of these two elements. Take for example
variability: you must examine whether that which exists in
something other than itself as in its subject, is necessarily
variable; if you discover that it is so, well and good ; you
will justly conclude that *variability* is a necessary property
of *accident*; in the opposite case, this conclusion will be
inadmissible. Should you, however, happen to find by
experience that there are variable accidents, you will have to
say that this is owing to some particular circumstance, and
not because it must necessarily and always be so. But as to
my own part, all I required—in order to prove to you that

---

deeply, we find that it is impossible to
conceive independently of a First Cause :
but in our *first concept* of things, we
think only of their *essence,* and not of
the *conditions* whereon their real existence depends. Hence in the *first
concept,* which is a knowledge of things
as it were in rough outline, their necessary connexion with the First Cause is
not conceived explicitly by us.

the Humist idea of sensible qualities *existing by themselves* is in reality composed of the two ideas of substance and of accident—was to make you see, that the two elements into which analysis has shown that idea to be divided, present respectively the notion of substance and that of accident, exactly in accordance with the definitions which the ancients gave to these notions: and I venture to hope that my efforts in this direction have not been unsuccessful.'

ARTICLE XI.

The sensible qualities do not exist by themselves (are not substances).

614. There only remains one question, namely, whether, notwithstanding all we have argued thus far, the speculations of the Scottish sophist have not contributed to improve upon the old notions of substance and accident in this, that whereas the ancients supposed some wholly invisible force to be lying under the sensible qualities and sustaining them, it would on the contrary be more accurate to say, that the sensible qualities exist by themselves; and that, although by analysing the idea we have of them, we can distinguish in it an element which exists in itself (the energy of existing, the substance), and an element which exists in something other than itself (the mode of existing, the accidents); yet in reality there is no secret or mystery about them, but everything is open and visible even as they are.

This difficulty also will disappear if we diligently consider that the energy by which the sensible qualities exist cannot be seen with the corporeal eye, nor in any way fall under the senses, but is a thing which is noted and abstracted purely through a mental operation. In fact, the follower of the old philosopher could very easily see this in his Humist interlocutor by addressing him in something like the following manner:—

B.—'Have we not agreed, that the sensible qualities have certain properties by means of which our senses enable us to distinguish them from one another, and to know which is which?'

A.—' Yes.'

B.—' Have we not also said, that these properties by which we distinguish the sensible qualities from one another, and which constitute the qualities themselves, are called *accidents* for the reason that they stand in need of an energy in order to exist, an energy which is not presented by the simple concept of them ? '

A.—' This also we have said.'

B.—' Now when I asked you to enumerate these distinctive properties, do you remember the reply you gave me ? '

A.—' I appealed to the senses ; I said that our senses showed us unmistakably that green is not yellow, that colour differs from sound, sound from taste, &c.'

B.—' You could not have answered better. But now tell me, are not yellow, green, red, sounds, taste, scents, &c., exactly the sensible qualities of which we are speaking ? '

A.—' They are, and nothing else.'

B.—' Now, can that be called a sensible quality which does not fall under the senses ? '

A.—' Certainly not.'

B.—' Conclude, then, that the properties by which we distinguish the sensible qualities from one another are *accidents*. But these properties are all that in the sensible qualities falls under our senses. Conversely, whatever falls under our senses is called a *sensible quality*, nor can this name be given to anything else. Therefore the name of *accidents* belongs of right only to the sensible qualities, and it would be a contradiction in terms to call them substances, although, as we have seen, they exist, *i.e.* have a force causing them to exist.

' Besides the sensible qualities, then, or the accidents, there is also a substance, which is non-sensible in itself, and yet constitutes that force which produces in us the sensations, and the sensitive perceptions of these qualities. This substance is noticed only by the mind, through analysing the concept of *sensible qualities existent* ; for it is only the mind that can perceive the *being* (*l' ente*) ; the senses cannot. The mind, by observing what strikes our senses, forms the concept

of a *sensible possessed of existence* ; then, examining this concept, separates from that which is " sensible " the *force* which
gives it existence ; and this force is what we call *substance.*

'It is therefore manifest, that this force, being an abstraction which we obtain by taking away from it all that falls
under the senses, is not a sensible thing ; and to call it so
would, as I have so often said, be a glaring contradiction,
for it would be tantamount to thinking and unthinking,
building and destroying the same thing at the same time,
in fact effecting nothing. Conversely, when we fix our
attention on the sensible qualities apart from the force which
makes them exist, we think of things essentially sensible, of
accidents, and not any longer of substance.'

CHAPTER IV.

ORIGIN OF THE IDEAS OF CAUSE AND EFFECT.

ARTICLE I.

Object of the present Chapter.

615. Considering that the idea of *Cause*, conjointly with that of substance, is the basis of the whole edifice of human cognitions, I deem it advisable to say here something on this idea also, by way of supplement to what I said on it in another place (350–352). What I wish is, that the origin and the legitimacy of this idea should be set forth in so clear a light, that no one, unless he be bent outright on bidding defiance to the plainest dictates of reason, could dare to dispute its force, and thus destroy this foundation of what is noblest in man—knowledge.

'Nothing happens without an adequate cause;' such is the axiom of the common sense of men.

I propose to inquire why it is that all men are agreed on this proposition; why they admit it as self-evident; why they take it as a rule of their judgments from the moment they begin to make use of reason, although it is only at a later period that they form a distinct abstracted idea of it, and bestow on it, in this lone and isolated state, a philosophical attention.

· I must therefore ascribe to the idea of cause such an origin as may suffice, not merely to show how it comes into our minds, but also to explain the facts I have just hinted at—namely, how it comes to pass that this idea is so easy of formation, that not only every adult person, no matter how little cultured, but even infants, possess it, as is proved by their very first attempts at speaking, in which they often make use of it—witness their lively curiosity to know the why of everything ; their ejaculations of wonder, and the questions they ask, sometimes importunately, as to the cause of what strikes their senses in a manner to them extraordinary.

For this end, I shall (1) Place clearly before my readers the proposition I have to demonstrate ; (2) Analyse it in order to know what in it is difficult and what is easy of demonstration ; (3) Demonstrate the part which is difficult.

ARTICLE II.

Proposition.

616. The proposition I have to demonstrate is this :—
' Every new fact (*i.e.* every change) necessarily implies a cause adequate to its production.'

By new *fact* I mean any *action* whatever joined with a change, or (generally) with a motion of some kind or other, whether its effect pass outside of, or remain within it.

I need not enumerate all the different species of *actions* that are possible ; but I wish it to be distinctly understood that under this term I include every conceivable species of action.

Now my contention is, that whenever we perceive an *action*, we perceive also an agent or cause of the same.   To account for this perception, to describe it precisely as it comes about ; to show how from the idea of new *fact* (event, action) we rise to the idea of *cause*—is to explain the origin of this idea.

ARTICLE III.

Analysis of the above proposition, directed to point out the knot of the difficulty.

617. The proposition I have undertaken to demonstrate is a judgment consisting of three parts, which are : (1) the *fact*, the event, the action to be conceived by us ; (2) the *connection* of this action with the agent or cause as yet unknown to us ; (3) the idea of this *agent* or *cause*.

In order to explain how we make this judgment, it is

necessary to show how we come to conceive each of the three parts of which it is the compound result.

618. Now, in the first place, we perceive the *action* or event by means of our sensitivity, internal and external.

Our consciousness tells us, that we are passive when corporeal things strike our sensitive organs,[1] and that we are active when we will a thing, and as a practical consequence think, move, &c.

Then, by means of the idea of being in general, we form the concept of *action*, whether coming from ourselves or produced in us from without.

Having thus acquired the concept of action, and also of several species of it, we can also be made cognisant of the existence of certain real actions through the testimony of other men,[2] or imagine similar ones at pleasure.

The way therefore in which we perceive an *action*, and form the concepts of diverse kinds of actions, is not difficult to explain; for we come to know what *action* is, first by that which we experience in ourselves (given the idea of being in general), and then by thinking the like of what we have experienced.

Again, as regards those actions of which we are ourselves the authors (the cause), our consciousness also informs us of them.

We are conscious that it is *we* who will, think, &c. As therefore we know the cause of all this species of actions through *perception*; so we know that *we ourselves* are that cause. Hence we can also, simply by analysing these actions,

---

[1] I say so in order in some way to determine this action: for the rest, the knowledge that our sensitive organs are struck by external realities is posterior to the consciousness of our passivity. The expression used in the text, therefore, refers to that which takes place subsequently to our being sensibly affected by that action.

[2] Language would be of no use to us unless we had already in our minds the ideas signified by it, or had the faculty of forming these ideas on occasion of the words we hear. On this S. Augustine has a beautiful observa-tion: 'Quemadmodum potest quivis digitum movere ut aliquid ostendat, non autem videndi facultatem conferre; ita potest homo exterius verba proferre, quæ veritatis signa sunt, non autem veri intelligendi virtutem, quæ a solo Deo est, impertiri.' 'In the same way that a man can move his finger for pointing out something, but cannot communicate the power of sight; so he can utter externally words significa-tive of the truth, but not bestow the power of understanding the truth. This power is from God alone.'

distinguish the EGO (cause) who acts, from the action produced by him ; and thus form the concept of the actions done
by ourselves.

In this also there is no difficulty ; and yet we have here
already an idea of *cause*.

619. But I must prove that in the idea of cause there is
something by which we see to evidence that without a producing cause there could be no event, no action ; for my proposition was, ' Every new fact necessarily implies a cause.'
This proposition affirms that between the produced and the
producer, the action and the agent, there is a necessary connection.　Now a necessary connection between two ideas
must flow from their very nature, from their standing to each
other as two correlatives, neither of which is thinkable without
in some way involving the thought of the other.　In other
words, to have a necessary connection, the two ideas must be
such that when we come to analyse the definition of either of
them, we find that the other is contained in it as the fruit
in its germ.

Now herein lies precisely the whole of the difficulty, and
in order to overcome it, I must submit to an accurate analysis
the two terms of the above proposition, namely, (1) the *action*,
(2) its *cause*; and I must demonstrate that by the fact of
conceiving the one we virtually conceive the other also.

If I succeed in this, I shall likewise have demonstrated
that it is impossible to conceive (1) a new fact or an *event*
without thinking a cause, and (2) a *cause* without thinking an
effect, at least as possible.

This done, all that remains is to explain how we acquire
either of these concepts ; since, by what I have just said,
the explanation of either of them contains the explanation of
the other.

But as regards the concept of action and the pure and
simple concept of a cause, no difficulty exists; for these
concepts, as we have seen, are furnished to us by experience
and our consciousness (618).

The difficulty is therefore reduced to a single point, namely,
to demonstrating that by conceiving an *action*, we implicitly
conceive a *cause*, and *vice versa* : let us make the attempt.

ARTICLE IV.

The one difficulty found in accounting for the origin of the idea of cause is explained.

620. Everything can be an object of the mind (603); therefore also actions.

But, by the principle of cognition (564, 565), every intellectual operation has *being*, either indeterminate or determinate (*l' essere o l' ente*), for its object.

Therefore whatever appertains to being, or to a being, and determines it, is thought by the mind, not *per se*, but only as a determination of being, or of a being.

Therefore in order to think of what appertains to a *being*, but is not that being itself, the mind must first think the *being*: thus and thus only can it conceive and understand those determinations.[1]

Now although what I now say is simply the outcome of the things that have been proved in the course of this work; nevertheless, in order that it may not present any difficulty (and those who have understood me will not find any), I think it right to request my readers not to be deterred by the somewhat abstract terms in which the doctrine here set forth is expressed, but to consider it in itself, divested of its verbal form. And that they may do this the more easily, I will present it here in as plain and simple language as I can.

In the first place, I would ask them whether when they think—no matter about what—the thing before their mind can ever be other than one of these two, (1) some being, or (2) some quality or attribute, in short, some appurtenance of a being.

I believe they will not be able to find anything between, but on attentively examining the matter, they will see that

[1] It is easy to see that this is not a *subjective* law of the intellectual faculty, but a necessity arising from the nature of the thing thought, and therefore an *objective* necessity; for the determinations of a being do not exist except through that being; and inasmuch as they can only be conceived by the mind in so far as they exist, it would be absurd to say that they can be conceived before, or independently of, the being to which they belong, and through which alone they are something.

nothing is thinkable which does not ultimately fall under one or other of these two classes; for anything which is not itself a being, must needs be something belonging to a *being*, or related to it.

Nor must they be misled by taking the word *being* in a wrong sense, that is to say, in a sense more restricted than it really has.

When I say *being*, I mean that which *is*. That which is not, is nothing. Therefore what is neither a being nor anything appertaining to a being, is nothing. The word *being*, then, embraces all the possible; and no one can say that outside of the possible anything remains. If therefore we think of any one thing whatever, it must be either a *being* or some appurtenance of a being. To say the contrary would be a manifest contradiction in terms, a speaking without making any sense.

It is true that, by a mental abstraction, we can consider the appurtenances of a being separately from it; but this kind of separation does not cause those appurtenances to be beings by themselves. We must have already conceived the being as a whole, since it is on the concept of it, that our abstraction is performed. Clearly, we cannot abstract or separate any part from a whole, unless the whole from which the part is abstracted be in our mind first.

That, therefore, which, by itself, is neither *a* being, nor *being*, but appertains to some being and is perceived in it, is purely an abstraction of our mind; and abstractions presuppose in us the entire idea of the thing whereon we have thought fit to exercise them. Hence the consequence, that 'Being is thought through itself, and the things that are contained in, or in any way belonging or related to being, are thought through it, by the use of our power of abstraction.'

The truth of this principle will likewise be understood, if we look at it from another point of view, namely, if we consider the nature of an abstract idea.

When with our thought we, from a being, separate a quality or relation or any part whatever, what we thus separate is indeed mentally divided from the whole, but this cannot lead us into error; for we cannot be ignorant of the fact of its still belonging in reality to that whole, to that being from which it has been abstracted. It is therefore impossible for us to think any appurtenance of a being, without first thinking the being itself. It is only after this that we fix our attention on whatever appurtenance of that being we please (which is to abstract), without ever forgetting (unless we wish to deceive ourselves) that such appurtenance is inseparable from the being wherein we know it to exist.

621. These most simple principles once well understood, it is no longer difficult to see how we form the idea of cause.

In our perceptions, as I have said, we are conscious of an *action* which takes place in us, but of which we are not ourselves the authors.

Were we the authors, we should perceive this action as a thing belonging to us, that is, we should perceive it in our own being. The intellectual perception would, in this case, have all the conditions necessary for its formation.

But when our consciousness tells us of an action without giving us any information as to the author of it, how can our mind perceive and understand it?

An action is not a being, nor what causes a being to subsist (substance); but it belongs to a being.[1]

We have seen that our mind cannot conceive anything except through the concept of a being in which it sees that thing.

Therefore the mind does not conceive an action otherwise than by referring it to a being of which it is not as yet cognisant, but to which it feels that the action must necessarily belong as its production; and this being is what we subsequently designate by the name of *cause.*

All these propositions are incontrovertibly true; and therefore it seems to be demonstrated beyond fear of contradiction that our mind must, together with the idea of an *action* of which we are not ourselves the authors, think a

---

[1] This proposition is proved by the definition of that kind of action of which I here speak, and which is not the *primal* and *immanent* act constituting existence itself, but an action subsequent to that act.

being distinct from us, as the author thereof, or, which comes to the same thing, it must think a *cause*.

All that remains to explain is, ' How our mind can think this being (cause), when consciousness or the interior feeling does not present it to us.' The necessity under which the mind is of doing this has been proved, but the manner in which the mind does it has not yet been explained.

Now this also will be clearly seen by a summary reference to what has been said in this Section.

The idea of a cause is the idea of a being which produces an action. The analysis of this idea shows in it three parts : (1) the action, (2) the being, (3) the *nexus* between the two.

Now the *action* is given to us by the external or the internal sense. Of what *being* is, we are cognisant by nature.[1] The *nexus* arises from the logical *necessity* which I have already demonstrated, a necessity springing from the nature of the mind or, more properly, of its objects, which cannot be conceived without being ; so that the being is the first thing which our mind conceives in every case, because it is the first thing existing, as well as that through which all other things are conceived, because it is through the being, whose appurtenances they are, that they all exist.

[1] The way in which I deduce the idea of substance agrees perfectly with that of the Angelic Doctor. He lays it down in the first place that the object proper to the intellect is *being, or common truth* (' Objectum intellectus est ens, vel verum commune '). Hence he deduces the proposition that ' Everything is knowable in so far as it *is*,' or has an existence of its own ; which is the very point I have done my best to establish, it being manifestly absurd to say that what is not can be the object of the understanding (' Unumquodque autem in quantum habet DE ESSE, in tantum est cognoscibile ') (*S.* I. xvi. iii). The obvious consequence of this is, that since the substance is that by which things are beings, they must necessarily be known or understood through their substance. Hence the other sentence of the Holy Doctor, that ' the *substance* is the object of the understanding,' precisely because the object of the understanding is BEING (' Quidditas rei est proprium objectum intellectus ') (*S.* I. lxxxv. v). And from this he, with his usual acuteness, draws also another consequence, viz. ' That *truth*, considered in particular things, is the same as their *substance*, their being ' (' Verum autem quod est in rebus, convertitur cum ente secundum substantiam ') (*S.* I. xvi. iii). In fact, the truth of things consists in the relation they have with our ideas of them ; but these ideas can only relate to their substance, because this is the object of the understanding ; therefore truth in so far as participated by things is nothing but their substance.

Let it be noted, that in the last passage but one I have rendered the term *quidditas* by *substance*, because this is the sense given it there by S. Thomas. For the rest, it is always true that the *quiddity* or essence of the *accidents* is cognisable only in the *substantial* quiddity or essence.

ARTICLE V.

Distinction between Substance and Cause.

622. When we, endowed with the faculty of understanding, supply *being* in the *sensitive perception*, we then form the idea of *substance*, that is, of a being which is conceived as existing in itself and not in another thing.

When we supply being in the *intellectual perception* of an *action*, we then form the idea of cause, that is, of a substance which acts.[1]

In forming these two ideas the understanding makes the same kind of act. This act, as I have just said, consists in supplying a *being*[2] to what is furnished to us by the sense or by the intellectual perception. Its possibility arises from our unity as human subjects, in virtue of which unity we possess at once the power of feeling, of perceiving intellectually, and of reflecting. WE who have the external and internal sense, are the very same who have also the intuition of being—the constitutive form of our intellectual faculty.[3] On experiencing

---

[1] Besides substances, we can also imagine other things as acting. Thus for example we say that one thought produces another. But this is only by way of abstraction ; for the true cause of all thoughts is invariably the substance of our soul.

[2] By supplying this being, we do not by any means create it, nor put it forth from our own selves, since it is given us as an object of intuition from the very first moment of our existence.

[3] I beg leave to subjoin a few more remarks on the teachings of S. Thomas. Seeing that this great master made his philosophical principles the groundwork of several sublime doctrines regarding religion—the greatest of all man's concerns—and it being of importance that as much light as possible should be thrown on these doctrines ; the principles of his philosophy, on which these proofs are based, ought also to be thoroughly known.

I have already remarked more than once, that the energy which *universalises* our sensations cannot, properly speaking, be the intellect as such, but must be the soul itself, which, possessed as it is at once of the intellectual and sensitive faculties, in virtue of its *unity* and *simplicity* conjoins in itself, as it were in a simple point, what it feels by the sensations, and *being*—of which it has naturally the intuition. Now, a careful study of the function attributed by S. Thomas to the *intellectus agens*, has convinced me that, according to him, this intellect is precisely that energy of the soul which unites together these two things. Thus the *intellectus agens* of the Schools corresponds with what I have called the *faculty of the primitive synthesis*, or the primary function of the *Reason* (64, 513). S. Thomas speaks also of a *particular Reason* which he terms *cogitative force*, and whose function consists in descending to particular things and arranging them in proper order.—' Mens regit inferiores vires ; et sic singularibus se immiscet mediante ratione particulari, quæ est potentia quædam individualis, quæ alio nomine dicitur cogitativa.' ' The mind directs the inferior powers, and thus mixes itself up with particulars by means of the *particular reason*, which is a certain

a sensation, we refer the *thing felt* to being, and by this reference we perceive, in that thing, a determinate being and

individual force otherwise called *cogitative* ' (*De Verit.* X. v). Since, then, according to him, the *Reason* is that force by which the soul, having on the one hand the sensations and phantasms, and on the other the intuition of being, joins together these two things, it follows that this same force which embraces the two extremes, when considered in relation to the particulars it has the power of regulating, is nothing but the *cogitative force* aforesaid. But when considered as a power of forming ideas in the manner I have stated, that is, of universalising the phantasms, it then corresponds to the *intellectus agens*, appropriately designated by the Angelical as ' Virtus quædam animæ nostræ' (*S.* I. lxxxix. iv). The thought of the Holy Doctor will be seen still more clearly by means of the following observations :—

In the first place, he lays it down that the sensations, as such, or rather the corporeal images (*phantasmata*), are not ideas, but that in order to become ideas, they require to be *illumined by the intellectus agens.* Now this illumination I have shown to be nothing but their *universalisation*, which is effected by our soul adding to them its *light*, namely *possible* or *ideal being.* The soul, having intellectually perceived a sensation, considers that sensation as possible to be repeated indefinitely, *i.e.* considers it no longer in its individual but in its possible existence, or which is the same, in general. Here are the words of S. Thomas : ' Formæ sensibiles . . . . . non possunt agere in mentem nostram, nisi quatenus per lumen intellectus agentis immateriales redduntur,et sic efficiuntur quodammodo homogeneæ intellectui possibili, in quem agunt.' ' The sensible forms . . . . . cannot act on our mind, except in so far as they are rendered immaterial through the light of the *intellectus agens*, and thus are made in a certain way homogeneous with the *intellectus possibilis* on which they act ' (*De Verit.* X. vi). Whence he concludes, that the principal agent in the formation of ideas is, not sense or the phantasms, but the *intellectus agens*, through its innate light. Now I say, if the *intel-*

lectus agens renders the phantasms immaterial (universalises them) it must act on them, or, according to the expression of S. Thomas, ' turn itself to them ' (' convertendo se ad illa '). This *intellectus agens*, therefore, can only be that energy which the soul possesses of seeing the sensations which it experiences, in possible being of which it has the intuition. But, that the nature of the *intellectus agens* is such as I here describe, will be better understood from the following passage in which S. Thomas explains how it is that this intellect renders the phantasms immaterial (universal) ; and it is, he tells us, precisely because of the *unity* of the human subject, that is, of our soul, which has, on the one hand the phantasms, and on the other the intellective energy. I will again quote his words : ' Anima intellectiva est quidem actu immaterialis, sed est in potentia ad determinatas species rerum.'—' The intelligent soul is indeed immaterial in act, but it is *in potentia* as regards the *determinate* species of things ' (I. lxxix. iv). This *immateriality* in act, belonging to the intellective soul, signifies exactly the intuition of *being* as having a universal act, free from all limitations and corporeal determinations. So true is this, that the Holy Doctor does not hesitate to maintain that we know the immateriality of the soul from its ideas, which we find to be *universal*, and therefore immaterial (*De Verit.* X. viii). He continues : ' Phantasmata autem e converso sunt quidem actu similitudines specierum quarumdam, sed sunt potentiâ immaterialia : unde nihil prohibet unam et eandem animam, in quantum est immaterialis in actu, habere aliquam virtutem, per quam faciat immaterialia in actu, abstrahendo a conditionibus individualis materiæ (quæ quidem virtus dicitur intellectus agens), et aliam virtutem receptivam hujusmodi specierum, quæ dicitur intellectus possibilis in quantum est in potentia ad hujusmodi species.'—' But contrarily the phantasms are indeed in act similitudes of certain species, but they are potentially immaterial ' (that is to say, they are not by themselves universal, but they can be universalised by our intellective soul).

therewith a substance. On perceiving an action, we attribute it to a being as its producer, and by so doing we perceive a being in action, and therewith a cause. A substance is a being producing something which we conceive as immanent in it (accidents);[1] a cause is a being producing something which terminates outside of the being itself (effect).

The necessity of a being antecedent to the accidents, gives us the idea of substance; the necessity of a being antecedent to the contingent being which has a commencement, gives us the idea of a being different from the latter, and which is termed a *cause*.

ARTICLE VI.

The understanding integrates the sense—perceptions.

623. A *sensible quality* cannot exist without a substance; an action cannot exist without a producing cause.

'Now there is nothing to hinder, that ONE AND THE SAME SOUL, in so far as it is immaterial in act ' (in so far as it has the intuition of possible being) 'should possess a certain virtue by which it renders the phantasms immaterial in act ' (*i.e.* universalises them), 'abstracting from the individual conditions of matter (which virtue is called *intellectus agens*), and also another virtue receptive of these species, which is called *intellectus possibilis*, because it is *in potentia* with regard to such species' (*S.* I. lxxix. iv). This passage seems to me to prove to evidence that the *intellectus agens* of S. Thomas is that energy which the soul possesses of *applying being* to the sensations, and hence that the *intellectus agens* is proper to the soul in so far as the soul feels at one and the same time its sensations, and the presence of being in general.

As regards, therefore, the nature of the two intellects—the 'acting' and the 'possible'—we may sum up as follows. The soul has an innate *light*, which is the idea of *being in general*. This idea may be considered under two aspects : (1) in so far as it is the means employed by the soul for universalising the sensations; and in this respect it takes the name of *intellectus agens* ; (2) in so far as it is always present to the soul, and has the aptitude to transform itself into all the other ideas (for, as I have so often said, all the ideas that can possibly be conceived by us are nothing but the idea of *being* furnished with various determinations) ; and when so considered, it takes the name of *intellectus possibilis.* This enables us to see in all its clearness the true meaning of the celebrated sentence of Aristotle : ' Est quidam intellectus talis qui omnia fit, et quidam qui omnia facit.'— ' There is an intellect which *becomes* all things ' (*intellectus possibilis*), ' and there is an intellect which *does* all things ' (*intellectus agens*) (*De Anima*, Lib. iii. c. vi). The *idea of being* becomes, as we have said, all determinate ideas ; behold the *intellectus possibilis* : by means of the *idea of being* the soul forms all determinate ideas ; behold the *intellectus agens.*

[1] Hence a substance is *cause* in respect of its accidents. But when we call it *substance*, we do not consider it as the producer of its terms (the accidents), but only as the *act in and by which* these terms (the accidents) *exist.* It must never be forgotten, that all these ways of conceiving are abstractions.

To the *sensible qualities*, or terms of our sensations, the understanding adds being, and thus conceives a determinate being ; to the *action* perceived it adds a being as the producer thereof.

It is therefore by integrating our sensations, that the understanding arrives at the idea of *substance*, even as by integrating our perception it arrives at the idea of *cause*.

When one reflects, that the understanding has *being* ever present to it, and that this vision is what constitutes it the nature of an understanding ; one cannot fail to see that this faculty must, in every one of its perceptions, see *a being* and nothing else.

But if it must see a being, it must also see what necessarily belongs to that being, or, as the Schoolmen expressed it, is *de ratione entis* ; for, if it did not see this, it would not truly see the being.   To say the contrary, would be a contradiction in terms.

We shall understand this fully, if we grasp well the fact that a being, and what necessarily belongs to it, are in truth one and the same thing.   No stronger proof can be had of this fact than to bear in mind that the idea of being is the most universal, and therefore the most simple, of all.

Hence it follows, that whenever we happen to perceive with our senses some appurtenance of a being, something which necessarily belongs to it, such as are the sensations, or the actions suffered by us, we, having already a permanent, fundamental and natural vision of *being*, at once perceive the *substance*, and infer the *cause*.

In fact, the perception of a substance, and the conception of a cause, are ' simply the perception of a being to which belong the sensible qualities, or to which we attribute the action suffered, or perceived by us.'

And since philosophy does not forbid us to illustrate a point by the use of similes when we have already proved it by argument, I would say that the indeterminate being which is abidingly and immovably present to us, is like to a sheet of blank paper on which our gaze is steadfastly fixed.   Now the determinations of this fundamental object of our interior vision are only an accidental addition to it, a writing made upon that blank sheet of paper (538). And these determinations, this writing, consist precisely of the sensations or perceptions referred to *being* as terms to the principle actuated in them.

By the same act, therefore, by which we contemplate *being*, we also see in it, and never without it, its determinations ; just as, when looking intently at a wall, we see the wall, and whatever shadows happen successively to be cast upon it ; or when in a *camera obscura* we behold the various figures which pass over the table.

624. It is, then, a fixed law of the understanding, a law flowing from the nature of its essential object, that it must complete whatever is presented to it by sense and perception ; for, to say it once more, the intellectual faculty consists in a permanent act by which it sees *being*, and consequently all that belongs to being, *i.e.* its determinations and conditions. When therefore the external or internal sense furnishes the determinations of being, these are naturally integrated and completed in us ; because with our internal vision we invariably associate *being* with them, and thus form to ourselves a determinate being, together with all that necessarily belongs to the same.

This intellective aptitude may therefore be called ' The integrating faculty of the understanding.'

ARTICLE VII.

Application of the above Doctrine on Substance to the internal sense.

625. The reasoning by which I have shown that the understanding cannot conceive the sensible qualities without at the same time thinking a substance in which they exist, must not be supposed to apply to the external qualities of bodies only. It is of universal application, and therefore holds good also in respect of the facts of the internal sense. I will try to explain how this is.

We have interior feelings : we are conscious of possessing ideas, of experiencing spiritual pleasures and spiritual pains ;

we also form *ideas* of these feelings, by referring them to a subsistent being, namely to ourselves whose modifications they are ; and thus it is that we can form the idea of our own substance.

626. It is, however, important to observe that the subsistence or reality of our own substance is also presented to our understanding antecedently to, and in a more expeditious and immediate way than, these partial feelings ; for the feeling of our OWN SELVES is, not an accidental, but a *substantial* feeling. The understanding therefore does not *supply* our substance, but *perceives* it immediately in the feeling wherein it is contained ; and it is by means of this immediate perception, that the understanding, abstracting subsequently from the judgment which is always united with intellectual perception, forms in the first instance a positive idea of substance.

627. There is therefore a most noticeable difference between intellectually perceiving the substance of *external bodies*, and intellectually perceiving the substance of *our soul.* In the former perception, all that the sense furnishes to us is a force acting on us in such a manner as to impress us with the feeling of those qualities which we therefore call *sensible*, dan which determine for us the force itself. But this force, acting as just said, although substantial,[1] is not by itself a *being*,[2] because it has not a *subjective existence.*[3] We therefore being obliged to consider that force as a *being* (the necessary condition for perceiving it intellectually), apply to it a subjective mode of existence, that mode by which it exists in itself and not simply relatively to us. Thus do we join with it that support or substance without which it would not be a being. As, however, this substance is, as I have observed, felt by us only in its *action*, so we conceive a *being* to which the action belongs, without defining exactly *what* that being is, but only defining it as the *proximate cause of that action.*

---

[1] Because it *really acts* (TRANSLATORS).

[2] The *sense* itself does not perceive *being*, but only the *sensible terms* of being ; not the *substance* but only the accident (TRANSLATORS).

[3] *I.e.* it does not exist by its own self, but only in the *being* to which it belongs (TRANSLATORS).

Hence some philosophers have declared that the substance of bodies is a thing hidden from our cognisance. They were induced to this by observing that we are under the necessity of considering as substance the *force in so far as it acts* on us, and that therefore we know nothing of these *bodies* except in that particular relation (though a *real* relation) which they have with ourselves. To me, on the other hand, it seems that the proper way to designate all this that relates to bodies, is by simply terming it *extrasubjective* ; because the idea we have of their substance does not present to us any subject in a positive form, but only something extraneous to us, to our subjectivity.

The case stands otherwise with the intellectual perception of our soul. Here the *substantial subject*, the *substance* (*i.e.* the soul), is actually present and intimately felt in its own real self. Consequently, for intellectually perceiving this substance, we have no need of supplying it through thinking a relation, but only of applying to it the idea of being.

628. Lastly as regards our own body, we can perceive it in two ways: (1) Like all bodies that are extraneous to us, and therefore *extrasubjectively* ; (2) As a term of our internal sense, and therefore *subjectively.* But this second way of perceiving our body is of such importance, that I must reserve it for fuller treatment in another place.

CHAPTER V.

A HINT ON THE ORIGIN OF THE IDEAS OF TRUTH, OF JUSTICE, AND OF BEAUTY.

629. To the class of *pure ideas* belong, besides those hitherto enumerated, the three most important ideas of *truth, justice*, and *beauty* ; and hence this would be a fitting place to speak of them.

But I abstain from doing so in this treatise on Ideology, it being enough for me to indicate their source, which is always *ideal being*. I consider that these three ideas constitute respectively the supreme principles of three most noble sciences ; namely, the idea of *truth* constitutes the principle of Logic ; the idea of *justice* that of Ethics ; and the idea of *beauty* that of Æsthetics. Nevertheless, to avoid repetition, I think it best to refer the reader to each of these sciences or an analysis of the principal idea on which it is based, and for the explanation of how it is that this self-same idea of *being*, viewed under different relations, takes the name now of *truth*, now of *justice*, now of *beauty*, and thus becomes the supreme criterion or the primary and certain rule for judging of all particular *truths*, of all particular *actions*, and of every species of the *beautiful*.

Moreover, having formerly had occasion to say something about these sciences, I did not omit to analyse such ideas and explain whence they are derived. Should anyone therefore wish to know what my views are regarding their origin, he can easily satisfy his desire by a reference to the places or treatises in which I have spoken of them.[1]

---

[1] Of the idea of TRUTH as the foundation of Logic, I treat in the present work, Section VI. ; of the idea of JUSTICE as the foundation of Ethics I have treated in *Principii della Scienza Morale* ; and of the idea of BEAUTY as the principle of Æsthetics, in the *Saggio sull' Idillio e sulla nuova Letteratura Italiana* (vol. i. of *Opuscoli Filosofici*, Milano, 1827).

PART V.

ORIGIN OF NON-PURE IDEAS, THAT IS, OF THOSE WHICH, FOR THEIR FORMATION, TAKE SOMETHING FROM THE SENSES.

630. Hitherto I have spoken of those ideas which are drawn solely from the idea of *being* itself—the *form* of all ideas—either by analysing it, or by considering it in some of its relations, wholly apart from the determinations of which it is susceptible, and which are suggested to us by the sense. To signify the perfect simplicity peculiar to these ideas, I have designated them by the epithet of *pure*.

I must now proceed to apply this *pure* portion of our knowledge step by step to the facts of *sense*, so as to explain the origin of *non-pure* ideas, namely, those which are derived not from the *formal principle* alone, but also from another principle associated with it in our subjective unity, and consisting of the sense both spiritual and animal.

631. I will begin by taking the pure idea of substance in general, and show how it becomes *specialised*—as the idea of *spiritual* substance by means of the spiritual sense, and as that of *material and corporeal* substance by means of the material and corporeal sense.

CHAPTER I.

ORIGIN OF THE DISTINCTION BETWEEN THE IDEAS OF
CORPOREAL AND SPIRITUAL SUBSTANCE.

ARTICLE I.

On the doctrine laid down above respecting substance and cause.

632. I have shown how, on occasion of the external and internal sensations, our mind conceives naturally the ideas of substance and of cause. This was in confutation of the system of Hume, who affirmed the possibility of the whole universe consisting of nothing but ideas, accidents, and facts, without any subject or substance to sustain them, and without any producing cause.

In this strange system we see a man who puts forth all his ingenuity to create for himself a huge fabric of delusion, an idol wherein to worship himself, thus bequeathing to the world one of the most memorable pieces of sophistry on record. Is it not sad, that so powerful a thinker, having reached the very summit of that culture on which his age prided itself, should, after the most daring and profound meditations, end by exhibiting in himself the humiliating spectacle of a scientist who does not know what is perfectly well known and perfectly clear, I will not say to every civilised man, no matter how scanty his learning, but even to the savage of the woods? The simplest and most elementary ideas, self-evident to all, are lost to the mind of Hume, who, thus left in intellectual darkness, gropes his way in search of them and finds them not. He therefore imagines them and makes them out anew for himself; but not having any exemplar to guide him, he falsifies them to such an extent, that a person out of his mind would express himself about them in a better way.

633. To come to details : (1) Hume talks of *substance* and *cause, accident* and *effect*, without knowing what they are. He does not even stop to inquire what men in general understand by these words ; but affixes to them an arbitrary meaning. He has conceived an aversion for them, and woe betide anything to which a philosopher takes an aversion; he then fights, not with the ideas which the words express, but with his own creations : (2) Hume jumbles up *sensible qualities, sensations, intellectual concepts*—three things entirely distinct—into one only thing—*ideas* : (3) by this kind of reduction, or rather by this three-headed monster, he has already lessened the number of the entities which compose the universe : (4) nevertheless, his admission of the existence of *ideas*, still left in the universe two elements—ideas and a subject (substance) in which they exist ; for no idea can exist except in a thinking subject. But this also must not be. The universe cannot attain to a regularity sufficiently philosophical until, by the magic touch of man's genius, it be brought to absolute unity, that is to say, until the subject and the idea become identified or, to speak more accurately, the subject be annihilated, and the idea alone remain. Thus did the *fiat* of Hume's Idealism mould this universe into perfect simplicity, and thus were all unseemly excrescences removed from the Creator's work, and all its imperfections healed at last!

634. But if I have demonstrated, (1) that it is absurd to admit the existence of sensible qualities without a substance or act by which they exist, and (2) that our concept of the universe embraces neither accidents alone nor substances alone, but accidents and substances combined ; I have not as yet examined what that substance is by which the sensible qualities exist ; neither have I shown the untenableness of the system of Berkeley, who maintains that the subject of the sensible corporeal qualities is not anything different from ourselves ; so that our soul is in reality the only substance which exists, and therefore the subject sustaining as well those sensible qualities as our own internal feelings.

Now it is certain that the common sense of mankind
repudiates this system, and that to men's minds generally
the subject of the sensible corporeal qualities, is quite different
from that of our internal feelings. This being a fact, we
must account for it. Let us therefore see what is the origin
of the distinction between the idea of corporeal substance
and that of spiritual substance.

ARTICLE II.

Argument of the following discussion.

635. Berkeley, then, does not, like Hume, deny that the
sensible qualities exist in a subject ; only he says that we
and we alone are this subject.

The common sense of men agrees with Berkeley in saying
that we are the subject of our sensations ; but it adds that
these *sensations* are produced in us by an external cause, in
which to the different species of sensations experienced by
us, there must be as many corresponding qualities fit to
produce those sensations, and which may therefore be called
sensible qualities ; and it says furthermore, that that cause
is a substance entitled to the name of *subject* of these
qualities.

In the Idealism of Berkeley, therefore, the fact of our
sensations consists of two things only : (1) the sensations
themselves, and (2) a subject of them (*Ego*), and nothing
more.

In the Realism of the common sense of men, on the contrary, the said fact consists of four things : (1) the sensations,
(2) the subject of the sensations (*Ego*), (3) the sensible
qualities (the thing felt), (4) the subject of these qualities,
which is called *body* : two subjects with their respective
qualities, instead of one only.

Now we must see which of the two systems is more in
accordance with nature ; whether the Idealism of Berkeley
does not perhaps overlook some real facts which ought to
be considered ; or else whether in the Realism of common

sense, the popular imagination introduces facts which have no existence.

636. But before entering into this examination, let us endeavour to throw some more light on the notions of *subject* and of *cause* ; for in debated questions the first condition for surely arriving at the truth, is to have a clear understanding of the notions upon which the question turns.

ARTICLE III.

Difference between the idea of ' cause' and the idea of ' subject.'

637. A thing which produces another thing, is *cause* in respect of that thing, but it is not always its *subject* also.

The thing produced may be such as to exist, and therefore be conceived by us, separately from the thing which produces it ; or it may not have any such existence, so that we cannot conceive it by itself alone, but only in union with that same act or energy by which its cause exists.

In the first case, the thing which produces, is *cause* only ; in the second, it is both cause and *subject*. Thus for example, the father is only the cause of his son,[1] inasmuch as the son, once begotten, has his own proper and separate existence. The intelligent spirit, on the contrary, is not merely the cause of its thoughts, but also their subject, because thoughts have not any other existence than that of the spirit which produces and preserves them ; hence they cannot be conceived existent except in it. And so of all the like cases.

638. The distinction between subject and cause is real and very important. It should however be observed, that when we say 'If the thing produced exists only in its cause and in such a manner as to be inseparable therefrom, then the cause is also *subject*,' we must be careful not to understand the expression in a wrong sense.

---

[1] I need not observe that a father is not wholly the cause of his son's existence, since man cannot be the creator either of matter or of a rational soul. Nevertheless, this example may serve in some way to make my meaning understood.

The word *thing*, used in this proposition, may give rise to ambiguity.

More generally, it is used to signify that which exists in itself; whereas that which is produced in a *thing* and exists only in it, is not usually called a *thing*, but a *modification*, an *appurtenance*, &c., of a thing. Let it be noted, then, that in that proposition the term *thing* has a most wide sense, and indicates whatever can be an object of thought, whether that object has a separate existence of its own, or not.

In this second case, the thought, the concept, is simply a mental abstraction; nor could we at the first conceive the thing produced, by itself alone without that which produces it (the subject). First, we conceive the two in one, and then, by analysis, we decompose that concept, separating the accident from the subject, from which it is not separable in reality, and we give that accident a name as though it were a *thing* standing by itself; in a word, we make it *mentally* an object of our exclusive attention (a dialectic being).

ARTICLE IV.

A further analysis of sensation.

§ I.

Object of this analysis.

639. Having thus drawn a clear distinction between *subject* and *cause*, we must now try step by step to arrive at the truth we are here in search of.

That we may proceed securely, we shall at the outset confine ourselves to proving one point, which is, that in both of those subjects (*i.e.* soul and body) upon which the common sense of mankind on the one hand, and the philosophy of Berkeley on the other are at variance, we may and indeed must, by a mental abstraction, distinguish a third thing intermediate between the sensations and sensible qualities, and the mere act by which they exist; so that it would be impossible and absurd to imagine them as united with that act only and nothing else.

This will be the same as to demonstrate, that that *subject* which I have shown to be necessarily conjoined with the *sensations* and *sensible qualities* (whether that subject be the soul only, as Berkeley maintains, or whether, besides the soul, subject of the *sensations*, there be also a body, subject of the *sensible qualities*), cannot consist purely in that act by which the sensations or the sensible qualities are conceived to exist ; but, in addition to such act, there must of necessity be an entity which, not only produces the act, but also has an absolute existence, that is to say, exists not simply relatively to other things, but in itself.

We will speak first of the subject of the sensations (*soul*), admitted by both sides alike ; afterwards we will treat of the subject of the sensible qualities (*body*), which is admitted by one side but denied by the other.

§ 2.

In the sentient subject there is something else besides the act by which its sensations exist.

640. I have distinguished the sensations from the act by which they exist, and which constitutes their substance. The concept of this substance is what I have now to submit to analysis.

My contention is, that this concept includes, not merely the act by which the sensations exist, but something else also. Let the reader keep well in mind the hypothesis upon which the whole of my argument is based, and I feel confident that he will agree with me.

The hypothesis was, that I did not as yet know whether *substance* exists or not. I knew only that the *sensations* exist.

Setting out from this knowledge which was granted, I demonstrated by means of analysis that the concept of a *substance* was necessarily implied in it.

Now, I say furthermore (and this is the second step in my reasoning), that by proceeding to analyse the *substance* thus found out, we discover in its concept, not simply an energy capable of making the sensations exist, but something besides ; and I prove this in the following manner.

The sensations exist ; therefore there is an energy which makes them exist.   Now what are the sensations—of colour, sound, taste, scent, smoothness or roughness, &c.—and how do they take place ?   If I observe the fact in myself, my consciousness assures me at once that they take place in me, namely, that they are so completely *my own*, that if I did not exist, or if I had not the sensitive faculty, not only should I be without them, but they would not exist at all ; for example, there would not be the sensations I feel in smelling this rose, in hearing this violin, in eating this orange, &c.   And what I say of my own sensations, I may equally say of those of other men ; for as their sensations are like mine, from which I derive their concept and understand the name which expresses them, clearly if the persons who experience them did not exist, or had no sensitive faculty, or were not actually feeling them, their sensations would not exist.   Now there is no sensation—of smell, taste, colour, &c.—but must belong to some one ; for a sensation is merely a modification of the sense of a sensitive being.

Such being the nature of sensations, I maintain that there must be in the sentient subject, besides the sensations and the energy or act by which they exist, something else in which that energy or act is rooted, and this is a thing so manifest as hardly to require proof.

In fact, when I say : ' I smell such or such scent, see such or such colour,' &c., I introduce, besides the sensations, the *Ego* who experiences them and is their subject.   Now the *Ego* is not simply the energy or act by which the sensations exist ; for in the mere concept of *existent sensation*, I do not as yet find the *Ego*.   Nay, were I not to conceive the sensations as existing in *me*, I should be obliged to conceive in them as many subsistent beings as they themselves are ; whereas, by thinking of them such as I experience them, I become convinced that, although many, they are equally centered in one and the same *Ego*.   This fact, that the *Ego* is one, while the sensations experienced by it are many, proves to evidence that the *Ego* is different from the sensations, even as the subject is different from the modifications incidental to it.

641. Again : I often experience many sensations at the same time, then many of these sensations cease, and others supervene ; nevertheless I continue identically the same. I have therefore the capacity of being variously modified, of feeling various sensations ; but this capacity is a thing wholly different from each actual sensation.

642. Lastly, the sensation is the *felt,* and I am the *sentient.* These, not merely different, but opposite characteristics show manifestly that the sensations, and the act by which they exist, cannot be conceived without a subject wherein, both, they and (before them) the act which makes them exist, are rooted.

643. It is important to notice in all this, that the existence of the sentient subject of which I speak, is not deduced through a long process of reasoning, but by a simple analysis of the concept of *existent sensation.*

As therefore by this analytical method it was demonstrated above, against Hume, that by the mere fact of conceiving an *existent sensation* (which Hume admitted), we conceive a substance (609) ; so here the application of the same method demonstrates that, by the mere fact of conceiving a *substance*, we conceive a something which exists in addition to the sensations (a subject of them).

The subject of the sensations, therefore, is not purely an act terminating in them, but it is a principle existing by itself, which has the *power* of feeling, and remains ever the same though it be divested of all special and accidental sensations.

§ 3.

The subject of the sensible qualities cannot be an act extending to them alone.

644. A similar process of reasoning will show that the Realism of the common sense of mankind is right in saying that the *sensible qualities* cannot be conceived as existing by an act which terminates in them alone ; but that the act by which they exist involves of necessity the existence of some other thing different from them.

In fact, according to the Realists, the sensible qualities are *powers* of producing sensations in the sentient subject (635).

Now it is absurd to suppose that these powers exist without something which cannot be mentally distinguished from them.

Let us analyse the concept or idea of *existent sensible qualities*, *i.e.* powers which produce sensations in us.

In the Realistic view, all these sensible qualities emanate from a sort of centre, which is called *body*, and is believed to be the subject of them.

Now if all these sensible qualities are thus united in, and referred to a being from which they proceed, we must perforce admit that in the concept of sensible qualities, this being (whatever its nature) which has the power of uniting them together in itself, is implicitly contained. Therefore, that concept includes, besides the existence of the sensible qualities, the existence of something else necessary for their existing in the way we conceive them.

645. Some one may object, that this reasoning is not founded on the concept of *sensible qualities* pure and simple, but on such concept of them as we obtain from experience; and that into the concept of sensible qualities pure and simple, the centre whereof I speak, the bond of union between these powers does not enter at all.

Let us then examine also the sensible qualities considered by themselves, in fact any sensible quality isolated from all others. I maintain that even in this concept we think something besides the sensible quality itself. To the proof:—

I define a sensible quality as a power which produces in us a certain species of sensations.

Now if this power really exists, we must think, and do really think, that besides the relation it has with us, it must also be something in itself. This subsistence in itself is different from the relation it has with us, that is, from the action it exercises in us; for it is impossible to think of a relation or action of a being, without thinking of the being itself; a relation and action between two beings necessarily implies both these beings. If, therefore, when I conceive a power of producing a modification in me, I conceive the real relation of a thing with me, it inevitably follows that the thing which has this power on me exists. Consequently, in a power which modifies me, I think (1) something which exists independently of me, (2) a relation or action which this something exhibits in me.

The analysis, therefore, of the concept of ' existent sensible qualities,' or of ' a power of producing sensations in us,' gives us as its result two ideas, (1) of a being really existing in itself, (2) of a relation with us, or of an action productive of our sensations.

Now, before proceeding to demonstrate that the two subjects, spiritual and corporeal, exist, I must say a few words on a matter the clear understanding of which is necessary for this demonstration ; I mean on *essence*.

ARTICLE V.

Distinction between the idea of substance *and that of* essence.

§ 1.

Definition of essence.

646. I call *Essence* that which is contained in any idea whatsoever.

The idea is the thing in so far as conceived by our mind in a state of pure possibility ; but if this same possible thing, instead of being considered in relation to the mind which conceives it, is considered in its own self, then it is the *essence*. The essence, therefore, is what we think in any idea.

§ 2.

Specific essence, generic essence, and most universal essence.

647. The ideas furnished with some determination are of two kinds, the *specific* and the *generic*.

To these correspond in our mind two species of *essences* : what we think in a specific idea, is the *specific essence* ; and what we think in a *generic* idea, is the *generic essence*.

Besides these two classes of ideas, which are more or less determinate, there is the *most universal idea* of all, the idea of *being in general.* What we conceive through this idea may be called the *most universal essence*, or simply *essence* (from *esse, to be*).   It is often so called by Plato.

§ 3.

On specific essence.

648. I have already observed that a thing may be considered in various states ; that is, either as entirely perfect in its kind, or as rendered more or less imperfect by privation. I say by *privation*, because it is now universally admitted, that evil is nothing but a privation of good.

The idea therefore by which a thing is conceived as complete in all the perfection suitable to its nature, is, alone, the entirely positive idea of that thing ; whereas the ideas by which one conceives the defective states of the same thing, are nothing but that same idea—which we may call the *typical* or *exemplar-idea*—less some of its perfection : in other words, they are *modes* of it (500–503).

Consequently, the *specific essence* of a thing is, properly speaking, what we think in the typical or exemplar-idea of that thing, to which are reduced all those other ideas wherein the thing is seen in its states of accidental imperfection.

649. But to understand well the nature of a *specific idea*, we must make another consideration.

The *modes* I have named arise from the imperfections to which the thing we think is liable.

But besides these *modes* which proceed from defects or deteriorations in the thing thought, there are also *modes* of the idea itself, proceeding, not from defects existing in it, but from the manner in which we conceive it.   I will explain.

The object seen by our mind in every intellectual perception, is always a determinate being (a possible reality) (491).

Every determinate being has in it something in virtue of which it is what it is, and without which it would not be.

This is its *primal act* (*actus primus*), immutable, immanent (587).

This first act produces others, namely, the *operations*, and various *actuations* of the being, which may be termed *secondary acts* (*actus secundi*) for the reason that they flow from the first.

We must however consider that these operations and actuations of the being, as also such effects or terms of them as remain in it,[1] and follow upon its primal act, are not all or always or necessarily conjoined with that act. They may sometimes be wanting; or if some of them are necessary, it is not necessary that there should be this particular one rather than another. Thus as regards bodies, though they cannot exist without some colour (in so far as it is a sensible quality), that colour need not be the blue any more than the white or yellow.

Now it is clear, that so long as I think the said primal act with all that it embraces as its term, I think the being ; because I think that in virtue of which that being is what it is.

But, as I have just said, that primal *act* is not necessarily conjoined with many of those particular operations and actuations which follow it, and with their terms. Therefore, these may fail or vary without my ceasing to think the being itself.

Suppose that *man* is the being in question. To think this being, all I require is to think what is comprised in the definition, *A rational animal.*[2] Why? Because that is all that the primal act in virtue of which a human being is a human being extends to. Any ulterior determinations of him, either are not necessary—as would be the case if, to constitute a human being, a fixed degree of intellectual culture, a fixed material weight, &c., were essential—or, if in the present order of nature some such qualities, for example,

---

[1] For instance, the inclinations, the habits, the objects and terms of thought.

[2] I do not here wish to express any judgment as to the merit of this definition ; in order to illustrate my meaning, it is enough for me that the definition is commonly adopted.

as material weight, size, &c., taken generally, are necessary, they are already virtually comprised in the definition.

If then my mind grasps the primal act of a being, it thinks that being.

If it does not grasp all that the said primal act extends to, the object before it is no longer that being, but another.

By repeating these observations on the nature of beings, we arrive at the conclusion : (1) that there is something which is *necessary* to constitute a given being what it is, and therefore to make it, as such, a thinkable object ; (2) that there is something which *does not necessarily* enter into the constitution of that being, and without which, therefore, it can be thought ; and (3) that this necessity springs from the *intrinsic order* of the being itself.

Let us now think of any being we please ; we shall find in it certain things which, though not necessary to its *constitution* and existence, are nevertheless necessary for its *perfection*.

Moreover, the things which are necessary for its perfection but not for constituting it what it is, are likewise not necessary for our *conception* of it. For this conception it is sufficient that we think that act which makes it possible for it to exist, because the object of cognition is *being*.

If therefore in our idea we think the being as furnished with all that is necessary to make its subsistence possible, but not with what is necessary for its perfection, we have then those *modes* of the exemplar-idea of which I have spoken above, and which arise from the defects of the thing thought.

If we do not think all that is necessary to constitute the being, we do not think that being.

If, on the other hand, we think that element by virtue of which the being exists, and at the same time do not think explicitly those things which are necessary for its perfection, without however denying or excluding them, but rather assuming them in an implicit manner as virtually included in the thought of the act which constitutes its existence ; in this case we have those *modes* of the *specific idea* which do not depend on the defects of the being thought, but on the particular manner in which our mind conceives it and on the being itself, whose nature is such, that, in order to conceive it, we require nothing further than to think that act which forms, so to speak, its root.

These *modes* of the *specific* idea, therefore, are the result of a species of *abstraction*, by which we do not, as in the former *modes*, think the being in a *defective state*, nor yet in the state of *perfection*, as we do in the case of the exemplar-idea ; but prescind entirely from what belongs to the perfection of the being, restricting our thought to what is necessary for its subsistence either actual or potential.

650. Again ; owing to the imperfection of our understanding, we can very seldom conceive things with that full and complete idea of which the *mode* last described is, as it were, a sketch or a germ initially including it.

Hence, not having to hand the *complete specific idea* (exemplar, or rather archetype), we take as the foundation of the species, that *abstract idea* which, properly speaking, is only a *mode* of the perfectly finished idea.[1]

[1] If we wish to state the order of the *specific ideas* distinguished in the text, according to the *time* in which we acquire them, we shall find that order to be as follows :

(1) First of all, we acquire the *full* or *concrete idea* of a given imperfect being, as is each of those we see in nature ; and not only imperfect, but sometimes *corrupted* as well ; for it is very seldom that · the beings we see around us have not some greater or less degree of corruption.

(2) Next, from this idea, full, but representing an imperfect being, we form the abstract specific idea by prescinding from the corruptions and imperfections of that being without adding to it any perfections, in a word, from all that is not necessarily connected with the conception of the being. It is through this abstraction that we obtain the *specific idea* of the being as it were in outline—that idea which is more commonly used in ordinary life.

(3) After this and last of all, we seek to rise to the *complete specific idea* (archetypal being)—a task, however, most difficult of accomplishment ; for it is extremely difficult for us to have the qualifications necessary for knowing all that belongs to the absolute perfection, natural or supernatural, of a being. Nevertheless, we continually strive to approach nearer and nearer this, the noblest of ideas, through that energy of our spirit which I have called the *integrating faculty of the human understanding* (623, 624). And even when we do not fully succeed, we still know that such idea must exist, and that we might attain to it had we only the requisite power. Hence, we aspire to it, at least as to a possible acquisition.

Such is the *chronological order* of the three kinds of our specific ideas ; but the order in which they stand when considered in their *nature*, is the very reverse of this. The *complete specific idea* (perfect exemplar, archetype) is the first ; the *abstract specific idea* is the second, and the *imperfect specific idea* is the third. Nay, these two last are only *modes* of the first, not ideas specifically different from it.

651. And this is the idea which contains what we in our common discourse are accustomed to call simply *essence*; so that when one speaks of the *essence* of things without any further explanation, the term must be understood as signifying that which our mind sees in the *abstract specific* idea.

652. Here I have to observe, that in forming this kind of specific idea, we make use, besides *universalisation*, of a sort of *abstraction*. But this is not that mental operation which, properly speaking, forms the *species*. It only forms the *abstract species*, which is already included in the *complete species*. And if the *complete species* also does not come to us through *universalisation* alone, but requires further the *integration* of that imperfect idea of the thing which we receive in the first instance; that does not depend on the nature of the idea itself, but on the accidental defect of the beings which we perceive, and whose first concept we obtain by detaching it from the judgment whereby we have, in perceiving them, affirmed their subsistence.

§ 4.

On Generic Essences.

653. Generic ideas are formed by *abstraction* (490-503); but specific ideas by *universalisation* only.[1]

654. As there are three modes and degrees of *abstraction*, so there are three kinds of generic ideas, and consequently generic essences, which may be called by the names of *real* genera, *mental* genera, and *nominal* genera.

655. The way in which these three genera are formed, and distinguished one from the other is as follows.

Abstraction may be exercised on the *abstract specific essence* in a twofold manner: we may abstract something from that essence in such a manner that in the portion of it which remains to us we still think a being possible to be realised; or we may so abstract as to take away all being, and have

---

[1] The *specific ideas* formed by universalisation alone are those which I have called *full specific ideas*, but *imperfect*; from which we afterwards form by abstraction the *abstract specific ideas*, and by *integration*, the *complete* or *perfect specific ideas*.

nothing left save an element purely *mental*, as the accident, or a quality or anything else which, by itself alone, does not convey the knowledge of a being. In the first case, our idea (relatively to the specific idea on which we have made the abstraction) is *generic real*. In the second case, it is *generic mental*, because what is expressed and represented in it has no existence outside the mind, or at least does not, as the mind conceives it, exist as a being.

Let us take an example. The idea of *man* is an abstract specific idea. On this idea I can practise abstraction in the two ways indicated.

In the first of them, I abstract the specific difference between a man and an animal, *i.e.* the *faculty of reason*. This gives me the idea of *animal*, which, relatively to the species *man* [1] is *generic real*, and includes a *generic real* essence.

In the second, I may abstract all that constitutes a being, and retain only an accident, for instance, colour. In this case, the idea of colour is *generic mental*, and therefore the essence of colour is called a *mental essence*, because colour in this abstract form is a purely mental entity.

Here I must again call attention to what I have repeatedly observed before, namely, that when I think abstract accidents by themselves alone, in virtue of the law of my intelligence which can only have *being* for its object, I consider those accidents as so many beings, although I know at the same time that they are not really such. Knowing this therefore, and that if my mind sees them as beings, it is only because this is its way of conceiving things, I call them *mental* or *dialectical* entities.

656. Lastly, besides these two modes of abstraction, there is also a third, which is when I so abstract and prescind, both from the *being* and from its *accidental qualities*, as to retain nothing but a relation, say, that of a *sign*. Thus, names arbitrarily imposed may be taken for the foundation of genera. For example, some one might introduce to my notice such genera as that of the Maurices, of the Peters,

---

[1] Relatively to *brute animal*, this same idea is *specific*.

&c. These I would call *nominal genera*, and the essence responding to them, *generic nominal essence.*

§ 5.

A more perfect definition of substance.

657. From all the above we are enabled to give a more perfect definition of substance in general.

We have seen the distinction between *abstract specific essence* and *full specific essence.* The first, we have said, when present to the mind, makes us know all which in a given *determinate being* is immutable, that is, which could not be changed without that being losing its identity, either by ceasing altogether to exist, or by becoming another before our mind.

Now, when in a given *determinate being* we think this immutable element which constitutes its abstract specific essence, and consider it in relation with the other element— the mutable—which is found united to it in the *full specific essence*, then the *abstract specific essence* receives the name of *substance* ; because it is regarded as the element necessary to make the being what it is, as the act through which it subsists as such a being, and by which the mutable element is supported.

The substance therefore may be defined as ' That by which a determinate being is what it is,' or as ' The abstract specific essence considered in a determinate being,' that is, considered in relation to the full specific essences of that same being.

658. But if there were some being which had no *abstract specific essence*, in other words, which had in it nothing mutable that could be abstracted, and which, were any change made in it by the mind, would instantly lose its identity, then the word *substance* could not with strict propriety be applied to it ; or we should have to say that in this particular case, the being was all substance, or that its substance and its *full specific essence* were identically the same thing. This is precisely the case with the Divine Being.

659. Now the diversity of the abstract specific essences is what differentiates substances. Should we therefore wish to apply the above general formula to express any special substance, it would be necessary, instead of saying 'Abstract specific essence in general,' to name that particular essence which represents the substance we wish to indicate.[1]

ARTICLE VI.

Resumption of the argument.

660. Let us now resume the thread of our reasoning.

All that we have said hitherto was directed to analyse the concept of substance in so accurate a manner as to preclude the possibility of any extraneous element being mixed up with it.

We have seen, that if a subject of the *sensations* exists (and its existence was proved in the preceding Chapter), this subject cannot have an existence purely relative to the sensations ; but must moreover be something subsisting in itself, antecedently to the sensations (639–643).

In like manner, if (as the Realists contend) there is a subject of the sensible qualities different from that of the sensations, this subject must be an energy which, besides and prior to giving subsistence to the sensible qualities, is itself something, so that these qualities are, in respect of it, what *powers* are to the being to which they belong.

But after thus showing that the subject of the accidents (the substance) is something existing in itself (since it is the act by which a determinate being is what it is), we went on further to inquire how it happens that substances are *specialised*, and distinguished one from the other ; and we found that this arises from the diversity of the terms in which the act whereby a determinate being exists as such or such attains its completion (649).

This enabled us to improve our definition of substance,

---

[1] The error of the Spinozists arose from mistaking *being* for *substance* ; whence they argued that since being, as being, is one, so there must be but one substance.

by reducing it to the following general formula : ' Substance is the abstract specific essence, considered in a determinate being.'

In order to remove all ambiguity, we explained, both, what *essence* is, and the various meanings of which the word is susceptible—including that of *abstract specific essence*, the basis of the substance of a being (649–652).

Our way being thus cleared, we will now continue our discussion about the different kinds of substances, that we may thus be in a position to refute the Idealism of Berkeley, as we have refuted that of Hume.

Something has already been done towards this by our having demonstrated that a substance which is the subject of the sensations (the *Ego*) exists. What still remains is to show, (1) that in the concept of this substance there is nothing of that which is comprised in the concept of corporeal substance ; and (2) that the corporeal substance exists. This second point, however, I must reserve for the next Chapter.

ARTICLE VII.

There exists a subject (the Ego) which perceives the sensations.

661. There are sensations external and internal : therefore, there is a subject which feels them ; and our consciences tell us that *we ourselves* are that subject.

This we have already seen (640-642).

ARTICLE VIII.

The concept of the Ego (percipient subject) is entirely different from the concept of corporeal substance.

§ 1.

There are in us two series of facts, in respect of one of which we are active, and of the other passive.

662. Anyone can see the truth of this by observing what takes place in himself.

When I deliberately will anything, and accordingly set

myself to do it, I feel that I move by a force which is my own, which is intrinsic to my nature. In these kinds of actions, therefore, I am not the patient but the agent or cause.

When anything takes place in me independently of and, as happens sometimes, even against my will, then I am a patient and not an agent.

663. This does not mean that when I am a patient, it is not *I* who suffer, nor that in what I suffer there is no cooperation from me. It is certain, however, that although the action is done in me, and I on my part contribute all that disposition which is necessary for my receiving it ; yet that force which produces it in me is not mine, nor would it be correct to say that I am the cause. This is not the place to enter into a searching investigation of the nature of the passion here referred to : it suffices to note the undeniable fact that the *passion* exists and that it is different from the *action* done of my own spontaneous will. Nothing more is required for establishing firmly the distinction of the two series of facts, in one of which we are rightly said to be active, and in the other passive.

664. To the passive facts belong the sensations which are produced in us from without ; and it is these that I have here principally in view.

We must, then, acknowledge the corporeal sensations as facts taking place in us, in which we are mainly passive, and of which we are the subject but not the cause.

Thus, if I, with my eyes open, turn to the sun, it is next to impossible for me not to see its dazzling brightness and feel the piercing effect of its rays. In the midst of a full military band, unless my ears be hermetically closed, I hear, even against my will, the sound of the music ; when severely pricked by a sharp-pointed instrument, I smart with pain ; in short, if in the sensations excited in my body, I were not passive, I should be able at will to stop every disagreeable sensation, to produce all those that are delightful, to shun every suffering, even death itself.

665. I adduce these extreme examples—although others of a simpler character would suffice—against those persons

who might be ready to say that we are able, by the force of mental abstraction or alienation, to obviate pain or any other feeling we do not wish to have; whence they would conclude that these things are attributable to ourselves, who by our own will lay ourselves out to receive these sensitive modifications.

To this I would reply, in the first place, that we cannot avoid all pain ; for if we could do this, we could also render ourselves immortal, or die without the least feeling of distress, however violent the mode of our death might be ; which is contradicted by experience.

In the second place, the mental abstraction and alienation alleged in the objection would be an effort on our part, and in some cases an effort too great for us to sustain.

It is therefore clear that in this effort, directed to neutralise the effect of a force which would act in a way disagreeable to us, our activity would be brought distinctly into play. But where a force is needed to impede a certain effect, there also is, unquestionably, the contrary force which tries to produce it. Reaction supposes action ; and the force which neutralises supposes that which is neutralised. The activity, therefore, by which we sometimes seek to avoid being passive, evinces our passivity.

Lastly, it also remains to be seen, whether the effort we make to withdraw ourselves from the sensible impressions aforesaid does actually impede in us the sensation ; or whether perhaps it is not simply a removal of our intellectual attention from that which we are suffering withal ; so that although we suffer in our sensitive part, nevertheless, not perceiving our passion intellectually, we are not conscious of it, and hence cannot say to ourselves that we have it ; for when our attention is suspended, we no longer think, or judge of what we feel.

§ 2.

In the active facts, we are both the cause and the subject; in the passive, we are the subject but not the cause.

666. All the facts which take place in us are modifications of ourselves. We are therefore the *subject* of every one of

them. Consciousness assures us on this point; we all say within ourselves: ' It is I who feel, who have the pleasure, who suffer, who think, will, &c.' Now this is the same as to say: ' I am the subject of all these facts.'

Nevertheless if in regard to *passive* facts we are the *subject*, we are not also the *cause*; for although produced *in* us, they are not, as I have said, produced *by* us, but by an external agent against, or at least independently of, our will.

This distinguishing of the facts which take place in us, into those of which we are both the cause and the subject, and those of which we are the subject only, coincides with the distinction established in the preceding article, between active and passive facts. But the analysis of that which is active in us, and of that which is passive, gives this result, that the idea of activity contains both a cause and a subject, whilst the idea of passivity contains a subject only.

The proposition at the head of this paragraph is therefore implicitly contained in the previous one, which simply states the fact.

§ 3.

That which we call body is the proximate cause of our external sensations.

667. We do not here require a complete definition of *body*; it is enough for us to know some property so characteristic of this substance that we cannot mistake it for anything else.

Now this object is sufficiently served by the definition which follows from the things I have said.

I, then, call *body* 'The subject of the sensible qualities,' namely, of those forces which produce sensations in us. Hence a body is the subject of extension, figure, solidity, colour, taste, &c., in so far as these sensible qualities exist in bodies, that is, in so far as they are forces which produce in us the sensations corresponding to them.[1]

[1] Reid has remarked and tried to explain at some length, that the words *smell, colour, taste*, &c., as commonly used, have two meanings entirely distinct; the first denoting the *sensations* which are in us, and the second the *perceptions* of the corresponding forces which produce them, and are in the

Now these forces, or sensible qualities, are the proximate causes of our sensations. We may therefore define *body* as

bodies. He, however, finds his task an embarrassing one; because what assigns to words their value is the general consent of men, and this consent is seldom or never chargeable with error. Let us hear, then, how he seeks to account for the twofold meaning attributed to these terms.

'Neither ought we,' he says, 'to expect that the *sensation* and its corresponding *perception* should be distinguished in common language, because the purposes of common life do not require it. Language is made to serve the purpose of ordinary conversation; and we have no reason to expect that it should make distinctions that are not in common use. Hence it happens, that a quality perceived and the sensation corresponding to that perception often go under the same name' (*Inquiry into the Powers of the Human Mind*, &c., Essay II. ch. xvi).

But however satisfactory this reason may appear at first sight, the satisfaction grows less when one examines it more closely. For in the first place, men, in imposing names, are not guided by their *wants* only, but much more by the *knowledge* they have of things. Thus, if they see two things distinct one from the other, they, without any further thought or inquiry, designate them by two different names; it being natural to them to express by a distinct word what stands before their minds as a distinct thing. Words are the portraiture of their inward thoughts; and the first *want* they have in this matter is, that the words they use be the faithful expression of those thoughts. In the second place, if the distinction drawn by Reid between the *sensations* and the *perceptions* of the sensible qualities really exists, how can he prove that it is of no consequence for men to express it in words? Or that the confusion of the two things cannot cause them any inconvenience? On the contrary, this confusion would lead to endless ambiguities; for as often as anyone happened to speak of what we suffer in our sensations, he could be understood as speaking of external bodies instead, and *vice versâ* : and this would evidently be a great hindrance

to our understanding one another and to the mutual interchange of ideas.

In Galluppi's system another reason is given for the employment of one and the same word to signify two ideas. Galluppi maintains, that every sensation is of its own nature *objective*; and hence that we do not pass, from the *sensation* to the thought of the *sensible quality* corresponding to it in the external body, by a leap, or, as Reid puts it, by a quasi-inspiration of nature. But while discarding this arbitrary passage, he would have us believe that there is an essential connection between the *sensation* and the *sensible quality*, so that the two are in reality indivisible, form one thing only—namely, that which he calls *objective sensation*. This theory is very ingenious, and would account for the application of the same term to the two things—*sensation* and *sensible quality*; or rather, that word would express but one only thing, and there would be but one only thing in nature, which we, through analysis and abstraction, would afterwards divide and decompose into two.

I will, however, make bold to say that Galluppi, in consequence of admitting, like Reid, the ambiguity of the words in question, has not been able to maintain all that propriety of expression which might have made him consistent with himself. 'This difficulty,' he says, 'arises from the *ambiguity* of the word *taste*. That word may denote as well a sensation of the soul, as the *object* of this sensation, which object is a quality of the saporific body : it is impossible that the word, if taken as meaning "sensation," should denote an external quality when the body itself is regarded as devoid of sensitivity'(*Saggio filosofico sulla Critica della Conoscenza*, Lib. ii. ch. vi. § 113). It seems to me that, having laid it down that *sensation* is *objective* (*extrasubjective* would have been the proper term, *i.e.* containing something extraneous to the percipient subject), he could have denied that there is any ambiguity in these words, and affirmed instead that they of their nature signify that identical *sensation*, which is at once subjective and extra-subjective : whence it arises, that they

'The proximate cause of our sensations and the subject of the sensible qualities.'

can with strict propriety be applied, now to the subject and now to something extraneous to the subject.

Here I cannot help making another remark on the system of Galluppi. I admit the *extrasubjective sensation*, although, in so far as it is such, I call it *sensitive perception*. But, I think that in proposing his opinion on this matter he has gone a step further than I am able to endorse.

His whole theory is based on two propositions.

First : 'All sensations are objective,' that is, in every sensation I perceive a something external to myself, but I perceive it as intimately united with *me*, and cannot perceive it otherwise.'

Second : 'The perception of *myself* is simultaneous with the perception of the modifications which take place in me, that is, I cannot perceive *myself* as apart from my modifications (the external sensations).'

Now, of these two propositions, I admit the first, saving the word *objective*, which applies only to the understanding (a fact unnoticed by Galluppi on account of his subjectivism), and in place of which I substitute the word *extrasubjective*; that is to say, I admit that the qualities of bodies cannot be perceived by us without our having perception of *ourselves*, and that therefore there is here a fact *subjective* and *extrasubjective* at the same time.

But the second proposition I do not admit, neither does it follow necessarily from the first. On the contrary, I hold that there is in us a *fundamental sense*, which, however difficult of advertence, is by its nature perceivable.

Lastly, I would remark that that intimate union of the extraneous substance with the percipient subject, in virtue of which the two are joined in one, was seen and noted by S. Thomas. In his opinion, the body felt and the sentient organ are one thing only ; and he says that the organ stands to the body felt by it, as a *faculty* stands to its *act*. 'Corpus sensibile est nobilius organo animalis, secundum hoc quod comparatur ad ipsum, ut ens in actu ad ens in potentia ; sicut coloratum in actu ad pupillam quæ colorata est in

potentia.' 'The sensible body is nobler than the organ of the animal, inasmuch as the body stands to the organ, as a being in act stands to a potential being ; as, for instance, what is coloured in act stands to the pupil of the eye, which is coloured only potentially ' (*S.* I. lxxxiv. vi. ad *2m*). And elsewhere he says, 'That the *sensible* in act is nothing but the sense itself in act.' 'Sensibile in actu est sensus in actu ' (*C. Gent.* I. li). This, however, according to S. Thomas, is true only in the act itself of sensation ; for it is in that act that the extraneous force felt, and the sentient subject are so united as to become one thing. Hence if the sensible body and the sentient organ are considered as separated from each other, they at once become two distinct things. Here are the words of the holy Doctor : 'Sensibile in actu est sensus in actu ; secundum vero quod (*sensibile ab sensu*) distinguitur, est utrumque in potentiâ :—neque enim visus est videns actu neque visibile videtur actu nisi cum visus informatur visibili specie, ut sic EX VISIBILI ET VISU UNUM FIAT ' (*C. Gentes*, I. li). 'The sensible in act is the sense in act ; but in so far as the sensible is distinguished from the sense they are both in a potential state : —for the sense of sight does not see in act, and that which is visible is not seen in act, unless when the sense is informed by the visible species, and thus the thing visible and the sense of sight are made one.'

Undoubtedly this union between the sentient (subject) and the extraneous force is mysterious and obscure. Hence if it had been proposed forty or fifty years ago (the author wrote this in 1828. TR.), when the modern philosophy both in Italy and France was as yet in its infancy, it would probably have been scoffed at, and rejected as an absurd piece of antiquated scholasticism.

Since that time, however, modern philosophy has undergone considerable improvements both in France and Italy. Speaking of Italy, the speculations of Reid in Scotland, and those of Kant in Germany, attracted, though somewhat late in the day, the serious

And even supposing that bodies did not exist, it is always true nevertheless, that this definition expresses the

attention of philosophers, and this led up to a train of thought which resulted in awakening their minds to the utter worthlessness of the Condillachian system then dominant. The work of reflection still progressed, and with it came fresh improvements to philosophical science, among which one of the most valuable was that made by Galluppi when he proved that in sensation there is an element extraneous to the sentient subject, and which he improperly called *object.*

Now to what has this course of laborious studies, so long pursued with the intent of advancing modern philosophy, brought us at last? To a *simple fact* which our fathers had noticed six centuries before us; a fact unheeded and despised by the proud philosophy of the eighteenth century, but which now a philosophy more mature and more modest finds it necessary to admit. There are some difficult truths which repel us by their apparent severity; but this is only for a time. The moment comes when we see the absolute need we have of them, and then it is that we face the difficulty and courageously dive into it.

To say something of that difficult truth which has given occasion to this long note, namely, respecting the perfect *unity* established between the thing felt and the *sentient* subject; I would here make another observation.

That mysterious unity is found to exist, not only between things felt and the sentient subject, but also in every other action exercised by one being on another, so that one of these beings is passive and the other active. Here please to observe well the simple fact (for I do not now seek to explain it), and you will find that it takes place as follows :—

The *passion* experienced by the one being, is the *term* of the action of the other. Now that *passion*, in so far as it is passion, is in the passive being; but the same is also the *term* of the action. In so far as it is in the term of the *action*, it is in the active *being*. We cannot therefore say that the *terms* of the action are two, one outside and the other inside the agent. This would be,

not to observe the fact, but to draw upon one's imagination. The passion is the *effect* produced by the agent: now where the effect is, *there*, evidently, must the agent have *acted*; I say *there*, but not a hair's breadth beyond. The action of the agent, therefore, terminates exactly in that effect; and the term of the action is necessarily conjoined with the action itself, just as the end of a rod is in the rod. The *agent* becomes indeed detached from the effect it has produced in the *patient*; but this occurs when its action has ceased. Here we consider it in the instant when the action is taking place; and in reference to this instant we must needs say, that the identical thing which for one of these beings is *passion*, for the other is the *term* of the action : in other words, in the instant of which I speak, the self-same thing is united with and belongs to two beings —to the one under one relation, to the other under another; nor is there anything between. Such is the concept of the mutual touch, so to speak, of two beings. It is, I confess, a difficult and singular concept; but it is true, even as a *fact* is true : and the difficulties presented by a fact are no reason for dissembling, or ridiculing it, much less for denying it. On the contrary, they should incite us all the more to do our best to verify it, ascertain its exact nature, and probe it to the bottom.

Returning in particular to the fact of sensation, which Galluppi finds to be composed of two elements, the one *subjective* and the other *objective* (*extrasubjective*), I cannot refrain from drawing attention to the sense in which I admit the fusion of these two elements into a single fact.

For this end, I would ask the reader to peruse again what I have written in the notes on n. 453.

I have there shown, that a sensation can, through mental *abstraction*, be decomposed into the two elements, *subjective* and *extrasubjective*; and that, in so far as it is *subjective*, we may appropriately reserve for it the name of *sensation*; while in so far as it is *extrasubjective*—that is to say, in so far as it is the term of the action exercised on

idea which men generally have of *body* ; and that is what we were in search of.

§ 4.

Our spirit is not body.

668. This is a corollary of the foregoing propositions.

Clearly, if what we call *body* is ' The proximate cause of our external sensations' (667) ; and if these sensations belong to that class of facts which take place in us in such a manner that we are not in any sense their cause, but only the subject which suffers them (666) ; it necessarily follows that WE (the human subject) are not body.

And since what is expressed by the monosyllable WE is a subject at once sentient and intelligent, therefore this subject is a substance entirely different from the corporeal.

669. It is by this process of reasoning that we come to form the distinct *idea* of the human subject, wholly incorporeal, and then denominate it *spirit.*

ARTICLE IX.

Simplicity of our spirit.

670. I have proved that our *spirit* is a thing entirely different from *body*—in other words, is incorporeal—from the difference, nay contrariety, existing between a being which suffers a sensation, and a being which causes that sensation.

671. Nevertheless, in confirmation of what I have said, I will add other evidences of the same truth, quoting them in the words of an Italian Philosopher now living (A.D. 1828. TR.). He writes thus :—

' I feel the *outside of Me* as a manifold.' Each part of

us by an external agent—the appellation of *sensitive perception* seems well adapted to express it.

From all this, however, it will be clearly seen that the *extrasubjective sensation*, as admitted by me, must never be confounded either with the *intellectual perception* or the *idea* of bodies. This, in very deed, is formed, not by the sense alone, but by the understanding in virtue of its possession of the idea of *being in general.*

Lastly I will observe, that the

words *smell, taste, sound,* &c., signify principally the *subjective* element, while the names of the *primary qualities* of bodies, such as *extension*, refer directly to the *extrasubjective* element. But of all this I shall have occasion to speak more fully later on.

' That we feel a manifold outside of us, is a fact, although one should not place the nature of body in *multiplicity*. I have not as yet made out nor examined in what this nature consists.

this manifold is felt by me as distinct from the others, and the modifications of one part are not, in my feeling, the modifications of the other parts. The trunk of a tree is distinct from the branches : each branch is distinct from every other : one branch may move while another branch, and indeed the whole tree, stands still. Such is the feeling I have of the *outside of Me.'*

'But let us see what sort of feeling is that of the *Me*, who perceives the *outside of Me.* The consciousness I have that I am reasoning is the perception of the *Me* who reasons : [1] the perception of the *Me* who reasons is the perception of the *Me* who says *therefore*; the perception of the *Me* who says *therefore* is the perception of the *Me* who judges in the inferences and in the premisses ; consequently, the *Ego* perceived or felt by the consciousness I have that I am reasoning, is the self-same *Ego* in each of the three judgments of which the reasoning (a syllogism. TR.) is composed. The *Ego* therefore who reasons is the same *Ego* in the feeling, as is the one who judges. But the *Ego* who judges is the *Ego* who says, *it is* or *it is not* ; therefore the same *Ego* perceives both the subject and the predicate of the judgment. The *Ego*, therefore, is but one in the notion, in the judgment, and in the reasoning.'

'The subject of a judgment may be physically composite, and logically one. For instance, when I say : "All the radii of a circle are equal," the subject of my judgment is physically composite, because the circle is a *manifold* ;[2] but it has a logical unity, because the subject of this judgment is one, and the act of thought which judges must embrace the whole circle ; it is therefore the thought that gives unity to the circle ; this unity springing from the act of thought, I call *synthetical unity*, that is, unity effected by synthesis. Consciousness therefore perceives the *synthetical unity.* But

---

[1] The *consciousness* I have that I am *reasoning* is not precisely the *perception of the Me who reasons* ; but the perception of the *Me* who reasons includes the consciousness of the reasoning as part of it.

[2] It is manifold potentially, that is, it can be distinguished into parts. But if instead of a *mathematical*, we mean a *physical* circle, Galluppi's reasoning is perfectly correct.

to perceive the *synthetical unity*, is to perceive the *Me* who *forms the synthesis* ;[1] to perceive the *Me* who *forms the synthesis* is to perceive the *Me* who joins into one the various perceptions I have of the logical subject.[2] Therefore the *Ego* felt in the synthetical unity of the perception is *one*, notwithstanding the variety of the perceptions to which it gives unity. Therefore the *Ego* who begins a reasoning, a demonstration, any science whatever, is the identical *Ego* who brings it to a close.'

'Let us try to make this important truth still more clear. "If," says Bayle, "a substance which thinks were one, only as a globe is one, it would never see a whole tree, or feel the pain caused by a blow from a stick."

'"Here is an easy way of convincing yourself of this. Look at the four quarters of the world as drawn on a globe; you will not see in this globe any one particular point containing all Asia, or all the kingdom of Siam, or even an entire river ; and if you cast your eyes on the part where the Euphrates is, you will notice a right side of it and a left, quite divided from each other. The obvious inference is, that if this globe were capable of knowing the figures with which it has been adorned, it would not contain anything which could say: *I know all Europe, all France, the whole city of Amsterdam, the whole course of the Vistula.* Each spot could only know the part which fell to its own share : and as this part would be far too small for representing any one place entire, so the capacity of knowing would be of no use whatever to the globe; the application of this capacity would not result in any cognition ; or at least the cognitions proceeding from it would be of a very different kind from those we have ; for our cognitions represent to us a whole tree, a whole horse, &c. ; which is an evident proof that the thinking subject, impressed by the whole image of these objects, is not divisible into many parts, and that therefore man, in so far as he is a thinking

---

[1] See above, note 1.

[2] It is true that the thinking subject *unifies* things that are manifold; but he does this, not in virtue of his own nature, but in virtue of the unity of the logical object (the *being*) in which he contemplates them. Nevertheless, this unity of the *logical object* leads us by a necessary induction to affirm the unity of the subject who contemplates it.

being, is not corporeal or material, or a compound of many
beings " (Bayle's Dictionary, art. *Leucippe*).

'The consciousness of the synthetic unity of perception
comprises, therefore, the perception of the *unity* or *simplicity*
of the *Me* who forms the synthesis.   By meditating on the
comparisons we make of the objects which act on our senses,
and on the judgments to which their impressions give rise,
the simple, indivisible, immaterial unity of the thinking being
will be seen to evidence.   When you warm your chilled hand,
you experience a certain pleasure : and if at the same time
an agreeable odour is wafted to your nostrils, you feel another
species of pleasure.   If I ask you, which of these agreeable
sensations is more to your liking, you reply in favour of one
or the other, as the case may be.   You therefore compare
these two agreeable sensations, and pronounce a judgment
upon them at the same time.   If after your having enjoyed
the feeling of warmth and of sweet fragrance, I cause you to
taste some savoury viand, you can certainly say whether or
not you prefer this latter pleasure to the others.   It is necessary, therefore, that the same principle which judges within
you should have felt all this.'

'Again, this same *Ego* who judges, knows also if a pleasure
of the senses is greater than the pleasure arising from the
discovery of a truth, or the practice of virtue, and he chooses
between the two.   Therefore, the identical *subject* who experiences the sensible pleasures, experiences also those which
are spiritual, and judges and wills.   This clearly proves, that
the consciousness of the *Me* who feels affected by all these
sensations, and then acts, is not the consciousness of your
nose that smells the fragrance, nor of your hand that feels
the warmth.   For, the nose and the hand being things entirely
distinct, it is as impossible for the one to feel the sensations
of the other, as it is, for us who are now in this room, to experience the pleasure enjoyed at this moment by those who are
at the theatre.   Therefore the consciousness you have of the
Me who at one and the same time feels the two sensations
of fragrance and of warmth, must needs be, not only the
perception of the nose or the hand, but also the perception

of a subject, one, simple, and devoid of parts ; for if he had parts, one of them would smell the fragrance, while the other would feel the warmth, and there never would be in you a thing which feels at once the odour and the warmth, compares them together, and judges that one is more pleasurable than the other.'

'The feeling, then, we have of *body* is the feeling of a manifold, a composite ; [1] the feeling we have of the *Me* is the feeling of the *one*, the *simple*, the *indivisible*. These two feelings are therefore mutually distinct. . . .'

'A science is a chain of reasonings directed to give us the most clear knowledge possible concerning any object whatever : a reasoning is a series of judgments : without the immediate synthesis of judgment, and the mediate one of reasoning, no human science would be possible. Now in reasoning the synthetical unity is necessary ; without a *therefore* there would be no reasoning, as without an *it is* or *it is not*, there would be no judgment. The *therefore* binds into a unity of thought the different parts of a reasoning, and the *it is* or *it is not*, binds into a unity of thought the different parts of a judgment. Now the consciousness of the synthetical unity of thought comprises, as we have explained, the consciousness of the unity of the thinking subject : this unity of the thinking subject, I call the *metaphysical unity of the Me*. The synthetical unity of thought, therefore, supposes necessarily the metaphysical unity of the *Me*. The first could not exist without the second. This metaphysical unity of the *Me* is the simplicity or spirituality of the thinking principle. Without this, no science would be possible, because a science supposes a unity effected between all the thoughts of which it is composed ; but since each thought is distinct from every other, how could these thoughts be linked into unity if there were no centre for them to be united in ? [2] Without a centre where would the different radii of the scientific circle meet ? A builder cannot raise his structure unless he has all the

---

[1] Or at least it is certain that there are composite bodies perceived by us ; this is enough for proving the unity of the spirit which perceives them.

[2] Nevertheless, this centre of union is also a *logical object*, the foundation and cause of the simplicity of the spirit which contemplates it.

materials necessary for it.   The *Ego* of the *Newton* who invents the *differential calculus* is the same *Ego* who had learned the numeration table.   *Without the metaphysical unity of the* Me, *there could be no synthetical unity of thought, and without the synthetical unity of thought, there could be no science for man.'* [1]

[1] Galluppi, *Elementi di Filosofia*, vol. iii. c. iii. §§ xxiv.-xxv.

CHAPTER II.

ARTICLE I.

A way to demonstrate the existence of bodies.

672. Having now shown that the sentient subject (the spirit, the *Ego*) cannot be that which we mean by the term *body* ; let us examine whether what is meant by this term really exists, or is a mere figment of the imagination. This is the same as to inquire whether the corporeal substance exists, as attested by the general sense of mankind, and whence our idea of it is derived.

If I can explain how we form the idea of *body*, and how it is, that in forming this idea we become reasonably persuaded that bodies really exist, the existence of the bodies themselves will also have been demonstrated.

But the whole force of this demonstration, drawn from the origin of our persuasion of the existence of bodies, depends on the supposition that reasoning, of which the intellectual perception is the first link, is valid for finding as well as proving the truth.

The generality of men admit this as the most certain of all things ; but there has now sprung up a school of Sceptics who attempt to call it in question.

With regard to these, I shall, in the next Section, be obliged to solve the objections that are preferred against the validity of reasoning; and that will set the seal on the demonstration which I am giving here of the real existence of bodies.

673. I have said, that the word *body* is that of 'A proximate cause of our sensations,' and 'A subject of the sensible qualities' (667).

I am therefore bound to show how we acquire a reasonable persuasion that 'A cause of our sensations external to ourselves' exists, and that 'This cause is the subject of the sensible qualities.' [1]

This can be very easily done by recalling to mind what has been said before.

ARTICLE II.

There exists a proximate cause of our sensations.

674. Our sensations suppose a cause distinct from ourselves.

Our external sensations are facts in respect of which we are passive (662–666).

Passive facts are actions which take place in us, but of which we are not the cause (Ibid.)

But, by the principle of causation (567–569), the actions which take place in us, but of which we are not the cause, suppose a cause distinct from ourselves.

Therefore our sensations suppose a cause distinct from ourselves ; which was the thing to be demonstrated.

ARTICLE III.

The cause distinct from ourselves is a substance.

675. Our sensations, then, suppose a cause distinct from ourselves (674).

But we have seen that a cause is always a substance (620, &c.)

Therefore the cause of our sensations is a substance.

ARTICLE IV.

The substance which causes our sensations, is immediately conjoined with them.

676. Our sensations are actions which take place in us, but of which we are not the cause (662–666).

---

[1] These definitions are based, as I said before, on the meaning which common usage attaches to the term *body.*

To experience in ourselves an action of which we are not the cause, is the same as to experience a force which has the power of producing a modification in us.

This force is a substance which acts and is called *body* (667).

Therefore the action which we experience from a body, is the effect, not of a particular power of that body, but of the body itself; and this in virtue of the definition. For, *body* is precisely that which acts on us in such a manner as to produce sensations in us; and we do not recognise any other co-ordinate powers in the agent designated by this word.

Now the action of a substance is always intimately conjoined with that substance, because the force or energy of a being is inseparable from the being itself.

Therefore the substance which causes our sensations is immediately conjoined with them.[1]

ARTICLE V.

The cause of our sensations is a limited being.

677. The energy or force which produces our sensations, and which we experience in ourselves, is limited; because the action it exercises on us is limited.

Now it is from this very energy or force that we derive the idea of corporeal substance; or, which comes to the same, it is in that energy or force, and nothing else, that we perceive the being distinct from us, and productive of our sensations.

Hence, as that energy whose action we experience in us, is limited; so is the being in which we conceive it; for, to us, this being is nothing but that same energy conceived as existent.

Therefore the being conceived by us as a substance and the proximate cause of our sensations, is limited.

ARTICLE VI.

We give names to things according as our mind conceives them.

678. This proposition is self-evident.

[1] For the better understanding this, see the note under 667.

We can only name the things we know, and in so far as we know them.

Rule to be observed in the use of words, in order to avoid error.

679. Words, then, express things just as the mind conceives them (678).

Therefore that which is expressed by any given word, is limited by our knowledge.

Consequently, if we attempt to use words in a more extended sense, to make them signify, not simply what our mind conceives in a being, but that also which *might* be in it, but of which we have neither perception nor knowledge of any sort, we shall be guilty of an abuse of language; and the reasonings founded thereon will be full of ambiguities, sophistical and misleading.

Bodies are limited beings.

680. To define *body*, is the same as to state what that is to which the name of *body* has been given.

In order, therefore, to define the meaning of this word, we may proceed in two ways, that is, either by analysing all the ideas which enter into that meaning, or by indicating only some one of them, but this so characteristically proper, that we cannot fail, by taking it as our guide, to identify the being which the word designates.

Now for our present purpose, it is sufficient to explain the word *body* in the second of these ways; later on we shall define it more fully and circumstantially.

We have seen, (1) that our idea of body is formed from the effect which bodies produce in us by their action, namely, from the force or energy we experience in our sensations (640–643);

(2) That, this energy being limited, we can obtain from it the idea of a limited being only (677); and

(3) That therefore all the knowledge we have of *body* is that of a limited being.

But words express things just as we perceive and know them (678).

Therefore the word *body* was invented to signify a limited being : and it would be an abuse of language to employ it in any other sense (679).

ARTICLE IX.

The proximate cause of our sensations is not God.

681. The proximate cause of our sensations is a body (667) ;

A body is a limited being (680) ;

God is not a limited being ;

Therefore God is not the proximate cause of our sensations.

ARTICLE X.

Bodies exist, and cannot be confounded with God.

682. The proximate cause of our sensations is an existent substance.

This substance is called *body*, and is not God (681).

Therefore bodies exist, and cannot be confounded with God.

ARTICLE XI.

Refutation of the Idealism of Berkeley.

683. The above demonstration of the existence of bodies is against Berkeley.

The sophism of this writer began in a falsification of the idea signified by the word *body*.

When once this idea is thoroughly grasped, there is no possibility of its being confounded with that of God ; for it is the idea of a thing altogether limited, namely, of that force which we feel acting on us in our sensations, and conceive as existent in itself.

In thinking this force experienced in us, all that our mind supplies is *existence* (623) ; nor has it any right to add more ; consequently, the force remains limited as it was before it became an object of our thought.

684. To confute the Idealism of Berkeley, this demonstra-

tion of the existence of bodies is enough. We may sum it up in the following series of propositions :—

(1) All that takes place in our sensitivity falls under the name of *fact*.

(2) In the *corporeal* sensations and feelings (I call them by the word *corporeal* in order to determine them ; let this word be taken for the present as an arbitrary sign), we experience in our sensitivity an action not caused by ourselves, but by an energy or force different from us.

(3) This energy or force felt by us, when intellectually conceived, is the idea of a being ; in other words, the mind conceives that energy as really existent ; and this in virtue of a necessary principle, that of substance (583, &c.).

(4) This energy is real as well as limited, and therefore the being conceived is also real and limited ; for that being is neither more nor less than this same energy considered precisely in that determinate existence which we conceive it to possess.

(5) Much less can this limited being which differs from the sentient subject (the *Ego*) and is called *body*, be GOD ; for GOD is only conceived by us as a Being every way Infinite.

(6) Therefore bodies, limited substances, the proximate causes of our sensations, exist.

All these propositions seem to me incontrovertible, and, as I fully believe, are endorsed by the common sense of mankind.

685. And here it may not be amiss to point out more clearly, how it happened, that the individual sense of Berkeley, leaving the beaten track of the general sense of mankind, wandered away into the path of error.

For this end let us carry our thought back to the time when Berkeley lived. Locke had placed the sources of human ideas in *sensation* and *reflection* ; but he had not understood the nature of the second of these faculties and had so described it that it could easily be confounded with the first.[1]

---

[1] S. Thomas, on the contrary, who is so unjustly classed with the modern Sensists, took the greatest pains to distinguish the faculty of *reflection* from that of *sensation*. He denied to the sense all power of reflecting on itself,

He himself declared it incapable of giving us the idea of substance.

Hence in England and in France the first step taken by Locke's philosophy was to suppress the faculty of *reflection*, and to reduce the origin of all ideas to the sense alone.[1]

and assigned this power exclusively to the intellect; thus distinguishing the two faculties in such a manner that it was thenceforth impossible to confuse them. ' Nullus sensus,' he says, ' seipsum cognoscit, nec suam operationem; visus enim non videt seipsum, nec videt se videre, sed hoc superioris potentiæ est. Intellectus autem cognoscit seipsum, et cognoscit se intelligere: Non est igitur idem intellectus et sensus.' ' No sense knows itself, nor its own operation; for the sight does not see itself, nor see that it sees: but to do this belongs to a higher kind of faculty. The intellect on the contrary knows itself and knows that it knows. Therefore intellect and sense are not the same thing' (*Cont. Gent.* II. lxvi.).

This doctrine, which S. Thomas took from Aristotle (*De Anima*, L. iii.), confirms the interpretation I have given (note 2, n. 246) of that *judgment* which Aristotle improperly attributes to the *sense*. For if the sense cannot reflect on itself, much less can it, speaking properly, *judge* of what it feels. Locke, however, assigned in some way a distinct place to reflection, although on the other hand he was inconsistent; for while denying in one place that we know anything whatever about substance, in others he felt obliged to admit that we have an obscure notion of it. But the adherents of his system who came after him confused everything, and attempted to identify reflection with sensation. Gallini, Professor of Physiology in the University of Padua, appears not to have recognised, between direct and reflex ideas, any other difference than a less degree of intensity in the attention we give to the impressions made on our sensories. To this alone does he ascribe the comparative clearness or obscurity of our ideas; not perceiving that the act of *reflection* is quite different from, and therefore not to be confused with that of *direct attention*; even as the *direct attention* of the mind is essentially different from *sensi-*

tive or *instinctive tension* (see *Considerazioni filosofiche sul Senso del Bello*, &c., by the Dottore Stefano Gallini, inserted in *Esercitazioni dell' Ateneo di Venezia*, vol. i.).

[1] Let an error, however small and as it were imperceptible, find its way into the fundamental principles of a philosophical system, and time will infallibly develop it. From that germ all sorts of errors will spring up, even such as are contrary to one another, and will steadily go on increasing until they reach proportions so gigantic as to inspire a horror of the system which has produced them. Then, in the light of those consequences, the baneful little seed being detected and extracted, the system will gradually be healed, and philosophy put on the way to perfection. The history of Lockism confirms this remark.

Locke did not place the existence of the faculty of reflection on a sure basis, owing to the vagueness of his description of it; and this was the little defect of his system.

But it sufficed to cause this vague faculty to be expunged, and the origin of all cognitions reduced to the more positive faculty of *sensation*. This change seemed at first of no consequence, in fact a step demanded by the nature of the system itself. What was the result? A complete revolution; a new system. For, Locke in admitting in a manner the faculty of reflection, was starting from an interior testimony: this being banished, and sensation alone retained, all philosophy was made to begin with external facts, and to end in them. Condillac, therefore, did not know what he was about when reducing philosophy to sensation alone. He fancied himself to be the interpreter of Locke, while in truth he was unconsciously changing the whole character and nature of his system.

At the present day, when the doctrines of Locke and Condillac have had full time to be leisurely compared

But if sensation is the only source of ideas, substance must be an illusion. This consequence was drawn by Hume in all its generality; Berkeley confined his attention to corporeal substances.

But what sort of idea could Berkeley have of bodies, when the senses were all he thought of in this connection?

Here is his definition of bodies: 'Sensible things are together, and the philosophical world is gradually being cured of that pitiable shortsightedness with which it seemed thirty or forty years ago to be affected, the gap which divides these two authors is fully seen.

In the Parisian journal *Le Globe*, 3 January 1829, we read: 'It is only necessary to compare the first pages of the *Traité des Sensations* with the beginning of the second book of the *Essay on the Human Understanding*, to be convinced of the singular illusion of Condillac in supposing himself to be a disciple of Locke. It is true that in both those treatises we often meet with the same formulas; but neither Locke in spite of his good sense, nor Condillac in spite of his love of perspicuity, has been rightly understood. Their standpoints are entirely different. Locke shuts himself up within himself, and lets images come to him from the external world; Condillac places himself externally by the side of his Statue, and composes for it a soul by means of the sensations which he successively imparts to it. What is a certainty to Locke, what he considers as so past all discussion that it need not even be spoken of, is the *Ego*. What is indubitable for Condillac, what he assumes as a thing altogether beyond the region of controversy, is the external world. The one is wholly occupied in finding out how the *Ego* comes to know the external world; the whole aim of the other is to discover how the external world, by acting on the sensorial organs, develops in the *Statue* what he calls the *phenomena of understanding and will*. Locke solves his question by declaring that we know the external world solely by means of *the ideas* of it, which are transmitted to us by the senses; Con-

dillac, in solving his question, protests that all that is in the *statue* is merely *transformed sensation!* The one is always *inside*, and the other always *outside*. Thus did they begin, and thus do they continue. Locke will not consent to go *out* in order to see bodies, he insists absolutely on finding them in the interior fact of ideas; Condillac will not consent to go *in* in order to observe the phenomena of the soul; he is determined at all costs to deduce these phenomena from the external fact of sensation.'

The defect of Locke's system suggested to Condillac the idea of remedying that defect in the manner, which, as we have seen, meant the total overthrow of the system itself. And here it may be noted, that a clear proof that Locke's teaching tended to dispose men's minds to reduce all ideas to sensation alone, is found in the fact that, simultaneously and without any mutual understanding, the sensuous philosophy appeared in England and France.

Nevertheless, having agreed thus far, the thinkers of the two countries soon parted company, and took to entirely different roads.

In France, *Sensism* became the *Materialism* of Cabanis and Destütt Tracy; in England it developed itself into the *Idealisms* of Berkeley and Hume.

But how could systems so opposite be deduced from one and the same principle?

For the reason I have already stated, namely, that one error is apt to engender others, and those of a most contrary nature.

In fact, from the moment that all the human faculties are reduced to the corporeal sense, man is nothing more than a corporeal faculty, because, to have sensations, a sensitive body is indispensable. This view once adopted,

nothing else but so many qualities, or combinations of sensible qualities.'[1]

With such a definition as this, and considering moreover that to his mind a *sensible quality* meant a *sensation*, it is clear that he could have no difficulty in proving that 'Sensible things are nothing but modifications of our sensitivity'; because this is certainly the case with our sensations.

Berkeley's Idealism, therefore, denied corporeal substances, because it started from a philosophy which, having divested man of the intellectual faculty and left him with nothing but the senses, had taken from him the only power by which substances can be perceived. If we take note of this fact, we shall see that it was not the Idealism of Berkeley that involved Hume's Scepticism, but that one and the same principle contemporaneously produced both these erroneous systems. And if Berkeley still admitted the existence of substances other than the corporeal, this was a remnant of that traditional good sense which cannot be wholly destroyed in a moment.

Nevertheless, *substances* as well as *causes* must have been preserved in the mind of Berkeley as isolated things, like those prejudices which we entertain without any proof or any connection with our other principles, for in his theory they were absolutely inexplicable.

Be this as it may, Berkeley denied the substance of bodies ; but at the same time he knew, by the principle of causation, that sensations could not be produced in us by nothing : he therefore attributed their production to God Himself. Now, in philosophy, substance and cause stand in precisely the same condition, and that is why I said that this was an inconsistency in the Irish philosopher.

686. The error of Berkeley, then, lay in ignoring the

---

it is very easy to pass to the belief that the body is the sole cause of that faculty which perishes with it : and this is pure Materialism.

Now take the thing from another point of view. Sensations exist only in the sentient subject ; if, then, there is nothing but sensation, there is nothing outside the sentient subject : and this is pure Idealism. Hence Galluppi has, with his usual ability, proved that even the Transcendental Idealism of Kant could be distinctly traced to the Sensism of Condillac (see the fourth of the *Lettere filosofiche del Barone Galluppi*. Messina, 1827).

[1] *Hylas and Philonous*, Dial. I.— Condillac gives a similar definition.

proximate cause of the sensations, and going direct to the *First Cause.*

Undoubtedly, God is, in the end, the First Cause of all that is and of all that happens, and consequently also of sensations; but the word *body* was not invented to signify this First Cause, and the philosopher's business is to discover, not the First, but the proximate cause of our sensations.

By confining our inquiry to this particular philosophical question, we arrive at the two results indicated above : (1) that bodies exist, (2) that bodies are the proximate cause of our sensations. This will receive further light from what I shall say in the following article.

ARTICLE XII.

Reflexions on the above demonstration of the existence of bodies.

687. To know if corporeal substances exist, we must first recall to mind the definition of substance.

Substance, I have said, is 'that which our mind sees before it in its first concept of any being.'[1]

On this definition, we may make the following observations.

(1) For a thing to be a substance it is not necessary that it should exist independently of everything else. Were this to be the case, there would be no created substances at all; for these can only exist dependently on the First Cause. A thing is entitled to the name of substance, provided that our mind can conceive it by itself alone. Not that the thing could, in point of fact, exist independently of its First Cause ; but when made to exist, it has a certain existence of its own, and this suffices to render it thinkable by itself, without the necessity of any other element entering into its *first concept.*

(2) It follows from this, that a thing may be legitimately

---

[1] This character of substance is relative to our mind, but it is founded in the nature of the thing conceived. My other definition has reference to the thing itself, namely, 'Substance is that in virtue of which a being is what it is,' or 'Substance is the abstract specific essence considered in the being relatively to its full specific essence.'

called a *substance*, although it be not such, that in reflecting upon it we cannot demonstratively prove the impossibility of its existing, or comprehend it fully without having recourse to the knowledge of something else, *e. gr.* of its cause. Undoubtedly, as I have said, no finite thing can be fully comprehended without the knowledge of its First Cause. But this is no hindrance to its being called a ' substance '; because we can form a ' first concept ' of it, see it by itself alone the very first time that our mind looks at it, without our being at all obliged to think of anything beyond it. In a word, its first concept is independent of every other concept ; it stands before us as, so to speak, an incommunicable essence, and mentally distinct from all others.

I have already observed, that if we give the word *substance* a more extensive meaning than is attached to it by common usage, we open the way to false reasonings and innumerable errors.

688. Bodies are, therefore, substances, because so soon as our mind begins to turn its attention to them, it can conceive them by themselves alone, quite irrespectively of our soul, or of God, or of anything else.

Accidents, on the contrary, are not substances because we cannot with our first concept think them by themselves alone, but can only conceive them after conceiving another thing conjoined with them, that is, a being in which they exist and to which they belong. Now, this is not the case with bodies, for the perception of them, as we have seen, terminates in them and calls for nothing else (515, 516).

689. The defect of Berkeley's theory, therefore, arose from a defective analysis of sensation, that is, from not distinguishing between the two elements thereof—(1) the force which acts upon us (in respect of which we are passive), and is of the same kind in all sensations ; (2) the various terms and effects of that force, I mean the various sensations it causes in us.

Both these things—the *force* and its *various effects*—are felt or experienced by us ; but with this difference, that while the force is felt to be the same in all the sensations alike, the effects are felt to be various, according to the different media and organs in and through which it acts on us.

Now since the variety of the terms and effects (the sensations in so far as they differ from one another) cannot be intellectually conceived without the force which produces them ; and since (by the *principle of cognition*, 536, 483–485) that force is not thinkable without the being which puts it forth ; it is clear that we have already arrived at ' substance,' because to say ' that which constitutes a being ' is the same as saying ' a substance.'

690. To sum up, therefore, in a few words all that I have said concerning the origin of our ideas of bodies :—

(1) We acquire the perception of bodies through that act whereby we judge that they subsist (528).

(2) By analysing this *perception*, we find that it is composed of two elements, viz. :

(*a*) A judgment on the subsistence of the particular body, and

(*b*) The idea of that body.

(3) By analysing this *idea*, we find that it consists of three elements, viz. :

(*a*) The *idea of existence*, because we cannot intellectually conceive anything, and therefore bodies, except by thinking their existence, thinking them as beings.

(*b*) The *primary determination* of the idea of existence, or that determination which is necessary to constitute the *essence* (abstract specific, 651) of what is called *body*, and without which therefore the idea of bodies would be impossible. This determination lies in that force or energy which is equally at work in all our sensations.

(*c*) The *secondary determinations*, or the sensible qualities, which are so many powers, into which that one force resolves itself, of producing different kinds of sensations in us.

(4) The way in which these three elements comprised in the idea of *body* come to be in our mind, is as follows :—

(*a*) The idea of existence is in us by nature.

(*b*) The force or energy which acts in us and produces

our various sensations, if considered apart from the variety of the sensations, is a mental abstraction (*abstract specific essence,* 651) ; but in so far as it acts in us, it becomes known through our consciousness ; and might therefore be termed a *common sensorium,* in this sense, that it bears witness to the fact of our being passive in every sensation alike.

(*c*) Lastly, the sensations are supplied to us by the external organs of sense.

We have, therefore, in us all the faculties that are neces- sary for explaining the origin of the perception as well as of the idea of *body* ; because we have, (1) the intellect or faculty of the abiding intuition of *existence* (first element of the idea of body) ; (2) the faculty (*common sensorium*) which perceives a *force* acting in us, but different from us, and which there- fore constitutes the essence called *body* (second element) ; (3) the five external sensories, which receive the *sensations* (third element) ; (4) lastly, the faculty of the *primitive synthesis,* or judgment by which we affirm that what we conceive in the idea of *body,* subsists.

691. Having thus pointed out the faculties which put us in possession of the several elements of which our intellectual perception of bodies is composed, we must now explain how we join these elements together.

In the first place, the sensations, in so far as they are various, and the force which acts in us, are linked together of their own nature, so much so that in order to conceive this force apart from its particular term, *i.e.* from this or that sensation, we must make use of abstraction : neither can the energy be felt by itself alone without the sensation, for it is the sensation itself considered in its general concept of an action done *in* but not *by* us ; whereas the same sensa- tion viewed in its entirety as it stands in our sense, namely as the feeling of a *determinate action,* is what I have else- where designated as *coporeal sensitive perception.*

Now we join the coporeal sensitive perception with the idea of existence or being in general, by virtue of the principle of cognition which involves the principle of substance.   This we do in the first instance through the same act whereby we judge that the body subsists, namely, through the intellectual perception of that body ; which perception, to state it briefly, takes place as follows :—

We are intelligent by nature.

As such, given that this or that thing acts in us, we perceive it as it is, viz. as a being.

The corporeal force which responds to the essence of bodies, acts in us :[1] therefore we perceive it as subsistent ; and this is the intellectual perception of bodies.

The formation of our ideas of bodies generally being thus explained, it remains that we also explain in particular how we perceive, first, our own body, and then the bodies outside of us.

---

[1] For this reason the feeling we experience of bodies is a substantial feeling, that is to say, we feel an immediate action of the bodies themselves on us ; hence to the first cognition we acquire of bodies the name of *perception* is appropriately given.

CHAPTER III.

ORIGIN OF THE IDEA OF OUR OWN BODY AS DIS-
TINGUISHED FROM EXTERNAL BODIES, BY MEANS OF
THE FUNDAMENTAL FEELING (SENTIMENTO FONDA-
MENTALE).

692. Bodies exist: they are substances different from
God and from us: they produce, as proximate cause, our
sensations: their essence consists in a certain *energy* which
acts on us and in respect of which we are passive ; an energy
different from our own constitutes a different existence :
Berkeley is therefore wrong in denying corporeal substances
(672, 686).

But men do not regard bodies merely as substances which
cause corporeal sensations. They attribute to them other
qualities also, namely, extension, form, solidity, mobility, divisibility, in short, all the physical and chemical properties
which bodies exhibit in relation to one another and in relation
to us ; but particularly, on the one hand, the aptitude to be
informed with life when a body is suitably united with a spirit
(668, 669), and, on the other, the aptitude to undergo those
modifications which tend to dissolve that union, *i.e.* to cause
death, or else those modifications which give us pleasure,
pain, perceptions of colour, taste, sound, &c. It becomes
therefore my duty to explain also how a body comes to be
known as the *subject* of all these properties and aptitudes ;
and this, if I succeed in it, will involve the explanation of how
we form the ideas of the various qualities which are generally
ascribed to bodies.

Here the reader already sees how from the purely intellectual order I find myself brought down to physical nature,
and what a vast field of inquiry is thereby opened up, since

I must now treat of life, of our corporeal fundamental feeling, and of the various kinds of sensations arising therefrom, in order thus to complete the doctrine concerning the ideas of matter and body.

ARTICLE I.

First classification of the qualities we observe in bodies.

693. Bodies have a physical relation with one another and with our spirit; and the facts which constitute and determine these two relations are known by observation.

As regards the physical relation of bodies with one another, observation tells us that when bodies are found respectively in certain positions, various changes take place in them according to uniform laws. This aptitude to undergo modifications or changes corresponding to the respective positions, constitutes what are called the *mechanical, physical,* and *chemical* properties of bodies.

It might be asked whether these mechanical, physical, and chemical properties—impulsion, attraction, affinity, &c.—are real forces belonging to the bodies themselves, so that the bodies must be considered as the true causes of all the modifications to which they are subject.

But this question I forbear discussing, as it is foreign to my present argument, and merely allude to it, lest the reader by having his mind preoccupied therewith, should turn aside from the main point now in hand. We do not here seek to know whether impulsion, attraction, cohesion, affinity, &c., be or be not true forces, but we seek to know *what are the true facts* as found by means of a vigilant observation.[1]

694. All these facts may be reduced to the following formula: 'When bodies are placed in certain positions relative to one another, certain *changes* take place in them which, given the same bodies and the same relative positions, are uniformly the same.'[2]

[1] Nevertheless, what I am about to say will throw light on this question also.

[2] Should there enter any new condition of such a nature as to change the uniformity of the result, that condition could only consist in an alteration in the relative position of the *bodies*; but this is excluded by the terms of the formula. I assume likewise that there is no action of spiritual substances intervening, and that the bodies are

How then are our ideas of these *changes* formed ? What ideas do they present to our mind ?

I answer: every change, mechanical, physical, or chemical, which happens in bodies owing to their being placed in certain positions relative to one another, is only conceived by us as consisting, (1) either in the body, which is the subject of the change, having acquired an aptitude to act on us in a new way, *i.e.* to cause in us interior or exterior sensations different from those which it caused before; or (2) in. its having acquired an aptitude to modify differently another body (which modification ultimately reduces itself to the different aptitude of the body so modified to act on ourselves).

When a body has changed colour, taste, hardness, extension, force, in short, any of its sensible qualities, this simply means that, relatively to us, the aptitude it had to produce in us certain sensations has been exchanged for that of producing sensations of another kind.

But when a body, without changing its sensible qualities, happens either to receive some new property or aptitude, or to lose some of those it had, how can we become cognisant of this new fact? Again, only by means of our senses. For if in a body there could be a change of such a nature as neither immediately nor mediately to fall under our senses, we could neither perceive it with them, nor think nor imagine nor affirm it.[1]

Keeping, therefore, simply to what observation tells us, we are bound to say that no changes which happen in a body can be anything relatively to us unless they be such as to fall in some way under our senses, that is, produce some effect, some action on them. The only difference to be found in these changes, consists in this, that some of them

---

considered alone in their mutual relations.

[1] If the change were reported to us by others, either it would be something of which we have already had sensible experience, and in such case we should have, together with faith in the word of the narrator, a positive knowledge of it ; or else it would be something of which we never had sensible experience, and then we could have nothing but a belief that a certain *change* had taken place, and our knowledge of this change would be purely negative.

may fall under our senses immediately, and others only mediately.

If a body in presence of another body changes colour, as for instance grass and foliage are made to look green when exposed to the action of the light, that body has undergone a change which reveals itself immediately to our senses.

If we magnetise a needle, the change that has taken place in it does not fall immediately under our senses, because neither by touch nor sight can we discover in it any difference ; and even if we could, we should not be able to divine from that difference the property which the needle has acquired of pointing to the north or of attracting iron. We only discover these properties by witnessing their effects. Now to witness those effects, to see the needle turn to the north or attract to itself a quantity of iron filings, is simply to receive a certain series of sensations, which we did not receive from it while yet unmagnetised. It can therefore be said with truth, that, relatively to us, the magnetic virtue newly acquired by that needle reduces itself ultimately to certain aptitudes to produce new sensations in us. And this applies also to every kind of action exercised by one body on another. For, even supposing that in a given series of bodies acting the one on the other, each of them successively underwent a change, all these changes would ultimately be nothing but so many aptitudes to act on ourselves. Let us assume that only the last of these bodies acts directly on us. This alone will suffice to make us know the changes which have occurred in the rest. To see how this is, we will designate these bodies by the letters A. B. C. D. E. F. Z.

The change undergone by Z, and which, as we have supposed, causes it to act on us in a new kind of way, might be defined as follows : 'This change consists in Z having lost the aptitude to produce in us one series of sensations, and acquired the aptitude to produce another series.'

How, on the other hand, should we define the change undergone by F? We could only define it thus : 'The change of F consists in having acquired the aptitude to cause the change described in Z.' The change of Z is known to us by what we experience with our senses; but the change of F is known to us only through the change of Z, so that if, in the definition of the change which has taken place in F, we should wish to substitute the known value of that which has occurred in Z, our formula would be somewhat cumbersome, yet, as I think, the only one available, namely: 'The change of F consists in having acquired the aptitude to cause in Z such a change as took away from Z the aptitude to produce one series of sensations, and gave it the aptitude to produce another series.'

In a similar way, we could not define the change of E except by referring to that of F, and so in due succession with all the other changes back to that of A.

Now, of all these changes, that of Z is the only one known to us by its immediate self: the others are known only mediately, that is, as causes, first, second, third, &c., of that one ; so that whatever we can know respecting the properties which bodies have of modifying one another, resolves itself into the aptitude they have acquired to modify us. By knowing the modification actually felt by us, we know the aptitude which produces it ; and the knowledge of this aptitude leads us to infer the causes which have, more or less remotely, produced it.[1]

It is clear from all this that, so far as observation (our only guide here) deposes, all the mechanical, physical and chemical qualities or properties which constitute the relation of bodies with one another, are, in ultimate analysis, nothing but powers to modify us, to produce sensations in us ;[2] since all the ideas which we have, or can have of these qualities or properties are, in ultimate analysis, reduced to different impressions which bodies make on us, and to the different sensations they cause in us by those impressions ; for we do not

---

[1] This our knowledge of the corporeal aptitudes or forces, derived from the experience we have of their action on us, is the *first* knowledge we can have of them ; but it does not follow that we may not, by subsequently reasoning on this same knowledge, deduce other truths concerning bodies.

All I mean to say is, that the *first* or experimental knowledge is the *basis* of all the reasonings we afterwards make respecting corporeal qualities.

[2] This does not take away from the sensations that *extra-subjectivity* which I have already spoken of, and shall explain more fully in due course.

conceive in bodies any powers, mechanical, physical or chemical, except such as modify us, or else modify and change other powers of a similar nature.

Consequently, the great point in the question now engaging our attention is, to examine well the relation which bodies have with ourselves. For if the origin of the ideas of the sensible qualities revealed by this relation is explained, the origin of the ideas of the other sensible qualities is also explained ; because, to say it once more, the latter qualities are all referable to the former.

ARTICLE II.

Classification of the corporeal qualities which constitute the immediate relation of bodies with our spirit.

695. In describing the relation of bodies with one another, I have not entered on difficult questions ; I have kept purely and simply to *facts*. In coming now to speak of the relation which bodies have with us, ·I purpose to follow the same rule, not to exceed by never so little the limits of observation. I beg the reader to take note of this, lest he might expect to find in my argument that which is advisedly excluded from it.

In this part, however, observation takes me further than it did in respect of the relation of bodies with one another. Here, we ourselves are one of the terms of the relation in question ; and as regards ourselves our observation can go deeper, since the facts which take place within us are testified to us by consciousness. Hence, if simple observation was unable to tell us whether bodies are the true causes of those modifications which, given certain relative positions, are seen to take place in them, it can, on the contrary, enable us to discern between those actions which are our own and those which are not so.

696. The relation, then, of bodies with us, as made known by observation, is of three distinct kinds, namely—

First : an intimate conjunction of our sensitive principle

with a body which becomes its term (matter); and this forms what I call *life*.[1]

Second : a *fundamental feeling*[2] which springs from that first conjunction, that is, from life, and by which we habitually feel all the sensitive parts of our body.[3]

Third : the aptitude which the sensitive parts of our body have of being modified in certain ways, to which correspond in us various kinds of external sensations, and in these the perception of bodies external to our own.

697. Now the connexion or relation of external bodies with us, according to the idea we have of it, consists precisely in their aptitude to modify the sensitive parts of our body, and hence to produce in us a variety of sensations.

ARTICLE III.

Distinction between life and the fundamental feeling.

698. First of all I must make clear the things I have just said : then I must prove them.

To make them clear, I shall begin by fixing with precision the difference between *life* and that habitual and fundamental *feeling* which springs from it.

I have said that life consists in an intimate conjunction, unique of its kind, of spirit with matter, in virtue of which conjunction matter becomes the permanent term of the

---

[1] I mean *animal life*.

[2] The reader will find later on the proofs of what I here assert.

[3] It is generally admitted that our body is composed of sensitive and insensitive parts. I hold that the nerves are the sensitive parts. The experiments made by Albert Haller in Germany, and repeated and confirmed by Leopoldo Caldani in Italy, are well known. These able physicists, sinking their natural feelings in the desire to benefit mankind, subjected to very painful anatomical operations a great number of living animals, in order to ascertain which parts of the animal body were sensitive and which were not. Subsequently, other physicists introduced such expressions as *vital contractility*, *vital force*, &c., in their attempts to establish the belief that in all parts of the body there is, together with life, a certain *latent* sensitivity. But Michele Araldi, referring to Haller's distinction between the sensitive parts, says : 'Whoever does not hold fast to this distinction, but listens instead to the vain systems that are abroad, will find himself involved in darkness and will fall inevitably into many errors ' (See *Saggio di un' errata di cui sembrano bisognosi alcuni libri elementari delle naturali scienze*, &c., Milano, Stamperia Reale, 1812, p. 53).

I cannot enter into this question at present. It suffices for me, that the nerves, when stimulated in a certain way, show unmistakable signs of sensitivity, while the other parts do not.

sensitive principle ; so that these two things make together one only subject (*suppositum*).[1]

To be convinced that *life* is not the same as *feeling*, or at least not the feeling which is observable by us, but that this feeling is an effect of life, it is enough to consider that all the parts of our body, so long as we are alive and in good health, have life in them, and are, each according to its condition, conjoined with us in the way which is necessary to entitle that union to be called *life* : hence all the animal parts perform the vital acts suitable to them, the chief of which are nutrition, heat, vital motion—whence incorruption—and the aptitude to perform their respective functions.

On the contrary, the feeling of which I speak resides not in all, but only in certain parts which I include under the name of *nerves* ; without thereby wishing to enter into physiological controversies foreign to my argument.[2]

699. To enable us to form a clear concept of the sensitive body, the following imaginary description may be of service. Let us imagine, that we see before us a human body, but in such a state that the bones, tendons, membranes, cartilages, the cellular tissue, in short, all the non-sensitive parts, have been removed from it, and that nothing is left except that admirable network of nerve-filaments which run in and out in all directions, and are so interlaced as to envelope the entire mass, themselves terminating (after they have been variously knotted together at the joints and ganglions) in the brain and the spinal marrow. Let us also suppose, that this stupendous and most complicated nerve-structure, with its every part just in its own proper place, is by some divine virtue, or rather by the force of our imagination which so pictures it, made to stand up erect and rigid, as though it were of iron or of steel. Now what we have thus before us is the sensitive body, which, when vitally conjoined with us, enables us to

---

[1] I do not here intend to give a description of this union ; it suffices to designate it by a proper word which prevents its being confounded with any other kind of union.

[2] Some physiologists would have us believe that there some anomalies in this law ; but, as I said before, it suffices for my present purpose that in the human body, given certain circumstances, and at certain moments, some parts are sensitive and others not.

receive sensations, and moreover, as I verily believe, is itself habitually and uniformly felt by us with a fundamental and innate feeling. Owing, however, to its being evenly diffused throughout the whole sensitive body, unchanging, and connatural with us, it is very difficult of advertence, so much so that oftentimes even philosophers seem to know as little about it as if it did not exist. The case is different as regards the changes which take place in this feeling, I mean as regards sensations. These, being neither universal nor constant, but partial, accidental, irregular, transient and more or less vivid, easily attract attention.

700. I must now therefore examine, (1) How our sensitive body, the seat of this fundamental feeling, is felt by us ; (2) How we come intellectually to perceive the external bodies which touch and excite our sensitive body.

And since, as we have seen, bodies are perceived, both as substances which cause sensations in us, and as the subjects of the corporeal qualities, it will be my duty, (1) to apply in particular to sensitive bodies, as well as to those which are not sensitive but only sensible, what I said above respecting the manner of perceiving corporeal substances in general ; (2) to treat of both these classes of bodies, considered as the subjects of the qualities hereinbefore mentioned, and which are either sensible or reducible to the sensible (393, 694).

ARTICLE IV.

Two ways of perceiving our own body; the one subjective and the other extrasubjective.

701. In the first place, I would observe, that our body (I always mean that part which in respect of us is sensitive) is perceived in two ways, viz.

(1) Like all external bodies, by the sight, the touch, in short the five sensories. When I perceive my body as *acting* on my sensorial organs, I do not then perceive it in so far as it is itself sensitive (mark this, reader, for it is a point of the greatest importance), but I only perceive it as I do any external body falling under my senses, and producing sensations

in them. One part of my body perceives another, and that is all. It is the same as when an anatomist perceives the nerves of the animal he is dissecting, which nerves are sentient, not to the anatomist himself, but only to the being whose they are.

(2) We perceive our body through that *fundamental* and universal *feeling* whereby we feel the existence of life in us (a feeling testified by consciousness, as will be seen more clearly later on), and through the modifications which the same feeling receives from adventitious and particular sensations.

These two ways of perceiving our sensitive body, may be appropriately designated by the terms *subjective* and *extrasubjective*.

By being perceived in the first way, *i.e.* through the fundamental feeling which springs from life, our body is felt as forming one thing with us ; so that, in virtue of its individual union with our spirit, it becomes part of the sentient subject. Hence one may say with truth, that we *feel it* as *co-sentient.*

When, on the other hand, we perceive our body in the second way, that is, as we perceive the external bodies which act on our sensitive organs, then, like all of them, it is outside the sentient subject, and quite another thing from our sensitive powers. We do not feel it any longer in so far as it is co-sentient, but only in its external data, *i.e.* in so far as it has the aptitude to make an impression on our sensitivity.

This distinction between the *subjective* and the *extrasubjective* way of perceiving our body should be well grasped ; because on it will depend in great part the doctrines I have still to expound in this connexion.

ARTICLE V.

The SUBJECTIVE *way of perceiving our body is twofold, namely, one through the* FUNDAMENTAL FEELING, *and the other through the* MODIFICATIONS *of that feeling.*

702. Again, the *subjective* way of perceiving our body is twofold.

We perceive the sensitive parts of our body subjectively, (1) by the *fundamental feeling* already referred to ; (2) by the modifications that feeling undergoes on occasion of the impressions made on the nerves :—

703. The means to discover the *second subjective way* of perceiving our body, is by accurately analysing our external sensations : we thus find, that in each of them there are two distinct elements, namely :—

(1) The change produced in the corporeal sensitive organ, which is therefore felt by us, for the time being, in a new mode. This is the same as to say that the fundamental feeling suffers a modification.

(2) The *sense-perception* of the external body which has acted on us.

Let us see this exemplified in the sense of touch.

If we rub the back of our hand with any rough-faced material, we feel two things simultaneously, *i.e.* the hand and the superficies applied to the hand. The first of these things is what I have called *modification of the fundamental feeling* we have of our body ; the second is the *sense-perception* of that rough superficies.

704. This *duplex nature* of our external *sensations* is never sufficiently insisted upon. But all that I require in this place, is to point out the relation which these two simultaneous and always conjoined feelings, included in every one of the sensations I speak of, have with each other.

I say, then, that if the sensation we experience when a change takes place in our corporeal organ [1] is simply a modification of our fundamental feeling, the *sense-perception* which accompanies that sensation, is, on the contrary, an entirely different thing. It indeed arises on occasion of that change and of that sensation, but, between the *sensation* (subjective) and the *sense-perception* (extrasubjective), we cannot discover any necessary connexion as cause and effect ; although, as I shall show in its proper place, we can prove that both these things are alike due to one and the same cause.

---

[1] The change which takes place in our sensitive organ is not, itself, a sensation ; but, given that change, a sensation arises in us, because the organ is habitually felt by us in whatever state it happens to be ; hence we also feel the changes which occur in it. One must not, therefore, confound the physical impression made on the organ with the sensation we instantly experience on occasion of that impression.

ARTICLE VI.

*Explanation of sensation in so far as it is a modification of the funda-
mental feeling we have of our body.*

705. But what do I mean by saying that the sensation we
experience on occasion of a change taking place in our bodily
organ is simply a mode of the fundamental feeling we have
of life?

The way in which I think this fact ought to be conceived
is as follows :—

By the fundamental feeling of life, we feel all the sensitive
parts of our body: this feeling begins with our life and goes
on continuously to the end of it.

What, then, do we feel by this feeling? What is its
matter?

Its matter consists of the sensitive parts of our body.   As
therefore it is natural for us to feel these sensitive parts, so it
is natural that we should feel them *in that state* in which they
are.

Such being the case, it follows that if any change takes
place in their *state*, there must necessarily be a corresponding
change in the feeling we have of them.

706. The activity of the said fundamental feeling, then, is
one, always the same, always on the alert and ever prepared
to feel the *state*, whatever it be, of our sensitive body.   Consequently, all the changes which happen in our bodily organism
must be perceived by us through that self-same fundamental
and primal act of feeling : and the modifications by which
this becomes affected on occasion of the changes produced in
the organism, constitute the first of the two elements whereof
our adventitious sensations, caused (I now assume this with
the common opinion) by the impinging of external bodies on
our own, are, as I have said, the result.

One and the same activity, therefore, perceives our body
as well in the first and substantial way as in the second and
accidental.   The primal feeling, and its adventitious modifications, are two facts ; whence I deduce, that our spirit, in the
very first moment of its being individually conjoined with an

animal body, must also emit from itself a certain energy
whereby it embraces, so to speak, its body and mixes itself up
with it, and so feels it, and continues thenceforth to feel it
without interruption (while the vital union lasts) *in whatever
actuation, or state* it may be found. Hence, as often as that
body with which the spirit is so closely united happens to
undergo a change by the action of an external force, the result
must be, that one mode is withdrawn from the sensitive
activity of the spirit, and another mode substituted in its
place ; and, as a consequence, the activity of the primal or
fundamental feeling must also suffer a modification, not indeed
on its own account, but because, without any action on its part,
an alteration has been made in the matter wherein it necessarily
terminates. The same thing happens here as when I keep my
eyes fixed upon a scene that changes while I am looking at
it. The effect of this change is, that although the application
of my gazing activity remains the same all through, the
objects I see are continually varying. Even so with the
activity of our fundamental feeling ; it is always the same, in
the first state of our body, in all the actuations and states
which supervene in it, and in all the partial modifications of
its sensories.

ARTICLE VII.

Explanation of sensation in so far as it is perceptive of external bodies.

707. When the nerves have all the conditions necessary
for sensitivity,[1] they feel in whatever part they happen to be
duly impressed or affected by external bodies.

In saying that the sensitive power of the soul is diffused
throughout the whole sensitive body, and that therefore the
soul is, by this its power, present to all the parts of the body,
my object is simply to state the fact as presented to us by
observation, and not to lay down any theory.[2]

[1] One of these conditions is communication with the brain ; when this is interrupted the organ ceases to feel.
[2] Galluppi describes this fact in a similar manner, thus: ' I say that the soul is intimately united with and present to the whole body' (*Saggio filosofico sulla critica della conoscenza* &c. (Lib. II. c. vi. § 112). Then he goes on to state that the mode of this union is *incomprehensible*. Now concerning this decision of Galluppi I would observe, that the exact knowledge of the fact is knowledge quite sufficient

Now if the sensitive faculty has a primal and essential act (fundamental feeling) which extends to all the sensitive parts of our body, this faculty or, to speak more accurately, the soul present in it, must of necessity experience a certain violence (I mean a passivity) when the sensitive parts are made to suffer a change by the action of a body external to ours.

The perception of this passivity, which the sensitive soul has in a given manner determined by the quality of the sensation, is the *sense-perception* of bodies, as I have already explained (674).

ARTICLE VIII.

Difference between our own body and the bodies external to us.

708. If the observations I have offered thus far are correct, it must be conceded that our spirit is affected by two different forces, namely, that which causes in us the fundamental and vital feeling, and that which modifies and alters the matter of this feeling, and produces the subjective sensation and, simultaneously with it, the corporeal perception.

Now, according to the definition I have given, the essence of *body* consists in a *certain* action [1] which we feel as being done in us, in an energy relatively to which we are passive, and which our mind perceives as a being acting on, but different from, us (674–684).

If then we experience two species of feelings, if we feel affected by two different actions, two different energies, there evidently exist two species of bodies, namely, our own body and bodies external to us.

Thus the existence of these two species of bodies is proved by the fact of our consciousness.[2]   It has therefore all the

---

of the union itself, as will be seen from what I shall say when coming to describe this fact, and all that I shall then submit will be directed to setting forth how the said fact takes place, and nothing more.

[1] See the next note but one (TRANSLATORS).

[2] It was necessary to define in what the first and substantial difference between our body and the bodies outside of us consists, and I have found it in this, that our body is perceived as *co-sentient* with us, whereas external bodies are perceived only as forces different from ourselves.   To justify this difference, I have had no further need than, (1) to appeal to the *fact* of consciousness, which carries its own proof; for to say *fact*, is the same as to say *thing beyond questioning*; (2) to apply the theory of *perception* which I had already expounded (528–536), and the principles of substance and causation (567–569).

certainty of a fact ; and no one, not even the Sceptic, denies the fact of consciousness.

But our own body, like external bodies, can be perceived also as *extrasubjective*. Now if we perceive our body as an *extrasubjective* term of our sensitive faculty, we can also discover other differences, secondary but important, between it and those bodies. But this mode of distinguishing our body, considered as extrasubjective, from external bodies, presupposes the real existence of an *extrasubjective* term of the said faculty, of which, however, I had no need when distinguishing our body from the others, on the substantial ground that, whilst the former is *subject*, the latter are *extrasubject*.

In the *extrasubjective* perception of our body as well as of external ones, I have noted three differences, which indicate that these two classes of bodies are distinct each from each. Galluppi describes these differences in the following manner.

First difference : ' If with your right hand glowing with warmth you touch the left which is cold, you will find the same *Me* in both ; you are conscious that the *Ego* who has the sensation of warmth in the right hand is the very same who feels the cold in the left ; the identical *Ego* therefore seems to you to exist in the one hand as well as in the other. But if with one of your hands you touch, for example, a ball of iron, you will feel the *Me* in the hand, but not in the ball ; the *Ego* therefore does not seem to you to exist in the ball, and this body seems extraneous thereto. The contact of the two hands gives you two sensations ; the contact with the ball only one. The *Ego* regards as parts of *his own* body the right hand no less than the left, because he is conscious of feeling in both alike ; and he regards the ball of iron as an *external body*, because he is conscious of feeling *the* ball, but not of feeling *in* the ball. The *Ego* therefore regards as *his own* that body which he feels, and in which it also seems to him that he feels or exists ; and he regards as *external* that body which he feels, but *in* which it does not seem to him that he feels or exists.'

Second difference : ' If you will that your arm move, it moves immediately. But if you will that the ball of iron

move, it does not move by your simply willing it : to make it move, you must apply your hand to it first. Therefore the *Ego* regards as *his own* that body in which he can produce motion immediately by his will alone ; and he will regard as *external* that body for producing motion in which he requires something besides the will.'

Third difference : ' You may have the ball of iron removed, so that it can no longer be seen by you or act on your senses. But you never can part with that body which you call your own ; it is impossible for you to withdraw yourself from its action, at least while you are awake. Therefore the *Ego* regards as *his own*, that body which is incessantly present to him, and as *external*, that body which can cease to be present to, and modify him ' (*Elementi di filosofia*, &c., vol. iii. c. iii. § 29).

From these observations Galluppi concludes that our body can be distinguished from external bodies by means of the two senses of *sight* and *touch*. But the sight and the touch perceive *extrasubjectively*. I do not content myself with proving that these two terms of sight and touch—*our own body* and *external bodies*—differ the one from the other ; I show moreover that our body is also an appurtenance of the *sentient subject*, while the other bodies are purely *extrasubjective* : herein lies the principal difference between the two.

Nevertheless, the three facts adduced by Galluppi may very well serve also for marking the distinction between a *subject* and an *extrasubject*, provided they are used and analysed with this particular intent.

In truth, in the first of them the *hand* feels itself sentient : here we have *subject*. *The ball of iron* does not feel itself, but is only felt : here we have a something *extraneous to the subject*.

In the second, the motion which I give to my hand by the act of my will, can be ascertained by me not only through the sight and the touch, but also and principally through my interior feeling and consciousness : here we have the *subject*. On the contrary, I do not clearly ascertain the motion caused by

It will be seen therefore, that in making out the existence of these bodies I do not rely on reasoning, but on observation alone ; even as I do not exceed the limits of observation in my definition of their nature, contenting myself with placing it in a *certain* energy [1] which we feel acting on us while at the same time we are conscious of not being ourselves its authors.

709. Nevertheless, the fact still remains that it is a very difficult matter to observe the fundamental feeling we have of our sensitive body. It seems therefore desirable that I should now try to remove this difficulty, not indeed by demonstrating the existence of that feeling through reasoning (which would be contrary to the method I have prescribed to myself in these inquiries), but by adding to what I have said some considerations calculated to assist the reader in reflecting on himself in the manner necessary to gain distinct advertence of a mode of corporeal feeling which, its great importance notwithstanding, has escaped the notice of so many philosophers.

ARTICLE IX.

A description of the fundamental feeling.

710. First of all, it is necessary to distinguish (and this point can never be sufficiently insisted upon) the existence in us of a feeling from the advertence which we give to it.

We may very well experience a sensation or a feeling without reflecting on and therefore being conscious of it. Now, given this case, we should not be in a position to say to ourselves that we have that sensation or feeling ; nay, if we did not know how to advert thereto, we might persistently

---

me in the ball of iron, except through the sight and the touch : here we have a something *extraneous to the subject.*

In the third, I feel my body as part of myself wherever I go with it, not because I see or touch it, but chiefly through an interior consciousness : here we have the *subject.* The removal of external bodies, on the contrary, is not ascertained by me except through the touch or the other senses ; which causes me to know that they are purely *extra-subjective terms* of my sensitive powers.

[1] I say a *certain* energy, and not *any kind* of energy ; because, as I have already observed, the corporeal force has characters proper to itself, which determine it, and distinguish it from all other species of force. About this, however, I shall have to make further investigation.

deny it. This fact was noted by Leibnitz, but entirely escaped the attention of Locke and a great many other writers (288–292).

When therefore I hear a person say : ' I have never yet been conscious, nor am I now, of that universal feeling of my body in which you would have me believe ; ' my reply is : This is no valid proof of the non-existence of that feeling.

You may have had it, and you may be having it still, and not be aware of the fact simply from the want of proper attention.

The more carefully philosophers have applied themselves to search what was passing within them, the more have they succeeded in detecting things which take place in our interior, but of which the vulgar know nothing, because they are not used to close self-observation. Hence the great precept, ' Know thyself' ; hence also the reason why the searching the hidden springs of our passions and the various affections and movements they excite in us, as also the noting of our habitual inclinations, and the motives of our actions, is esteemed an art so difficult and so meritorious that only those generous souls who devote their whole strength of mind and will to the attainment of perfect virtue can be credited with it.

Whoever therefore has not as yet noticed in himself the feeling to which I refer, will do well, instead of peremptorily denying its existence, to reflect on himself better and more calmly than he has done heretofore.

Whoever has not grasped the distinction between *feeling* and *advertence* to feeling, has yet to learn in what the essential difference between *sensation* and *idea* consists. Sensation can never advert to itself ; the *understanding* alone adverts to sensation. This advertence is nothing but the intellectual perception of what we feel, or else an act of reflection on that perception itself. Hence the act of *knowing* a sensation is essentially of a different nature from the act of *feeling* it. From this it follows that if a being affected by sensations should not perceive them intellectually nor be aware of their presence, he could not name them to others or to himself ; and this is why brutes cannot speak, namely, because they have not the faculty of reason.

711. Should any one, on the other hand, look upon advertence to the fundamental feeling now under consideration as a very easy thing, he might readily be deceived in another way regarding the nature of this feeling.

We ought to remember, that this feeling is such that it always remains in us even though we should have no sensations from without.

If I shut myself up in a perfectly dark room, and keep perfectly still for a long time ; and if I seek, moreover, to forget every sensible image I ever received, I shall find myself at last in a state in which I shall seem to have lost all knowledge of the outlines of my body, of the position of my hands, feet, or any other part. Making this experiment in the best manner I can, and, through abstraction, carrying myself back as nearly as possible to a condition anterior to all my adventitious sensations, I find that there still is in me a vital feeling of my whole body.

It will thus be seen, that although this feeling exists, it must nevertheless be very difficult of detection ; for we do not, generally, advert to anything which takes place within us unless stimulated thereto by some change. When there is no change, there is no advertence, no comparing, no exercise of our powers of reflection.

But if advertence is conditional on a change, *feeling* is not.

Suppose that we pass from a temperature to which we are used, to another many degrees warmer : this sudden change will instantly excite our attention, and we shall perhaps complain of the discomfort caused by the excessive heat. Those persons, on the contrary, who by always living in that atmosphere are thoroughly habituated to it, perceive nothing singular in the temperature, but find it quite natural and genial. How comes the difference, when the degree of heat felt is the same in both cases ? Simply from this, that in the first case there is something new to arouse attention, but not in the second. Now, to be reasonably satisfied that we feel a certain thing, it ought to be enough for us to know

that the thing truly acts on the senses. We must argue thus :
' The heat of that atmosphere acts physically on the senses ;
therefore it is felt even when not adverted to.'

712. But some one may say : 'Well, I agree with you in
this that a certain vital feeling—that by which I feel that I
am alive—always exists in me, and can never abandon me
until death comes to put an end to it. But what I cannot
admit is that this vital feeling extends to all the sensitive
parts of my body. If it did, I should perceive by it the size
and configuration of my body, without having need, for this
purpose, of the sight and the other external senses.'

Whoever speaks thus, evidently supposes me to have said
what I have not.

The size and configuration of our body as perceived by
the sight and the touch, are not comprised in the vital feeling.
I mean that we never could, through this feeling alone, have
formed to ourselves the image, either visual or tactile, of our
body. In order to form that image, we must necessarily have
seen the body with our eyes or touched it with our hands ;
for the image is simply a sort of reproduction or an imitation
of the representation received through the sight and the
touch. Nothing of this is to be found in the primitive feeling ; consequently, neither the visual nor the tactile representation is in any way its matter : in fact, the reader has
already seen the great difference there is between perceiving
bodies by the (supposed) *representations* of the external senses,
and perceiving our own body by the *fundamental feeling*.
We must not, therefore, confound, but keep perfectly distinct
and separate from one another, the two, or rather three, ways
in which our own body is perceived (701–707). Neither must
we say : 'When I perceive my body in the first manner (by
the fundamental feeling), I do not perceive it in the third (by
the sensitive representations) ; therefore I do not perceive it
at all.' This would be about as good a piece of reasoning as
to maintain that two things, because specifically different,
must be possessed of the same characters.

In fact, the whole difficulty here consists in forming a
precise and genuine concept of the fundamental feeling ;

because if we expect to find what is not in it, the result will be that we shall at once be tempted to reject it, though unreasonably, as an absurdity.

713. There is also another obstacle to be overcome. Generally speaking, men's attention occupies itself exclusively with the third way of perceiving bodies, namely, with the *sensible representations*; and this for several reasons. (1) The external sensation is more vivid, and, as it were, brilliant, so that in comparison with it the other two ways of perception seem to be non-existent. (2) The external sensation is constantly changing; and, as I have said, it is *change* that awakens and attracts our attention, and leads us to institute comparisons and find out differences—a thing so important for us, that, without it, we do not seem to ourselves to have gained any true knowledge of an object. (3) The *direct* act of thought is the first, the most easy, and the most *natural* to us; and it is by a direct act that we intellectually perceive external bodies, whereas thus to perceive our *subjective* body we must reflect, that is to say, concentrate the attention of our mind on our own selves. Now, this turning of the intellectual activity inwards, while the natural movement is continually carrying it outwards, is a matter of no small difficulty. Indeed it is the last thing we do; and this, probably, is also the reason why the reflection we make on ourselves seems to be so wanting in light as compared with the perception of external things.[1]

[1] Hence, the *chronological* order of our feelings runs inversely to the *advertences* we give to them.

First, we have the fundamental feeling; next, we have the external sensations.

On the contrary, we advert, first, to the external sensations and next to our fundamental feeling.

Moreover, that we may advert to our fundamental feeling, we must have acquired the free disposal of our will; for it is by a free act, that we reflect on and advert to this feeling. Now I have demonstrated, that we do not acquire the free disposal of our will (and therefore of our thoughts) until we have arrived at the formation of abstract ideas

(525, 526). Before adverting therefore to the fundamental feeling, we must (1) have *adverted* with our mind to the external sensations and *perceived* external bodies; (2) have drawn from these perceptions the *specific* ideas; and (3) have exercised on these ideas the *abstractions* which result in *generic* ideas. When our mind has reached in succession these three kinds of development, and through the last of them (which is generally obtained only by the aid of language, 521, 522) has given us full dominion over our thoughts, then we are in a position to reflect on the interior and fundamental *feeling*. Thus we see that in the *chronological* order this thought comes last, and must be

714. The primitive feeling, then, does not enable us to know either the form or the size of our body as visible to the

preceded by all the operations which the mind performs on the external sensations.

This explanation enables us to reconcile many passages of S. Thomas regarding the necessity of *phantasms* in order that we may think of anything. For he sometimes absolutely affirms this necessity (*S.* I. lxxxiv. 7); and he even goes so far as to say: 'Quidditas rei materialis est proprium objectum intellectus' (lxxxv. 5), or again : 'Natura rei materialis est objectum intellectus' (lxxxvii. 2); whence he concludes that habits are not present to the understanding as *objects*, but *ut quibus intellectus intelligit*. This doctrine, taken purely and simply by itself, seems the very opposite of that which I have attributed to the Angelical Doctor and, as I venture to think, proved from his own words in this very volume (See notes to Nos. 478 and 528); namely, that the *matter* of our cognitions is supplied, not by the external sensories only, but also by the internal feeling. It will therefore be well to give here a further elucidation of this difficulty, since the question whether human ideas have two sources or one only, is of the greatest relevance in philosophy. Let us then try to explain S. Thomas by himself. According to him, the *material thing* is not the *sole* object of the understanding, but only the *first* in the *chronological* order; and this agrees perfectly with what I hold. In one place in the *Summa Theologica* (I. lxxxvii. 3), he inquires 'Whether the intellect knows its own act,' which is certainly not a material thing, and he answers in the affirmative; only he adds, that it knows it subsequently to its knowledge of *material things*, differing in this from the angelic intelligence, which by its very first act understands both itself and the act by which it understands itself. His words are : 'Est autem alius intellectus, scilicet humanus, qui nec est suum intelligere, nec sui intelligere est OBJECTUM PRIMUM ipsa ejus essentia, sed aliquid extrinsecum, scilicet natura materialis rei. Et ideo id quod PRIMO cognoscitur ab intellectu humano, est hujusmodi objectum, et SECUNDARIO cog-

noscitur ipse actus quo cognoscitur objectum : et per actum cognoscitur ipse intellectus.'—' But there is another intellect, namely the human, which neither is the act by which it knows itself, nor has its own essence for the first object of its cognition; but that object is something external to it, namely, the material nature of the thing. And therefore that which the human intellect knows *first* is the object here spoken of, and that which it knows *next* is the act itself by which the object is known; and by the act, the intellect itself is known.'

This same teaching he propounds still more openly a little further down in the same article, where he sums it up thus : —' The object of the understanding is something common, viz. *being* and *truth*; under which is comprised also the act itself of understanding. Hence the understanding is able to know its own act, but not first of all; because in this our present state the first object of our understanding is not every kind of being and truth, but being and truth considered in material things.'—' Objectum intellectus est commune quoddam, scilicet ens et verum ; sub quo comprehenditur etiam ipse actus intelligendi. Unde intellectus potest suum actum cognoscere, sed non primo ; quia nec primum objectum intellectus nostri secundum praesentem statum est quodlibet ens et verum, sed ens et verum consideratum in rebus materialibus' (*Ibid.* art. 3, ad 1m). And in confirmation of all this, he refers to a sentence of Aristotle, who says : 'The objects are known *before* the acts (PRÆCOGNOSCUNTUR), and the acts *before* the faculties'(Lib. ii.*De Anima*, text 33). Whence it is clear that he is speaking of a priority of *time* and nothing else. This is precisely what I say ; only that I observe further, that in order to arrive at that state of intellectual development in which man reflects on his own interior and fundamental feeling, it is not sufficient that he know external bodies first, but it is, moreover necessary for him to draw from this cognition abstract ideas (for which the aid of speech is usually needed), and, by

external eye. The perception it gives is quite of another kind, and we have no means of forming a genuine idea of it except by concentrating our whole attention on our inner selves and calmly observing that feeling of life which animates us throughout. And even while doing this, we must be careful not to indulge in any speculations as to what this feeling may be.

means of these abstract ideas, acquire dominion over his powers of *attention*, so as to be able to direct it to them at will. Then only is man in a position to reflect upon himself and to advert to the acts which take place within him. According to me, the *first* of these acts is the fundamental feeling ; and I say, that man reflects upon this *last of all*, that is, after he has reflected on his accidental acts. Hence I describe the *chronological* order of man's ADVERTENCES as follows : (1) he adverts to the corporeal things which act upon his senses ; (2) he forms *abstract ideas* ; (3) he adverts to the ACT OF FEELING (the *sensations*) and to the act of understanding (the perceptive cognitions) ; (4) lastly, he adverts to the *fundamental feeling*—the first act, and the common root as well of the sensitive as of the intellectual faculty.

After what has been said, we can also easily reconcile some other passages wherein S. Thomas says clearly that the senses are not the only sources of our cognitions. Let me quote a few of them.

'The sensitive cognition,' he says, ' is not the WHOLE CAUSE of the intellectual cognition ; and hence it is no wonder if the intellectual cognition extends further than the sensitive.' ' Sensitiva cognitio non est TOTA CAUSA intellectualis cognitionis ; et ideo non est mirum si intellectualis cognitio ultra sensitivam se extendit ' (*S.* I. lxxxiv. 6). Amongst the things to which the intellectual cognition extends, and which are wholly beyond the sensible cognition, there is, first of all, what takes place in our understanding. Hence he writes : ' That which is known intellectually, is known *per se*, and for knowing it the nature of the knowing subject suffices without any external means.'—' Quod intellectualiter cognoscitur, per se est notum, et ad ipsum cognoscendum natura cognoscentis sufficit ABSQUE EXTERIORI ME-

DIO ' (*C. Gent.* i. 57). How, for instance, could we know our affections except by consulting our heart ? External and material things can tell us nothing of this. On this account he says : ' Although faith is not known by means of the external movements of the body, nevertheless it is perceived also by him in whom it is, by means of an internal act of the heart.'—' Etsi fides non cognoscatur per EXTERIORES CORPORIS MOTUS, percipitur tamen etiam ab eo in quo est per INTERIOREM ACTUM CORDIS ' (*S.* I. lxxxvii. 11). Again, if we had no knowledge except of *material things*, we could not form to ourselves any idea of *spiritual substances*. This idea must therefore be drawn from the feeling we have of our soul, as we are told by S. Augustine, and after him by S. Thomas, who comments thus :

' From that authority of S. Augustin we may see, that what our mind receives in reference to the cognition of incorporeal things, it can know by *means of itself*. And this is so true, that even the Philosopher says that the knowledge we have of our soul is a certain PRINCIPLE which enables us to know separated substances (Lib. i. *De Anima*, text 2). For, through the knowledge which our soul has of itself, it comes to have such knowledge of the incorporeal substances as it can have in this world.'—' Ex illa auctoritate Augustini haberi potest, quod illud quod mens nostra de cognitione incorporalium rerum accipit, PER SEIPSAM cognoscere possit. Et hoc adeo verum est, ut etiam apud Philosophum dicatur, quod scientia de anima est PRINCIPIUM quoddam ad cognoscendum substantias separatas ' (Lib. i. *De Anima*, text 2). ' Per hoc enim quod anima nostra cognoscit seipsam, pertingit ad cognitionem aliquam habendam de substantiis incorporeis, qualem eam contingit habere ' (*S.* I. lxxxviii. art. 1, ad. 1).

We must act the part of spectators and nothing more. Neither the imaginative nor the reasoning faculty must be allowed to add any thing to what we see before us.[1]

715. Again, we can be convinced that the fundamental feeling must extend to all the sensitive parts of our body, by observing the movements which are incessantly going on within it. Thus the circulation of the blood, the continual current of the humours, the manifold assimilations, and that universal vegetative process to which the body is subject, must of necessity continually act on our sensitive parts, touching or pressing them on all sides, and therefore exciting them in some slight degree. This ought to be enough to satisfy us that there is in us a multitude of little sensations, habitual and not adverted to, which uninterruptedly succeed one another; it being manifest that, ' Given a touch or modification in a sensitive fibre, a sensation must follow, even though, by reason of our being habituated to it, we should be unable to give it distinct advertence.'

Here nothing could be further from my thoughts than to enter upon an investigation of the mystery of life—how life springs up in us, and how it comes to keep in a continuous act. The only thing I wish to say is, that if it could be reasonably believed that some internal movement is essentially necessary to life (and certainly in our present state this move-

[1] The author, in a conversation, gave one of the translators of this work to understand that he could, when in the prime of life, while his health was perfect, observe distinctly and without much difficulty his corporeal fundamental feeling. By it he felt his body wholly divested of those attributes which fall under the external senses—in fact, felt it lost in space. And so, the translators believe, would the subjective body be felt by any one who could successfully perform the experiment. Besides following strictly the directions laid down in the text, the person should place himself in the easiest possible posture, and also be wholly free from physical ailments ; in a word, he should avoid everything which, by tending to *localise* the attention of the mind, would increase the difficulty of the operation, if not render it altogether impossible. Should the experiment not be successful at once, let it be tried over and over again, at fairly distant intervals. Success would amply repay the trouble, and furnish much food for thought, and particularly in connexion with the highly interesting question about the nature of *space* (TRANSLATORS).

ment is, to say the least, a necessary condition of it), then our habitual and fundamental feeling would be easier to understand; since there is no difficulty in conceiving that where changes occur in sensitive parts, there is sensation.

716. And as to our continually feeling our body, I could cite a great many facts which leave no doubt about it. Take for instance the following.

(1) The atmosphere presses upon each of us with a weight which, on the estimated average surface of the human body —fifteen square feet—has been reckoned at something like 32,400 pounds, or 16 tons! Now, of this enormous weight, far exceeding that of the heaviest cloak of lead and pressing upon us within and without, and even on the most delicate parts of our frame, we are not in the least conscious. Nay, it would be no easy task to persuade, for example, an illiterate countryman that he is actually carrying such a load. His first thought on hearing our assurance to that effect would most probably be, either that we are fools, or that we want to impose on his credulity. Adopting the same mode of reasoning which is so common among superficial philosophers, he would reply : ' I know better than that ; I am full certain that I could never carry a load like this without feeling it.' He does not understand, that the reason of his not adverting to the pressure in question, is because the feeling he has of it is equally distributed all over his body, as well as constant and habitual, so that it forms as it were part of himself, of his substance. For a similar reason, a fish, pressed though it be on every side by the waters in which it lives, would, if it had thought and speech, deny feeling any pressure at all. But were our countryman to have personal experience of a considerable diminution in the density of the air, and consequently in its pressure ; if, for instance, he were, from the plain in which he now stands, taken up to the summit of a very high mountain,[1] where the atmosphere is much thinner, he would soon see what a change takes place in himself. He would find himself affected with attacks of vomiting, nausea and giddiness, and the blood

---

[1] The variation of a single line in the barometer supposes a variation in the atmospheric pressure equivalent to 138 pounds.

would ooze from the pores, simply because the vehement and continuous rush of this fluid is now stronger than the resistance with which its outflow was checked by the greater density of the air at the lower level. Then, perhaps, by confronting his present with his former state, he would be made sensible of the fact that, unawares to himself, he had felt the air-pressure all along.

(2) And must not the circulation of the blood itself, propelled as it is with so impetuous a force through the whole body in so many winding and intricate channels, cause an habitual sensation of some sort? For, the vital fluid, thus driven and compressed within its narrow vessels, cannot but push and strike against their sides, and especially at those numberless turnings where it is obliged, by the reaction it suffers, to alter its course. Nevertheless, of all this motion you seem to have no feeling, or next to none. Let, however, a change occur by the circulation being quickened or retarded under the influence of sudden anger or fear ; and you will feel your heart jerk violently, and your pulse beat irregularly in the first case, and, in the second, you will experience a fainting sensation. Had you not some feeling of the circulation of your blood before ? Undoubtedly ; but you did not advert to that feeling for the reason that there was nothing new (no change) to draw and direct your attention to it.

(3) Our body contains a certain amount of heat. Now this heat is certainly felt by us; and yet how seldom do we give any advertence to it unless when a change occurs in its degree ! Suppose that all the degrees of heat from zero up to boiling point were applied in succession to a part of our body, say the hand : we should feel every one of them, and also perceive that we feel it. Now among all these successive degrees of heat there is also the one which our body contained originally. Therefore we felt that heat before the experiment took place, but were not aware of it. We notice it during the change, because there is then a transition from one sensation to another, and hence the occasion for making a comparison between them and observing their differences. It is unnecessary for me to say, that the sensations are not

felt by us because they are compared with one another, but they are compared because they are felt. Each sensation is felt independently of the other, and independently of all comparisons. Comparisons are needed only in order that we may advert to them. They exist even when there is no comparison, no transition from one to another. It must then be conceded, that, whatever be the degree of heat connatural to our body, it is habitually felt by us, although this our habitual sensation remains in us unnoticed.

(4) All the molecules of which our bodies are composed incessantly gravitate to the earth by the force of attraction, whatever this force may be. Now here is an action continually exercised on each of these molecules, but of which we have not the least consciousness. And yet it must give us some sensation. Were it not so, why should corpulent persons feel specially hampered by their weight, or why should walking produce a sense of fatigue in the whole body? Unquestionably we always have that sensation, caused by attraction to the earth ; but from the first moments of our existence it has been equally spread all over us ; then, as we were gradually growing up, it only increased by imperceptible degrees, nor was there at any one moment a leap or transition striking enough to draw our attention to the addition made to our weight. But were a material diminution in the earth's attraction to take place suddenly, the result in us would be a new universal sensation which, being both novel and extraordinary, would not fail to arouse reflection. We should then observe in ourselves a feeling of lightness, agility and freedom of motion such as we had never before experienced, and, together with this, a disturbance, wholly unexpected, in the general economy of our health. Conversely, under a sudden notable augmentation in the attractive force, we should feel as though we were loaded with a most oppressive and fatiguing burden, and our body would be contracted even to the extent of changing its form ; and we should, of course, advert to this great change. So, on the other hand, should the attraction cease altogether, our body would (not to speak of other possible mishaps) quickly gain an

accession of stature quite unusual, in as much as all its parts, instead of pressing, as they now do, one upon the other, would stand loosely in their respective places, without any downward tendency. If, then, each of these several changes in the intensity of the attractive force would cause a distinct sensation in our body, it is manifest that this would be due to the fact that attraction really produces a sensible effect in us ; and, if so, it is equally clear that such effect is produced also by that degree of attraction to which we are now subject, although, for the oft-repeated reason that it is habitual and, as it were, connatural to us, we do not give advertence thereto.

The same mode of reasoning might be applied to cohesion, and to the continual movements and changes which go on in us through respiration, digestion, the incessant vegetative process, and those numberless chemical actions of which the human body is the scene. In short, everything goes to prove that our body is felt by us with a feeling *sui generis* and made up of a multitude of little particular and habitual sensations, even from the first moment of the union of our spirit with it.

But besides all this vast aggregate of particular sensations which are fused into an universal and constant feeling of our body (I do not pretend, as I have already said, to decide as to whether they be or be not essential to our life ; all I know is that in our present state they are conditions of it), I believe that our spirit itself, conjoined on the one hand with matter, and on the other with *ideal being*, has in it a special feeling of its own, one and most simple in itself, and yet the foundation of all other feelings, mixing itself up with them all, and making of them an undivided whole ; a feeling whereby the spirit is felt together with its body. I say a *feeling*, to signify that it is pure feeling, and not *idea*, according to the distinction [1] I have laid down between ideas and feelings, from which distinction we learn that the latter are only realisations of the former.[2]

---

[1] The reader will remember, that in the system of the Author this distinction is of cardinal importance, a *categorical* distinction (TRANSLATORS).

[2] And therefore not knowable through themselves, but only through ideas (TRANSLATORS).

ARTICLE XI.

The origin of our sensations confirms the existence of the fundamental feeling.

717. Feeling, then, exists in man as an original fact.[1]

There is no longer any question, therefore, of inquiring how feeling arises in us, but only of discovering how it comes to be modified so as to give us particular sensations.

718. Those philosophers who imagine man as wholly devoid of feeling at the first, make him a veritable statue : and when, further, they pretend that this statue, not being a sensitive subject at all, when touched by external bodies *feels* their actions, they then describe a process which is simply unintelligible, a mystery contrary to the usual order of nature.

I say an unintelligible process, because a sensation beginning of a sudden where no feeling of any kind exists is as much above our powers of understanding as creation from nothing. Again, according to these philosophers, the sensation which is suddenly excited and created in the statue on occasion of the impression made on it by external bodies, informs us also of our own existence. They suppose, therefore, that it is possible for us to feel a thing different from us, while at the same time we cannot feel ourselves !

This hypothesis (for it is nothing but a mere hypothesis) is also entirely at variance with the established order of nature, which does not work by leaps ; and there would certainly be a wonderful leap if we, while having absolutely no feeling of ourselves, were, through the mere touch of an external body, suddenly made to feel *it* as well as ourselves. Simultaneously with that mechanical action which does not bear any the least resemblance to sensation, a spirit would, so to speak, be enkindled and created in us. For what kind of spirit can that be which has in it nothing whatever in the nature either of feeling or of thought ? A spirit has no extension nor any other corporeal qualities. If, then, you

---

[1] Not deduced by theoretical reasoning, but certified by observation and consciousness (TRANSLATORS).

deprive it also of its characteristic properties, which are feeling and understanding, you annihilate it, or certainly the idea of a spirit has completely vanished from your mind : unless indeed by drawing on your imagination you invent for yourself a species of spirit about which neither observation nor consciousness knows anything, or take this for the true spirit of which you have cancelled the idea.

719. All these observations confirm the existence in us of a fundamental feeling ; but even apart from them, we might be convinced that this feeling exists simply by bestowing a careful attention on the nature of what is termed *myself*; for we should thus find that the *myself* is, at the bottom, a substantial feeling constitutive of the human subject, a subject at once sentient and intelligent.

ARTICLE XII.

Explanation of the saying of S. Thomas, that 'the body is in the soul.'

720. The above considerations will enable us to see the meaning of that formula of the ancients which we find repeated by S. Thomas, viz. that ' The soul is in the body, not as contained, but as containing : '—' Anima enim est in corpore ut continens, et non ut contenta ' [1] (*S.* I. lii. 1).

I have said that the word *body* means a thing known, inasmuch as we name things only in so far as we know them (678) ; and hence, that in order to know the value of this word, we must not proceed to speculative reasonings, nor deduce our notion of its value *a priori*, but consult experience (672, 673).

Now the fact given us by experience is, that we feel in us a certain action of which we are not ourselves the cause. Accordingly, I have placed the essence of *body* in a certain force which modifies us (676).

This force is felt by us from the first moment of our existence, although we do not advert to it at once (715, 716).

---

[1] Later on, the value of this word *certain*, which is like an unknown quantity, will be determined and substituted in the formula ; and that will perfect the definition of body.

It is felt habitually and uniformly in a determinate mode, and this is what we call *our body*. Now although the same force is essentially different from *Us* (668, 669), nevertheless it is *in us*, in our soul, that it acts. Hence, strictly speaking, it would be more accurate to say that ' Our body is in our soul,' than to say that ' Our soul is in our body.'

In the sequel I will give the reason why men generally use the second formula in preference to the first.

ARTICLE XIII.

The physical commerce between the soul and the body.

721. From what has just been said, we can also see that the celebrated question of the commerce (*influxus physicus*) between the body and the soul does not require a course of elaborate reasonings for its treatment.

Its solution must be drawn from the fact of consciousness itself. By attentively observing this fact, we find in it a soul and a body, a patient and an agent ; therefore our body, by virtue both of the *fact* and of the *definition*, is a substance acting on the soul in a peculiar mode. Thus the physical commerce here spoken of is included in the very notion of body, and has therefore no need of being proved by argument.

CHAPTER IV.

ORIGIN OF THE IDEA OF OUR BODY BY MEANS OF THE MODIFICATIONS OF THE FUNDAMENTAL FEELING.

ARTICLE I.

The analysis of sensation is resumed.

722. In order to form a genuine notion of what a sensation[1] is, we must forget entirely the idea of external bodies, which we always imagine as impinging upon our sensorial organs, and thus producing or exciting sensations in us. These causes of sensation must not be thought of any more than if they did not exist : our whole attention must be concentrated on the sensation alone, which is the fact given us by consciousness, and be kept steadily fixed thereon.

723. By analysing in this way any particular sensation, we shall find it to consist of two elements, namely, (1) a special feeling which, as I have already shown, is a modification of the fundamental feeling (705, 706), and has for its matter the organ in which that modification has taken place ; (2) a representation or rather, to speak more correctly, a *perception*[2] of something extraneous to us and to our body (708, 709).

The first of these two elements is *subjective*, *i.e.* a modification of the sentient subject ; the second I have termed *extrasubjective*, *i.e.* perceptive of something different from the *subject*.

On the accuracy with which these two elements are dis-

---

[1] Generally speaking the word *sensation* is taken to signify the particular sensations acquired by us.
[2] *Sensitive* perception, of course, which differs essentially from the *intellectual*, as the author has so lucidly explained in this work (TRANSLATORS).

tinguished one from the other depends the genuineness of the notion we form of the nature of bodies and of the manner in which they are perceived. It will not therefore be amiss to add here a few words with the object of fixing well the distinction between these elements, which always are, in the concrete fact itself, conjoined and fused together. And I would ask the reader to bear in mind, that it is the first of them (I mean the partial modification of our fundamental feeling) that is wont, through being as a rule the weaker of the two, to escape observation, which, commonly speaking, takes note only of the second, and believes this to be the all.

ARTICLE II.

Definition of the fundamental feeling, and distinction between it and the sensitive perception of bodies.

724. In every corporeal sensation we feel our sensitive organ in a new way (705).

Moreover, as often as a change or modification is suffered by the sensitive organ, there arises in us a sensitive perception of some agent different from ourselves (703, 704).

The particular perception which we have of the *percipient* organ itself, is a modification of the fundamental feeling (704). This last I have made to consist in an abiding perception of the sensitive parts of our body in their natural and original state (696, 698). Every modification of it is a perception we have of some part of our body as modified, that is to say, as changed with more or less force from that equable and original state.[1]

In order therefore to understand and notice clearly the particular perception we have of our organ as modified, and to distinguish it from the accompanying perception of an agent extraneous thereto, we must consider the nature of that fundamental feeling whereof the said particular perception is only a new mode.

[1] By thus describing the particular way in which we feel our sensitive organs, I make no gratuitous suppositions. It is true that the description takes in the *change suffered by the organ*; but this change is not assumed gratuitously, seeing that the organ is itself part of our body, and therefore of that force which acts in us and concurs in producing the fundamental feeling.

725. Given that we are in a sound normal state of health, the fundamental feeling which springs from life is a *pleasurable* feeling.

It extends equably and softly through all the sensitive parts of our body ; but there does not appear to be in it any thing different from itself. Hence if we could conceive a person who has never in his life experienced any particular sensations, but has always been left with the fundamental feeling alone, it would certainly be impossible for him to form that image or representation of his own body—of its form, its size, &c.—which is furnished by the sight and the other external senses.

The fundamental feeling, then, is nothing else than pleasure diffused in a determinate mode ; [1] hence the modifications of that feeling are simply *sensations* of *pleasure* or of *pain* with a *mode* proper to them.

726. By the aid of these considerations, we can now give a more complete definition of the fundamental feeling, thus : ' It is a fundamental action which we feel to be exercised in us immediately and necessarily by a force different from ourselves ; which action is naturally pleasurable to us, though it may suffer variations according to certain laws, and become successively more or less pleasurable, or even painful.'

ARTICLE III.

Origin and nature of corporeal pleasure and pain.

727. The action experienced by us in the corporeal fundamental feeling constitutes the very essence of corporeal pleasure and pain.

[1] Although the pleasure which springs from life be really diffused throughout every part of our sensitive body, nevertheless, it would hardly be right for one to say, without a word of explanation, that ' We refer that primitive feeling to the different points of the *extension* of our body.' For, common usage applies this expression to the body as known externally, whereas that primitive feeling does not cause us to know our body in this way at all : in it we neither see nor touch the *extra-subjective extension*, and still less the several parts thereof. Consequently the expression is susceptible of being understood in a wrong sense. In speaking therefore of the feeling of our whole sensitive body, we must always remember that this signifies purely a *mode* of that pleasure and nothing more. It is only when we come to perceive our body by the external senses, that we clothe, so to speak, this mode with the external and figured extension. But of all this, I shall have occasion to say more hereafter.

The particular perceptions we have of our sensitive organs when they affect us with some new pleasure or pain, are partial modifications undergone by the said action, according to a law which it is not necessary here to investigate.

Thus pleasure and pain are feelings which we must distinguish from whatever is external and figured in sensation.

I will describe this second element of our sensations later on, after I shall, if possible, have presented to my reader so accurate an idea of the first, that he may no longer be able to confound it with any other.

Corporeal pleasure or pain is purely an affection of our soul ; it does not represent anything, nor figure anything ; it is simply a fact ; it is what it is ; it has nothing in common with anything but itself ; and hence he who does not experience it in himself can neither know its nature, nor define it.

728. Nevertheless, *corporeal* [1] pleasure as well as pain (1) terminates in the *subjective extension* of our body (which I therefore call *matter* of corporeal feeling) ; and (2) it is susceptible of greater or less intensity.

ARTICLE IV.

The relation of corporeal pleasure and pain to extension.

729. As regards *subjective corporeal* extension, it is not difficult to prove that corporeal pleasure and pain terminate in it. [2]

Suppose I place a small square plate of iron on the palm of my hand : I feel the touch of that plate all over the part impressed by it : and if the plate were larger or smaller, or of

---

[1] By saying *corporeal*, I merely wish to indicate by a sign, the difference between this and all other feelings ; without going any deeper into this difference, the examination of which would reveal a third element of the sensation.

[2] Although corporeal pleasure and pain are *passions* of the soul, there is in them also a certain *activity* put forth by the soul itself. I cannot here stop to describe how these two conditions are combined together ; I have said something on them elsewhere. Suffice it to observe, that in so far as pleasure and pain are acts of the soul, they may be said to terminate in extension ; but in so far as they are *passions*, it is more correct to say that the corporeal extension terminates, by its *action*, in them. The truth of these two seemingly contradictory expressions will be seen by considering that perfect *unity*—mysterious yet perfectly true—which takes place between the *subject* and the *extrasubject*, between the agent and the patient, in the instant of the action.

another form—round, triangular, &c.—my sensations would vary accordingly.

730. So with the *fundamental feeling*: embracing as it does all the sensitive parts of our body, it must necessarily extend to, and be present in, every one of them, and this must be its *mode* of being.

This, however, does not, I repeat, mean that we do not also know by the use we have made of our eyes the form and size of the parts affected by pleasure or pain : nothing of the sort. Nevertheless, in dealing with the present question all the knowledge we have thus acquired must be banished entirely from our thoughts. It is through feeling alone— feeling pure and simple, and divested of all such images as could be furnished to us by the sight or the other senses— that the extension I speak of is perceived. And it is precisely in order to distinguish this kind of extension from that which we externally perceive, that I designate it by the epithet of *subjective.*[1]

731. Nor will any difficulty be found in this, if we re- member, as I have already said, that the extension in question must be taken purely as the *mode* in which the feeling exists, so that it can never be entirely separated from it, but only undergo modifications.

The reader must not therefore suppose that the feeling and the subjective extension are two things disjoined by their nature from one another, or that the feeling, concentrated at first, becomes subsequently diffused through the extension as through a thing different from it. Such a supposition would be not only gratuitous, but wholly at variance with the fact as it presents itself to an attentive observation.

It would be to introduce images taken from the sense of sight, whereas all these images must be rigorously excluded, and the attention restricted to the subjective feeling, and to that only.

If the reader adheres strictly to this rule, he will easily see

---

[1] This denomination, however, does not indicate its nature ; for in the ordinary sense of the word all extension is *extrasubjective* ; but it indicates its intimate union with the sensation itself, which, being subjective, takes its mode from that extension.

the impossibility of the soul perceiving in its purely subjective feeling an extension different from that which is found in the feeling itself.[1]

To conclude: the first requisite for being able to thoroughly grasp the true nature of the fundamental feeling and its modifications, consists in disengaging our mind completely from every sensible *figure* as well as from the idea of that extension which is perceived by the external sensories; and in shutting ourselves up in ourselves, and there taking note of the feelings—whether of pain or of pleasure, whether equable or marked by variations—which we experience in the different parts of our body. By acting thus, we shall discover that these feelings have no *figured* extension whatever, though they have a certain limitation or *mode*, which, when mentally abstracted from the feelings themselves, and compared with the extension outwardly perceived, is found to agree with it, and is also called *extension*.

ARTICLE V.

Refutation of the opinion of Ideologists, ' that we first feel everything in the brain, and then refer the sensation to the different parts of our body.'

732. To perceive that the feeling we have of our own body must extend to and diffuse itself through all the sensitive parts of the same, it is enough to consider what follows.

Ideologists declare that 'The fact of our seeing the corporeal objects as outside of us is due to the use of the sense of touch; otherwise they would be adhering to the retina of our eye, like a veil spread closely over it.'

So far they are perfectly right, and I agree with them.[2]

---

[1] Hence extension is the *matter* of the subjective feeling, inasmuch as matter and form make together one thing.

[2] Here I feel bound to dissent from Galluppi, who thinks that the eye sees bodies that are at a distance from it immediately. He compares the globules of light which come in a continuous stream from the illuminated body to strike our retina, to the various parts of a smooth walking-stick felt successively by the hand as it glides over it from knob to point. But the simile will not hold. The hand moves, and the eye does not. Now it is *motion* that causes the hand to feel the length of the stick. And were the stick to be drawn across the hand while the latter remains motionless, I do not think that we could ever perceive the length of that stick, except perhaps through habit and memory. I allow indeed that the eye feels the *outside of itself*, but only

733. But then they add : ' In like manner all our sensations are felt in the brain; for if the communication between the organ and the brain happens to be interrupted, we no longer feel anything; therefore it is only through habitual judgments, that we refer our sensations to the organ affected.'

Now here I am entirely at variance with them. To my thinking, it would be impossible for us, when feeling with our hand the bodies we see, to refer them to a distance from us, unless we first referred the sensation we experience from that touch to the extremity of the hand itself rather than to some central place in our brain.

734. In fact, if it is by means of the touch of our hand that we see a body as at a distance from our eye, how is it, I ask, that we see the hand in a similar way? and that the sensation we experience in that touch, made, for example, with the tips of our fingers, is felt by us, not in our head, where the sensitive nerve is supposed to respond, nor in our soul only, nor along the arm, nor in another part of the hand, but only in the tips of the fingers with which we have touched that body? I contend, that this cannot be the effect of a habit we have contracted ; for, in order reasonably to maintain this, it would be necessary to prove that there was a time in our life when we did not refer our sensations to the various parts of our body ; and that, subsequently, we were supplied with a *means* for learning so to refer them. Now, no such proof has ever been produced by anyone, nor do I believe it can be produced.

in so far as this sense has also the nature of touch, and not otherwise. Hence the eye never perceives *distance*, but only a something *different* from or, if you will, *external* to itself (for I suppose the eye to be felt through the fundamental feeling). Nevertheless, this *outside thing*, though not the eye, would be adhering to the eye. In support of Galluppi's opinion one might quote such facts as that of the young man from whose eyes a cataract with which he had been afflicted from birth was removed by the oculist J. Janin, or of those persons born blind, whom Professor L. de Gregoris partially cured. It is said that none of these individuals had any suspicion that the bodies were things adhering to their eyes, but that all saw them at once as at a distance. (See the pamphlet entitled *Delle catteratte de' ciechi nati, osservazioni teorico-chimiche del Professore di chimica e di oftalmia Luigi de Gregoris.* Rome, 1826.) But such allegations notwithstanding, Cheselden's experiment appears to me too solemn and too well ascertained to be summarily rejected ; and thi̇s all the more as, on its being repeated with the most scrupulous care by Professor Jacobi of Pavia, it was fully corroborated in every detail by the result.

For if the eye stands in need of the touch in order to refer to their proper distances the things it sees, and if from this it is pretended to infer, that the same must be the case as regards those parts of our body which we feel by means of the touch; it will clearly be necessary to attribute to the soul another sense of touch, which causes the different parts of our body to be seen as outside the brain ; a thought as absurd in itself as it is contradicted by experience.

It must therefore be conceded, that there is in our soul a power by which, immediately and not through the intervention of any contracted habit, it refers the sensations to the various parts of the body, and feels them there.

ARTICLE VI.

The two subjective ways of feeling and perceiving the extension of our own body,[1] are compared together.

735. The extension of our own body is, then, a *mode* of the fundamental feeling.

Now as this *fundamental* feeling is either in its *primitive* and natural state or in a state of adventitious and accidental modification, and as in both these states it has always extension for its *mode* ; even so the extension of our body is felt by us subjectively in two ways, viz. :

(1) Through the fundamental feeling, and

(2) Through the modifications of that feeling, or the particular sensations we experience from the impressions made on our bodily organs.

736. The differences to be noted between these two ways of feeling subjectively our sensitive body may be reduced to the following :

(1) By the fundamental feeling the extension of our sensitive body is perceived in *all its entirety* ; by a modification of that feeling, *i.e.* by an adventitious sensation, a *part* only of that extension is felt, the part affected by the sensation.

(2) By the fundamental feeling the extension is felt in an

---

[1] Let it not be forgotten, that this *subjective extension*, is not known to us like that of the external bodies, *i.e.* under a *figured* form, but only as a *mode* of the fundamental feeling.

abiding manner ; by an adventitious sensation the part affected is felt in a *new* manner, more vivid than, or certainly different from, that in which we feel the other parts of the body ; so that, in that feeling, the part is as it were detached from or outside of the rest—it stands alone and isolated.

(3) By the fundamental feeling we feel *necessarily*, so long as life continues ; by a sensation the organ affected is felt in an *accidental* and adventitious manner.

(4) By the fundamental feeling the extension is felt in an almost invariably *equable* manner, or at all events the inequalities are not distinctly present to our consciousness ; by sensations the organs are felt in widely different ways, according to the different degrees of pleasure or of pain, and to the different phenomena of colour, sound, taste and smell.

737. These four differences are quite enough to explain why the fundamental feeling does not, as a general rule, attract attention.   It is connatural to us, and so intimately conjoined with us as to form part of ourselves.   Hence it never presents to us anything new, and therefore calculated to excite that curiosity which prompts us to observe and give advertence to things.

Adventitious sensations, on the contrary, not being essential to our nature, but *partial, new* and *vivid, accidental* and *diversified*, are apt in every way to arouse curiosity and attention, and thus to make us aware that we perceive the several parts of our body with a subjective perception.

Under these circumstances, it is no wonder that there are but few who have a distinct consciousness of the fundamental feeling, whilst the sensations affecting particular organs are patent to everyone.

ARTICLE VII.

Another proof of the existence of the fundamental feeling.

738. But the sensations we have of our bodily organs, when affected, afford a fresh proof of the existence of the fundamental feeling, which precedes those sensations.

For how could we refer a sensation to a particular part of our body, if that part were not felt by us at all ?

This point deserves attention : to say that on occasion of a sensation we feel the part affected contemporaneously with the sensation itself, is not sufficient ; for to feel that part is nothing but to refer the sensation to it ; and hence the assertion will amount to saying that we refer the sensation to a part of our body, of which we have no feeling whatever. How could this be ?

739. The same thing applies to the power we have of moving the members of our body. If these members were not of their nature habitually felt by us, they would be wholly extraneous to us ; consequently we could not by an act of our will set in motion whichever of them we please.

Without the fundamental feeling, therefore, the two species of interior acts of which I speak would be inexplicable, if not altogether absurd, namely, that by which we refer our sensations to the different parts of our body, and that by which we cause those parts to move at pleasure. For we must recollect that it is WE, the human subject, who refer the sensations and produce the movement ; both things are effects of the activity of our soul.

ARTICLE VIII.

All our sensations are at once subjective and extrasubjective.

740. I call a sensation *subjective* in so far as we therein feel our sensitive organ itself as co-sentient with us, and I call it *extrasubjective* in so far as we feel, simultaneously with the organ, an *agent* extraneous thereto.

I say moreover, that, by attentively observing the fact, we find that this duplex nature—subjective and extrasubjective —belongs alike to every one of our external sensations ; that is to say, in each such sensation we at one and the same time feel our sensitive organ modified and have perception of something extraneous to the organ itself. The second of these things is what I have termed *sensitive corporeal percep-tion* ; and it is very often so strong and vivid as to draw our whole attention to itself ; so that we neither think of our sensitive organ, nor of the sensation occurring in it.

741. Nevertheless, the distinction between the *sensitive*

corporeal perception, and the *feeling* we experience in our sensory, is of such importance, that no amount of pains taken in fixing it accurately can be excessive. On the thorough mastery of this distinction depends the solution of a great number of psychological problems.

To make the co-existence of these two perceptions clear to the reader, I will begin with the sense of sight.

Respecting this sense, everybody understands that it is one thing to feel one's own eye, and quite another thing to see the bodies which are presented to the eye.

The bodies perceived by the eye give a representation so vivid and attractive as to draw to itself all our curiosity and excite our admiration, especially if the eye has already been, so to speak, taught and trained by the touch. Hence when we happen to be intensely absorbed in contemplating, for instance, some beautiful natural scenery, or some exquisite works of art, we do not give the least advertence to our eyes, or to the sensation which the light proceeding from those objects causes in them.

The sensation, however, is none the less real on that account. But suppose that your eye is suddenly struck by an intense burst of light, too strong for it to bear. You will immediately feel, and be conscious that you have a distressing pain in the eye. It is in such cases as these that we advert also to the organ affected, namely, because the unusual and comparatively much livelier feeling of pleasure or of pain, then experienced causes us to forget the external agent perceived by that organ, and to notice the percipient organ itself instead.

Meanwhile, what I have said of the eye shows to evidence the fact—easily overlooked indeed, and yet true—that given a suitable modification in the sensitive organ, we experience the two things above mentioned, namely (1) we feel the organ modified, (2) we perceive the external *agent* in that way in which corporeal sensitivity is able to perceive it. And this *perception* is quite a different thing from the *sensation* felt in the organ ; although the two always go inseparably together as parts of a single whole.

742. The same is found to be the case with the sensations of hearing, smell and taste.

By the hearing we get the sensation of sound ; but the sound is neither the modification we feel in the acoustic organ, nor yet the external body by which it has been occasioned. It is a phenomenon which arises in us when that organ comes to be modified, but it has no resemblance with the feeling of the organ itself. In this phenomenon we experience an exciting action of a kind entirely different from the action produced in us by the organ affected.

The former action with its attendant phenomenon of sound, is much stronger than the feeling we experience in our organ, and has great power to attract us to itself, especially if it be endowed with peculiar qualities. Thus, if I hear an extraordinarily sweet melody from a flute, or the stirring harmonies of a harp, played in a masterly manner, I am so enchanted with that music that I lose all thought about my ears. To cause me to transfer my attention from it to these, there must supervene in the latter some modification of a very disagreeable kind, such, for instance, as is produced by the firing of a cannon, at which my hands would instantly rush to close the ears, as a protection against that terrific noise, thus clearly showing my perception of the organ.

743. The same must be said of smelling and tasting, which are the phenomenal parts of the sensations we experience whenever the olfactory nerves or the palate are modified by the agents respectively suited to their nature.

In the fragrance of a carnation and in the taste of honey, the two things I have spoken of may be noticed.

The odoriferous particles of the carnation being wafted on the air to our nostrils, gently titillate the olfactory nerves. Whether this titillation consist in a slight tremulous motion excited in these nerves, or in a tiny wound or mark left on them, I do not care to inquire. But I ask : what do we perceive by smelling ? Is it the little motion or the slight puncture or impression which the odoriferous particles must have caused in those nerves themselves ? Certainly not. Smell is utterly unlike all that. It neither represents nor reminds us

of any motion or form undergone by the olfactory nerves. It is a thing which stands wholly by itself, and arises instantaneously in us on occasion of those slender and perhaps indistinguishable nerve-modifications to which I have referred ; in a word, it is purely what I call the phenomenal part of the sensation of smelling. But should the odoriferous particles be extraordinarily offensive, such as those which assafœtida emits, I need not say that, for the reason stated before, our advertence to the state of the organ thus modified would be shown in no uncertain manner. If this does not always happen, owing to the slenderness of the impression, the fact always remains, that the phenomenon of smell (which is the term of an action from without) has nothing in it resembling our feeling of the organ of smell.

The same must be said of the taste ; for the alteration caused in our palate by the touch of the honey is not by any means the flavour we experience in tasting : *flavour* is but the phenomenal part of that sensation, and is altogether independent of the perception we have of the palate itself.

ARTICLE IX.

Description of the touch as a universal sense.

744. *Touch* is the universal sense : it extends equally to all the sensitive parts of our body.[1]

745. The four other sensories are also touch. How, then, are they distinguished from this sense ?

By the adjunct of the phenomenal part of sensation.

When these sensories are touched, they perceive just in the same way as the touch itself.[2] But together with this, they also, if touched in the proper manner, yield to the soul four

---

[1] The fact that all our sensories are ultimately reduced to that of touch did not escape the notice of the ancients : hence S. Thomas writes : ' Omnes autem alii sensus fundantur supra tactum ' (*S.* I. lxxvi. 5).

[2] We have seen that the perception belonging to the touch is of a *duplex nature*, that is, *subjective* and *extrasubjective* at the same time, inasmuch as in the sensation of touch we perceive (1) the sentient organ (subjective part), and (2) the external agent which impresses the organ (extrasubjective part). What I shall say further on will show yet more clearly how this *duplex nature of sensation* belongs also to the four particular sensories of which I speak, and how, besides this, there are in them the four *phenomena* I have indicated.

different species of phenomena, *i.e.* colour, sound, smell, and taste.   These phenomena distinguish each of the four from the others, and all from the touch, which is common to every one of them, and diffused through the rest of the body.

ARTICLE X.

Origin of the sense of touch.

746. The sense of touch, considered in its *subjective* element, is nothing but the susceptibility which our corporeal fundamental feeling has of receiving modifications.

Now, since the fundamental feeling extends to all the sensitive parts of our body, or in other words, since this extension is nothing but the *mode in which that feeling exists* (735), it follows that if a change takes place in this *mode*, the fundamental feeling must also undergo a change.   It is for this reason, that on the suitable impressions being made in our body, we experience the sensations of touch.

Moreover, with some of these sensations are conjoined the four different species of phenomena I have mentioned, as also others which it is unnecessary to enumerate here.

ARTICLE XI.

Relation between the two subjective ways of perceiving our body.

747. All our particular sensations, then, rest on the sensation of touch as their basis, and hence in all of them there is a modification of the sentient organ, which is felt by us, though not always with advertence.   Nay, we very seldom advert to it in the case of the four sensories to which the above-named sensible phenomena belong ; for the vivacity and singularity of those phenomena, as also their advantage and their necessity, draw our whole attention to them and divert it from the perception we have of the organ itself—a perception generally of no practical use to us.

But this is not applicable in the same degree to the sense of touch, a sense less phenomenal, and therefore more apt to let our attention fall on the organ itself.

The second way, then, in which we perceive our body, that is to say, by means of particular sensations, does not differ essentially from the first. And it is also subjective, inasmuch as by it we perceive our organs, not only as *felt*, but also as *co-sentient* with us, or as forming one thing with OURSELVES, the sentient subject.

748. Nevertheless, in both these two ways of feeling and perceiving our body, the matter of the fundamental feeling and of the particular sensation, is always the same (*i.e.* our own body). Consequently there can be no contradiction between them.

What makes the two consistent with and equal to each other, is the fact of our referring them to the same points in space (731).

CHAPTER V.

CRITERION OF THE EXISTENCE OF BODIES.

ARTICLE I.

An improved definition of bodies.

749. The analysis we have made of the fundamental feeling and of the adventitious sensations (in their subjective part), places us in a position to improve our definition of *body*.

First of all let us pass in review the most celebrated definitions which have been proposed in modern times.

I. Berkeley and Condillac defined body as ' An aggregate of sensations.'

But, as we have seen, *sensation* can be nothing else than an effect of the action of a body on a sentient subject. Hence in this definition the *agent*—that is, the corporeal *substance* —is wanting, and nothing is retained but an accidental effect of it. Now the corporeal substance is the body itself. Consequently the definition given by these two philosophers excluded the body and included Idealism, or the negation of bodies.

750. II. Des Cartes and Malebranche placed the essence of body in *extension.*

But the concept of extension does not present to us any activity, any force. Rather than an activity or force, extension is the term of an action. Observation tells us that the first thing we experience from bodies is the sensation they produce in us by acting on us in a certain mode ; and it is only by afterwards analysing this sensation that we find it to refer to certain points in space, to diffuse itself and terminate in extension. Hence, at the outset, extension presents itself to us simply as a *mode* of that feeling which bodies produce in us.   It is true that the analysis (to which I shall come presently) of this *mode* of feeling shows that it must also have a real counterpart in the cause which has produced it, and that therefore bodies must be extended.   But this is merely a secondary discovery ; and the *essence* of a thing, according to Des Cartes, is that which our mind conceives first in a given object.   Now we could not think of extension, unless we first thought of an *action* which is done in us, and through which the extension itself is brought to our cognisance.

751. III. Leibnitz perceived that the essence of bodies must consist in a *force*; but in making this out he omitted to start from observation, the one sure guide in inquiries of this sort.   Hence instead of restricting himself to the fact certified by our consciousness, which presents to us the substance called *body* simply as a force acting on us, and by that action causing in us a corporeal feeling in respect of which we are passive, he imagined that this substance (like all his other monads) must be a force acting, not on us (although it acts *harmoniously with* us), but only in itself, by an energy intrinsic to it.   He thus deprived himself of the only means he had of knowing the true nature of that force ; for we cannot know it otherwise than by observing the effect which the force produces in us.   The hypothesis that this knowledge springs up, and is developed purely from within our own selves, independently of what we experience, is, as I have said, a mere imagination, wholly unsupported by fact, analogy, or any valid intrinsic proofs.   Now if our idea of bodies must be formed, not upon what observation tells of them, but according to our imagination, there was nothing to prevent our philosopher from picturing to himself the forces which we call *bodies* in any way he pleased.   Hence he could suppose them [1] as *simple* and endowed with *perception*, that is, as substances not *sensiferous* but *sentient*.   Thus, the Leibnitzian idea of bodies is entirely different from that which I submit to my readers.

752. In all that I say about bodies my starting point is

[1] Further on I shall have the opportunity of giving a direct disproof of the *simple points* of Leibnitz and of Boscovich.

observation, and I do not wish my description of them to contain anything but what is in accordance with the depositions of this guide.

Whether in bodies there be anything which does not fall under our experience, or does not enter as an essential into our concept of them, is a point I have now no thought of investigating; the inquiry would be foreign to my purpose.

Observation, then, deposes that in our sensations we are passive. To be passive, means to suffer an action of which we are not the authors. The consciousness of an action done in us, but of which we are not the authors, is the consciousness of a force acting on us; and a force acting on us and conceived by our mind, is a being, a substance. Hence the first definition, as yet imperfect, which I gave of *body* was this: ' Body is a substance which acts on us in *a certain mode.*'

In order to perfect this definition, it was necessary to ascertain the precise value of that vague phrase *a certain mode*—the mode in which the corporeal substance acts on us —and, having ascertained it, to substitute it in the formula.

The action of this substance consists in causing in us a sensation or feeling : this sensation or feeling had therefore to be analysed.

I attempted this analysis; and I found that there is a fundamental feeling, constant and uniform,[1] and again there are partial and adventitious feelings (sensations) which modify the fundamental. Hence two actions, two forces, two substances, two bodies—our own body, producing in us the fundamental feeling, and external bodies, producing the modifications of that feeling ; in other words, the body which is both felt by and sentient with us, and those bodies which are only felt.

The fundamental feeling is a pleasurable feeling, and not only pleasurable but also characterised by a mode or limitation proper to itself—a mode or limitation which is in itself distinct from pleasure considered purely as such, and is called *extension.*

All adventitious sensations are a species of touch.

[1] With the natural growth of our body, the fundamental feeling becomes modified.

The sensation of *touch* is at once *subjective* and *extra-subjective*: that is to say, in this sensation we feel two things at one and the same time.

We feel the sentient *organ* itself, and this is the *subjective* part; and we feel the *external agent* which by coming in contact with us has produced the sensation, and this is the *extrasubjective* part.

The *subjective* part is a modification of the fundamental feeling, and by it that part of our body which has been affected is perceived with a feeling more vivid and new, but which is found to refer to the same points in space as the fundamental feeling.

There are, however, four classes or species of sensations proper to four of our sensitive organs, to which belong four species of phenomena—*i.e. colour, sound, taste* and *smell.*

The action which the corporeal substance exercises on us being thus analysed, I say that the essence of *body* must consist in that which in such action is common and invariable, namely, (1) the feeling of pleasure or pain, (2) the extension where this feeling is experienced. Hence the definition of body quoted above may be improved in the following manner: 'Body is a substance which acts in such a way as to produce in us a feeling of pleasure, or of pain, characterised by a constant mode which we call *extension.*'

And it may also be added: 'and which may be accompanied by the four species of phenomena called colour, sound, smell and taste;' taking note, however, that this addition does not import the necessity of these phenomena actually taking place, but only that bodies have the *aptitude* to excite them in us, given all the requisite conditions.

753. Wherefore, if such a substance be permanently conjoined with us by that union which is called *vital* (in *what* this union consists, it is none of my duty here to investigate), that substance is our subjective body, and exercises on our soul a constant and uniform action resulting in what I call the *fundamental feeling.* But if it be not so conjoined with us, then it is an external body and can only produce in us particular and transient sensations.

ARTICLE II.

General criterion for our judgments concerning the existence of bodies.

754. Having now found the definition of *body* (752), we possess the criterion by which to judge of its existence. It is this :—

'We are certain of the existence of a body when we are certain of the existence of that which constitutes its *essence* and is expressed in the definition.'

ARTICLE III.

Application of the general criterion.

755. In the primitive perception of our body we experience a pleasurable feeling, I mean the feeling which springs from life or the individual conjunction of a body with ourselves.

This feeling refers to different points of space,[1] in other words, it has *extension* for its mode of being. Therefore by that first perception we perceive a body.

756. In the same way is proved the existence of external bodies, namely, from the fact that in the adventitious sensations we perceive the two elements expressed by the definition of body.

The extension through which our first or fundamental feeling is diffused, suffers modifications from a cause which is not ourselves, and in these modifications there takes place in us, (1) a particular sensation of pleasure or of pain, and (2) this sensation diffused over an extension more limited than the first, but, so far as it goes, conterminous with it.[2]

These conditions, again, make us certain of the perceptions of external bodies.

757. The pleasurable (or disagreeable) sensation which we

---

[1] To say that the feeling refers to different points of space, is a form of expression which easily suggests the thought of space as perceived *extra-subjectively*, that is, *figured* space : on the other hand, to call extension purely a *mode* of the feeling, is a form of expression which does not indicate anything beyond the *subjective* perception of the same extension.

[2] In addition to this, there are the phenomena of the sight, the hearing, the smell and the taste, supposing these to be the sensories affected.

experience in us does not, by itself alone, indicate the presence of a body. It informs us indeed that an action is being exercised on us, and has therefore a cause other than ourselves ; but it could never tell us (I mean if it existed purely as sensation) that that cause is a body, inasmuch as extension—one of the essentials of bodies—would be wanting. To betoken the presence of a body, that sensation must be such as to make us perceive an extension. It is by extension that a sensation is constituted in the nature of those feelings which are called *corporeal* or *material*.

On the other hand, extension alone does not constitute a body, because the first element necessary to constitute a body is the *force* capable of producing in us a feeling.

That we may not, therefore, fall into error as to the existence of a body, we must make sure of the two essentials of the corporeal substance, viz. (1) the *feeling* (passion caused by an external force acting on us), and (2) the extension characteristic of that feeling (*mode* of that feeling). Let us come to the application.

758. There is a *force acting* in us in such a manner as to constitute the fundamental feeling : and this feeling has extension conjoined with it as its mode.

Consequently, there is a body permanently united to us. Thus the existence of our own body cannot be a matter of doubt ; because the two essentials of a body—viz. a *force* acting in us, and extension—are facts certified by our consciousness. We cannot mistake as to our being alive or not.

And as regards the adventitious sensations, we distinguish in them, (1) a modification of the fundamental feeling, or a new and more vivid feeling in some part of our body ; (2) the perception of an agent external to the extension embraced by the fundamental feeling.

The modification is the second *subjective* way of perceiving our body ; the perception constitutes the *extrasubjective* perception of external bodies.

The certainty therefore of the existence of our own body is always based on the testimony of the fundamental feeling.

759. And so is the certainty of the existence of external

bodies ; for the action which they exercise on us, is inseparably conjoined with the modification of this feeling, and their extension is measured by the very same extension which is previously occupied by it.

ARTICLE IV.

The certainty of the existence of our own body is the criterion of the existence of other bodies.

760. It follows from the above, that our body as perceived by the fundamental feeling is a *criterion* of the existence of all other bodies.

And it is to this first kind of perception that the other two kinds must be reduced, namely, the second *subjective*, because it is only the fundamental feeling itself modified ; and the third or *extrasubjective* (for external bodies), because the *extrasubjective* extension is ascertained by comparing it with the subjective.

ARTICLE V.

Application of the criterion to the errors which sometimes occur in reference to the existence of some particular member of our body.

761. About the existence of our body as perceived by the primitive or fundamental feeling, there can be no error (755–759).

But in the perceptions obtained through adventitious sensations (viz. the second *subjective* perception and the *extrasubjective*, 760), we may be deceived as to the existence of some part of our body.

762. Respecting the error which may happen in connexion with the third or *extrasubjective* way of perceiving our body, I shall say nothing now, because this error is common to the perception of all bodies external to ours, and of this I shall have to speak later.

But with regard to the error into which we may fall concerning the existence of some part of our body as perceived in the second subjective way, here is the case and its solution.

A man who has lost a hand or a foot, even long after the

wound has been perfectly healed, is at times made unhappy by distressing pains felt, not at the stump where the amputation took place, but in the hand or foot itself, so that it seems to him as if he had it still. He refers therefore his pain to a part or extension which does not exist.

Such is the error.[1] Let us see how it can be detected by applying the criterion as above.

This man does not feel the amputated hand or foot through the fundamental feeling, but through the adventitious sensation of those pains. To see, therefore, whether this sensation tells the truth or not, we must, as I have said, test it by the fundamental feeling.

We are sure that an adventitious sensation is reduced to the fundamental feeling from the moment we discover that it is a modification of this feeling. Let us see, then, how this discovery is made in the case in question.

Undoubtedly, the pain felt in the amputated hand or foot is a modification of the fundamental feeling, but this does not yet prove that these bodies (the hand and the foot) exist (757).

To prove their existence, it is furthermore necessary that the extension felt in that sensation of pain be reducible to the same extension as that of the fundamental feeling.

Now what are the characteristics of the extension of the fundamental feeling?

We have seen two of them: (1) its uniformity and permanency; (2) its aptitude to undergo modifications. Let us take the second, and see if the extension of the hand or foot we have lost can stand the test of a comparison with it.

Is the hand which we feel in the manner stated, the same as is perceived in the fundamental feeling? If so, it must be susceptible of many modifications, because such is essentially

---

[1] The cause of this error does not lie in the sensation, but in a judgment resulting from *habit*. While we had the hand or the foot, we used to refer the pain to these parts of our body; nor could we do otherwise, for it was they that were affected by the pain. Now this necessity has induced in us a *habit* of referring that pain to those parts; and the habit remains even after the necessity has ceased. When, therefore, we feel a painful sensation much of the same kind as that which we formerly experienced in the hand or foot, we confound it with the former sensation, and refer it to the same place, not adverting to our mistake.

the property of a hand perceived in the extension characteristic of the fundamental feeling. We shall therefore be able to
touch it, see it, move it and so forth. But the missing hand
admits of nothing of this. Therefore we do not perceive it
by, nor, consequently, can reduce the sensation in question to
the fundamental feeling, or prove it to be a mere modification
of the extension thereof. Consequently that sensation is a
deceptive phenomenon. In fact, when I feel my real hand
through a particular pain I happen to experience in it, the
mode of this sensation—viz. its extension—is identical with
that of the fundamental feeling, nor can there be any difference, save this, that in the fundamental feeling itself the
sensation is permanent and less vivid, while the adventitious
sensation is transient, partial and much more lively.

ARTICLE VI.

Refutation of the idealistic argument drawn from dreams.

763. From this we can see how vain is the argument
drawn by Idealists against the existence of bodies from the
illusory nature of our dreams. They ask : may not life be
nothing but a continuous dream ?

They fail to observe that if dreams deceive us as regards
the existence of external bodies, they are a confirmation of
the existence of our own.

We could not be subject to the illusions of dreams if we
had not a body which, being affected in certain ways, gave
rise in us to this class of phenomena. Obviously, for dream-
ing we must have a body. Further on we shall see by what
means we can distinguish real from deceptive external phenomena.

CHAPTER VI.

ORIGIN OF THE IDEA OF TIME.

ARTICLE I.

Connexion of the doctrines already explained with those which are to follow.

764. Having seen how we perceive our own body in two *subjective* ways, it now remains for me to speak of the third or *extrasubjective* way. This holds good for all bodies which act externally on our sensorial organs, and hence for our own body in so far as perceived like all the others, that is, not subjectively, but in an external manner.

But before entering upon this subject, I must treat of certain *abstract ideas* which can be derived, at least in part, through abstraction, even from the body subjectively perceived [1]—I mean the ideas of *time, motion* and *space*.

765. *Time* is connected with all the facts, active or passive, which are certified by our consciousness. *Motion* has no need of the external senses in order to be perceived by us, because, as the same consciousness testifies, our *motive faculty* is *internal* to us and subjective. Lastly, *space* or *extension* is but a mode of our subjective corporeal feeling,[2] from which it cannot be separated in point of fact, although it can be distinguished by a mental abstraction, even as in every being the *mode* of its beingness can, by abstraction, be considered

---

[1] Our mind does not make this abstraction until it has attained a sufficient degree of development, which is only acquired through the use of the external senses. This, however, does not prevent the subjective perceptions of our body from being the foundation of the abstractions to which I refer.

[2] So far, we have not made out anything further concerning *extension*; later on we shall learn more of its nature, and see that it exists, not merely in the sentient subject, but in the external agent also.

apart, although in the real fact it is indivisibly united with the being itself.

Of the ideas therefore of *time, motion* and *space,* we have already, to a certain extent, the source in those ideas which I have thus far endeavoured to expound. It will, nevertheless, be well to make use also of the *extrasubjective* perception of bodies and of the service rendered by the external senses, in order not to disjoin that which is so commonly united together in our mind. Let us see, then, how these ideas are formed.

ARTICLE II.

The idea of Time as acquired from the consciousness we have of our own actions.

766. Our every action is marked by two limitations;[1] and the same consciousness which tells us of an action being done by us, informs us also of these limitations.

The first of them is the *degree of intensity* in the action ; the second is a certain *duration* of that action. But it must be remembered that the terms *intensity* and *duration* signify the two limitations in an abstract state, that is, after we have divided them in thought from the external and internal actions themselves which they limit, and thus converted them into two mental entities.

767. Up to a certain point, we can increase the *intensity* as well as the *duration* of our actions, and we can also conceive this duration to increase indefinitely. Now the idea of *successive duration* is the idea of *Time.*

768. As my present action has a successive duration, so has every other action whether done by me or others.

Hence the duration of one action, when compared with that of other actions, gives a certain relation. This relation is called the *Measure of time.*

769. Generally we take for the measure of time some

---

[1] The action called *life* is the first which we feel as going on in us, and to this action also belongs the limitation of *duration.* In the *fundamental feeling,* therefore, the feeling of *time* is also comprised. But the analysis of the fundamental feeling would be a task too long for me to undertake in this place ; suffice it to indicate respecting this feeling what is necessary for my present purpose.

action of a glaring, uniform, and permanent character. Such
is the revolution of the earth on its axis, and round the sun :
and the several parts of this action form the parts or divisions
of time in common use—years, months, days, hours, &c.

Any other action might have answered the same purpose,
provided its duration had been taken as the standard of the
duration of all other actions.

770. Although I can diminish or increase the duration of
an action done by me, yet if I wish to maintain the same
quantity of action I can only do so on condition of making
up in intensity for what I lose in duration; or if I increase
the duration, I must proportionately diminish the intensity.
Therefore, between the *duration* of a given action and its
intensity, there is a constant relation.

In the case of motion, the *intensity* consists in *velocity*,
which is greater in direct ratio to the space traversed, and in
inverse ratio to the time consumed in the transit ; hence the
formula : $V = \dfrac{S}{T}$, or $T = \dfrac{S}{V}$.

771. The constancy of this relation is founded on two
constant data, that is to say, (1) the constant quantity of
the effect or action which it is sought to produce; (2) the
limited quantity of the forces employed in the production,
which quantity is also determinate and constant.

Hence the following law, issuing from the nature of
things: 'If a given quantity of action is wanted within a
given time, there must be a given and fixed intensity of
action to obtain it.'

772. Again, let us suppose that the quantity of action
wanted is undetermined, and the intensity of the action
variable, but the duration constant. By applying to this
duration successively an intensity of action varying in degree, we shall have a series expressing as many quantities of
actions or effects as correspond exactly to the several grades
of intensity. We may therefore say in general, that 'Given
a certain duration, the quantity of action will be proportionate
to the intensity of the action, neither more nor less. Hence
the idea of the *Equableness of time.* Whatever may be done

within a given time, there is a constant relation between the intensity of the action and its quantity, so that if I were to see but little done in that time, I could indeed always imagine that more might be done, but only conditionally on the supposition of an increase in the intensity of the action. In short, I can think the possibility of doing a thing within a certain time by means of a certain intensity of action ; and I can think precisely the same of any similar duration.

773. Should we wish to express in a general formula the relation between the *quantity of action*, the *intensity* and the *time*—designated respectively by the letters Q, I, T, we should have : $T = \dfrac{Q}{I}$; that is, assuming that there is but one agent at work ; for if the action proceeded from many agents together—indicated by the letter M—the formula would be $T = \dfrac{Q}{I\,M}$.

ARTICLE III.

The idea of time as suggested by the actions of beings other than ourselves.

774. What has been said in respect of actions whereof we are conscious of being the authors, applies equally to those of which we are not the authors, but the percipients only.

Thus time is a *limitation*, not merely of actions, but of passions also ; and this because *passion* and *action* are very often but one and the same fact considered under two different and opposite aspects.

ARTICLE IV.

The pure idea of time.

775. In all the actions and passions of finite beings, our mind can by abstraction take away that limitation which I have termed their *successive duration* (766), and then, by applying the *idea of possible being* (which, as we have seen, is innate in us), conceive the action purely in a state of *possibility* : this gives us the pure idea of time, *i.e.* the idea of time, not in a real, but in a possible action.

ARTICLE V.

The idea of pure time as indefinitely long.

776. The pure idea of *time*, then, or, which is the same thing, the idea of time in general, as supplied to us by observation, may be expressed by the abstract formula : ' Given a certain degree of intensity in the action, a certain quantity of action will be the result.'

777. Supposing therefore that the intensity is constant, the *quantity of action* produced will be the *measure of time* ; and the *equableness of time* simply means ' The same quantity of action obtained by a constant degree of intensity.'

778. But given this quantity of action so obtained (of whatever kind the action or the force engaged in producing it may be), we can always, by means of the idea of possibility, conceive it as repeating itself an indefinite number of times. Hence the idea of the *indefinite length of time*. This idea therefore, when analysed, is found to be composed (1) of the idea of *possibility*, indefinite by its nature ; (2) of the (abstract) idea of one of the two limitations to which all actions successively repeated are subject.

ARTICLE VI.

On the continuity of time.

§ 1.

Everything that happens, happens by instants.

779. At whatever instant we may observe anything in which there is succession—that is, which begins, increases, comes to perfection, grows old and perishes—we find in it a determinate state.

In fact, by the principle of contradiction there cannot be in that thing any part or degree of perfection existing and not existing at the same moment.

For example, we observe a child that is cutting its teeth, or a youth at the period when his beard is growing. If we are asked : are the teeth cut? or is the beard grown? we answer : not yet ; they are *beginning*. This word *beginning* implies a mental relation with that state in which the teeth or beard will be when full grown. Yet it is certain that each particle of the growing teeth or beard, considered in itself, already exists, nor is there any middle term between its existing and its not existing.

780. This simple observation of the fact gives us a consequence, singular indeed, but nevertheless true. It is, that ' All that happens, happens in an instant ; ' meaning of course by *All that happens*, not a complex thing, that is, a nature already complete in all its parts (and this is what men usually think of), but only such part or element of a nature as comes to exist in each instant ; for no matter what that part or element may be which is found to exist in a given instant, it is complete relatively to itself, to its own existence, although it is incomplete when considered as a part, element, germ, or beginning of a thing greater than itself.

781. But here arises a serious difficulty. If, as just stated, all that happens, happens in an instant, whence comes our idea of *continuous* time ? Do we get this also by means of abstraction from the actions observed by us ? Clearly not ; for, by thinking of a series of things each happening in an instant, our mind conceives indeed a series of points, a succession of instants, but not a *continuous* duration.

§ 2.

In the idea of time, as supplied by observation alone, we can find no solution of the above difficulty.

782. Let us return to the example of the growing beard, and see if it be possible by means of observation alone to form a concept of time characterised by true continuity.

A single hair a palm in length took, we will say, two months to grow.

This growth is one of those which I have called *complex actions*, because it presents itself to us as composed of many small actions, each of less duration than the whole.

It would be the same with every other kind of production.

Thus the growth of a flower, the carving of a bas-relief, or any other operation by which a thing has been brought into being, or made to undergo a change, all are *complex actions*, inasmuch as our thought can always subdivide each into several parts, which are so many lesser actions, or 'things that happen.'

Now be it noted in the first place, that the time that hair took in growing maintains a constant ratio with all the other actions which occurred within the two months, as has been explained above (764, 765), that is, account being taken of the intensity of the operation.

Assuming the intensity as fixed, any force operating during those two months could only yield a certain *quantity of action*, a determinate effect.

Let us see, then, how this complex and successive action, or total effect, can be conceived as divided into instants in the period named.

Let us make any arbitrary distribution of these instants we please. Let us suppose the hair to have grown a palm in 5,184,000 instants, so that in each one of them it acquired a corresponding increase. I say, that if at the end of two months its total length must be a palm and no more, it is necessary that the intervals which divide those instants from one another be of a determinate length ; and assuming all the intervals as equal, each will be precisely of one second.

Intervals so minute (and they might be still more minute) would entirely escape our observation. Therefore we could neither measure nor perceive them by means of observation, but solely by means of reasoning, that is, we could judge of their length by knowing the total effect or quantity of action produced in a given noticeable time (when we can fairly observe the action), for instance, two months, or even less ; and the measure of that total effect or quantity of action is nothing but the relation in which it stands to all other total effects or quantities of action obtained within the same period.

But let us dwell a little longer on the supposition of the existence of these minute intervals. If they were really observable by us, how could they fall under our observation ?

Certainly not by themselves, because intervals, as such, are a mere negation, a cessation from action, and consequently there is nothing in them to observe. Therefore we could only observe them through the relation of the different frequency with which the instants occur in different actions. If then it were possible for us to notice the successive instantaneous increases which we have supposed to accrue to the hair every second, we could not, by looking at this action alone, have any measure of this interval. In order to have such measure, we must compare that action to some other which goes on in us in a corresponding interval, such as the beating of the pulse or a degree of fatigue, &c. On the other hand, by comparing several actions together, for example, by noting how a hair grows respectively in an old man and in a youth, we would perceive that while in the old man the hair receives one increase, in the youth it receives two or three. Hence the measure of the little interval aforesaid—a measure, be it understood, always drawn from the quantity of action produced within two instants (given the intensity equal). Therefore the measure of those most minute intervals of which I am speaking, if it could be obtained by observation, would consist simply in the relation seen by the mind to exist between two forces acting in the same two instants—and thus could not differ in kind from that of a series of instants or of a noticeable time, at the end of which we confront together quantities of action or total effects large enough to fall under our observation.

I conclude then : seeing *first*, that everything that happens, happens in an instant, and *secondly*, that the idea of time which observation can give us is merely a relation between the different quantities of action produced within the same instants, it follows necessarily that :—

Observation—even were its powers indefinitely more keen and penetrating than at present—never could by itself alone supply to us the idea of a *continuous* time, *i.e.* a continuous succession : it could only give us the idea of a series of instants more or less proximate to one another, and show us the relation existing between them.

And yet, it is a fact that we do possess the idea of *continuous* time. The question, then, still remains, *how* we come to have it.

§ 3.

Necessity of having recourse to the simple possibilities of things, and importance of not confounding them with real things.

783. Let us therefore, in our ideas concerning time, separate those which are suggested to us immediately by observation, from those which we form through reasoning—abstract indeed in itself, yet always based on observation.

Observation presents to us nothing but *facts*; whereas ideas express not facts, but *pure possibilities*.

Nevertheless, *ideas* should not on this account be despised, as they were by the hasty temerity of the eighteenth century ; but should be given their proper place, *i.e.* should always be kept perfectly distinct from the cognitions of *real* things and of facts.

Ideas or possibilities are most valuable for two reasons : (1) because without them we could not make any reasoning whatever even about real things or facts, as is evident from the whole theory of the origin of ideas, which shows that the element of *possibility* is a necessary ingredient of every idea (470); (2) because amongst all contradictory propositions conceivable about anything, there must needs be a true one, and this one may sometimes be discovered by means of reasoning.[1]

The confounding of possibilities with realities is the root of all errors ; since it corrupts method itself, *i.e.* the means of arriving at truth.

Let us therefore proceed to separate with due diligence such cognitions about time as we get immediately from observation, and which inform us of facts, from those which express simple *possibilities*.[2]

---

[1] Which, of course, consists of ideas (TRANSLATORS).

[2] These cognitions are the same as the intellectual perceptions of things, which perceptions are composed of *ideas* and of *judgments*. The ideas detached from these judgments, and not submitted to any other mental operation, express indeed *possibilities*, but such as have cases of actual realisation.

§ 4.

Time, as known by observation alone, is simply a relation between the respective quantities of actions, given the same acting intensity.

784. By observation, then, we perceive *great actions* only (782); for when an action is divided or attenuated beyond a certain point, it entirely escapes detection.

The same observation which presents to us these great actions, gives us also the relation [1] of their respective quantities (the acting intensity being, however, taken into account).

Now from the difference in the quantities of action (given always an equal intensity) there arises a circumstance which is precisely what enables observation to give us the idea of time. I will explain.

The action which (given the intensity equal) has less quantity, is completed, and therefore can be observed by us while we are still unable to observe the greater action, *i.e.* the total effect, because this has not yet been produced.

Now the aptitude which the minor action—a part of the greater—has of being observed by us at a moment more or less distant from that in which the whole will be completed, constitutes what we call the *successive duration of the action*, which is identical with our idea of time as derived from observation.

§ 5.

The idea of pure time, and that of its indefinite length and divisibility, are mere possibilities or mental concepts.

785. So far the *fact*. Now what are the *possibilities* which, this fact being presupposed, present themselves to our mind? And be it remembered that, in the deduction of *possibilities*, the mind goes on as far as ever it can, that is, until it comes to something where it sees logical contradiction.

I. In the first place, observing that within two given instants [2] many real actions take place, differing in quantity,

---

[1] I mean, of course, a relation already conceived by the mind.; for, as I have shown (180-187), it is only by the mind that *relations* are noticed.

[2] These instants are nothing but the *beginning* and the *end* of a possible complex action which we take as a standard of measurement.

but maintaining a certain relation to their respective intensities and to one another, the mind proceeds by means of abstraction to conceive these same actions, not in their real, but only in their *possible* existence. The conception of this possibility is the *pure idea of time* (775).

786. II. After this, the mind notices, that among the several actions observed by us, there are some which within two given instants repeat themselves twice, thrice, or it may be a thousand times as often as others. Hence, by abstracting as before, it conceives those actions as *possible* to be *indefinitely* repeated even beyond those instants—or which is the same thing, it sees no contradiction in that thought. This second *possibility* conceived by the mind, gives the idea of the *indefinite length of time* (778).

787. III. Moreover, from noticing that certain actions take longer in their production than others, so that while one is done once, another is repeated many times over, the mind very naturally concludes, that by the instant that the shorter action is fully completed once, the longer action can only be done in some part. It considers therefore an action as the result of many parts, or a compound of many minor actions. It is true, that when these have dwindled down to an extreme minuteness, our powers of observation fail us ; but the mind conceives the *possibility* of a keener observation than is now at our command ; and then of another yet keener, and so on again and again, without an assignable limit ; for even in this it finds no contradiction. Whence it infers that, had we only observing powers keen enough, we could discover an action of yet shorter duration than the least that is observable in our present condition. Thus the mind conceives the *possibility* of actions indefinitely shorter and shorter ; and this gives the idea of the *indefinite divisibility of time.*

788. IV. Therefore the *indefinite divisibility of time* is nothing but the possibility which the mind conceives of a series of instants always nearer and nearer to one another—or in other words, of actions always shorter and shorter, and the beginning and end of which are precisely the instants of that series, in the same way that the two extreme points of a

line are its terms.　Nevertheless, this is not yet the idea of *continuity* of which we are now in search.　Let us see, then, how this idea also is a mental *possibility*; and let us proceed herein with special care, because this idea is not less important than difficult of explanation.

§ 6.

The phenomenal idea of the continuity of time is illusory.

789.　The most minute intervals which divide from one another those small actions of which we -have seen that the greater actions are composed, entirely escape our observation (782).　Hence the total result of the numberless little actions aforesaid presents itself to us as though it were a single and *continuous* action (784–788).　This, however, is only an appearance.　The idea, therefore, which observation gives us of the *continuity* of time is purely *phenomenal* or apparent.

That it is not anything else, is evidenced by the fact indicated above, namely, that 'All that happens must necessarily happen by instants' (779–781): for a series of instants can never be joined together into a truly continuous time, however near the instants may be brought to one another.

790.　But since this truth is of the very greatest consequence, I wish to corroborate it by a new demonstration, carried up even to the principle of contradiction—I mean such a demonstration as will show that the notion of any of those actions which can fall under our observation being performed entirely without interruption, or, which comes to the same, in a *truly continuous time*, involves contradiction.

As I have already observed (785), our mind, in its speculations within the world of possibilities, never stops until it comes to a point involving contradiction.　There it is bound to stop, because contradiction, being impossibility itself, cannot possibly form an object of thought.

Now I add, that a perfectly uninterrupted or *continuous* succession is neither more nor less than a contradiction, and therefore the mind cannot see it as a possibility.　This I shall prove by the following propositions : —

First proposition : ' To think that an indeterminate number actually exists, is a contradiction in terms.'

In the idea of a number actually existent, the determination of that number is included as a necessary condition. The mere fact of my thinking any one number, proves that that number is determinate. If it were not, I could not think it as a number, for it would not then be a particular number, but simply, number in general, a purely mental entity. To see this more clearly, let the reader consider, that if I write down on paper the series of numbers in their natural order—1, 2, 3, 4, 5, &c.—and suppose it carried on indefinitely, this series will be a formula which expresses and enumerates all the particular numbers possible. If, then, I think a particular number, I must necessarily think one of the numbers comprised in the said formula. Now every one of the numbers contained in that series is determinate, *i.e.* each is itself, and is not another. For instance, 3 is 3, neither more nor less, not 4, nor 2, or any other number that could be named. Determination is of the specific essence of number. An indeterminate number, therefore, neither exists nor can exist.

Second proposition : ' If a number of things, in order that it may exist, must be *determinate*, it must also be *finite.*'

This also is clear ; for the *determination* of a number necessarily includes its *finiteness.* In fact, as I have just observed, the word *determinate*, when applied to a number, means that that number is itself and not any other, and therefore that its existence is entirely distinct, both from the number which precedes and from that which follows it. Take any number you please from among those of the series we have supposed to contain all particular numbers ; and you will find that it is always the number immediately preceding it, *plus* a unit. But the preceding number is certainly finite, since, like this one, it is nothing but the number previous to itself, *plus* a unit. And so you may go back in succession from one number to the other until you have come to the beginning of the series, *i.e.* to the unit alone. This will make it evident, that every particular number is, and cannot be anything else than the unit *plus* other units, *i.e.* a sum of finite numbers, and therefore finite. Any determinate number, then, is necessarily finite ; consequently the actual existence of things truly infinite in number would be an absurdity.

Third proposition : 'A succession of things infinite in number is a contradiction in terms.'

The proof of this proposition is contained in the preceding two.

A succession of things infinite in number is unthinkable for the same reason that an infinite number is unthinkable, namely, because it involves contradiction.

That which is unthinkable because involving a contradiction, is an impossibility.

Therefore a succession of things infinite in number is an impossibility or, what comes to the same, a contradiction in terms.

Fourth proposition : ' The production of an entity by means of an action at once successive and continuous would involve a succession of things actually infinite in number.'

In a continuous succession, we can assign an indefinite number of instants.

But this number of instants, no matter how great we may choose to suppose it, can never form the *continuous*, nor yet diminish it by ever so little. The reason is, that an instant, being but a point, has no length, and therefore cannot cover any. Consequently, whatever number of instants we may with our mind assign in a continuous time, and then subtract from it, the length of that time will not thereby be lessened in the least, because we have not subtracted any *lengths*, but *points* only. By this mode of reasoning one arrives at the conclusion, that inasmuch as the continuous length in question remains ever the same (for although it may be divided into many parts, yet each of these parts is still continuous), it would be impossible for us to exhaust it, even if we could multiply the instants *ad infinitum* ; for an infinite number of no-lengths can never make a length. Nevertheless, it is not this nature of the *continuous* that involves contradiction ; since, *in it*, there is no such thing as an infinite number of points. These points exist only in our imagination.[1] However mysterious this nature of the *continuous* may be, it involves no contradiction.

On the contrary, if, as the proposition now under consideration supposes, a truly *continuous succession* really existed, we should be obliged to admit, not only that it is possible *mentally* to assign in such succession an indefinite number of instants, but also that there really exists in it *an infinite number* of instants each distinct from the others. Here is my proof.

The instant in which a thing first is, is really distinct from the instant immediately preceding it, in which the thing was not.

Let us imagine, then, that the hair which we have taken as an illustration has grown to the length of a palm by a *continuous* motion. We can divide the time that has been taken in performing this operation, into any number of instants we please. Now be it observed, that this division would not be merely the work of our imagination, but would have a division corresponding with it in the real fact. To be convinced of this, let us, in the series of instants we have decided on, think for example of instants 2, 3 and 4. Since the hair is supposed to grow *continuously*, it will as a matter of course be longer in the 4th instant than in the 3rd, and in the 3rd longer than in the 2nd. Here then we have minute lengths coming out respectively in different instants, and therefore really distinct and different one from the other. Now, if the growth of the hair is *continuous*, the consequence will be, that while on the one hand we can augment the number of instants indefinitely, on the other, the augmentation, even though carried to infinity, could never exhaust that continuity either wholly or in part. But what unanswerably proves my thesis is, that given the *successively continuous growth*, that division which we cannot succeed in making with our mind, *i.e.* by assigning an infinite number of instants, would be actually made by the nature of the thing itself; and thus

---

[1] That in the idea of the *continuous* there is no intrinsic contradiction, will be seen more clearly when we come to speak of the *continuous* in space.

nature would be chargeable with an absurdity. In fact, we have just seen that, whatever be the number of instants which we now or at any time choose to assign in that continuous growth, these instants are not merely mental entities, but have really a corresponding number of different lengths or states existing in the hair itself, wholly independent of our thought. And we have seen, moreover, that for the same reason for which the number of instants assigned, even if it were infinite, can never equal the *continuous*, there must also, of necessity, be in that hair an infinite number of differences corresponding with this infinite number, each of them really distinct from the others, and each still forming a continuous length by itself. Hence it follows, that if the growth has been at once successive and continuous, the hair will actually have in it an infinite number of lengths, according to the infinite number of instants through which it has successively had to pass. Here we must remember, that if this conclusion —namely, the existence of a number actually infinite—involves contradiction, the contradiction springs direct from the premisses, I mean, from the assumption of a *continuous* growth. Given this assumption, an infinite number is a *necessity.* As therefore an infinite number is an absurdity, we must needs admit that the assumption is erroneous.

Fifth proposition : ' The production of an entity by means of continuous succession is an absurdity.'

This follows as a corollary from propositions fourth and third, and is what I had to demonstrate.

The logical outcome of all this, then, is, that the continuity of time as supplied to us by observation alone, is purely *phenomenal* and illusory, because demonstrably proved to be impossible.

§ 7.

The continuity of time is simply a possibility or a mental concept.

791. If we have not an idea of really continuous time from observation, we have nevertheless an abstract, although vague, idea of continuity, which is obtained by reasoning on *possibilities* in the following way.

Within two given instants, *i.e.* during the same time which a great action occupies in being brought to completion, we see also many other actions done, or at least commencing, of greater or lesser duration than that one. Now, by reflecting on the commencements of these actions, we find that the instant in which they respectively begin is in no way determined by their natures. This naturally suggests to our mind the *possibility* of an action beginning at any of the instants assignable within the span of time aforesaid. Hence, as regards this beginning there is not in all that duration any one particle different from the others, any interval of any sort; but a point can be assigned in it wherever we choose, and the action be supposed to commence there. This aptitude of the said duration, this its perfect indifference to admit of the commencement of an action in any part of it whatsoever, this absence from it of all interval, of all exclusiveness, no matter at which of its instants we consider it, is precisely what gives us such abstract idea as we possess of the continuity of time, an idea, therefore, which reduces itself to a pure *possibility* conceived by our mind.

792. I have said that this *abstract* idea of continuity is *vague*, because if we submit it to analysis we discover that, although it is perfectly true that the commencement of an action may be placed at any instant assignable within a given period, yet the sum of these instants is impossible to define; and even if it were defined, the result could never be a continuous time.

§ 8.

Distinction between the absurd and the mysterious.

793. *Absurdity* is that which involves contradiction.

Mystery is that which we cannot explain.

Sophists have attempted to confound these two concepts together; but in vain : they will for ever remain distinct.

That which is absurd must be rejected as false.

That which is mysterious, so far from having to be rejected, is very often impossible of denial; for it is very often a fact, and facts cannot be denied.

Material nature teems with mysterious facts : where, then, is the sense of pretending that there shall be no mysteries in the spiritual nature, so much more sublime, active, immense and profound than the material ?

794. I have shown that *continuous succession* is an absurdity.

But as to *simple continuity*, I believe it indeed to be mysterious, but not absurd ; and I believe, moreover, that it exists as a manifest fact. Hence, while rejecting the *continuous* as applied to *succession*, I do not consider that I have either the right or the power to exclude the *continuous* itself from the nature of things; for I see no intrinsic contradiction in it.

As I have proved that continuity as applied to *time* is absurd, so I shall in due course prove that there is no absurdity in continuity as applied to *space*. The same thing may be said of that *duration* in which there is no succession.

§ 9.

In the duration of completed actions there is no succession, and therefore that duration does not give us the idea of time, but only of continuity.

795. We find that actions, or beings, when fully completed according to their nature, endure, and sometimes unchangeably.

In any nature which exists unchangeably, there is *duration*; but we cannot assign in it a *succession*, as we can in those actions or beings which are in course of production and generation, and therefore are not fully completed.

Now since in the duration of a completed thing there is no succession, nothing forbids its being *continuous*; for, as we have seen, the only reason why continuity is incompatible with succession is that the co-existence of the two would, of necessity, involve an actually infinite number of things really distinct each from the others ; which is an absurdity.

796. Hence the existence of God, of our soul, and of all things which endure, is *continuous*.

On the other hand, the succession which is found in the

gradual generation of things is not continuous ; and it is this succession that gives us the idea of time as well as its measure.

Nevertheless, it is extremely difficult for us to conceive *duration* without *succession*; for, as I have said so many times, we are generally in the habit of seeking light for our thoughts from changes and limits.

§ 10.

The idea of being in general, which constitutes our intelligence, is exempt from time.

797. The idea of time is the idea of a succession considered in reference to duration.

Succession is found only in such actions as are transient, that is, in the production or generation or, which comes to the same, the changes of things.

The idea of being in general—which constitutes our intelligence—is immutable, simple, uniform.   It is therefore wholly exempt from time.

798. Hence the idea of time is not known *a priori*, as Kant supposed, but is obtained only *a posteriori*, namely, drawn through the use of our reasoning powers from those finite things which we perceive as mutable.

799. Hence also we see how right the ancients were in placing the highest part of our intelligence outside of time,[1] and in saying that this faculty, when reasoning *a priori*, abstracts altogether from time, because it does not find time in itself, I mean in that primal idea which constitutes it and the analysis of which furnishes the whole subject-matter of its reasonings *a priori*.[2]

[1] This highest part is, properly speaking, what we call the *Intellect.* S. Thomas says : ' Supremum in nostra cognitione non est ratio, sed intellectus, qui est rationis origo' (*Cont. Gent.* I. lvii.).

[2] S. Thomas also derives the idea of time *a posteriori*, that is, from the phantasms. ' Ex ea parte qua se (intellectus) ad phantasmata convertit, compositioni et divisioni intellectus adjungitur tempus.' Hence that loftiness of tone which is so noticeable in the Fathers of the Church when speaking of the nobler portion of the human mind ; those expressions, consecrated by an unchanging tradition, which they repeat one after the other from age to age, and wherein they declare that our spirit is *conjoined with eternal and immutable things,* enjoys the vision of an *immutable truth*, and, as says the author of the *Itinerarium*, beholds eternal things and in an eternal manner—' videt sempiternalia et sempiternaliter.'

CHAPTER VII.

ORIGIN OF THE IDEA OF MOTION.

ARTICLE I.

Motion is perceived by us in three ways.

800. One of the great actions which take place with succession, and constitute as well as measure time,[1] is *motion.* It is of the idea of motion that we have now to speak.

As regards ourselves, motion is either *active* or *passive.*

We have *active* motion when we cause our bodies to change their place by walking, or by any other use of the locomotive power belonging to us.

We have *passive* motion when the change of our bodies from one place to another is caused by the action of a force external to ourselves.

801. Besides our own motion there is also the motion of the bodies around us, in which we have no part either actively or passively.

802. Now since *motion* is an affection of bodies, whether our own or not, it follows that we perceive it together with the bodies themselves (hence it might be called a *co-perception*), and consequently that we perceive it in as many ways as there are ways of perceiving bodies ; and these we have found to be three (701, 702, 708), namely :

(1) A *subjective* way by means of the fundamental feeling ; and this holds good for the *active* motion, of which our consciousness tells us that we ourselves are the cause.

(2) Again a *subjective* way by means of the adventitious

---

[1] *Succession* in general constitutes time ; but each particular *succession* is called a measure of time, when we take it as a standard with which to confront other successions.

sensations, which cause us to feel a change in the sensitive organ affected ; hence by this way we may be said to perceive subjectively a kind of *passive* motion.

(3) An *extrasubjective* way by means of the several sensories which, as they cause us, each after its fashion, to perceive our own as well as other bodies, so also do they cause us to perceive the motions which take place in all bodies. Speaking, however, of our own motion, whether active or passive, although the fact of the motion itself can be perceived *extrasubjectively*, the feeling which we have of it is not perceivable otherwise than *subjectively*.

Now, according to strict method, I ought not here to speak of any except the *subjective* ways of perceiving motion, because so far I have treated only of the subjective perceptions of bodies, and said nothing of the extrasubjective. But as this separation would render the present discussion incomplete, I do not think it advisable wholly to disjoin the subjective ways of perceiving motion from the extrasubjective.

ARTICLE II.

Description of active motion.

803. It is not, however, my intention to go too deeply into the question on the nature of motion ; I only purpose to explain how our ideas of motion originate.

Here also observation, and first of all the fact of our consciousness, must be my guide.

I will speak first of active and then of passive motion.

We have the faculty of moving our own bodies.[1] What is this faculty ? How does observation present it to us ?

The fundamental feeling by which we immediately perceive our bodies has a *mode* of its own, which I call *extension*.

Now the faculty of moving our own bodies, as presented to us by observation, is a power which the soul has over the fundamental feeling, I mean the power to change in a given manner the *mode* of that feeling.

[1] We could never spontaneously begin to move any part of our body if we did not feel in ourselves the power of doing so. In the fundamental feeling, therefore, of our body there is included also the power we have over it.

To say that the fundamental feeling undergoes a change in its mode, is the same thing as to say that it diffuses itself in a new *space*, or, as we usually term it, a new *place*.

It is because the soul can effect a change in the mode of the fundamental feeling, that we predicate of it power over its body, the power of moving it.

In truth, if the *body* is the agent from whose action the soul receives the fundamental feeling—a feeling terminating in extension; the soul must needs be admitted to have an active power over that agent, since we find by experience that it can directly cause the action thereof to be modified in the manner stated.

ARTICLE III.

Description of passive motion.

804. But besides having the power of self-motion, we may also be moved by a force external to us.

In the case of self-motion, the *amount of effort* we make in moving gives us the perception and, to a certain extent, the measure of the motion.

But when we are moved by an external force, we do not always perceive our motion.

For either the motive force produces a change in our sensitive organs—as, for instance, when a force is applied only to a particular part of the body, but with a power strong enough to compel the whole to move—and in that case we suffer a sensation in the part affected, and at the same time perceive the motion, to which the other parts of the body not immediately affected by the said application oppose, owing to their *vis inertiæ*, a greater or lesser degree of resistance : or else that force acts in such a manner as to transport the whole body simultaneously, yet without causing any disturbance in the relative position of its sensitive parts ; and then our interior feeling cannot, by itself, give us any information either about the motion or about its quantity.

Thus although, as a matter of fact, we are continually revolving with the earth and being carried with it through space with a velocity to which the highest railway speed is as nothing, nevertheless we have no consciousness whatever of this motion. The reason is, that we do not move ourselves, but are moved by another force, and so equably, that no particular sensation, internal or external, arises in us to make us aware of the motion.

805. While therefore our active motion is, as we have seen, perceived in two ways, namely through the interior feeling testified by our consciousness and through external sensations ; our passive motion is perceived through external sensations only.

ARTICLE IV.

Our motion does not, by itself, fall under our sense-perception.

806. As a corollary of the above, it follows that our motion does not, by itself, fall under our sense-perception.

Observation shows that we may be moved without in any way feeling it.

We know motion, as I have said, through its *cause* subjectively, and through its *effects* extrasubjectively. But if we are not our own movers, if we are carried away bodily in such a manner that no alteration is made in our sensitive organs, we can have no knowledge of this *motion*, because no change has taken place in our fundamental feeling.[1]

[1] I avail myself of this occasion for solving a doubt which might occur to some respecting the distinction between the *idea* of a thing and the *judgment on its subsistence.* I have said (398-401), that even if an object were conceived by our mind complete in all its characteristics, essential as well as accidental, it would not necessarily follow that that object should *subsist*; whence I concluded that, by judging it subsistent, we add nothing whatever to the idea of it. Now one might ask : are not place and time characteristics, however accidental, of corporeal things? When therefore you judge that one of these things subsists, you add to the idea of it place and time, two elements which were not previously contained in that idea.

To this I reply, that place and time are not, by themselves, characteristics of the thing. In whatever place and time it may subsist, the thing remains always the same ; nothing is added to or subtracted from its nature. This must be attentively considered. We may see a proof of it in what I have before observed respecting sensitive beings. A sensitive being may be transported even to enormous distances without having the least perception of the fact. Why so? Because the circumstance of its being found in this place or in that (and the same would apply to time) is wholly immaterial to it. Place it where you will, its nature suffers no alteration. Time and place, therefore, are no elements of the idea of a thing. On the other hand, the judgment we make on the subsistence of a corporeal thing which has fallen under our sense-perception determines the *place*; for if we perceive a body with our senses, we must perceive it somewhere. But what is this place occupied by the body so perceived? *Place*, I maintain, is

ARTICLE V.

The motion which takes place in our sensitive organs falls under our
sense-perception. ·

807. It is a fact that when a certain motion is produced in any of our sensitive organs, we feel the sensitive particles of that organ in a form different from that to which we previously referred our fundamental feeling.   In this fact, therefore, we sensitively perceive two things at once, *i.e.* a

something belonging to *reality*, and for this reason it does not enter into the *idea* but falls under the judgment together with the *subsistence* of which, in the case of corporeal things, it forms an element.   It may be rejoined : have we not, then, the *idea* of place?   Yes, we have ; but in the same way that we have the *idea of subsistence.*   The idea of subsistence is an universal like all other ideas, since by it we conceive subsistence only as *possible* to be realised.   When, on the contrary, we affirm that a being really subsists, the subsistence thus affirmed is indeed the same thing as we saw in the *idea*, but determined by our *judgment* to a particular.   In like manner we have the idea of a *place.*   By this idea we see the possibility of a being possessed of *extension* (a body) existing in that place.   When we perceive a body actually subsistent, that which we conceived only as possible is affirmed by us as a reality, and so the place is filled.   Thus the *place*, considered by itself alone, is a pure abstraction ; in other words, the *subsistence* is the act itself by which the body really exists, and the place is simply the *mode of that subsistence.*

This distinction between what is contained in the idea of a thing (*i.e.* its *essence*) and what we are made to know about it by *judgment* (the particular, the subsistence), was not unknown to the ancients ; although they oftentimes forgot it, owing doubtless to the great difficulty of keeping it clearly before the mind. Hence it happened, that when they came upon questions that could not be solved without it, they had recourse to other distinctions, which have indeed a great analogy with it, but at the same time, when presented as different there-

from, cause embarrassment to philosophical science by a needless multiplication of entities. One of these distinctions was that which I have had occasion to notice elsewhere, between *universal* and *particular matter.*   They said, that for the *ideas* of corporeal things the universal matter was necessary ; not so the particular.   To speak accurately, however, they should have said, (1) not that there are two matters, but one matter only, namely the particular ; and (2) that of this particular matter we have the idea.   The idea is nothing else than the particular matter itself considered as possible : hence it seems to be a universal matter, because the *possible* is universal.   A similar distinction was made by the ancients between universal and particular quantity ; and the same observation holds good in reference to it.   Universal quantity is nothing but the *idea* of quantity.   That they had an inkling of this, is evidenced by the fact of their terming it *quantitas intelligibilis.* Let us hear how this distinction is stated by Simplicius in his Fourth Book on the *Physics* of Aristotle.   He writes : 'I think it better to say, that there is a *specific extension*' (in the Greek κατ' εἶδος, that is, *according to the idea*, which precisely coincides with the view I am expressing), 'such as is seen by the mind in the *exemplars* ; — and there is another extension which is perceived by a passive discernment of a substance indivisible and without parts.'   Thus the *intelligible quantity* is described as that which is *according to the idea* ; which the mind sees in the exemplars, *i.e.* the first ideas of things.   What is this but *the idea of quantity* or, what is the same, possible or universal quantity?

modification excited in our fundamental feeling, and the motion through which that modification has been brought about (the change effected in the *matter* of the said feeling).

It must be noted, however, that the motion is perceived, not on its own account, but solely through the peculiar circumstance of its altering the *state* of the sensitive organ, which is always felt by us in that *state* in which it happens to find itself.

This kind of motion, then, consists in an alteration of the respective position of the molecules which compose the sensitive organ. For, the mode in which we feel that organ is determined by the same law which determines the position of its molecules ; and hence, if the position requisite for a certain *sensible state* of the organ happens to be altered, the organ assumes a new *sensible state*, and, by consequence, is felt in a new mode and in a new place, according to the nature of the alteration suffered by it.

Our sensitive organism might therefore be transported even to immense distances (as it actually is by the daily revolution of the earth) without being at all affected thereby.

It is not, then, exactly the motion of the organ that is felt by us, but its *sensible state*. But I must try to explain this a little more.

Clearly, the sensitive and sensible particles which compose the organ, by being respectively joined together in different ways, proportions and positions—being, for instance, brought closer by compression or driven further apart by distension—give a different form to the *whole* organ. We must therefore feel that organ in a different mode, with varying pleasure or pain ; and this implies a feeling of the change that has occurred in it. Now the new pleasure or pain, in other words, the new sensation, has reference to all the sensible points embraced by the new form of the organ where the change-producing force has operated. And whereas previously the form was different, so the pleasure or pain previously felt in the organ had reference to different points. Properly speaking, then, it is not the change of place befalling each sensitive molecule, considered irrespectively of the rest (the *absolute* motion of the molecules), that is felt by us; but it is the change of form in the organ taken as a whole, *i.e.* the change of place effected in many molecules together (the *relative* motion of the molecules), that change which causes the individual particles of the organ to be matter of sensation in new places.

808. Coming therefore to analyse that subjective feeling whereby we perceive the sensitive parts of our body on occasion of a sensible motion, we find :

(1) That this feeling is either a pleasure or a pain, varying according to circumstances, and diffused through a given extension which has a certain form or figure ;

(2) That the form or *figure* of this extension is susceptible of changes by means of certain relative motions in its parts ; but whatever those changes may be, the feeling invariably diffuses itself through the new extensions respectively created by that motion ;

(3) That therefore the *subjective feeling* perceives the particular *motion* which takes place as often as the form or figure of the organ is altered, but perceives it only in that part wherein the force applied operates in the way which is necessary in order that a sensation may be produced in it.

The subjective feeling, therefore, perceives motion simply in so far as it is an alteration undergone by its matter.

ARTICLE VI.

Relation between motion and sensation.

809. Hence we may lay it down as a general principle,

(1) That *absolute* motion, or motion considered *per se*, has nothing whatever to do with sensation ;

(2) That the *relative* motion which takes place in a sensitive organ whenever the form or figure thereof happens to be changed, is 'An affection of the matter of sensation,' and is felt as the matter affected is felt.

ARTICLE VII.

On motion considered relatively to the perception of the touch.[1]

810. By the sense of touch we perceive the hardness and the surface of bodies ; but what about their motion ?

Suppose that while we keep one of our arms stretched out and motionless, some thinly-pointed instrument is drawn steadily along it from shoulder to wrist, do we perceive that motion with our touch ?

It would seem at first sight that we do ; and certainly we perceive something similar to motion.

But against this there is the following difficulty : although it is true that we feel in our arm a sensation which moves on according to the length of the arm, and, together with that sensation, we perceive the body which produces it ; nevertheless it does not seem that we can by this means alone be unmistakably certain of the unity of that body, because the same kind of sensation might be equally caused by substituting, instead of it, a number of similar bodies successively applied to the arm at intervals too minute to be noticed.[2]

[1] In the operations of the external senses, I have distinguished (1) the *sensation* we have of the sensitive organ itself, (2) the *corporeal perception* of something different from the organ (740-743). Of motion considered relatively to the sensation, I have already spoken (806). Now I proceed to speak of motion considered relatively to the corporeal perception.

[2] It may be laid down in general, that when we touch external bodies with different parts of our own, we do not perceive their identity ; because the extrasubjective perceptions corresponding to the different parts affected are different from one another, and hence there seem to be as many bodies acting upon us as are the perceptions themselves, and this especially if these perceptions are simultaneous. Nevertheless, when we are touched in a continuous extension (I mean *phenomenally* continuous), the surfaces thus coming in contact with us are perceived as forming one continuous whole—as in the case of solids. But if the tactile sensations are not continuous—as when a body touches us in the hand and also in the foot—then we can only think that two bodies are acting on us. It is only by the aid of sight, or, as I have just said, by the continuity of the sensation of touch, joined with the force of habit, that we judge of the identity of a body which comes simultaneously in contact with different parts of our own. Hence the judgment respecting that identity is the result of a *habit* formed by experience ; and this causes it sometimes to be deceptive. For example, if you touch a button with two fingers, one thrown across the other, you feel two buttons. Why so ? Because you have two sensations, and in a form quite different from that to which you are accustomed when touching one and the same body in the ordinary way. The natural position of the fingers is, not to be thrown one across the other, but to be straight and go smoothly together. When therefore you touch a body with two fingers in their natural posture, the two sensations thereby produced run in close proximity, so as to seem continuous ; but when the fingers are thrown

ARTICLE VIII.

On motion considered relatively to the perception of the sight.

811. If we move on from place to place, we see that the scene of the objects around us is continually changing ; and these changes indicate to us that we, as well as the surrounding scene, are moving.   How this happens, I shall explain when I come to treat of the third way of perceiving bodies.

But suppose that the things seen by us move, while our eye remains steadily fixed on one point, does the eye then perceive a motion ?

A black speck gliding along a white surface gives us the concept of a motion ; but this alone does not suffice to make us absolutely certain that it is the selfsame black speck that runs all through ; because there are apparent and illusory motions as well as true ones : nevertheless the concept of motion is here presented to us.

The difficulty about our being certain of the identity of a body, which I have noticed in connexion with the sensation of touch, exists also in that of sight, though in a lesser degree ; because the characteristics of a body as seen by the eye are much more numerous than those of a body as felt by the touch ; hence the simultaneous union of the former characteristics in different bodies is very difficult, whereas the touch may easily be affected in the same manner by many different bodies.

across each other, the proximity of these sensations is entirely broken, and moreover you feel them in an order opposite to the usual.

In the case mentioned in the text, of a thinly-pointed instrument drawn all along our arm, there is the (phenomenal) continuity of the gliding sensation ; and this induces the belief that the whole of that sensation is caused by one and the same body : but in strict truth the touch, taken by itself alone, witnesses to nothing further than that we have a series of sensations similar to one another and succeeding one the other without perceptible interruption ; and this would not be enough to prove indubitably that the instrument is in motion. On the contrary, when, taking a body in my hand, I remove it from one place to another, the identity of that body is proved by the continuity of the perception I have of it ; for I keep holding it in my hand.   In this case I do not perceive the motion with the touch alone, but with the touch aided by the consciousness I have of moving my arm.

ARTICLE IX.

On motion considered relatively to the perception of the hearing, the smell and the taste.

812. In so far as these sensories agree with the touch, we must, in regard of the perception of motion, say of them the same as we have said of the touch itself (810).

In so far as they differ from the touch and have, conjoined with them, the phenomena of sound, smell and taste, they do not perceive motion ; but, iike all the other senses, they give us a clue to its measure, by means of time. For, from the time it takes a body to come near us, so that we can touch or see it, taste or smell it, or hear its sound, we infer the distance intervening between us and that body, and therefore the quantity of motion necessary for reaching it.

This mode of measuring motion is available also for persons born blind, or who are bereft of some other sensory, provided not of all.

ARTICLE X.

On the continuity of motion.

§ I.

Observation does not reach exceedingly minute extensions.

813. Experience tells us that our observation does not reach exceedingly minute extensions.

The invention of the microscope has thrown open to observation a world which was entirely hidden from it before.

But, increase as we may the appliances for observing nature, it is evident that her subtilty far exceeds our ingenuity. So fine is the texture of bodies, that we may well give up the hope of ever seeing it fully as it is, and in the continually decreasing scale of extensions, which that texture exhibits, we must come at last to a minuteness that will baffle all attempts at detection.

§ 2.

*The continuity of motion as presented to us by observation is purely
phenomenal.*

814. Hence all that observation tells us about the continuity
of motion is of no value except as applicable to a *phenomenal*
or apparent continuity.

But inasmuch as there can be most minute intervals which
escape observation, we are bound to say that it is impossible
to draw from observation any absolute proof of the real continuity of motion.

§ 3.

The real continuity of motion is an absurdity.

815. If observation can tell us nothing certain about the
real continuity of motion, it remains for us to try the way of
reasoning.

Reasoning cannot be a sure witness as to facts, but it can
pronounce as to whether they are intrinsically possible or not,
because possibility is the proper object of the mental and therefore of the reasoning faculty.

Now we have proved already, that a truly *continuous
succession* is an absurdity (779–799).

But in motion, as in every action which goes on increasing
or decreasing, there is succession.

Therefore a true and real continuity in motion is an
absurdity.

Thus it is that the mind by reasoning on mere *possibilities*
draws sometimes conclusions which bear on facts. It can
deny facts if it sees in them an intrinsic or logical repugnance ;
if it does not see in them any such repugnance, though it cannot affirm their real existence, it can affirm its *possibility.*

§ 4.

*Solution of the objection drawn from the admitted fact that ' Nature
does nothing by leaps.'*

816. It may be objected : If there is no true continuity in
motion, then motion takes place by leaps. But this cannot

be, because by the universal consent of philosophers in all ages there is no leap in the action of nature.

817. I fully admit that nature does nothing by *leaps*, and, in fact, that to say the contrary would be an absurdity. But I also maintain, that from the absence of continuity in motion it does not at all follow there are *leaps* in it.

There is not, and there cannot be a *leap* in that which happens in an instant.

A *leap* supposes two points, from one of which a *passage* is made to the other without touching the intervening space. Now the idea of *passage* necessarily includes the idea of *touching* the space between ; since to pass from one place to another without touching the middle, would be passing without passing. To assume, therefore, that there are intervening spaces, and then to say, that they are passed over without being touched, is a manifest contradiction; and it is in this sense that I call a ' leap in the action of nature ' an absurdity.

But there is nothing of this in real motion. The concept of this motion, if not distorted by the imagination, presents to our mind nothing more than a body existing in many places successively, nor does it in any way oblige us to think that the body leaps from one place to another, however near. The necessity of this *leaping* is a mere fiction of the imagination, which, being habitually preoccupied with the *phenomenal* continuity of motion, deceives us into believing that we see a continuous passage when, in point of fact, all we see is the existence of a body, first in one place, then in another, then again in another, and so on, these places standing in such close proximity that their distances are wholly unobservable.

The reader will find it easier to understand what I say, if he bears in mind that, according to the explanation already given, extension is nothing but the term of the action of a force. Now a force may vary the term of its action, *i.e.* it may act in one part of space rather than in another, without there being any need of our supposing a truly continuous passage from the one to the other ; for it can with the utmost rapidity withdraw its action from one place, and at the same time put it forth in another. This, I venture to affirm, implies no contradiction.

818. Nevertheless, I can very well foresee how extremely difficult of comprehension this thing will prove for the generality of men, whose minds are always more or less embroiled with and obfuscated by the imagination. Neither can experience be of any help here; for, as I have just remarked, the different spaces in which the corporeal force acts in succession are (by a law of the Author of nature) so very near one another that no division is perceivable between them: hence the seeming continuity of motion, and the difficulty of conceiving how it can be any other than continuous.

To those of my readers who can follow up an argument with strict philosophical accuracy, I very willingly leave the decision as to whether my proof of the non-existence of true and real continuity in locomotion be conclusive.

§ 5.

Mental continuity of motion.

819. The difficulty of realising to oneself the truth of the view I am advancing, is still further increased by the fact that we really have in our minds the abstract idea of a certain *continuity*, as of *time*, so also of motion.

This *mental* and abstract *continuity* consists in the possibility, conceived by us, of motion beginning or ending at any point of time or of space without any exclusion or difference whatever.

This perfectly even *possibility* of motion beginning or ending at any conceivable instant of time and at any conceivable point of space, produces or rather constitutes the vague idea we have of an *abstract* continuity in the motion of a body passing between any two instants or any two points. I say *vague*, because this idea, when submitted to analysis, vanishes from us, inasmuch as we then discover that no number of points summed up together can form a continuity.

CHAPTER VIII.

ORIGIN OF THE IDEA OF SPACE.

ARTICLE I.

Distinction between the idea of space and that of body.

820. I have defined *body* 'A substance capable of producing in us an effect which consists in either a pleasurable or a painful feeling characterised by a constant mode called extension' (749–753).

Extension, therefore, as known through reflection on the nature of bodies, is, like pure *time* and pure *motion*, a mental abstraction: in other words, it is conceived by us as the particular mode of that feeling which the body causes in our soul.

When, however, this abstraction has once been formed, it can continue to exist in our mind independently of bodies, in the same way as all other abstract ideas.

ARTICLE II.

Extension or space is unlimited.

821. Extension or space, taken either in this abstract way or in any other, is *unlimited, immeasurable* and *continuous.* ·

But how is it that we come to conceive space as indubitably endowed with these characteristics of *unlimitedness, immeasurableness* and *continuity*? and this even in the case of that knowledge of space which we derive from bodies by abstraction?

Let us see how this happens, commencing from the first two characteristics.

There exists in us a power by which we can move our body (672–692).

To move our body is nothing else than to repeat over and over again the *mode* of the feeling we have of it, that is to say, the extension or space which it occupies.

Now the acts of our faculties can be repeated by us indefinitely; and when, owing to the limitation of our strength, we are no longer able to repeat them in reality, we can still imagine and conceive them as repeated indefinitely at our pleasure, by reason of that idea of *possibility* which is always in our mind, and which we can apply to all that is conceived by us (403).

This intellectual operation by which we can apply the notion of the 'possible' to whatsoever event or object is conceived by us, and with the aid of that notion can imagine it as indefinitely repeated, I have already explained by means of the idea of being in general (469, &c.).

It is this power of imagining and conceiving the extension of our body as repeated indefinitely, that enables us to form the idea of an unlimited extension or space.

The idea therefore of *unlimited extension* is, in its first formation, nothing but 'the abstract possibility imagined and conceived by us, of repeating indefinitely the mode of our corporeal feeling, I mean the extension of our body.'

822. Thus from the extension subjectively perceived we derive the notion of its unlimitedness.[1] But this same extension, which we perceive subjectively, can also be perceived by us extrasubjectively, *i.e.* in external bodies : I say in *external bodies*, for it is through their externality that these bodies are perceived in the extrasubjective way.

Given thus the perception of bodies, we obtain by means of abstraction the idea of corporeal extension.

Hence the unlimitedness and immeasurableness of space, which may be defined in general as ' The possibility of conceiving the extension of bodies as indefinitely repeated.'

---

[1] Extension is found in external bodies as well as in our fundamental feeling and in our adventitious sensations, but with a difference. In and relatively to the fundamental feeling, extension is both *matter* and *term* ; in the sensations, it is *matter* ; and in external bodies it is the *external term* of the sensations.

ARTICLE III.

Space or extension is continuous.

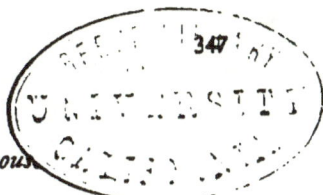

823. The idea, then, of unlimited space, which first
presents itself to our analysis, is an abstraction, namely, the
conception of the possibility of the extension of a body being
successively repeated without end

But, more than with external bodies, we must occupy ourselves with our own ; for we have as yet treated only of subjective perception. But whatever we shall say about space
subjectively perceived, will be no less applicable to external
bodies, *i.e.* bodies perceived extrasubjectively.

In the inquiry 'Whether perfect *continuity* be included in
the idea of space,' we must, first of all, be careful not to confound our corporeal feeling as it now exists, with the possibility of its existing in other states.

Concerning the state in which it now exists, a very difficult
question might be suggested, namely : Does the feeling we
now have of our body comprise in itself the feeling of perfect
continuity ?

The solution of this question, if it were attempted by
means of experience, would not only require the keenest
observation and the utmost vigilance, but also, I verily believe,
be at last found impossible. So far as I can see, one would
have to be content with mere conjecture, or else to depend on
reasonings more subtle and ingenious than apt to carry
absolute conviction. For the question here is as to whether
sensation can be excited indifferently at all conceivable points
all along each of the nerve-filaments of our system, thus
implying that all the sensitive molecules are placed in mathematical contiguity : and on this matter observation does not
reach far enough to be able to tell us anything.[1]

This inquiry, however, is not necessary.

For explaining the continuity of space, it is irrelevant to
know whether all the mathematical points observable along
the course of a nerve, are really possessed of sensitivity ;

[1] Reason finds no intrinsic contradiction in this.

since the question is not about a concrete fact, but about an abstraction, that is, an idea formed by applying the notion of ' possibility.' And in truth we can very well conceive the possibility of referring a sensation experienced by us to any one of the points in question. For, assuming that in the most delicate texture of the nerve felt by us there are pores and minute voids, it is a mere accident that these fall in their present places rather than elsewhere ; and there is nothing logically repugnant in the thought of an entire reversal of position between the places that are now filled up with sensitive molecules, and those that are vacant. We have the power to imagine and think this whenever we please, and consequently to conceive ' the possibility of a sensation being excited at any point assignable in the whole length of the nerve :' and this is precisely the idea of continuity.

The *possibility* of our referring a corporeal feeling to any point assignable in a given space, arises from the fact that space is by its nature perfectly indifferent as to whether that feeling is diffused in one part of it or in another. Owing to this absolute indifference, it is possible for the sensation to terminate anywhere within the space occupied by our sensitive body : and the conception of this possibility includes, or rather, as I have said, is the abstract idea of continuous space.

The acquisition of this idea is facilitated for us by the power we have of self-motion ; for the use of this power supplies us with a practical proof of the indifference which every part of space has to our corporeal feeling being diffused in it.

Imagine that you anatomise one of your hands : that you lay bare the whole network of nerves running all over and throughout it in all directions, and that by the aid of a powerful microscope you have their exquisitely fine texture fully laid open to your observation. You thus see where the nerve-molecules adhere together, and where they are divided by those minute voids in which there is, of course, no corporeal feeling. If you now give even but a slight movement to the hand, what will be the result? The place that was occupied by the sensitive molecules will be left vacant, and that which was vacant, filled up with them instead. Consequently in this new position of the hand you will feel a sensation where you felt none before. Thus, even in point of fact, we can, by means of self-motion, cause our corporeal feeling to be diffused in any mathematical point of space we think fit : and this possibility enables us, as I have said, to conceive space as absolutely and perfectly *continuous.*

It is true that the motion which has taken place in the sensitive organ does not cause the feeling we have of the organ itself as such to be altered in the least from what it was ; since motion does not, by its own self, fall under sense-perception (806). But this does not prevent our mind, especially when assisted by the extrasubjective perception of bodies, from forming an idea of continuous extension or space in the way I have described.

ARTICLE IV.

Of real continuity.

824. The idea of continuity of which I have thus far spoken is the result of a mental combination of *possibilities.* But is there such a thing as *real* continuity in corporeal extension ?

I think it better to delay the answer to this question until we come to speak of the extrasubjective perception of bodies, because that kind of perception seems more open and therefore better calculated to afford us light in such an investigation. For the present, be it enough to know that in the continuity of bodies as well as of space there is no intrinsic contradiction.

ARTICLE V.

The continuous has no parts.

825. That is said to be ' continuous ' in which there is no interval or division, nothing disconnected.

The ' continuous ' therefore can have no parts, because parts suppose some separation of the one from the other.

ARTICLE VI.

The continuous may be mentally limited.

826. The idea of *continuity* as hitherto described consists in 'the conception of the possibility of a body terminating simultaneously with its action at any point whatever assignable in a given extension.'

The idea of *unlimited continuous space* consists in 'the conception of the possibility of a body repeating indefinitely its continuous extension.'

But we may also restrict our conception so as to embrace with it, not all the repetitions that are possible in general, but only a certain quantity of them.

In this way, there arises in our mind the idea of a *limited continuous space*, for example, of an area of a thousand square feet, or of some other dimension.

The area so conceived has, however, no parts in it, and hence, although limited, it is still continuous.

Now of these continuous and limited spaces, we can imagine as many as we please ; but each of them, whether it be large or small, remains always continuous, that is to say, without parts.

827. Hence all these ideas of continuous limited spaces are comprised, so to speak, potentially[1] in the idea of unlimited continuous space. Moreover, each of them bears a certain proportion to every other, so that one is double or treble, &c., the size of another, or else there is between them one or other of the ratios known to mathematicians, whether commensurable or not.

828. This causes us to consider the lesser continuous spaces as parts of the greater, although they are not so in

[1] That which exists only potentially, does not as yet truly exist : hence in the continuous there are such limits as we actually assign to it, but no others. Therefore it would be a pure imagination to suppose with Malebranche that in the conception of space and of figures our mind possesses an infinite number of ideas, nay, an infinite number of infinities (*Recherche de la Vérité*, Book iii.). The idea of the continuous is but one, and it is simply by assigning sundry limits to this self-same idea that we form other ideas, always, however, finite in number, because in this process one must come to a stop at last, and can never succeed in assigning an actually infinite number of limits.

reality. They are only *mental* parts, *i.e.* formed by the diverse acts of our mind, which has the power of limiting in various ways its conception of the continuous.

829. Wherefore, all these mental parts, placed in juxta-position to one another, do not, so long as they are considered as parts, form a continuous whole, but each makes a separate continuity by itself. Nor can we conceive them as forming together one continuous whole, unless we cease to look upon them as distinct parts, and, with our imagination, remove from them every division as well as every limit, even purely ˙mental ; for, as I have remarked, the two ideas of *continuous* and of *part* are essentially in contradiction to each other.

ARTICLE VII.

In what sense it can be said that the ' continuous' is divisible
ad infinitum.

830. It follows from the above, that the continuous cannot be said to be divisible *ad infinitum* except in the sense that it is indefinitely limitable by our mind.[1]

This its capability of being indefinitely limited arises from its nature, and also from the nature of our faculties, which can always repeat the acts proper to them ; and prin-cipally from the faculty of thought, which by means of the notion of possibility can imagine and conceive as possible every thing which involves no contradiction.

Thus infinite divisibility is nothing but the possibility of going on indefinitely restricting the limits of a space present to our thought. Hence the saying of S. Thomas, that ' The continuous has infinite parts *in potentia*, but none *in act.*'

[1] The continuous cannot be said in a composite sense to be *divisible*, be-cause from the moment that it is *divided*, it is no longer *continuous*.

CHAPTER IX.

ORIGIN OF THE IDEA OF BODIES BY MEANS OF THE EXTRASUBJECTIVE PERCEPTION OF THE TOUCH.

ARTICLE I.

The analysis of the extrasubjective perception of bodies in general begins.

831. We have seen that in every adventitious sensation there are two elements :

(1) A modification of our fundamental feeling, causing us to feel in a new way the part where our sensitive organism has been affected.

(2) The sensitive perception of an external body, or, as I call it, the *extrasubjective* perception.

It is with the analysis of this kind of perception that we must now occupy ourselves.

This analysis, carefully conducted, shows it also to consist of two elements :

(a) The feeling of the action exercised on us, and which may be termed a species of violence done to us.

(b) The extension to which we refer that feeling, and which comprises a something extended outside of us.

832. Hence it may be concluded that we can be said to have perception of a body by means of adventitious sensations, when we perceive a something, both different from us and having extension.

Let us, then, explain how our external senses furnish us with a subject combining in itself these qualities. We will begin with the sense of touch.

ARTICLE II.

All our senses give us the perception of a something different from us.

833. All our senses are susceptive of being acted upon.

But the fact of our being acted upon supposes a something which acts on and is different from us.[1]

Therefore all our senses perceive a something different from us.

ARTICLE III.

All our senses give us the perception of a something outside of us.

834. To proceed clearly in this matter, we must first of all distinguish between what is *different* from us, and what is *outside of us.*

The concept of *diversity* neither includes, nor is in any way connected with *extension.* The word *outside of*, on the contrary, taken in its proper sense, has relation to extension. To say that a thing is outside of another, is the same as to say that it does not occupy the same *place* as the other. Hence the phrase, OUTSIDE OF ME, signifies *outside of the sensitive parts or organs of my body,*[2] and does not apply to the spirit except in a metaphorical sense.

As, then, the expression *different from Me* indicates a distinction from my *spirit*, so the expression *outside of Me* indicates, properly speaking, a distinction from my *body* in so far as it is co-sentient by reason of the intimate union it has with my spirit.

In order, therefore, to demonstrate that each of our senses perceives what is outside of us, I must demonstrate that each sense perceives a something different from our body as subjectively perceived.

[1] (See n. 672). Hence it is impossible to admit the distinction which Royer-Collard endeavoured to draw between our senses, some of which he supposed to be purely instruments of sensation, and others of perception as well as sensation (See *Fragments de Leçons*, &c., of Royer-Collard, published by Jouffroy). All the senses have perception, all have their *extrasubjective* part, although in some this part is more vivid than in others, as we shall see in due course.

[2] Every part, even sentient, of our body may be said to be OUTSIDE OF US in so far as we perceive it *extrasubjectively*; for this perception presents it to us only in that which it has in common with all external bodies. In this sense, therefore, it is outside of us the percipient *subjects*, that is to say, the *part perceived* is perceived as outside of the *perceiving part.*

835. Now, that such is really the case, is clear from the things we have said.

We have said, that our fundamental feeling is produced by a force different from that which causes in it changes or modifications. Hence two species of force: (1) our own body which acts immediately on the spirit; (2) the external bodies which act on ours.

In every sensation, therefore, we perceive the action of a body different from our own; since every sensation is a passion we experience from something which is not our body. Therefore, each of our senses perceives a something outside of us.

836. And that on this point there may be no doubt, it will be well to corroborate the proof just given by some further remark.

Our body is felt in the fundamental feeling; whatever is felt outside that feeling is not our body.

Now let us fix our attention on the four phenomenal sensations of colour, sound, smell, and taste, and also on hardness and such like tactile qualities of bodies; and let us ask ourselves whether all these things be peradventure nothing else than our own sensitive organs. Consciousness will at once answer us in the negative. Most assuredly, the scent which affects our nostrils is not the nostrils; the flavour is not the tongue or the palate; the sound is not the ears; and so of all the other qualities. Therefore those sensations cannot have for their sole matter our body; and if in them we feel our body also, this is certainly not all that we perceive by them. Consequently, they bear witness to the presence of an active principle exterior to our body, of a term different from that of the fundamental feeling.

ARTICLE IV.

The touch, taken by itself alone, perceives only the surfaces of bodies.

837. When we are touched in a sensitive part of our body, we feel a certain pleasure or pain in the part affected,[1] and

---

[1] There are sensations which differ essentially from either pleasure or pain.

we feel also an action exercised on us by something external ; in other words, we perceive an agent outside of us (834–836).

Moreover, the feeling we have of this action is found to terminate or be diffused in no other than a *superficial* extension.

In fact, if you happen to be pricked in the arm with the point of a needle, the pain you feel corresponds exactly with the exceedingly diminutive surface of that point ; but if a larger body circular in form, for example a coin, is pressed down with force on the arm, your sensation is then conterminous with the size and form of the new surface, neither more nor less. And a similar change would happen if, instead of the coin, a thin plate of steel cut in the form of a cross were pressed down on the arm in the same way.[1]

ARTICLE V.

The touch combined with motion gives us the idea of solid space.

838. On being touched, then, in some part of the surface of our body, we experience a sensation terminating in a superficial space.[2]

Let us now add to this the faculty we have of locomotion.

Through the use of this faculty we can repeat at pleasure the space in which our fundamental feeling is diffused (803) ; and we can, also at pleasure, repeat the surface felt by us in the sensation of touch.

Now, by moving that surface in such a manner as to make it change its plane in certain ways, we obtain this effect that, while our tactile sensation remains unchanged, the sur-

---

For example, does not the sensation of *tickling* seem a something wholly *sui generis* ? And the same may be said of many other sensations. I do not here intend to enter upon this inquiry ; I only wish to observe, that it seems to me indubitable that all the corporeal feelings we experience, either are accompanied by a certain degree of pleasure or of pain, or else are *modes* of pleasure or pain. For this reason I say, 'a certain pleasure or pain,' or 'corporeal pleasure or pain,' using the word *corporeal* to indicate in general those dif-

ferences which I do not submit to analysis in this work.

[1] In short, a touch impresses only the outer extremities of the nerves, and hence the sensation corresponding to that impression has only a superficial extension. This holds good in all cases of external touch.

[2] I speak here of adventitious sensations, and not of the fundamental feeling, as regards which I am, on reflection, convinced that there is continuity in the parts wherein it terminates.

A A 2

face describes a solid space, namely, a space with the three dimensions of width, length, and depth.

Thus by the exercise of the faculty of moving ourselves and with ourselves other things also, we come to be made aware of the possibility of the same tactile sensation being experienced in any of the surfaces of solid space.[1]

Now the conception of this possibility, that is, of changing and repeating indefinitely the surfaces in which our sensations of touch terminate, is the idea of indefinite solid space—an idea acquired by means of the touch associated with motion.[2]

ARTICLE VI.

Recapitulation of the ways in which we form the idea of solid space.

839. From what we have said, it is manifest that our idea of indefinite solid space is formed in two ways : (1) by means of the fundamental feeling combined with the faculty of self-motion ; (2) by means of the sensations of touch, aided also by that same faculty.

In the first way, this idea is produced by our conceiving that solid space in which our corporeal fundamental feeling is diffused, as capable of being moved in all directions indefinitely.

In the second way, the idea is produced by our conceiving a given surface felt by our touch, as capable of being moved, also indefinitely, in all directions outside that of its actual plane.

[1] Not that this solidity can fall under our sense-perception; for motion is not perceivable by its own self, as I have already observed ; but it is a means by which we form the *conception* of sensible solidity.

[2] Our self-motion is the principal cause of the cognitions we acquire respecting distances and determinate spaces. The touch (in combination with time), and the sight, serve only to make us gauge with accuracy the *terms* of the various distances (*a*). Hence a very acute sense of touch is not necessary for measuring great distances. This we can see in the case of birds, which glide swiftly through the aerial spaces and measure them, although they have but a very obtuse sense of touch in their talons. The vulture, for instance, takes a correct measure of the space, the time, and the swiftness necessary for alighting on and seizing his prey ; and this by no other means than his imperfect sense of touch conjoined with great quickness of glance and great locomotive power.

(*a*) *I.e.* they serve us as a guide for estimating *how far* a certain object lies from us or from some other object (TRANSLATORS).

From this we can see how it is that persons born blind have the idea of indefinite space and can understand mathematics.

ARTICLE VII.

The idea of space, as formed by means of the touch combined with motion, is more easily adverted to than that formed by means of the fundamental feeling combined also with motion.

840. I have already shown how difficult it is to advert to the fundamental feeling, and, on the other hand, how easy to advert to adventitious sensations (710–721).

For a similar reason, indefinite space, as conceived in the first of the two ways just named, is less apt to stimulate advertence than that conceived in the second way, because the sensations of touch, being adventitious, more easily attract our attention both to themselves and their translocations.

ARTICLE VIII.

The space perceived through the motions of the sensation of touch is identical with the space perceived through the motions of the fundamental feeling.

841. The external sensation of touch terminates in a surface more or less extended (837).

Now this surface is identical with the external surface of our body ; for we only feel the sensation in the extremities of the nerves where we are touched.[1]

In the very same surface[2] wherein terminates our *subjective sensation* of the organ affected, terminates also the action suffered by us from the external agent or body, and the consciousness of which bears witness to what I have called the *extrasubjective perception* of the senses.

---

[1] In the identical surface, we must always distinguish the sensation we have of our body from the perception of the external thing. Although the surface is but one, two things are simultaneously felt therein : (1) our own body, at once co-sentient with and felt by us ; (2) an external agent, felt by but not co-sentient with us.

[2] It is in the unity of this surface that the nature of touch consists, as well as that mysterious unity which is effected, as I have observed before, between the agent and the patient in every kind of action (See note to No. 667).

In the act of touch, therefore, that identical surface is the term, not merely of our body, but of the external body also.

Now I have shown, that we have the idea of indefinite space, when this surface, common to our own and to the external body, is conceived by us as capable of being moved or changing its place in all directions indefinitely (839).

Therefore space, whether it be perceived through a motion in the organ felt by us, *i.e.* through a modification brought about in our fundamental feeling, or through the motion of the surface perceived in the external agent, is always one and the same.

Again, since the modification of the fundamental feeling (the adventitious sensation of our organ) has no other extension than that of the fundamental feeling itself, it also follows, that the space is one and the same, whether perceived in the two *subjective* ways or in the *extrasubjective*.

ARTICLE IX.

The identity of the extension of our own body and of the external body forms the link of communication between the idea of the one and the idea of the other.

842. In the act of sensible contact, then, the superficial extension of our body, considered as *co-sentient* with us, and that of the external body which we feel only as acting on us, make together but one extension.

This communion of the two bodies as to extension, is the passage that takes our minds from the idea of the one to the idea of the other : it is the so-called *bridge of communication* between them ; since by the selfsame act by which we perceive the mode of the existence of our own body, we perceive also the mode of the existence of the external body.

ARTICLE X.

Continuation.

843. The above consequence is of great importance.

In fact, we have placed the essence of *body* in the presence of two elements, *i.e.* (1) a force acting on us, and (2) an extension in which the action of that force diffuses itself and terminates.

Now, our own body exercises on us a permanent internal action resulting in the fundamental feeling, and this diffused in an extension. Here, then, we have both the essentials of a body. Therefore, as to the truth of the perception of our own body, there can be no mistake; and the presence in it of the essence of this body is as certain as the fact of consciousness.

844. Let us now come to the perception of the external bodies. In the first place, by this perception we feel an action exercised on us ; but the first effect of this action lies in a modification of our fundamental feeling and nothing more.

By this effect alone (the adventitious sensation) we do not go outside ourselves : although we feel our body in a new way, it is only the same subjective body that we felt before.

We can indeed from this effect infer a cause, but a cause the nature of which is as yet unknown ; since, according to the hypothesis, we do not as yet know by what kind or mode of action the modification or sensation in question is produced.

This alone therefore would not suffice to give us the perception of a *body* outside of us. What more, then, is required ?

It is necessary that that action should also have an *extended* term. Then indeed should we perceive a *force acting in extension*, which is what we mean by the word *body*.

Now, how is it possible for us to perceive the *extension* of the action exercised on us by the said force ?

The provision made for this by the All-wise Author of nature is as follows :—

We habitually feel extension, I mean the diffusion of our fundamental feeling.

We could, therefore, feel also the extension of the action of which I speak, provided such action were diffused in the *same extension* as that of our fundamental feeling.

And so we find it to be in the real fact. The superficial extension of our fundamental feeling, and the superficial extension of the external body, become compenetrated so as to form together one single surface, but of such a nature that, wonderful as it may appear, we feel in it two different things at once —*i.e.* our own fundamental feeling as modified in a certain portion of its extension, and the action of the external body which causes and is conterminous with that modification ; so that the same consciousness which assures us that the action proceeds from without, assures us also that it takes place in an extension which we already felt by nature.

Thus in the extrasubjective perception we feel (1) an external *force* acting on us, and (2) acting in that mode which is called *extension*. We perceive, therefore, the two properties necessary to constitute a *body*—properties which, being common to our body as well as to the external one, make us certain that both are *bodies*, both equally possessed of the corporeal nature, although in many other respects the effects which we respectively experience from them are widely different.

ARTICLE XI.

The subjective perception of our own body is the medium of the extra-subjective perception of other bodies.

845. We can see from the above, that the extrasubjective perception of bodies is founded on the subjective.

The first element in the extrasubjective perception consists in a force acting on us so as to cause a subjective modification in our fundamental feeling. We perceive the presence of this force, together with the said modification, in that species of violence which we are conscious of suffering.

The second element consists in extension, an extension which we feel by nature, the extension characteristic of the fundamental feeling. But inasmuch as the modifying force acts in every point of the extension where the modification of this feeling is taking place, so we perceive that force as extended in its term.

This is why I say that the criterion of the perception of external bodies ultimately resolves itself into the subjective perception of our own body (843, 844).

ARTICLE XII.

Of the extension of bodies.

846. Before proceeding further, I must dwell a little on the real extension which I have sometimes attributed to bodies. This is a very grave question, and it has given rise to a greal deal of controversy. I shall, therefore, demonstrate that the *extension* which we perceive in bodies is real, and not apparent or illusory.[1]

§ I.

Multiplicity is not essential to the corporeal nature.

847. Some philosophers have thought that multiplicity is essential to the corporeal nature.

But it is easy to see, as Leibnitz has observed, that the idea of multiplicity cannot be the idea of any nature, but only of the co-existence of many natures. It is a relative idea,

[1] Philosophical science, coming down, not through one but through many channels, has ended at last by losing itself, so to speak, in the boundless sea of modern Scepticism. I have already given a rudimentary sketch of the history of this system, or rather negation of system, through Locke, Berkeley, Hume, Reid and Kant, as also through Condillac and the French Sceptics. Another way by which this destruction of philosophy was gradually accomplished, may be traced through Des Cartes, Bayle and Kant as follows. Des Cartes had, by the great prestige of his name, succeeded in securing the universal acceptance of Galileo's opinion that the secondary properties of bodies existed only in the sentient subject ; and he placed the essence of bodies in extension alone. His error consisted in not having observed that all our sensations, although subjective, as in the case of colour, taste, sound, smell, &c., have always of necessity an *extrasubjective* part. This part being forgotten, and all sensations without exception represented as purely subjective, Bayle, who came next, found no difficulty in applying the same mode of reasoning which Des Cartes had employed with regard to the secondary properties, to prove that the primary properties also were nothing but subjective phenomena, and, among these, the property of *extension*. His argument was simple enough and quite *ad hominem*. It ran thus : 'Extension is perceived only by means of a sensation ; but all sensations are subjective ; therefore extension is subjective.' In starting from this point, Kant had only to invent his 'categoric' name of '*Form of the external sense*' for expressing the aptitude which the sentient subject has of perceiving space : this sufficed to give to the belief in the real existence of external bodies its final overthrow in the eyes of *critical* reason. Such was one of the consequences of that dismal spirit of scepticism by the strong current of which Kant had, whether consciously or not, allowed himself to be carried away, and which, being worked out by his active mind into a complete scientific system, took the name of *Transcendental philosophy*. Extension could no longer be defended after the slip made by Des Cartes in overlooking the *extrasubjective* element which is invariably mixed up in all our sensations.

which supposes and is founded on an absolute one. In short, where there are the many, there must be the one; because the multiple is only an aggregate of units. Therefore the nature of things must be sought in unity,[1] and not in multiplicity, which simply means many natures agglomerated together.

848. Therefore, neither the nature of *body* nor the nature of anything else, can ever consist in *multiplicity*, which is purely a mental entity. It is only the Idealists, and principally those of the Transcendental school, who are consistent in placing in it the corporeal nature, because, according to them, bodies are only a certain emanation of our mind.[2]

§ 2.

Complex unity of our sensitive body.

849. Our organs, in order to be sensitive, must have certain conditions.

One of these conditions is communication with the brain.

This leads to the conclusion, that the sensitivity of each part of our sensitive organism depends on the structure of the whole sensitive system, namely, on a fitting arrangement and organisation of the several parts, which, in virtue of being thus harmoniously disposed, give a whole which is sensitive throughout.

It is, therefore, from the whole or rather, from a certain unity which pervades it, that the various parts of our organism derive their sensitivity; and thus we may say, that our body, in so far as it is sensitive, has a certain complex unity, namely, that it is one by reason of the order and harmony of its parts.

850. This would have to be held as certain, even if we could not decide the question as to whether there be precisely a centre in the brain, and if there be, whether it consist of a

---

[1] If the corporeal nature is to be placed in the elementary molecules of which bodies are composed, these molecules must not on this account be considered as devoid of extension. In order that they may have the nature of 'body,' it suffices that they have a con-tinuous extension, for, as we have seen, the continuous is one (825).

[2] Here I speak of *actual multiplicity*; nevertheless the nature of the 'extended' always involves the idea of a *potential multiplicity*; but this does not as yet constitute real multiplicity.

single molecule to which all the nerves converge, or of many such molecules.

For, even apart from the intelligent spirit, the unity of the human body is sufficiently proved by the fact that a certain state of organisation is necessary to it, in order that it may be vivified and inhabited by the soul, and that the various powers may be duly fitted for the performance of their respective functions.

§ 3.

About the unity of our body we cannot be mistaken.

851. To see this truth, let us for an instant suppose that we had, not one, but two bodies. We should then have two fundamental feelings, with two separate extensions; because these are the two essential constitutives of our body. Our consciousness, therefore, by bearing witness to one fundamental feeling only, diffused through a certain extension, bears witness also to the unicity of our body.

Again, let us suppose, that we had two fundamental feelings, each with its own extension. In this case, we could not have one body only; because we should be perceiving the two constitutive elements of a body duplicated. Even then, therefore, we could not be mistaken as to whether we had one body or two.[1]

[1] No one who keeps in mind the idea I have presented of the corporeal substance will fail to see the unreasonableness of the following words of Reid : 'We ought not, therefore, to conclude that such bodily organs are, in their own nature, necessary to perception ; but rather, that by the will of God, our power of perceiving external objects is limited and circumscribed by our organ of sense ; so that we perceive objects in a certain manner and in certain circumstances, and in no other ' (*Essays on the Powers of the Human Mind.* E. II. Ch. I.).

That other beings devoid of corporeal organs may have a more perfect *knowledge* of bodies than we possess, is quite true ; but that there could be a better *sensitive perception* of bodies without the use of bodily organs, is a proposition which can be maintained only by a person who has not sufficiently analysed the said perception. I have shown, that what we call *body* is precisely what we perceive with our bodily organs, so that, in order to have the sensitive perception of the corporeal nature, these organs are fully as necessary, as the corporeal nature itself. It is manifest that the concept which Reid, like all the modern philosophers who preceded him, had formed of bodies, was that of a certain unknown and mysterious something. From an idea of bodies so vague and confused, nay altogether mysterious, which gives room for any amount of theorising, have arisen, we may fairly say, all the strange things broached by modern philosophy, and especially by Idealism. The truth, on the contrary, is, that the word *body*, does not and cannot express anything except that which we know and perceive

§ 4.

Multiplicity of the feeling we have of our body.

852. Now although our body is *one* because of the harmony of its parts, and we therefore feel its *unicity*, while all that lies outside that harmony is no more felt by us than if did not exist; yet neither that unity nor that unicity is such as to exclude from it a certain multiplicity.

With regard to this multiplicity, I have to observe, that as, owing to the organised state of our body, the soul feels by the fundamental feeling *all* the sensitive parts, so by the adventitious sensations it feels *in* all the sensitive parts; and this gives a certain multiplicity, at least conceivable by the mind.

853. I will confine myself to the sensations; for what is said of them can be easily applied by any one to the fundamental feeling also.

What, then, can we say for certain respecting the multiplicity of sensation, and what can we not?

Speaking of tactile sensations we can say for certain, that if the part affected is of a certain extension (and impressed with sufficient intensity), we have a sensation in all that part, and in the majority of cases advert to it.

But if that extension be reduced beyond a certain degree of minuteness, it altogether escapes our advertence.

This extension of the sensation, which if it became at all smaller, would no longer have power to excite advertence, we may designate as the *minimum* of extension.

Now let this *minimum* be regarded here as the elementary unit of extended sensation.

It is certain that one such unit is not the other; because

---

by means of the corporeal senses. Hence our idea of bodies is conditioned to and closely linked with the sensitive organs. On this point, the error of Reid is the opposite of that of Newton, who thought it necessary to attribute a *sensorium* even to God himself, that *sensorium* being 'Infinite space.' Reid considered that organs possessed of extension are not indispensable for the sensitive corporeal perception. Newton regarded extension as indispensable even for the Divine *knowledge*. These errors will for the most part vanish when once we thoroughly grasp the difference between *sensation* and *sensitive perception* on the one hand, and on the other the *idea* and the *word* of the mind.

in each of them we have severally, (1) *feeling* (sensation), (2) *extension* ; and these are the two constitutives of a body.

Hence we may legitimately consider these *elementary units* as corresponding to as many minute bodies, each subsisting separately from, that is to say, outside of the other ; nor is there any possibility of the one of them confounding itself with, or filling the place of the other. Consequently, in our body we perceive *multiplicity* as certainly as we perceive *unity*.

§ 5.
Multiplicity perceived by us in external bodies.

854. The same mode of reasoning is applicable to external bodies. A body may be so exceedingly small, that any further diminution in its size would entirely withdraw it from our advertence.

Taking this *minimum* (the smallest corpuscle capable of exciting advertence) as the elementary unit, we may safely affirm, that in the perception of a large body our mind can distinguish and separate those *elementary* perceptions in such a manner as to conceive them (when taken each by itself) as distinct from one another in reality also.

Now since in each of them we find the two constitutive elements of a body, it follows that we can mentally distinguish a corresponding number of corpuscles—whether as divided or as united together, it matters not.

And that these corpuscles have also a subsistence independently of one another, is seen from this, that each has an action separate and incommunicable. For each of those minute spaces which we have distinguished is outside every other. Therefore one agent is outside the other agents, and is a substance with its own separate existence, although it may lie in material contiguity to the others. *Multiplicity* is, therefore, perceived by us in external bodies also.

§ 6.
Distinction between body and corporeal principle.

855. We 'give names to things according as we know them' (647).

Hence to inquire what *body* is comes to the same as to inquire what is the notion commonly attached to the word *body* (653–656).

We have found this notion to consist of two elements, viz. a *force acting* on us, and an *extension* in which the action of that force, and the passion corresponding to it on our part is diffused.

If that force did not act on us at all, we could neither know it nor give it a name. We know it, therefore, and name it only in so far as it acts on us. Consequently, the meaning of the word *body* is determined by the *immediate effects* which the said force produces in us, and by the laws in accordance with which it produces them.

But the same force might also have aptitudes and be subject to laws which are hidden from us, not indeed contrary to, but different from those we can now see by its action. If such were the case, we should not know that force, nor name it, with respect to any of the effects it could produce by means of the said aptitudes, and to the laws it would follow in that production. Until, therefore, these effects are revealed to us, the word *body* is not applicable to them, because ' Words must not be used in a wider sense than they were invented to express' (648–652).

Nevertheless if, in the event of a change taking place in the present order of things, new effects and new laws were discovered to belong to the same principle by whose activity are produced the effects which now determine the value of the word *body* ; the common use of that word would then undergo a modification.

But so long as that word is used in the present condition of things, its meaning is limited by the immediate effects aforesaid, and by the laws in conformity with which those effects (the *bodies*) reveal themselves to us.

856. Hence I think it meet to draw a distinction between *corporeal principle* and *body* ; and, in the definition of the latter, to comprise that principle only in so far as it is accompanied by those effects and laws whereby we now know it ; leaving to it at the same time all that it might have in itself

beyond or different from what now constitutes its nature for us.

857. It is therefore of the *body* taken in the sense here explained, that I have had no hesitation in affirming that we know for certain the *multiplicity* of bodies.[1]

§ 7.

Assuming that corporeal sensation terminates in a continuous extension, we are bound to admit a really continuous extension also in the bodies which produce that sensation.

858. Let us suppose that that portion of the surface of our body wherein an adventitious sensation, or at least some small part of it, diffuses itself, is truly continuous.

I maintain that the body which produces that extended and continuous sensation must also be itself extended and continuous.[2] This is but a corollary of what I have said just now, and oftentimes before.

I have said, that 'the body is the *proximate* cause of our sensations' (639–645); and I have explained, that by *proximate cause* is meant a being which takes its name from the immediate effect constantly produced by it, and not from anything else (*ibid.*).

Hence I have concluded, that the constant sensations—*i.e.* the fundamental feeling and its modifications—are not produced by any one particular *aptitude* of the body, but by its very *substance*, by the body itself; because the meaning of the word *body* is taken solely from those immediate effects, and therefore is wholly exhausted by them.

Starting from these truths, I found that wherever we experience a sensation diffused in extension, there we must admit the presence of an acting force furnished with all the

---

[1] Whatever new properties might be discovered in bodies, or whatever changes they might be made to undergo by a force superior to nature, the new properties could not nullify the truth of the old : hence the extrasubjective qualities which we at present perceive in bodies do not deceive us, and are true notwithstanding that it would be possible for them to be changed.

[2] It would be just the same if we supposed that the fundamental feeling diffused itself over some space, superficial or solid, of a continuous nature, that is, where there are no interruptions.

characteristics necessary to constitute a body : and hence the *multiplicity* of bodies deduced from the multiplicity of sensations in the multiplicity of extensions. For we can always imagine a certain sensation as ceasing in one of the little extensions while it continues in another, and again as reappearing here while it ceases there : so that all we know about these sensations felt in different extensions is, that they are each entirely independent of, and capable of existing without the others.

This essential difference in the effects authorises, nay obliges us to admit a substantial difference in the causes, and hence the multiplicity of these causes. Now this smoothes the way for demonstrating that if there is a continuously extended sensation, there must be a continuous extension also in the body which has produced it.

859. In fact, a large extension pervaded by sensation has been imagined by us as divided into a quantity of minute extensions; and we have seen that for each of these little extensions there is a force or corpuscle operating in it and producing a sensation.

Let us now, in thought, bring these little extensions together, so as to leave no division between them. By so doing, we make of them one large and continuous extension. But will the argument I have put forward lose its force on this account? Certainly not; for no alteration whatever has been made in the little extensions themselves. Whether, therefore, they lie wide apart from or are placed near to one another, and even in immediate contiguity, there must, so long as they are distinct, be a corpuscle corresponding to each of them. As therefore this their contiguity results in a large and continuous sensation, so it proves the presence of a continuous body.

In fact, the whole force of my argument lies in the principle that 'Wherever we suffer a sensation, there is an acting force which causes it.' If therefore the sensation is continuous, and equably diffused in every assignable point of a given extension, the acting force, the body, must be present co-extensively therewith. Hence, no division in the sensation means no division in that body. The one continuity calls necessarily for the other.

This necessity flows from the nature of continuous extension—marvellous indeed and mysterious, but undeniable. No space, however small, can be assigned in it, which has not an entity proper to itself, that is to say, an entity external to and wholly independent of the other spaces. Hence each of the little spaces can be distinguished from the whole, at least mentally; and hence the property which the 'continuous' has of being *indefinitely limitable* (826–830). And the fact of each little space being outside of all the others, renders it impossible for the action which is enclosed within one to operate in another. Therefore each of these spaces, no matter how diminutive we conceive it to be, supposes a force operating outside of that which operates in those next to it. Consequently, in the external body, there must be as many parts operating contiguously on our body, as there are contiguous little spaces assignable in the portion of extension where our sensation is felt.

860. But here an objector may say : Your argument will not hold. The so called *sympathetic pains* are certainly sensations, and yet everybody knows that they spread much beyond that part which has been actually impressed by the external body. Therefore it is not true that every sensation must of necessity be precisely co-extensive with the body that excites it.

To this objection I have two answers to make.

(1) I wish to observe that in all the places really embraced by a sympathetic pain there must be sensitive parts. Now, to these parts the reasoning I have made is certainly applicable. If that pain is diffused in a continuous extension, the parts which through being molested produce the pain, must needs be continuous.[1] But if they are continuous, there is, as I say, continuity in bodies.

(2) The sensation propagated by sympathy falls under

[1] Sometimes we are mistaken concerning the place to which we refer a sensation, as for instance in the case of a limb which has been amputated and which still seems to pain us : but this kind of error is not attributable to the sense, but to a *judgment* resulting from habit (762).

the same law as all other sensations, which is, that ' Where a sensitive being is acted upon by a force, there it feels.' In truth, why is the sensation propagated except because the force whose action causes a change in the state of the parts of the sensitive organ affected is itself propagated ? Let us suppose that the alteration of the organ, which is followed by pain (whether that alteration be produced by a mechanical, physical, or chemical force, it makes no difference), communicates itself from one part of it, or, if I may say so, from one stratum to another. Obviously, the third of these strata will receive its motion from the second. What body, then, will this third stratum feel ? The external body ? No, but it will feel the internal part of the organ itself, I mean the second stratum which presses upon or draws it, in a word, acts on it. The pain diffused in the sensitive fibre by sympathetic propagation, does not bear witness to an *external body* ; it only makes us feel more vividly the organ affected, that is, the parts of it which by their immediate action produce the pain. Whether therefore a sensation be caused immediately by an external body, or whether it take place by sympathetic propagation from one part of our sensitive organism to another, the principle from which I started in my demonstration of the continuity of bodies, remains unshaken. In either case, it is always true that ' Wheresoever we feel a sensation being produced in us, there a corporeal force in action (a body) is present.'

§ 8.

The sensitive parts of our body do not produce a sensation more extended than they are themselves.

861. This is clear from the preceding paragraph, and the definition of the sensitive parts of our body proves it also.

For how do we come to know these parts ? We perceive a sensitive part where we experience a sensation, and then by reflection we make sure as to the reality of that sensation.

Therefore sensation is never more extended than the sensitive part affected, and the sensitive part affected is never more extended than the sensation.

§ 9.

The extension of external bodies is neither larger nor smaller than that of the sensations which they produce in us.

862. This proposition is proved in the same way as the preceding one.

How do we measure the size of external bodies ?

By our sensations, and chiefly by that of touch: as we have seen elsewhere, the extension of our own body perceived subjectively is the measure of the extrasubjective extension of external bodies.

Therefore the extension of external bodies is neither larger nor smaller than the extension of the sensations which they produce by coming in contact with us.

§ 10.

In our tactile sensations there is a phenomenal continuity.

863. It is certain that when we, with our hand or any other part of our body, touch a surface which is perfectly smooth, we are not able to notice in our sensation any vacant spaces.

Hence a sensation of this kind seems to us continuous ; and this is the same as saying that its continuity is phenomenal.

For if that same surface, which when felt by the touch appears to be continuous, be observed with a microscope, it will be found full of pores and rugged all over. This fact would seem to be in contradiction with the statement I have just made to the effect that a tactile sensation never exceeds the size of the external body by which it is produced. But we must always bear in mind the essential distinction between *sensation* and *advertence*:[1] and we must also, by careful

[1] I have on many occasions drawn attention to the distinction between *sensation* and *advertence* to sensation. To me it seems most certain (and what I shall say in the sequel demonstrates it), that in order to produce a sensation fit to be adverted to, at least with a fair degree of facility, the corporeal stimulus which acts on us must be stronger than that which is sufficient to make us simply *feel* a sensation. I mean to say, that the slighter and more restricted a sensation is, the less easily can we advert to it. Hence, in the case of a most slender sensation, it must be exceedingly difficult to notice it, or at least to notice its extension.

observation, realise to ourselves the plain fact that there are in us sensations so exceedingly slight as entirely to escape advertence ; hence our utter unconsciousness of those incredibly minute voids and interruptions which exist in our sensation of the said surface, and as a consequence, the belief in, or rather the assumption of its continuity.

§ 11.

The elementary sensations have a truly continuous extension.

864. Sensations of notable extension, then (like that of the surface just referred to), have not a perfect continuity, being in every part of them interspersed with a multitude of vacant little spaces or interstices.

These break, as it were, the large sensation into so many small and elementary sensations, placed in very close proximity to one another, but not actually in contact at every point.

Now I maintain, that these minute or elementary sensations fill an extension truly continuous ; and I prove it in the following manner.

Let us suppose the contrary, namely, that these sensations are not continuous : they will then be mere mathematical or unextended points.

865. These points would necessarily leave intervening spaces more or less minute, but always continuous as well as contiguous. I say *contiguous*, because a mathematical point does not break contiguity.

Now we must take note of a special law which governs our sensations, namely, that ' Whenever there are in our bodies two or more sensations, with a space intervening between them,' we are conscious of the fact ; because we refer them to different points. Consequently, if these spaces are notably extended, we are aware of them, principally through comparing the place affected by the sensation with that which is not so affected.

Now let it be assumed, that the sensation is felt only in a number of mathematical or unextended points ; I ask :

Would it be possible in that case to have the phenomenal continuity we now have from our sensations?

I say it would not be possible, and here are my reasons:—

I. If we were able to advert to sensations wholly without extension, *a fortiori* we should be able to advert to the little spaces interspersed between them, and which have an extension infinitely greater than mathematical points. Therefore the sensation never could, in the supposition now made, appear to us continuous; but we should be obliged to notice it distinctly as composed of unextended points placed apart from one another; and thus the phenomenon of continuity which we have at present in our sensations would be inexplicable.

866. II. On the self-evident principle that ' Non-extension cannot make extension,' no number of unextended points added together, even though it were infinite, could ever cover the smallest particle of a line, much less of a surface. All those points, therefore, which we have supposed as felt by us would not cause any diminution whatever in the size of the surface over which they are spread. Consequently, we should have to feel not one, but two sensations, namely, that of the unextended points, and that of the whole surface just as it was felt before by the fundamental feeling: or rather we should have to feel no continuity at all; since all the minute spaces in which there would be no sensation would, taken together, form precisely as much extension as there was before our sensation of the said points had begun. As, then, the extension felt by us in these points would be *nil*, it remains that we should have to advert to the extension left between them, an extension, as just said, fully as large now as it was before the new and totally unextended impression took place: and so we never could have either the perception or the idea of anything continuous.

867. III. Moreover, if simple or unextended points were felt by us, we should be experiencing an aggregate of sensations, which, not having any extension, would not be of the corporeal kind (754), since it is essential to corporeal sensations to terminate in extension; nor, consequently, would they supply us with the material requisite for the idea of body.

868. IV. Lastly, granting even that unextended points only were felt by us, how could we refer them to different places on the surface of our body, as experience tells us that we refer our corporeal sensations? We could not do this except by measuring in some way the distances from one point to another. Now, if we felt these distances, we should be feeling the *continuous*—which is against the hypothesis—or if we did not feel them, we should not have any means of referring those points to the places we now refer them to: hence these would be sensations outside of all place, and referred perhaps to nothing else than the simplicity of our spirit. Most assuredly, only the *continuous* can serve us for measuring distances. A simple point cannot be a measure. But given that we perceive the *continuous*, we shall also be able to measure the intervals between one point and another, that is to say, to ascertain their length, since all that is wanted for this consists simply in comparing in our mind each such interval with that *continuous* extension, which we take as the standard of measurement, and finding out how many times each can admit of it in itself.

It must therefore be conceded that the minute elementary sensations, whether they are adventitious or are those composing the fundamental feeling, terminate in continuous extension.

§ 12.

The elementary bodies have a continuous extension.

869. That the *corporeal principle* may be simple, is a point which we can neither affirm nor deny; for this principle may be in part unknown to us (855–857).

But to say with Leibnitz that bodies are an aggregate of simple points, would be a manifest error.[1]

We have seen, (1) that the elementary sensations are extended as well as continuous; (2) that the size of bodies,

---

[1] The error of Leibnitz seems to consist precisely in this, that he meant to speak of the *corporeal principle* rather than of the *bodies* themselves, of the unknown rather than of the known. And how can a man speak securely and without error of what he does not know?

which are the *proximate causes* of the sensations, is equal to the size of the sensations themselves.

The necessary consequence of this is, that the elementary bodies have a continuous extension.[1]

§ 13.

Refutation of the opinion that the elementary bodies consist of simple points.

870. Simple points, because unextended, cannot, whether taken as units or as aggregates of units, be sensitively perceived ; therefore they are not *bodies*. To call them so would be a glaring perversion of the use of language ; for the word *body* has been invented to signify only what is known as being capable of falling under our senses, of making a sensible impression on our corporeal organs.[2]

Wherever there happens to be a sensation, there is, on the one hand, a passion felt by us, and, on the other, an action exercised by a force which excites the sensation and is called *body*. Now if, as we have seen, there are in certain minute spaces continuously extended sensations, this implies that the said force diffuses its action respectively over the whole of each of those minute spaces ; that it is present in every point of them ; that it is continuously extended. Consequently, the elementary bodies must be admitted to be truly continuous, and not simple points only, unless, instead of standing upon the safe ground of observation, one chooses to be led by mere imagination.[3]

[1] The elementary bodies, besides having a certain continuous extension, must also have certain regular forms, after the manner of crystals, and be perfectly hard and not subject to change.

[2] See numbers 647–652. Nevertheless, it must always be borne in mind that the things we designate by words are *true*, although only in that limited aspect under which we know them.

[3] If the action of simple points were to terminate in a point only, these agents could pass from one part of our body to another without causing the least disturbance. And if we assign to them a little sphere to which their action extends, then this sphere so filled with their action will be precisely an extended body. But before we could affirm that they are constructed in this manner, we should have to demonstrate that the force of elementary bodies operates in a way similar to that of rays emanating from a centre. This may perhaps be one of the questions destined to engage the attention of some future inquirer ; but it has not been investigated as yet. Should the demonstration of which I speak not be given, there would be no difference between

ARTICLE XIII.

The definition of BODY *is perfected.*

871. Having found that the thing called *body* is really possessed of continuous extension, we can perfect its definition by including in it this quality.[1]

A *body*, therefore,[2] is 'A substance possessed of extension, and causing in us either an agreeable or a painful feeling which terminates in that same extension.[3]

ARTICLE XIV.

External bodies are perceived by means of the touch combined with motion.

872. Since a *body* is a force terminating with its action in a solid continuous space, we must now see how we can perceive it by means of the touch.

Space has three dimensions —length, breadth and depth.

the centre and the sphere ; because the acting force would be numerically the same in the one and in each several point of the other. If, on the other hand, the *centre* of the supposed sphere were purely ideal, it would not constitute any real nature, but be simply a mental postulate. Again, in the supposition of the said centre radiating a force in all directions, the primitive or elementary bodies would have to be spherical in form ; and this cannot be true of all such bodies. But if they are not spherical, the result will be, that the law of the centre of gravity must clash with the centre of the force. Be, however, all this as it may, the word *body* can never mean anything else than a force possessed of extension.

[1] I gave in the first instance an imperfect definition of *body*, taking it from the notion which is commonly attached to this word (635). I say an *imperfect*, not a *false* definition, because the whole essence of *body* was contained in it ; but that essence was not as yet analysed into its component elements. By making that analysis, I have, as I think, been enabled to improve the same definition heretofore (749-753), and more so in

this place. Now this seems to me exactly the method to be pursued by those who wish to help on the progress of philosophic knowledge. The philosophical student should begin from those natural and synthetic ideas which constitute the common knowledge, I mean such knowledge as the generality of men ordinarily express in their everyday life. The analysis of these ideas will gradually lead him to the formation of that knowledge which is completed by *scientific synthesis*. Those therefore who say that one ought not to begin with definitions, seek to avoid one error by running into its opposite. We must begin with definitions if we wish to make ourselves understood : but there are definitions taken from the common manner of speaking, and there are scientific definitions ; and both are true. It is necessary to begin with the first in order to be able to end with the second.

[2] I say *a* substance, meaning *one* ; and this I do to indicate that the corporeal substance is *continuous*.

[3] How this happens I have shown before.

In our own body we first perceive these three dimensions by the fundamental feeling (692, &c.).

When external bodies act on the surface of our own, we cannot in that action feel and perceive anything more than a surface, that is to say, the two dimensions of length and breadth. The depth of external bodies is not perceivable by this means alone.[1] So far, then, we have not the idea of a solid body.

To form this idea, we must consider the external surface perceived by our touch in relation with the power we have of moving it.

Even as the idea of solid space is obtained by our conceiving a surface as movable in all possible directions outside of its plane (839), so the idea of solid body is derived from the motion—partly experienced by us, and partly expected, or at least conceived as possible—of a corporeal surface moving also outside of its plane.

873. The thought of such a motion as is here described leads us to conceive as a possibility that all the surfaces assignable within a given solid space will be fully as perceivable by our touch as the external surface is.

An example will make all this clear.

Let us imagine a body made in the form of a cube, and perfectly hard.

We feel this cube in all its six faces, and what do we find? Press it as hard as we will, our touch never perceives anything else than the outer limits of a solid space, that is, corporeal surfaces.

With this experiment we begin to have an idea of *body*; but this idea is as yet imperfect, because only two of these dimensions of a solid space have thus far been perceived.[2]

---

[1] Sometimes an external body seems to act on ours contemporaneously in all the points of a solid space, as for instance in the action of a corrosive and powerfully searching fluid, or of some other similar agent. Supposing this to be so, we should then indeed perceive the solidity of our own body, but not that of the external one. This observation may help the reader to distinguish between the extensions of these two bodies, which, in the sensation of touch, are perceived conjointly, and may be easily confounded together. It is only by the different relations they have to the two agents (the one felt as co-sentient with us, and the other not. TRANSLATORS), that we can distinguish them from one another.

[2] The reader need not be told that

Let us now take in our hand another cube, not hard nor impenetrable, but soft and yielding, or otherwise composed of such frail material as easily to admit of changes of form and divisions into parts. By touching this body in all its sides, we can compress it, or give it any shape we please, or break it even into fragments. As a result of all these experiments, we discover that a very great number of fresh surfaces are successively laid open to us which we could not feel before, because they were covered over and hidden inside the cube, and were not therefore, to us, surfaces at all.

By multiplying such experiments indefinitely, we come at last to the conclusion that the aforesaid cube, besides presenting a corporeal substance at the outside, has also from within the capacity of presenting numberless other sensible surfaces in all those directions in which we may choose to open and divide it. It is through experiments and thoughts of this kind that we arrive at the concept of corporeal solidity, and so complete the idea of *solid body*, namely, of a substance which expands its activity, according to certain laws, in the three dimensions of space.

ARTICLE XV.

Origin of the idea of mathematical body.

874. By the above experiment, we have come to know, that inside that space bounded by corporeal surfaces, it is possible to obtain other and other corporeal surfaces through the application of a force sufficient to make the cube change its form or to break it into parts.

Now, reflecting on this fact, our mind can see no necessary reason why each of the several surfaces which we gradually lay open should occupy one particular part of the solid cube rather than another.

There is therefore no intrinsic contradiction in the thought that each of the said corporeal surfaces might equally be dis-

in describing this operation the author supposes that we have not as yet acquired that habit by which we judge of the solidity of a body at sight (TRANSLATORS).

covered in *any* part of the cube, that is, in any plane assignable within it.

Now this possibility of conceiving corporeal surfaces as intersecting that cubic space in any plane, is the idea of *mathematical body*, which is always conceived as perfectly continuous.

ARTICLE XVI.

Origin of the idea of physical body.

875. So long, then, as we think of the simple *possibility* of a corporeal surface being found in any of the planes assignable within *e.gr.* a cube, we have the idea of a *mathematical body* (874). But when, instead of stopping at this possibility deduced by analogy from experiment, we set ourselves to make out, in the best way we can—by the touch and the other senses, assisted also, if need be, by suitable mechanical appliances—the forms of a particular and real body ; and to note also—as we go on discovering in it fresh sensible surfaces—the porosities, the irregularities and all the minute divisions between one stratum and another, one particle and another ; we then form the idea of an aggregate of small corpuscles, variously fashioned, not in perfect contact, but with interstices or clefts interposed and, nevertheless, adhering together at certain points, in such a way that they cannot be separated except by force. This is what we call *physical body.*

And thus is explained how persons born blind, can form the idea of mathematical as well as of physical bodies, namely, by means of the touch and of motion, joined with the use of the faculty of thought.

CHAPTER X.

THE PARTICULAR CRITERION OF THE EXISTENCE OF EXTERNAL BODIES.

ARTICLE I.

The criterion of the existence of external bodies is only an application of the general criterion of the existence of bodies.

876. We have seen in what the general criterion of the existence of bodies consists (749, &c.). By applying it to external bodies, whose nature we have now discovered, we shall have the criterion of their existence.

This application gives as its result, that in order to be certain that we have perception of an external body, we must perceive four things, namely,

(1) That we are being *sensibly affected* by a force acting on us;

(2) That the action by which the force thus affects us is distinctly characterised by *extension*, and therefore gives us an extended sensation;

(3) That the said extension is in its nature *permanent*, namely, such that, through it, the force is capable of repeating in us at any time the same kind of sensation which it has first given us, as it is necessary it should be in order that we may legitimately call it a *substance*; and

(4) That the same extension is possessed of *three dimensions*.

It will not therefore be sufficient that we perceive corporeal surfaces; we must, moreover, perceive a solid space, which, when broken asunder, presents to our senses fresh corporeal surfaces.

ARTICLE II.

Applications of the criterion of the existence of external bodies.

877. I. Take a silver coin and press it briskly against the forehead of a rustic, as if you were going to fix and leave it there. You may then remove it without his perceiving the fact ; nay he will still believe that he has the coin adhering to his forehead, and will shake his head to make it fall off. But if he puts up his hand to feel the spot, he finds nothing. Thus, although a sensible impression has been produced on his forehead, the substance which produced it is no longer present ; for if it were present, not only would he still feel that impression,[1] but he could also, given the proper conditions, have it repeated and intensified.[2]

II. In feeling with our hand a column apparently of silver, we may be apt to take it for solid silver throughout. To make sure of the truth, however, we must examine its interior,[3] when we shall perhaps find it empty or filled with some other substance.[4]

---

[1] According to the third of the essentials assigned by the author to the criterion (TRANSLATORS).

[2] The sensation excited in the nerve continues for some time after the cause of the sensation has been removed, as we see in the case of the eye, when a piece of burning charcoal is whirled round before it with great velocity. The pure sensation bears witness to itself only ; and the consciousness of a sensible impression made in us bears witness to the existence of a cause, but not to its actual presence. This must therefore be inferred through a judgment, which, if not safeguarded with all the requisite conditions, will prove deceptive. The sensation, however, does not deceive us in its deposition, (1) regarding the existence of the part of our body which is affected, in so far as the affection is a modification of the fundamental feeling, and (2) regarding the existence of a cause which has produced that modification.

[3] According to the fourth essential of the criterion (TRANSLATORS).

[4] Here also it is the *judgment* which deceives us, not the sensation ; and the judgment deceives us because it goes beyond where the sensation has gone, *i.e.* into the interior of the column.

CHAPTER XI.

DISTINCTION BETWEEN WHAT IS SUBJECTIVE AND WHAT
IS EXTRASUBJECTIVE IN EXTERNAL SENSATIONS.

ARTICLE I.

Necessity of this discussion.

878. Having, under the guidance of observation, described the *extrasubjective* perception of bodies as given us by the touch, I ought now to do the same thing in regard to the other four sensories, by trying to ascertain precisely how far the perceptions of each of them can take us in the same direction.

But as we have seen that in all sensations the subjective part is mixed up with the extrasubjective, the task of which I speak ultimately reduces itself to sifting and distinguishing with great care the one part from the other. When this separation shall have been so well made that we can feel perfectly sure that the extrasubjective perception stands before us in its pure self alone and isolated from every element foreign to it, we shall then be able to understand its authority and, by consequence, the extrasubjective value of each sensory.

ARTICLE II.

Some truths recalled to mind.

879. I have demonstrated the two following points :—

(1) Sensations are in us, and not in the external agents (632, &c., and 672, &c.).

This fact has been abused by modern Idealists in this, that, in giving their attention to it, they forgot to consider other facts equally necessary to be taken into account.

Hence, the error of their deductions arises from imperfect observation.

(2) Sensations are in us as terms of an action proceeding from something different from us (*ibid.*).

This fact also has been overlooked by the Idealists, although it is not less manifest than the first. For in every sensation we indeed experience a modification, but of the kind called *passive*; since, as our consciousness tells us, it is a species of violence brought to bear on us ; and that violence bespeaks the term of an action from without. Such is the singular nature of sensation. It is *in* us and yet deposes to a something *outside* of us. Either we must deny the difference between activity and passivity, or we must concede that our consciousness of a passion is also the consciousness of an action done in us, but not by us.

ARTICLE III.

The mind analyses our sensations.

880. In every adventitious sensation, our consciousness, simultaneously and as it were by one and the same word, informs us,

(1) That we are being modified, and (2) that this modification is an action produced in us, but not by us.

Reflection supervenes, and noticing, by means of analysis, the two elements conjointly expressed in that interior deposition, considers the one separately from the other.

Then the mind applies to the second element, namely, to the consciousness of the action done in us, but not by us, the idea of substance ; and this is how external things become objects of thought, on which the mind afterwards exercises its powers in sundry ways.

ARTICLE IV.

General principle for distinguishing between the subjective and the extrasubjective part of our sensations.

881. The principle to be followed in distinguishing in sensations the subjective from the extrasubjective element,

is this : 'All that enters into the concept of sensation considered by itself (and not in the manner of its production), is subjective : and all that enters into the concept of our passivity, certified to us by consciousness, is extrasubjective.'

ARTICLE V.

Application of the general principle to find the extrasubjective part of our sensations.

882. The extrasubjective elements which we find in our sensations by applying the above principle are as follows :—

Firstly, our consciousness testifies that in every sensation we suffer what I call a species of violence, that is to say, we feel acted upon by a *force*, in which our mind sees a *being different from ourselves*, namely, a *body*. A *force* is therefore the first part of the extrasubjective perception of bodies.

Secondly, our consciousness testifies that the *forces* which we feel acting upon us, are many ; hence the *multiplicity of bodies* constitutes the second part in the extrasubjective perception of bodies.

Thirdly, our consciousness, combined with reasoning, testifies also that, within a given extension, no one point can be assigned in which a *force* is not found acting ; and this leads us to infer with certainty the existence of a *continuous extension*, which extension is therefore the third part of the extrasubjective perception of bodies.

883. Now these three first extrasubjective properties of bodies, when submitted to analysis, are seen to contain numerous other properties. On this point it will be enough here to observe what follows.

By the *force* which is first among all the properties of bodies, we must not understand any kind of force capable of acting on our spirit, but only a force which acts in a particular mode—I mean the mode determined by the subjective effects it produces in us, or, which is the same thing, by the subjective part of our sensations, such as pleasure, pain, warmth, colour, taste, smell, &c. Now, if the force produces these different species of effects, it must necessarily have in it as many *aptitudes* or powers capable of producing them. Therefore the first among the properties of bodies generates many others, that is to say, all the aptitudes of which I speak, and in which it diversifies itself according to the variety of its effects (determinations of the force).[1]

884. *Multiplicity* is not a real property of the corporeal nature except in this sense, that it is *possible* for us to imagine it in the continuous extension of which bodies are possessed. Such real *multiplicity* as we find in the world of fact is accidental, and consists of a relation conceived in our mind between several bodies.

885. · Finally, *extension*, especially if united with *force*, gives rise to a great number of the properties we see in bodies, such as *mobility, configuration, divisibility, impenetrability*, &c. All these properties are comprised in it, and are therefore, both real and extrasubjective, *i.e.* existing in the bodies themselves and not merely in us.[2]

ARTICLE VI.

On the distinction between the primary and the secondary properties of bodies.

886. It will be seen from the above, that the celebrated distinction between the primary and the secondary properties of bodies has its foundation in nature.

Only it would be more accurate to call the former *extrasubjective*, and the latter *subjective.*

Considering, however, that our idea of *corporeal substance* is derived from the former, while the latter are attributed

---

[1] These determinations explain that element which I have hitherto passed over in order not to make my argument too complicated, contenting myself with designating it by the term *corporeal* added to that of *force.*

[2] From this we can see in what sense the ancients were right when they said that the phantasms are *similitudes* or images of external bodies. The saying was true in relation, not to the subjective, but to the extrasubjective part of the phantasms ; and it is by the extrasubjective part alone that we perceive external bodies. Hence it is true that the *multiplicity* and *continuity* of the phantasms are similar to those of the corresponding external bodies. As regards, however, the *force* proper to these bodies, it is felt by us as passive recipients only, whereas in the bodies it is active. But, whether in us or in the bodies, it is the selfsame force in action ; for our sensations are the term as well as the immediate effect of it.

to that substance as its accidents, so to speak, the denomination of *primary* and *secondary* properties does not seem to be altogether unreasonable.

ARTICLE VII.

Application of the general principle to discover the subjective part of our sensations.

887. I have said, that whatever is found in a sensation considered purely by itself is subjective (881).

Hence, all that we can discover in sensations after having separated from them the *force* which produces and keeps them in existence, *multiplicity* and *extension*—and likewise everything which the analysis of these three parts discloses to us—will be subjective.

Here it must be observed that, although our fundamental feeling is characterised by unity—the unity of the sentient principle in which all the various modifications are equally centred—and although we may reasonably believe that it is by the very nature of that principle and of the animal fundamental feeling that those modifications are generated and their different characters fixed and determined; nevertheless, we are not sufficiently acquainted with that nature to see how they come to be so united together; hence the most diversified changes which we notice in the fundamental feeling seem to us arbitrary and like facts wholly isolated from and independent of one another, and therefore not deducible *a priori*. So, at least, it appears to me.

888. Whether, therefore, it be that this my impression is simply the effect of ignorance on my part, or that there really is in the thing itself something occult and mysterious ; I shall content myself with indicating the most diversified species of sensations to which we are liable, as so many primitive facts, without stopping to inquire how or by what necessary laws it happens, that facts so different and so utterly beyond our power of forecasting, can all be generated by, or flow out of one and the same primal feeling.

What induces me to believe that in the fact to which I

am referring there really is something hidden from our knowledge, is this, that one species of sensation never causes us to imagine another which we have never experienced. For instance, a man born blind never succeeds in forming to himself the image of colour, no matter with what other sensations he may be familiar. And speaking in general, persons who have come into the world bereft of one sensory, find the other sensories—which in them are perhaps even more active than in others—absolutely of no use for constructing any image whatever of the species of sensation they never had. It appears, therefore, that, so far at least as regards the external and adventitious sensations, we can lay it down as a certainty that there is in them something essentially incommunicable, and that each stands entirely divided from the others—a conclusion which seems furthermore suggested by their great simplicity.

889. So much being premised, I say that the first subjective element of sensation consists in that pleasure which is diffused in all the sensitive parts of the animate body by means of the fundamental feeling.

This is caused by our body, and its nature is determined by the *state* of the body itself, life being of course supposed.

That the *modifications* of the fundamental feeling are determined by the *state* of the body is beyond all controversy ; but this takes place according to laws, the reason and principle of which I do not, as I have said before, feel myself competent to investigate.

890. Hence, as the various parts of our body have each a different *state,* so each receives the sensible impressions differently, and modifies the self-same fundamental feeling in a different manner.

This difference of *state* between the several parts of our body has been so ordained by the infinitely Wise Author of all things, that the various sensitive organs should be found exactly suitable to that species of sensation for which they were respectively intended. Thus, the wonderful structure of the eye fits it for receiving modifications of the fundamental feeling different from those which are received by the ear, the nostrils or the palate.

891. Nor are these the only organs which produce different *modifications* in the fundamental feeling. Other parts of the body also are susceptible of other modifications, according to the greater or lesser delicacy of the substance of which they are made, and of their texture, or according to the peculiarity of their organisation. Thus the sensations of hunger, of thirst, of sleepiness, and the sexual inclination, are all totally different from one another; and if we do not regard these as so many sensories, this is not because they are not really such, but because we reserve the appellation of sensory to signify those organs which aid our understanding in a more special manner to gain the knowledge of external things.

892. It is, then, by its state and speciality of organisation, that an organ is fitted to receive that kind of modification of the fundamental feeling for which it was destined and fashioned. But this is not enough. In order that such modification may actually take place, there must be, in addition to a suitably-formed organism, a stimulus to act upon it, and to act in a proper manner.

Thus the eye, to give us the sensation of colour, must be acted upon by the light: the hearing in its turn stands in need of air; the smell, of odoriferous effluvia, and the taste, of savoury particles. In short, without an agent every way suitable both as to matter and form, no special sensation or modification of the fundamental feeling can be produced.

893. Moreover, the agent must, as I have just said, operate in the *proper manner*. The air must undulate, the light must vibrate, the effluvia must be diffused, and the savoury particles dissolved and applied—all in such and such a way, and no other.[1]

894. For the production, then, of special sensations three

[1] Even as regards the touch, what a variety of sensations there arises simply out of the different ways in which it is impressioned! Who would ever imagine unless he had had experience of it, that a slight tickling of the skin could produce so singular an excitement as it does! Is there any sensation like this, which by a power as strange as it is unique of its kind, makes you laugh in spite of yourself?

. things are requisite, besides life : (1) the suitable structure and state of the organ ; (2) a suitable *agent* ; and (3) a suitable mode of action in that agent.

895. Hence it follows, that the effect, namely the subjective sensation—proceeding as it does from three joint principles —will be no certain indication of the state of one of these principles taken apart from the others ; and therefore an attempt to infer from the said subjective sensation the nature of the external cause of it, must inevitably lead to error.

Thus, for instance, we find that the sensation of heat, which is subjective—*i.e.* is in us and not in the external body which has produced it [1]—affords no accurate measure of the

---

[1] It is supposed by some, that before Des Cartes no one had ever noticed the fact of the *subjectivity* of sensation ; but they are mistaken. All antiquity had knowledge of it, and even then sophists were not wanting who abused it by converting it into a pretext for making all truth purely subjective, that is relative to man, and thus introducing universal scepticism. Leaving aside, however, the Sceptics and coming to the Epicureans, let us see how Lucretius denies the property of colour to elementary bodies, namely to the corporeal nature :

' Nullus enim color est omnino materiai
Corporibus, neque par rebus neque
denique dispar.'

The same he applies to cold and heat, to sound, smell and taste :

' Sed ne forte putes solo spoliata colore
Corpora prima manere : etiam secreta
teporis
Sunt, ac frigoris omnino, calidique
vaporis :
Et sonitu sterila, et succo jejuna fe-
runtur :
Nec jaciunt ullum proprio de corpore
odorem : '

And he proves this by some clever observations (*De Natura Rerum*, ii. 729–863).

The tradition of this truth was not lost in the palmy days of Scholastic Philosophy. S. Thomas takes it for granted, that when the sun is spoken of ' as being hot,' no intelligent person understands that the sensation of heat is in the sun itself, but that the sun simply *causes* in us this sensation (*Cont. Gent.* I. xxix. xxxi.). And so the Italians say : ' una medicina è sana' (' a medicine is *healthy*'), to signify only that it is health-giving. And here I may observe in passing, that in this teaching of the Angelical Doctor we have a proof of the distinction of those two periods through which Scholasticism has successively passed. The first is the period of its vigorous manhood, the age of S. Thomas Aquinas and other great celebrities ; the second is that in which, like all things human, it fell into decrepitude and decay. When it came to this, divine Providence committed the cause of philosophical truth to other hands ; and the particular truth of which I am now speaking was revived by Galileo. He treats of it in his elegant work entitled *Il Saggiatore*, from which the following extract may perhaps be quoted here with advantage : ' I do not believe ' (he says), ' that in order to excite in us the sensations of taste, smell and sound, external bodies require anything beyond size, form, multitude, and motion, slow or fast, as the case may be. And I think, that if our ears, tongues, and nostrils were taken away, the sizes and forms of bodies, their number and their movements, would indeed remain, but not the scents, the flavours, or the sounds ; for I am persuaded that, outside the living animal, these sensations are nothing but names, as also are tickling and titillation, if we do away with the arm-pits and the membrane which covers the nostrils.' And a little

degree of heat. Of this any one may convince himself by a very simple experiment. Let one of his hands be made bitterly cold and the other intensely hot. If he places the former in cold water, the water will seem to him warm; if he places the latter in warm water, the water will seem to him cold. This arises from the different disposition of the hand in which the modification of the fundamental feeling must take place.

ARTICLE VIII.

How far minute extensions can be perceived by our sense of touch.

896. Although, as we have seen, the elementary sensations of the touch, as also the corpuscles which correspond to them, are both extended and continuous; yet we cannot conclude from this with any certainty that the touch is able to perceive every, even the most minute extension.

It is true that in an elementary continuous sensation no space can be assigned, however small, which is unfelt; but what is said of the several minute spaces considered as ideal parts of one continuous whole, cannot be equally said of each minute space considered by itself alone.

Might not nature have so disposed that, sensibly to affect the touch, an extension of a certain size, and not anything under, should be required? On the other hand, in a fact like

further down he applies the same doctrine to heat in the following words: 'I am much inclined to think the same of the sensation of heat, and that those agencies by which heat is caused in us, and which we call by the general name of *fire*, are nothing but a multitude of minute corpuscles with such and such a form, and moving with such and such a velocity. These corpuscles coming against our body, penetrate it by their extreme subtilty, and through this kind of touch produce in us the affection which we term *heat*, pleasant or painful, according to their quantity and to the degree of velocity with which they stir and penetrate our substance. When the impression goes no further than to assist our necessary insensible perspiration, it is pleasant; but when it causes our substance to dissolve too violently, it is painful.

The action of fire, therefore, considered in itself, consists simply in a motion whereby it penetrates with its extreme subtilty all bodies, dissolving them more or less actively in proportion to the multitude and velocity of t e igneous particles, and to the density or rarity of the bodies themselves: among which bodies there are many, the greater portion of which, as the dissolving process goes on, passes into other igneous particles, and so the dissolution continues while there is proper matter for it. But that, besides the form, number, motion, penetration and touch, which I have described, there is in fire any other quality, namely, the quality of *heat*, is a notion I utterly repudiate; and I believe heat to be an affection so exclusively ours, that if the animate and sensitive body be taken away, heat is nothing but a name.'

this, in which no light can be obtained from observation, we cannot speak with any assurance except as to what is possible, or what is probable. Wherefore, there being nothing absurd either in the thought that a tactile sensation can be indefinitely more and more restricted, or in the thought that there is a *minimum* of extension absolutely necessary for it, we cannot reasonably exclude either opinion, but must leave this an open question.

897. But whichever of the two opinions be the true one, this much seems at all events indubitable, that, ordinarily speaking, our power of *feeling* the tactile sensation very much exceeds in subtilty the power of *adverting* to it ; so that the sensation reaches to spaces far more minute than we have any consciousness of feeling.[1]

Of the truth of this we have an evident proof in the case of persons born blind. It is commonly said, that in these persons the sense of touch grows *refined.* We all know how by means of the touch alone they can tell the differences of coins, of playing-cards, of cloth-stuffs, and even of colours. They perceive from a great distance the breath of a person who approaches them silently and stealthily, nay, the very motion caused in the air as he walks along. In short, they do wonders in this way. But is it correct to say, that their touch grows *refined*, or is by nature more acute than in others? I think not. What grows refined, what is more acute in them, is the *advertence* they give to their sensations. The touch is the same in all, without difference between blind and not blind.[2] But the blind are peculiarly circumstanced. They have none of those distractions which the sight causes. They

---

[1] All this will assist us in seeing more and more clearly the difference there is between *sensation* and *intellection.* *Advertence* is an act, not of the sensitive but of the intellectual faculty ; for it is nothing but the attention which the mind bestows either on what we feel or on what we understand. So well did the ancients know that *reflection* is an act, not of the sense but of the mind, that they sometimes characterised this latter faculty by it. Thus Dante, wishing to designate the three powers — of life, of sense, and of understanding – says :—.

. . . ' un' almå sola
Che vive, e sente, e *sè in sè rigira.*'
(PURG. xxv.).

[2] In the animal there is also to be noticed a certain power over its nerves, whereby it protrudes and applies them, the better to receive sensations. And the use of this power may be perfected by art and by the habit of applying it.

feel keenly the need of turning their touch to the best account
as a make-up for the want of sight. They live perpetually in
the dark. These things combined produce in them such a
habit of self-concentration, and an attention so constantly
wide-awake to all the impressions which happen in their sense
of touch, as to render them great experts in noting those even
that are the slightest and that escape everybody else's notice,
and in descrying their most minute differences. Hence it is
allowable to hold, that if human advertence could proceed still
further, we should find, that our touch is possessed of a delicacy,
if not indefinitely exquisite, certainly stupendous and such as
hardly to be believed.[1]

[1] As a further confirmation of what I here say, namely that many things are attributed to a greater or less perfection of the senses, which ought rather to be attributed to a more or less perfect *advertence* and wakefulness of the attention, I beg to submit the following remarks.

Is the hand the part of our body where the sense of touch has the greatest delicacy? Observation says no, but that other parts of the body are more largely supplied with nerves, and possessed of a much greater sensitivity than the hand. Nay we may even affirm, that almost every other part of the surface of the body is more sensitive and delicate than the hand; nature having wisely provided that the hand should not be over-sensitive, in order that we might freely use it without the inconvenience constantly arising from pain. Then also the continual use we make of our hand has the effect of rendering it callous and obtuse. Our hand does not therefore gain in delicacy of touch by exercise; but it gains in a greater actuation and tension of the nerve-fibres in such parts of it as are most used—which I have no doubt is due to the action of the will. But leaving this aside (which proves, however, the need of a greater attention, or at least, a greater *sensitive actuation*), is not the hand the member best adapted to make us perceive and distinguish the slight inequalities on the surfaces of bodies, the minutest particles, and all the tactile differences which bodies exhibit? Most assuredly it is. But if this apti-

tude of the hand cannot be ascribed to a superior natural delicacy in its touch, to what then? My reply is, to the habit we have acquired of *adverting* to the finest differences in its sensations, but have not acquired with regard to the sensations of other parts of our body. Again, have not persons who were deprived of hands been known to do marvels of this kind with their feet? Now was this owing to the feet being in them more sensitive than in other people? I do not believe it, at least to the extent here indicated. The true explanation I believe to be, that these maimed persons, under the pressure of necessity, directed their attention most particularly to the sensations received in their feet, and thus mastered the art of distinguishing those sensations from one another, and noting their differences with a precision unknown to other men.

Again, how is it that a skilful doctor, after long practice, is able to detect even the least shades of variation in the pulse of his patient in a way no one else can? Should we say, that the touch of the doctor's fingers has been *refined* in consequence of feeling a very great number of pulses? By no means; for another man might have felt quite as many pulses as he, and yet have learned nothing. Or, if the frequent feeling of pulses has the effect of refining the touch, I should wish to kn w why the touching of precisely that part of the vein should increase the sensitiveness of the physician's hand, more than if it had been applied to any other part; or why the same hand which is highly re-

898. As I have already observed, it is more difficult for us to advert to our sensations when they continue unchanged, and have little or no variety in them.

fined in regard to pulses, is perhaps found very dull when applied to the minute intricacies of a goldsmith's work. For if the perceiving of the variations of the pulse depended on the physical sensitivity of the skin, and not on the acquired ability of adverting to what is felt by the touch, every exquisite touch would equally serve for all purposes alike, and thus a person born blind, whose touch, as we have said, is in the highest degree exquisite, could at once discern the differences of a pulse without any need of special practice. It is, therefore, in the *advertence* to the sensations that improvement takes place, much more than in the senses themselves. That the senses improve even physically by use, I am ready to admit, but not to anything like the extent necessary to account for the immense difference which is seen to exist between those who have exercised their sensitive powers with proper discernment and those who have not. As a matter of fact, the degree of physical sensitivity in an organ depends on its texture ; and this is determined originally by nature, nor does it therefore admit of any great increase. The sense whose quickness and delicacy of perception seems most capable of being improved by training, is the sight. But when we bear in mind that all that the sight tells us about distant objects is due, as I shall hereafter prove, to *habitual judgments*, we shall easily see that, as regards distances, it is principally the aptitude for making these judgments that increases in us, and, as regards surfaces, it is to the development of the capacity for observation that we must in great part attribute, for instance, the nice and delicate eyesight of the jeweller, or that peculiar knack which some medical men have of reading in the countenance of a patient, the condition of his system. Moralists, politicians, and, in general, men gifted with keen insight can, from a similar indication, judge of the affections of the soul. I need not dwell on the most minute differences in colours and in paintings which are discerned by the artist ; for here it is evi-

dently his skill in the art that enables him to discover such varieties as pass unobserved by others, not because they do not see them, but because not being aware of their importance, they do not think of directing their attention to them. We may say the same of accomplished musicians who, in a concert, seem to hear many more things than are heard by other listeners, whereas all hear precisely the same sounds, but with an attention differently attuned. A musician displays greater sagacity than the rest of the audience, because he has learned to divide the sounds and note their natural differences as well as their beauties and defects. Hence that marvellous power of musical appreciation, from which it would almost appear as if his acoustic sense were of a kind different from that of his neighbours, whereas it is the same, or certainly not much better, and possibly it might not be so good, as, for example, if he were far advanced in years. Those Red Indians who, as we are told, could distinguish by scent the track of the Spaniards, caused great astonishment by the acuteness of their olfactory sense. But what in my opinion should have been much more wondered at, was the perfect attention they must have given to observing the minute sensations of smell, and their differences.

Again, what can be the improvement produced in a palate by frequent contact with different sorts of food ? Very slight in comparison with that marvellous nicety which epicures exhibit in discriminating between one flavour and another. And perhaps the constant use of sauces and luxurious dainties had deteriorated the palate of that *gourmand* of whom we read in Juvenal, that by dint of paying the closest attention to his viands, he had become such a *connoisseur* in the taste of oysters, that he could tell at the first bite whether they were from Circia, or Lake Lucrine, or the Sea of Rutupe ; as he discerned at a glance on what particular shore an echinus had been caught.

Hence whenever we wish to notice by means of the touch the minute inequalities and projections in the surface of a body, we do not content ourselves with placing our finger thereon and pressing it down separately, first in this part and then in that; for by so doing, even if we felt those things, we should perhaps never advert to the fact that we *feel* them. In order to gain this advertence, we go on rubbing the surface with our finger to and fro in all directions. This causes the sensations we have of those little hollows and projections to be more diversified and more acute; and so we find it easier to advert to them.

899. Hence a solid body, in so far as felt by the touch, is one thing; and in so far as *adverted to* by the mind, is another. In so far as adverted to, it will, perhaps, be perfectly continuous and smooth in all its surfaces; whereas, in so far as touched, it is perhaps most rugged, and full of cavities and inequalities, as we know in fact to be the case in all bodies when viewed by means of a powerful microscope. For, as I have already remarked, it is impossible to fix a limit to the subtilty of the sense of touch.

But the same microscope which to our surprise shows us the body in the state I have mentioned, reveals also in it many parts which are closely joined together so as to present a number of small extensions seemingly continuous. Now the continuity so observed is not yet the continuity of the elementary bodies of which we spoke before (ch. ix.). For, beyond all doubt, the minuteness of these bodies is such as to defy all our powers of distinct advertence. Neither can we say with certainty that the continuity seen with the microscope is a true continuity; because though not actually contiguous, these bodies may still very well be divided by interstices too small for detection. On the other hand this continuity cannot be pronounced impossible, because there is nothing impossible in a real contact.

900. Leaving aside, however, this hidden world concerning

The best fruit my readers can gain from all these observations is, to be firmly convinced of the immense difference between *sensation* and *advert-* ence, and to be persuaded that there are innumerable things perceived by our senses without our being in the least conscious of them.

which we can gain no knowledge from observation, and on which, therefore, it would be very hazardous to make assertions either way, I say that the solid bodies touched and *adverted to* by us have certain *configurations* which we very clearly distinguish, as may be seen from the fact that, passing over their minor differences, we can, by the force of our imagination, assort them in such groups as we find most convenient or necessary for the objects we have in view. Owing to their regularity and simplicity, these forms are easily perceived by us, satisfy the mind, and seem full of distinctness and of light.[1]

ARTICLE IX.

On the extrasubjective sensation of the sight, the hearing, the smell and the taste.

901. What we perceive immediately with the eye is the light, and the light indicates to us external things.[2]

---

[1] The regular figures—such as the triangle, the square, or any other figure of a perceptible number of sides—are grasped by our mind without difficulty because they consist of few elements only. If, on the contrary, we multiply excessively the sides of a polygon, our mind can no longer *advert* distinctly to their number, although they are all equally perceived by our *senses*. If we suppose those sides unequal, the difficulty of forming a *distinct idea* of them is increased. And again if the same multiplicity and variety should exist in the planes of a solid body, our power of distinct advertence would be still more at fault. The reason of this is, that figures are conceived only through our seeing the relation of unity which their parts have with one another. Now when these parts are too many or too diversified, our mind either cannot think them simultaneously, or it cannot give to each that degree of attention which it could if they were less in number.

[2] The hearing and the smell serve to indicate distant objects. Here, however, I do not consider them in this aspect, but only as the recipients of the immediate sensations of sound and of scent.

Of the sense of sight, in so far as it serves to indicate distant bodies, I shall speak in the next chapter; and what I shall then say of this sense may easily be applied by the reader himself to the hearing and the smell. Here it will suffice to remark that one of the principal sources of error in the reasonings commonly made about the senses, lies in confounding the immediate perception with the *indication* it furnishes to us, and expecting from the first what can be had from the second only; as also in confounding together the knowledge which we obtain of bodies by means of different sensories. For instance, Reid, wishing to combat the opinion of Locke, that 'The primary qualities of bodies perceived by us are similitudes of the bodies themselves,' argues thus: 'According to Locke, these qualities are sensations: now if the sensation of sound be the idea of that vibration of the sounding body which occasions it, a surfeit may, for the same reason, be the idea of a feast' (*Essays on the Powers*, &c., Essay II. ch. xvii.).

I shall not inquire what Locke might have to say to this; but for my own part, I think this language very much beside the purpose. It should be considered, (1) that the sensation of sound is immediate, whereas the vibration of the sonorous body is not perceived by

Now I do not intend here to treat of the eye in so far as it gives us an indication of distant bodies which do not come in contact with it ; but only in so far as it perceives the light which is the agent operating immediately upon it.

We have seen that the extrasubjective part of sensations consists of three things, namely, force, multiplicity and extension.

Force is felt by all the senses alike.   But on the other hand, although the word *force*, taken by itself alone, suggests the notion of an agent of some sort, it in no way specifies the nature of that agent.   It remains therefore to be seen how by the four sensories in question we perceive *multiplicity* and *extension*—the two elements by which the nature of the agent is, in some way, determined.

902. As regards *extension*, we find that the corpuscles which act upon the said sensories are so prodigiously fine and subtile, that if only one such were to present itself to them, it would be impossible for us to detect and observe it.   Who has ever been able to say that he has seen or touched one of those atomic particles which compose light, or fire, or air, or odour, or flavour?   All these are so inexpressibly minute as to elude all our powers of observation and advertence.

Let us now consider their multitude ; how they crowd upon our organ in such quantities, that even if we could notice their extensions, we could never reckon up their number, nor keep it distinctly before our mind.

Now from these two circumstances combined, namely, on

the hearing except through an association of ideas, which, on our hearing the sound, say of a pianoforte, reminds us of the oscillation of the chords, which we have perceived on former occasions by means of the touch and the sight. It is therefore impossible that the sound should be a representation or imitation of that which it only recalls to our memory.   And when I say that the primary qualities perceived by us are a similitude of the bodies, my meaning is very different from that here expressed by Reid.   (2) By the hearing, the smell and the taste, the primary qualities of bodies are not perceived save in a con-fused manner.   It is not therefore to these senses that we must look for that *similitude* of which I speak.   (3) It is not true that the primary qualities perceived by us are sensations ; they are only one of the elements of the sensations, namely, the *extrasubjective* element.   (4) Finally, it is wholly inaccurate and erroneous to say that a sensation is the idea of a thing.   Tolerated as this expression might have to be by a follower of Locke, it is absolutely inadmissible in itself; and I have already shown what an immense distance there is between an idea and a sensation.

the one hand the utter impossibility of our observing the
sizes, and consequently the forms, motions and changes, of
the said atomic particles, and, on the other, their overwhelming
multitude—what must follow? Simply this, that our perception of these particles will indeed be vivid, but at the
same time very *confused*. In other words, the extrasubjective
part of the sensations of which I am speaking, must be
devoid of *distinctness* and as it were blind.[1] These sensations,
therefore (their great vividness notwithstanding), will not be
of much service in giving us clear information as to the precise nature of the agents by which they are immediately produced. Hence it is that they seem to have in them something
more mysterious than the sensation of touch; because whatever our understanding fails to perceive with anything like
clearness has for us an air of mystery: and we must not
forget that it is from the extrasubjective part of the sensations,
that our understanding draws its perceptions; so that if this

[1] Reid had caught some glimpse of this truth when he placed the difference between the *primary* and *secondary* qualities of bodies in this, that the primary gives us *distinct*, and the secondary *confused* notions. The fact was so, but he was unable to give any explanation of it. In answer to the question, whether the distinction between primary and secondary qualities be a real one, he says: 'There appears to me to be a real foundation for the distinction, and it is this: That our senses give us a direct and a distinct notion of the primary qualities, and in-form us what they are in themselves. But of the secondary qualities our senses give us only a relative and ob-scure notion. They inform us only that they are qualities that affect us in a certain manner, that is, produce in us a certain sensation; but as to what they are in themselves, our senses leave us in the dark' (*Essays on the Powers*, &c., Essay II. ch. xvii.).

Locke had placed the distinction be-tween *primary* and *secondary* qualities in this, that the first are *similitudes* of bodies, not so the second. Now, Reid rejected the opinion of Locke entirely, which he would not have done, had he properly understood the true principle whence the distinction of the said quali-ties must be drawn. This principle lies in the duplex nature of sensation, namely, in its being at once subjective and extrasubjective. Now the extra-subjective element lies, as we have seen, in the perception of the primary qualities, which are in truth *extrasub-jective*; and hence we are justified in saying, that our sensation is, in this part, a *similitude* of the external agents, because it has the qualities of multipli-city and continuity in common with them, and to have qualities in common is the same thing as to be similar. On this point, therefore, I adhere to the opinion of Locke; but at the same time I limit and explain it. Nay, I hold that if all similitude between the external bodies and our sensations be taken away, scepticism in regard to sensible things is inevitable, and no answer can be given to the objections raised by Bayle against the primary qualities, all which objections arise from his not having observed their ex-trasubjectivity and his consequent at-tempt to treat them as if they were, like the secondary, subjective.

part be confused, the intellectual perceptions also will be hazy and indistinct.

903. It is also important, in this connection, to mark the difference there is between the four sensories of which I speak and the sense of touch which perceives the larger sizes of solid bodies.[1] The particles of a solid body which fall under the perception of the touch, adhere together either by actual contact or at least by a very close proximity ; and I believe in both these ways. Hence, they present to this sense a form or *configuration* which is both observable and felt as one ; since the vacant interstices as well as the extremely minute irregularities and projections escape our notice.   Thus with regard to the observable agents operating on the touch, we clearly apprehend their extension, and easily conceive their regularity of form.   On the contrary, the particles which strike and affect the other senses are disjoined, and so mobile that they never remain in the same state or place.   Hence they do not coalesce into one form, but, continually changing, they come and go, float about, oscillate, evaporate, strike upon this thing or that, and, being wafted away, disappear.   In short, even if they were very few in number, and not of that extreme minuteness which precludes the possibility of our adverting to them, they would still evade our observation, by reason of the amazing quickness and changeableness of their incessant movements.

904. But there is another observation to be made, which will show still more clearly, that the agents which immediately operate on these four organs of sense, are not such that we can observe their size or form,[2] and thus gain a distinct perception of them, failing which perception, all these sensations, however pleasant and vivid,[3] must necessarily appear to us confused and, by this very confusedness, excite our wonder.

---

[1] Liquids also, in so far as they act on our touch, occupy a certain solid space, and exhibit forms defined and precise, because stable, bulky and regular, although most easily altered by motion.

[2] As I have said, it is the *size* and the *form* that give us a distinct perception of the agent, because they are the *extrasubjective* parts of the sensation.

[3] The vivacity of these sensations depends on the elementary particles producing a very strong impression on the organ, by reason of their multitude and velocity, and, as regards light, perhaps also their elasticity, which causes

We have, in all adventitious sensations, distinguished two parts, the subjective and the extrasubjective. We have also seen, that when an external body impresses some sensitive part of our own so as to cause in it a sensation, the part thus impressed must be distinguished from those adjacent to it, in which by a kind of sympathy the motion sometimes diffuses itself, and with it the sensation. But the sensation which spreads in this way beyond the parts actually impressed, has nothing in it of the *extrasubjective* ; because the motion sympathetically communicated is different from that impulse or species of violence which the nerve suffers in the first instance, when it is made to pass from a quiescent to an active state. Now it is by this first impression, this sort of violence, that the presence of a force acting from without is indicated ; whereas the motion sympathetically communicated and continued does not betoken any fresh violence or force, except that of the parts of which the nerve itself is composed, and which spread that motion from one to the other in virtue of a certain force belonging to their nature (860). Hence it follows, as I have already said, that the whole of the sensation thus propagated must be attributed exclusively to the sensitive member in which the motion expands itself in the manner described. Consequently, that sympathetic increase of feeling is purely subjective, or certainly is not conjoined with the perception of an external body, but rests solely, as in its seat and matter, in the nerve so moved and affected.

905. Now let us take note of the singular nature of the sensations of the four organs now under consideration. Could one particle alone of air, striking against the acoustic

it to touch and rebound most quickly, without its impression being too strong to bear. A strong impression of this nature must necessarily produce a great movement—perhaps a tremor—throughout the nerves, and consequently a strong *subjective* sensation. And in general, the following may be laid down as a law certified by observation : 'Given a quick and frequent movement in the nerve without its parts being severed or broken, a most agreeable sensation will follow.' Now this result is obtained whenever the stimuli acting on the nerve are exceedingly minute and at the same time multitudinous, provided their multitude be not excessive, and the percussion given by each be moderate and gentle. Hence we see why a bed of roses, or of some downy material, is so pleasant to recline upon, and why soft surfaces are so delightful to the touch ; the vivacity here being similar to that which causes the beauty of colour to please the eye, or a sweet melody to delight the ear.

nerve, produce in it the sensation of sound?   Assuredly not; for it is only by the undulations of a considerable volume of air that this sensation is excited.   So in like manner, I am not at all sure that a single atom of light would be capable of exciting the visual organ.   I believe, on the contrary, that to have the sensation of colour, our eye must have, poured into it, a copious supply of that which some one has grace-fully described as 'the soft liquid light' ('il dolce liquor della luce ').

In the same way, it does not seem to me probable that the sensations of taste and of smell arise in us from the action of elementary corpuscles, saporiferous or odoriferous, taken one by one.   I rather believe that what causes these sensa-tions is, that the said atomic particles, by coming in great quantities and as it were tumultuously for a simultaneous attack on the palate or on the acoustic nerves, excite them in such a manner as to produce and keep up over their whole surface a state of tremor.   If this is so, we shall have to say, not that each of these most minute agents has produced a sen-sation of taste or of smell, &c., but that each has given its own percussion, so however that the sensation, saporiferous, odori-ferous or otherwise, does not begin until the tremor propagated along the whole nervous membrane or cartilage, has risen to the degree which is necessary for exciting that sensation.

Now, assuming this to be correct (and, as regards the hearing, I do not think there can be any doubt of it), I say that these four species of sensations would, to a great extent, be of the sympathetic kind, *i.e.* the result of a communication of motion; and this would make the *extrasubjective* part of these sensations still more confused and involved in obscurity. For there would be question of particles which escape all observation; and the sensations would be a reflex, not so much of the impulse given by the parts, as of the tremor which has affected the sensitive organ taken as a whole; or if it were a reflex of both together, the first mixed up with the second would be almost impossible to discern.

CHAPTER XII.

ORIGIN OF THE IDEA OF BODIES BY MEANS OF THE EXTRASUBJECTIVE PERCEPTION OF THE SIGHT.

ARTICLE I.

The eye perceives coloured surfaces.

906. Suppose a man perfectly still, and with his eyes open : he sees surfaces variously coloured, which having, so far as his sight is concerned, neither depth nor perspective, adhere to his eye, and nothing more.

ARTICLE II.

Coloured surfaces are corporeal.

907. What is perceived by our sense as extended is corporeal ; because extension is essentially the term of corporeal action.

But coloured surfaces are perceived by the eye as extended.

Therefore coloured surfaces are corporeal.

ARTICLE III.

The coloured surfaces are identical with the surface of the retina of the eye affected by the light.

908. All the sensories are touch (744, 745) : they are also subject to the laws of the touch, and do not differ from one another except by certain accidental phenomena which accompany them.

In seeking what these phenomena are, we found in all of them alike this feature, that they consist, on the one hand, in the peculiarly high degree of subjectivity characteristic of the

sensations of the four organs to which they respectively belong, and on the other in their very feeble and confused
extrasubjectivity (887–895).

These phenomena, therefore, are simply the mode of those
four species of sensations. The touch itself yields a certain
number of similar phenomena (*ibid.*), although we do not
usually give them a distinct attention. Consequently, they
do not add anything to, or imply any change in those laws
to which the sense of touch in general is subject.

But in the touch, the surface of the external body which
impresses it, becomes identified with the surface of our body
which is impressed, so that the said surface is perceived in
two ways at once—*i.e.* subjectively, or as affecting our body,
and extrasubjectively, or as the term of an action exercised
on us from without (841).

Such being the case, it is evident that ‘the coloured surface perceived by our eye, is identical with the surface of the
retina touched by the light.’

We must carefully take note of this fact, that the eye perceives the coloured surface in the same way that the touch
perceives the hardness and resistance of a solid body.

In the corporeal sight, therefore, two things must also be
distinguished : (1) the sensation affecting the retina, (2) the
very confused perception of innumerable globules of light
crowding pell-mell upon the retina.

ARTICLE IV.

*The coloured surface perceived by our eye is of the same extension
precisely as the retina touched by the light ; but in that surface
the colours are distributed according to constant proportions.*

909. This singular but undeniable truth is a corollary of
the preceding proposition.

What may cause it to be disbelieved by those who do not
pay proper attention to these things, is the habit we have of
attributing to the bodies perceived by means of the eye the
same size which we perceive in them by means of the touch
and of motion. But later on I shall explain how this habit is

contracted, and it will then be seen, that it belongs, not to the sensation of sight itself, but to the *judgment* we add to that sensation.

910. Here I shall begin by observing, that, whatever be the size of the agents perceived by the eye, it is always true that they are perceived by it as having a certain constant proportion relatively to one another. For instance, whilst receiving into it the colours of all the agents around, the eye receives also those of the pupil of the person who happens to be right opposite, and it perceives that pupil as very much more diminutive than the person's whole body, just as it perceives his body as much smaller than the room in which he is. The reason is because the pupil occupies a much smaller part of the retina than the body, and the body a much smaller than the room.

The eye, therefore, perceives the *relative dimensions* of the bodies equidistant from it, although it does not perceive their *absolute* dimensions.

The case of persons who, having been born blind, receive the power of sight, affords a confirmation of the truth of these remarks. When first beginning to see, they experience a sensation as of something adhering to the retina of their eye. They perceive no distance, no real distinction between external bodies ; in short, nothing but a painted surface, or the tissue of their retina overlaid with various colours (811 [1]).

ARTICLE V.

The coloured surface cannot give us the idea of solid space, even by means of the movements which take place in its colours.

911. I have elsewhere proposed the question as to whether the eye perceives motion, and answered it in the affirmative.

But whatever motion may take place in a coloured surface perceived by us, it is always reduced to a change of surface. One coloured surface goes, and another comes in its place, then a third, and so on. This succession of surfaces gives us

[1] See also note to n. 732 (TRANSLATORS).

no idea either of depth or of distance. Each of them in turn appears in the eye in a certain order, like the slides of a magic lantern : that is all.

The eye, then, taken by itself alone, and without any other aid, can never give us the idea of solid space.

ARTICLE VI.

The sensations of colours are so many signs of the sizes of things.

912. Hitherto I have abstracted from the use of the touch and from motion, assuming that the sight only was employed ; for my object was to ascertain how far the capabilities of the eye taken by itself alone can extend.

As a result I discovered, that, apart from motion and touch, the eye could perceive only a coloured surface adhering to it, and that not larger than the retina on which the light strikes and thereby produces sensation (910). But I also observed, that in this small surface, the colours, and likewise the movements which take place in them, are not scattered at random, but distributed in a certain order; and that certain proportions are maintained between the colours, corresponding precisely with those existing between the sizes which the touch finds in external things (*ibid.*).

Now the constancy of these proportions, and the order kept up in the movements of the colours perceived, are of invaluable service to us in this sense that we can take those colours as so many signs whereby to know the true sizes of things,[1] as well as their distances, and consequently the quantities of motion necessary for us to get at them.

913. Let us see how this comes about, first as regards the sizes of external things, then as regards distances and the quantities of motion.

External things pour the light into our eyes from every point of their surface. Those that are larger reflect a greater number of luminous rays which, therefore, supposing the several things to be at the same distance from the retina,

---

[1] *I.e.* those given us by the touch, as we have seen, and shall still more clearly see in the next chapter.

cover in it a larger space, in that proportion exactly in which the real sizes of the things themselves stand to one another.[1]

The same principle obtains here as we see carried out in a well traced map of a tract of country. The whole is drawn in it on a very small scale comparatively, but the proportions of the parts are perfectly maintained. Even so the external bodies are delineated on our retina, much less indeed in size, yet with exactly the same proportions as they have outside of us.

In this operation the light and the eye accord so well together, that those mechanical contrivances which modern science has invented for reducing the representations of objects from larger to smaller scales, are after all only an imitation of what is done, and in greater perfection, by nature.

914. Let us consider attentively how well suited to our purpose is the simile I have quoted.

In a geographical or topographical chart there is not much stress laid on colours, or on the other qualities of the objects there delineated. What is principally kept in view is their size ; and this is very accurately known through the proportion which carries our thought from the lesser scale to the greater and natural one. So also in the variations incidental to the sensation of the colours perceived by the eye, it is not the colours themselves that give us a correct and immediate knowledge of the things seen ; for, as I have already observed, colour, as such, is only the subjective part of sensation.[2] On the contrary, the size and proportion of the various

---

[1] With this theory of vision, the problem proposed by Molineux—'Whether by sight alone we can distinguish a sphere from a cube which we had discerned before by the touch '—is easily solved. The eye is also itself touch. Like the touch, it perceives figures, but it perceives them so to speak in miniature. Of the signs, therefore, of the sphere and of the cube, which the light impresses on the retina, one is circular in form and the other rectilinear, that is, they are distinguished from each other in a way similar to that which has been found by the touch. Therefore Leibnitz was perfectly right in solving this problem in the affirmative.

[2] The qualities of things are also made known to us by colours, not, however, because colours have any *resemblance* with those things (for they are only the subjective part of sensation), but because we learn by experience to take them as so many *signs* (not *resemblances*) of the same. Thus writing is a sign of spoken language, though it has no similarity with it ; whilst a *portrait* is a sign of the person depicted, because it resembles him. In this way many things are known by their colours. How do we know, for instance, that fruit is fully ripe, or otherwise ? By its colour. By colour we judge of a man's healthy or sickly

coloured spaces is the extrasubjective part, and that which informs us of the size of external things. With the dimensions of these things, that size and proportion have a true resemblance; for instance, a small triangle or square truly resembles a large triangle or square; and the very same proportion which exists between the size of a city and that of a house, exists between the two coloured spots respectively corresponding to those two objects on the retina.[1] Thus it is that the eye, while informing us of the extension of things through a resemblance which the sensation bears to them, does not inform us of their other properties.

Now, that we may see how from the sensations of colour we come to know the sizes of things, we must call in the aid of the touch, and assume that by this sense combined with motion we' have already perceived the external bodies, their absolute dimensions and their relative proportions. By simultaneously making use of the touch and the eye, we discover a singular relation between the parts of the body perceived by the first, and the colours perceived by the second. As often as our hand is laid on a body, it takes away from our eyes a coloured spot. Each part so touched is a little space withdrawn from sight; for, instead of that space, we see the hand which covers it. By repeating these experiences we come to learn at last that the tactile and visual sensations have a connection which never varies, and we

---

condition, of the passions by which his soul is agitated, in fact of the perfection or imperfection of almost everything; and yet colour has not the slightest resemblance to health or sickness, or to any of the other qualities which it reveals to us. But this revelation is purely the result of an association of ideas. Experience has taught us, that in a given object such or such colour accompanies such or such qualities. Whenever therefore we see that colour in the object, we at once infer its qualities. The sensation, therefore, in so far as it is *subjective*, may be a sign, but not a resemblance; whereas, considered as *extrasubjective*, it is at once a sign and a resemblance of external things.

[1] I wish to observe once for all, that when, here and again later, I speak of little spots formed on the retina by colours, I do not use the expression in a literal sense, as if I meant that the eye is really marked with spots such as could be gazed at by a looker-on. They are nothing of the kind. They are purely and simply subjective sensations, which I indicate by the word *spots*. For instance, to designate a yellow sensation of a certain size, I say a *yellow spot*, and so of the other colours. The reader is particularly requested not to misunderstand this figure of speech, which I employ simply for the sake of facility and brevity.

become aware that to every coloured part in our retina there corresponds a sensation produced by the touch of a body outside of us ; so that the larger any one of the spots which colour the retina happens to be, the larger in the same proportion is the space which our hand can cover with its touch. Through this connexion, therefore, the spots variously cast on the retina by the rays of light, become to us sure indications and signs of the external bodies and their sizes ; I say *sure*, because the touch has immediate perception of these bodies and correctly measures their sizes. Thus it is that we, in course of time, form the settled habit of passing with the utmost rapidity from the thought of the sensation felt by the eye to the persuasion of the existence of external tangible bodies. And this habit, while it keeps going, grows also daily in strength and perfection, until at length we take the sign for the thing indicated by it, and, on perceiving with the eye a coloured spot, we no longer say : ' I perceive a coloured spot, therefore there must be a tangible object outside of me ; ' but we say straightway : ' I see a body, I see a tangible object.' [1]

Whoever looks at a topographical drawing, knows the sizes of the places there represented, provided he has a clear idea of the scale to which they are drawn, namely, of the proportion between this scale and their respective natural sizes ; but he does not know this so readily and as it were so intuitively as when he perceives the places themselves through their image being directly impressed on his retina. The reason of this difference is because the retina—our natural chart so to speak—is always present to us, and we are

[1] Be it carefully noted that when the *sign* is perfectly well known to us, and we are accustomed to its use, we do not stop at it, but go straight to the thing signified, as if we saw and perceived that thing itself. The sign seems to us so identified with the thing, that we find it extremely difficult to distinguish the one from the other. Hence such expressions as, ' I have heard such and such truths from a learned man,' as though we had heard the truths themselves, and not the words, which are all that has really fallen under our hearing, and which have not the slightest similarity with the truths signified by them. So in looking at the portrait of a person, we speak of it as if it were the person himself, and call it by his name ; because our mind does not stop at the portrait. To be brief, *in the sign we think the thing*. This is what happens generally in almost all the operations we make as intelligent beings.

continually exercising ourselves in the use of it ; and because
the touch, continually and with little or no trouble, rectifies
and confirms our judgments on the sizes in question.

915. There is also another difference between seeing a
country delineated on a chart, and perceiving external bodies
by means of the variegated spots which the light, refracted
by and reverberated from those bodies, impresses directly on
our retina.   The chart and the country represented on it are
two things entirely detached from each other ; whereas the
lineaments depicted in the eye have a marvellous physical
connexion with the bodies perceived by the touch.   In consequence of the luminous rays being reflected from the bodies,
the latter become associated with the impressions suffered
by the eye ; not indeed that the eye, in being struck by those
rays, goes outside of itself, or perceives anything save their
extremities ; but because those extremities are altered and
changed with wonderful quickness and fidelity by every
motion which takes place in those bodies, and particularly
by the hand being laid on them here or there.   In this way
a child learns by experience, that to every part touched by
his hand, there corresponds a coloured sensation, and that
therefore the coloured spots felt by the eye, are commensurate to the parts so touched.   And so he gradually comes to
identify the two measures—that given by the eye, and that
given by the hand—by super-imposing, as it were, the one
on the other, point on point, line on line, and surface on
surface.   Thus does nature itself set the human being on the
way to find with the greatest ease, by means of the coloured
spots seen by him, those same dimensions which he perceives
in bodies by the touch.

916. The better to understand this, it may be well to
note a third difference between the chart, and the places
drawn on it, on the one hand, and, on the other, our retina
spotted with various colours, and the tangible bodies.   The
places and the chart are two terms of the sight, one larger
than the other ; but the external body and the colours, whilst
also two terms of the touch, refer to two different senses—
the one to the common organ of touch, and the other to the

special organ of sight, which is incomparably more delicate, and of a complexion wholly peculiar to itself. Now so long as there is question of two terms of one and the same sensory —I mean the eye—for instance, of two triangles one immensely larger than the other, it is easy for us, owing to their *similarity*, to take the one as the sign of the other; but the difference of their sizes is so openly manifest, that we cannot easily overlook it. On the other hand, the coloured surface perceived by the eye, and the surface felt by the touch, are so very different in their sensible qualities, that their similarity of form and disparity of size, cannot be well ascertained, unless by super-imposing, as it were, one on the other. But nature has rendered this impossible. It has, on the contrary, arranged for us a singular kind of super-imposition, quite the reverse of what it seems to us; that is to say, it has so provided that, when touching with our hand the bodies seen by us, we imagine that we apply to the terms of the touch the *apex* of the luminous pyramid which enters our eye, whereas in truth we always apply to them the base, which is not perceived by the eye. What produces that impression in us is the connexion which (as I have shown in the preceding number) this base has with the apex perceived by the eye.

This is why we find it more difficult to recognise the difference between the dimensions seen by the eye and those touched by the hand, than to believe in their equality.

ARTICLE VII.

The sight, associated with touch and motion, perceives distances and the qualities of the motion of our own body.

917. Let us now consider a man, who, with his eyes wide open, moves about.[1]

What changes does his motion cause in his visual sensations?

A continual shifting of coloured surfaces, a variation of

---

[1] How it is possible for animals to move in space before they have acquired the perception of space by the use of the external senses, is a question which the reader may see treated in my work entitled *Antropologia.*

colours, the clear lights turned into shade, and the shade into lights. If you gaze on the colour and form of a large building from afar, it will perhaps seem to you a little speck shining white on the blue distance of the mountain rising behind it. But as you go nearer, the little white speck expands before you, it takes shape, its outlines become marked, and by the time you have come close up to it, you see it in its full dimensions. Now all the changes that have taken place in this coloured surface on which your sight has been concentrated—the points or various coloured spots which expand—appear more and more distinct, take definite forms in proportion as you move on, hold, as I have said, a constant relation with the whole of your various movements.

Clearly, motion has no likeness to colour; it is as different from it as taste is from sound. Nevertheless the constant relation which the colours, and especially the lights and shades, bear to the movements, causes the variation of these colours to be a sure indication and sign by which to know and measure the movements themselves.

918. Thus colours become, as it were, a language wherewith nature speaks to us, informing us of distances and of sizes; and this natural language proceeds on the same principle as artificial language.

In artificial language words are used to express ideas; but words, being but material sounds, have no resemblance to ideas, which are thoughts of the mind. Still, they serve as *signs* of ideas, and the instant we hear the words spoken, it seems to us, by the force of habit, that with them we receive the ideas also; and we join them together so intimately as to form of them as it were the object of one and the same thought. All this arises from that constant and analogical relation which we have established in our own mind between articulate sounds and ideas, most dissimilar though these things be in their own natures. The very same takes place in respect to colours, by means of lights and shades. These act as so many words which tell us the distances of bodies from us and what locomotion has been made, or must be made, in order to reach them; and they do so in virtue of the relation which experience has shown us to exist between these things.

We shall find it easier to understand how the eye, or rather the animal sagacity, is able to gauge distances, by having recourse to another simile. Let the various colours which speckle, as it were, the retina of our eye, be likened to the letters of the alphabet. The letters which I write with ink on a sheet of paper have no resemblance, much less community of substance, with the articulate sound which I form in the air by speaking. Nevertheless the strokes and curves and points I put down on the paper have power to recall words and ideas to the mind of the reader, who therefore weeps or laughs, as the case may be, just as if events of a most heartrending, or else most joyous nature were being related to him or actually passing under his eyes. Now this happens simply because between those ink-marks, and the sounds which are connected with ideas, there is a constant relation, partly arbitrary and partly analogical. This relation enables the mind to pass most rapidly from the perception of the ink-marks to the thoughts which I by writing intended to communicate.

So with colours and motion: there is no similarity of nature between them ; but there is a relation of analogy. Hence we make use of the colours as so many signs for knowing and measuring our movements ; and the same thing that we do by an act of the mind, is done by animals by the sagacity of instinct.

919. As however we must learn to speak and to write, so must we learn to discern distances and movements with the eye. The first is learnt under the tuition of society, the second under the tuition of nature.[1]

[1] It would be useful if one could accurately ascertain the time it takes infants to learn this correspondence of the sizes perceived by the eye with those perceived by the touch, and with distances. Be it noted, that the same result can be obtained in two ways—instinctively and intellectually. I mean, that the training necessary for correctly perceiving the correspondence in question, is acquired, (1) by the *sensitive faculty*, and this takes place in animals also ;

(2) by the *intellectual faculty*, which belongs to man alone. The sensitive faculty learns that art practically through the associations of *sensations, phantasms, feelings, instincts* and *habits.* In the case of man, all this is accompanied by *judgments.* The experiments instituted for this object should, therefore, aim at distinguishing in infants the progress of these two faculties respectively, which is, however, extremely difficult to do. Cabanis tells us that he had known an

When we have learnt the art of reading distances at a glance, and of judging of the quantity of motion through the signs given us by the colours, and this art has grown into a settled habit; we then seem to see distances, and to measure the motion required to traverse them, immediately with the eye itself, although in truth the eye never sees anything more than a surface. But the rapidity with which the varying colours of this surface are conjoined by us with the idea of depth is so great, that in the end it wholly escapes our advertence. We then suppose that our eye sees immediately depth itself; even as a reader fancies that he perceives the articulate words themselves, and a listener that he receives with his ears the images and ideas, whereas in point of fact he receives nothing but the words.

ARTICLE VIII.

The smell, the hearing, and the taste compared with the sight.

920. Odours, flavours, and sounds cannot indicate to us the presence or the distance of bodies so precisely and so universally as colours do ; and this for two reasons : (1) because these three species of sensations do not, like the visual sensations, immediately delineate in us a corporeal surface at once distinct and continuous, but rather give us corporeal points wanting in distinction, changeable, perfectly homogeneous and uniform ; (2) because they cannot, like the sensations of the eye, be as it were validated by the touch ; since the objects usually perceived by this sense have not that close relation with the hearing, the palate, or the olfactory nerves, which they have with the eye.

921. With regard to the hearing, however, there is a specialty to be noticed. The hearing gives us a variety of sensations, which, though not so intimately connected with those of the touch as the visual sensations, are nevertheless governed by laws constant as well as simple. Hence they

idiotic youth who, although perfectly sound in his organ of sight, could never be brought to discern distances by sight alone (*Rapports du Physique et du Moral de l'Homme*, &c. Mém. ii.). If this be true, that youth must have been deficient not only in his intellect, but also in his animal instinct.

are particularly adapted for the formation of languages. As, then, the eye, aided by the touch, becomes a limited natural language (for the things we see speak to us as it were of themselves by means of the order maintained in colours), so the hearing affords facilities for the invention of an universal language. ·

CHAPTER XIII.

CRITERION OF THE SIZE AND FORM OF BODIES.

ARTICLE I.

The criterion of the size of bodies consists in the size perceived by the touch.

922. When we wish to know if a thing is true or false, we must compare it with that idea which is known to express its genuine essence.

Now this idea is supplied to us by that faculty which perceives immediately, not merely a sign or image of the thing, but the thing itself.

We have seen that *extension* is essentially the mode of our fundamental feeling.[1] Therefore our fundamental feeling is a faculty which perceives immediately, not matter only, but extension also. Hence by this feeling we are unmistakably put in possession of genuine extension, and, with it, of the first measure of all that comes under the name of *size*.

923. But we have also seen that the extension of the fundamental feeling commensurates itself with the several extensions felt and perceived by the touch (841).

Consequently, the touch also gives us the true and genuine size of bodies. This is, in fact, the measure we advert to and regularly make use of; nor could the case be otherwise, for the extension of the fundamental feeling, so long as left to its pure self alone, could not be a measure of anything.

924. The eye, on the contrary, and the other sensories in so far as they differ from the touch, (1) do not immediately

---

[1] The philosopher who said that our body is the measure of all things, would have expressed an excellent truth, if he had restricted his meaning to the size of spaces and of bodies.

perceive the sizes of things at a distance, and (2) do not perceive distances, but only the signs of them.

Hence it follows, that in order to avoid our being led into error, the sizes of things as presented by the sight, must be continually tested and rectified by a reference to those perceived by the touch, in accordance with the beneficent provision made for us by nature.

ARTICLE II.

Application of the criterion to illusions concerning the visible size of things.

925. Habituated, then, as we are to accompany the visual sensations with most rapid judgments, by which, regarding these sensations as signs, we instantaneously infer from them the sizes of bodies, it seems to us that we perceive those sizes immediately with the eye itself.

This mistake is so universally prevalent among all classes of men, that it may not improperly be called an error of the *sensus communis.*[1]

[1] The erroneous notions universally prevalent are all perhaps of this description; they depend on habitual judgments into which men slip as it were involuntarily, irresistibly. Judgments become habitual when experience has shown an almost constant connexion between two facts. The generality of men do not notice very rare exceptions to the ordinary rule. They are exceedingly prone to extend the meaning of *ordinarily* to that of *always,* and have not sufficient self-control to suspend their judgment. For instance, did not all classes of men in every place go on for ages in the erroneous persuasion that the sun really travelled round the earth? Whence the error? Not certainly from the eye, which deposed only to an *apparent* motion, but from a *judgment* which they added to the sensation of the eye. But how could they withhold this judgment when an almost universal experience told them that the two motions—the apparent and the real—go hand in hand? True, this law of experience had its anomalies. One such anomaly, patent to all, was the case of the man who, rowing in a boat, sees the banks of the river glide swiftly past him, though he knows for certain they do not move at all. But a particular case is much too small a matter for the multitude, for whole nations, for all mankind to weigh it carefully and turn it to account. If the suspension of judgment is difficult for an individual, to the multitude it is a trial beyond endurance. The multitude judges according to its bent, and no power on earth is able to restrain it in this. Who ever taught a people the art of curbing its judgment? At what period, or in what part of the world have the masses shown themselves possessed of this art, which requires a prudence, a calmness, a thoughtfulness, a sobriety of mind very seldom attained even by philosophers of the highest order? This would be to expect too much from human nature such as we find it. When things have come to such a pass, that an error is not avoidable except by suspending a judgment to which the multitude has been fully and long habituated, and which has all the

The existence of this error gives rise to certain questions, which, however, are found to be wholly superfluous when the error itself has been dissipated.

One such question is the following :—

I am gazing at a scene. I see before me, the boundless spaces of the heavens, a vast plain teeming with fertility, mountains, lakes, rivers, animals, plants, herbage—an infinite variety of objects. In the midst of all I descry a human being like myself—a mere speck as compared with the rest. Now in the forehead of this man I see his eyes, minute parts of a minute object. In the centre of the eyes I notice a dark little aperture at the end of which there is the retina, an exceedingly fine and sensitive kind of membrane, into which the light penetrates with its marvellous and exciting action.

Now it is precisely here, in this tiny little spot, at the far extremity of the eye, that this person sees me, and all other things, even as I, in a similarly most diminutive space, see him and all this vast and magnificent scene.

But how can this be? How is it that the objects appear to me of so large a size, while the ground on which I see them depicted is so exceedingly small? Is there not some deception here?

The whole difficulty disappears if we remember what has been explained before, namely, that the eye does not perceive either the sizes or the distances of things, but only *signs* of the former, and that from these signs our mind infers distances by means of most rapid judgments, even as the sagacity of instinctive habit causes mere animals to act as if they conceived distances intellectually.

appearance of truth, because founded on a law of common experience attended with extremely rare exceptions, no force, no power of persuasion will be of avail; the erroneous judgment is certain to follow. A sage may foresee it, predict it, but impede it —never. It would be easier to stop the downward dash head-long of an overwhelming avalanche, than to keep in check the judging propensity of a multitude under such circumstances. Only after the lapse of many years, perhaps of centuries, is the error corrected. A time comes when some extraordinary man arises to demonstrate its falsehood. At first he is fiercely contradicted, is crushed, so to speak, under the immense weight of an adverse public opinion. But, in the oppression of the man, the germ of that truth to which he falls a martyr does not perish. It outlives him, and by slow degrees makes its way in the world, until it comes to master the multitude itself, repentant at last and ashamed of its foolish presumption, and of that conceited ignorance which is now seen to have been as full of conceit as it was cruel.

A *sign* need not be of the same nature or size as the thing signified. All that we require in order to estimate correctly the size of the thing, is to be cognisant of the ratio in which that of the sign stands to it.

In the case of the eye we habitually know that ratio, because by means of the touch we perceive the true sizes of things, and form the habit of using those sizes as a test of comparison for such as appear to the eye.

926. But another difficulty presents itself, which deserves every attention. As I have repeatedly observed, the eye also is an organ of touch, and the light really comes in contact with it. Why then should not the law of touch be applied to the eye as well? Now what is the law of the sense of touch? This: when we feel a body with our hand—the part of our organism best adapted for the purpose—it is with the hand itself, laid on the body, that we measure it, as, so to speak, with a rule or compass. And in this touch and application, I have distinguished the *subjective* sensation of our hand from the *extrasubjective* perception of the external body, and I have said that the extension of the former is the measure of the extension of the latter. Let us, then, apply the same law to the eye. The luminous globules really touch it; therefore it will have 1st a *subjective* sensation of the several parts of the retina affected by diverse luminous rays, some thicker than others; 2nd, the *extrasubjective* perception of those rays, *i.e.* of the luminous globules by which it is struck. Consequently, the eye will, with the extension of its *subjective* sensation, measure the extension of those agents, that is, if not of the fractional portions which compose each ray, at least of each ray taken as a whole. Continuing therefore to speak of the sight as a tactile organ, we ought (on the principle that 'The whole is greater than the part') to perceive in its sensation the comparative diminutiveness of each of the tiny little images depicted on the retina; and we ought also to be cognisant of the exact ratio in which each of them stands to the size of the retina itself, their common container. It is true, that on our subsequently making use of the touch, those minute images will be capable of serving us as so many signs

of the real sizes that have been ascertained by means of this
sense, in the same way that a topographical chart, once we
know the proportional scale to which it is made, serves us for
judging of the size of the various places sketched on it. But
this does not in any way exclude the knowledge previously
acquired—*i.e.* the knowledge we had obtained of the real size
proper to each of the tiny little images impressed on the
retina, by comparing it with the retina itself as with its
standard of measurement, even as is done with everything
else which falls under the touch. And yet experience gives
us nothing of this.

927. Having thus stated the difficulty, I proceed to give
its explanation.

In the first place, it is not correct to give the name of
images to the coloured spots in our retina, before the touch
has made us aware that these spots are signs of the external
bodies. Before then, they are spots felt by us, and nothing
more. They neither indicate, nor represent anything outside
of themselves; consequently they can in no sense be called
either *images* or *signs*. But when the touch comes to be used
simultaneously with the eye, we discover that constant relation
which I explained above (915), and which, to say it once
more, flows from the fact that the spots in the retina are
always observed to vary exactly according as our touch covers
the bodies in these or those parts. It is then, and then only,
that the spots assume, so to speak, the nature of signs, and
seem to us true images of the bodies placed at a distance
from us.[1] Such is the change produced through the touch
being applied in combination with the sight. The little spots
or coloured sensations, then, and the visual *images*, considered
in their own entity, are one and the same thing; but under
the aspect in which we are here considering them, they are
two; for, the self-same sensation considered as a spot felt
in the retina, presents to our attention one term, but presents
to it another and entirely opposite term when considered as
the image of an external object. In the first case, the atten-

[1] I say *seem* true images, because
the coloured sensations have no likeness
to the external things except in the
extrasubjective part.

tion stops in the sensation of the retina alone ; in the second, it goes direct to the object represented, and rests in that alone. Thus for example, he who looks at the portrait of a friend, thinks straightway of that friend, without at all stopping to examine the picture in its own proper entity. He does not dwell on the consideration of the canvas or the texture thereof, of the quality of the colours or the oil in which they were mixed, of how the painter proceeded in executing his work, &c. Neither does he dream of submitting to analysis the chemical ingredients of which that canvas and the whole painting are composed. Let us then try to understand well how the fact here spoken of takes place. I repeat it, the little spot felt in the retina becomes an image only in consequence of the use of the touch ; but the moment it has become an image, our thought starts from this new point, takes a new direction, goes outside of, and to a distance from us, to fix itself on the object of which that spot is an image.

Perfectly to comprehend this important fact, it is necessary to master that most vital distinction on which the whole of philosophical knowledge may be said to depend—I mean the distinction between *sensation* and *advertence* to sensation.[1]

928. The law of advertence may be thus stated : ' That to which we advert constitutes the term of our intellectual attention.' A thing is said to be adverted to when our attention turns to it in such a manner as ultimately to terminate and rest in it alone. All the intermediate links through which the mind passes, but in which it does not rest as in its term, are fugitively perceived by us, but not *adverted to*. If we desire to advert to any of those links, we must turn back,

---

[1] This advertence, I sometimes call *observation*, sometimes *attention*, sometimes *consideration*, and at other times, *notice*. All these terms express an act of the mind which fixes itself on the sensation, and by so doing forms the idea of, and adverts to the sensation. Galluppi says very appositely that ideas are formed by *meditation* on the sensations. But I should like to know what this meditation, this reflection, this operation of our mind really is, by which he would have ideas be formed ? On this, Galluppi says nothing. I maintain, then, that it consists in the application of an universal idea to the sensations (482-494) ; that it cannot consist in anything else ; and that if this be not admitted, the *meditation* of which he speaks has no meaning, the act of *reflection* is inexplicable.

retrace the course our thought has rapidly traversed, and convert the link itself into a distinct and ultimate term of attention. Although, then, many other things are felt by our sense and perceived by our mind, that alone is an object of *advertence* on which our thought is bent, and wherein it finally terminates.

To come now to the sensations felt in the retina of the eye ; when these sensations have acquired the quality and condition of *images*, they are such as no longer to admit of being by themselves alone the term of our attention. As I have before observed, it is the nature of an image to take us outside of itself—to direct our thought from it to the object it represents For, when I say *an image*, I necessarily imply a special relation of one thing to another whereunto that relation carries our thought. From the moment, therefore, that the sensation felt by the eye has assumed for us the nature of an image, our mind is, *ipso facto*, debarred from regarding the sensation as *sensation*. It regards it as *image*, and so is carried elsewhere, namely, to the external thing expressed by the image. Thus it is that the sensation remains unobserved, escapes our advertence.

929. Add to this another observation. As a matter of fact, 'we advert more easily to distinct than to confused perceptions.' Now what causes a sense-perception to be distinct or confused ? I answer : A sense-perception is distinct in the proportion in which the bodies perceived in it are (1) fewer in number, (2) of sufficient size to be fully embraced, and (3) more constant in the configuration they present to our senses. Now the globules of light, being of a number, a minuteness and a quickness of mobility beyond all calculation, can only cause in us a perception extremely confused, though at the same time vivid because of the great and sudden impetuosity with which they strike the retina in such overwhelming multitudes. When, therefore, we perceive a body in a confused manner, we hardly seem to perceive it at all. Thus, for example, when gazing only at aerial spaces illumined by an equable light, we are wont to say that we see nothing. On the contrary, the perception of the touch is most distinct in

its nature ; and so are the signs which correspond to it in the eye, these signs being (their marvellous minuteness notwithstanding), not only vivid, but likewise perfectly distinct the one from the other, as well as perfectly precise in their several outlines. Hence it is that in the visual sensation we give little if any advertence [1] to the immediate perception of the particles of light themselves, and to their varieties, but are, instead, wholly taken up with the bodies as presented to us by the touch, whereof that sensation is an image and a sign ; and this attention is no vain speculation, as would be the observing of the spots in the retina, but is extremely useful, and required by the continual wants of our life.

ARTICLE III.

Application of the criterion to the visual illusions concerning the distances of things.

930. The objects delineated in our retina by the light, when not equidistant from us, do not maintain their proportional dimensions ; but those that are further away project relatively smaller images than those that are nearer.

This arises from the law which regulates the convergence of the luminous rays. The greater the distance from which these rays take their departure, the more acute must be the angle into which they are prolonged, so as to reach the eye where they excite the sensation. As a result, the tracing they produce in the retina is smaller than it ought to be. This kind of deception, however, is not to be attributed to the visual sensation itself, which in truth tells us nothing about the object, but solely to the judgment whereby, taking that sensation as a sign, we infer from it the size of the external body.

931. But this error also can very soon be corrected ; because the images coming to us from various distances follow

[1] I say 'little if any advertence,' because in point of fact we have some consciousness of the sensations felt in the eye. Does not every one of us feel the light striking into his eyes? And if we close our eyes, do we not perceive a difference also in the pupil ? But, as I have said, we do not particularly care to attend to what takes place within our eyes, when there are so many delightful objects to attract us outside of them.

another kind of proportion, which serves us as a sure index and measure of the distances themselves.

The proportion I allude to consists in this, that the image in our eye grows larger according as the distance at which the bodies are placed diminishes, and *vice versâ*; so that the apparent sizes and their distances are seen constantly to proceed in a contrary ratio. The constancy of this ratio is the foundation of the art of perspective.

By spontaneous motion combined with the use of the touch we ascertain the true distances, and by habitual observation we come to know the relation between the apparent size of the bodies, and their distance thus ascertained. Hence we very soon acquire the art of passing with the utmost rapidity from the first to the second, and of estimating at a glance, at least approximately, from the apparent size, the distance of the bodies from us.

Imagine yourself standing before a long avenue of ilexes, poplars, or other trees. As you look down, you see the apparent heights of the trees on both sides gradually diminishing. Now it is precisely by means of this diminution that you become aware of the greater distance of the trees following in order those next to you, down to the end of the line.

When you have contracted the habit of judging of the height of the trees in this way, you no longer miscalculate; for, in observing that gradual diminution, you understand at once, that it is nothing but the effect of distance, and you thus correct the apparent inequality in the heights by reducing with your thought all those trees to the same nearness to you as the foremost ones, and thus seeing them all as of much the same height—that is, supposing that the trees are all of the same kind.

ARTICLE IV.

Application of the criterion to the illusions concerning the position of things.

932. The light delineates bodies in our eye upside down. How is it, then, that we see them the right way up?

This happens because the inverted position in which the

images of bodies are depicted in the eye never is and never can be in contradiction either with the different parts of the images themselves, or with the perceptions of the touch, but only with the fundamental feeling by which we feel the eye, and with the modification of that same feeling by which also we feel the eye subjectively.

933. I say in the first place, that the fact of our eye receiving the image of a body upside down, is not in contradiction with the different parts of the image itself, and that it is therefore impossible that we, by means of the image alone, should be made to notice the reversed position.

In fact, whence is it, that if a body—a small statue for instance—is reversed, we forthwith notice the new position assumed by it? Only from its relation to the bodies around it, the position of which has not been reversed. But let us suppose the opposite case, namely, that all the surrounding bodies, and we with them, had also been turned upside down, without any disarrangement or change being caused in the relative position of the several parts. We should not then, and could not, advert to the new position taken by that statue and by ourselves with it; for the whole scene has been reversed together, and there is no other body left around us to serve as a sign or test whereby to perceive the change. As I have already observed, motion is not perceivable by the senses except through its relation to the bodies that are moved and of which we have perception. The fact of the daily rotation of the earth proves this clearly; for that rotation causes all things, and ourselves with them, to be turned upside down once every twenty-four hours, and yet we cannot by means of our senses notice this inversion, because the relative positions remain unchanged; so that, in order to find it out, we must make use of arguments supplied, not by the senses, but by the intelligence only. It is just the same with our eye. No matter in what position the images may be found there—whether upside down or transversely, &c.—we could never be informed of that position by the eye itself, because those images are all inverted alike, and retain their true relative proportions; and we ourselves, in so far as perceived by the eye, are also placed inversely like every other object. In our eye, therefore, the whole world is placed upside down ; but as there is neither change nor contradiction between the different little images, so we cannot notice the inversion of particular bodies, even as, for the same reason, we cannot perceive the circular motion caused in them on our planet by its daily revolution on its axis.

934. But not only is the eye unable to see the objects otherwise than in their true and natural positions; but even the sense of touch cannot give us any indication of the inverted posture they have in our retina ; because, as I have said, the position of the visual images, whatever it may be, can never be found in contradiction with the position of the bodies as felt by the touch.

In fact, as the eye sees the relative position of bodies, so the touch feels that same position, and not any other. For instance, that which is over my head (here is the relation which fixes the position of things), is found to be over my head by the touch no less than by the sight. So with that which lies under my feet. It is perfectly immaterial that I stand upright in one absolute direction or in another, at this point of the globe or ninety degrees away, in which latter case my position relatively to the present one would be horizontal : the 'over,' the 'under,' and the sides would be precisely where they now are, as well for the eye as for the hand. Whatever, then, be the direction of the tiny images traced on our retina, the positions indicated respectively by the sight and by the touch are always in complete harmony.

935. On the other hand, as regards the fundamental feeling and the adventitious sensations, by both of which we feel the same retina, there is really a contradiction between the images aforesaid and the posture of the bodies as presented to us by the touch. To understand how this is, we will suppose that the image is felt adhering to the retina in such a way that we perceive it is as conjoined with the sensation of the retina itself whereon it is laid ; just as is the case with the tactile sensation, which has always a duplex nature, because in it we feel two conterminous surfaces in one—the surface of

the hand affected by the touch, and the surface of the external body covered by the hand.   In this supposition, we should feel the image as upside down, *i.e.* placed inversely to the position of our eye.   Hence, if the image of another person's eye were reflected into our eye, the brows of that miniature eye would, relatively to those of ours, be 'under,' while those of ours would be 'over.'   In the one sensation, therefore, the position of the *extrasubjective* part would be directly contrary to that of the *subjective* which corresponds to it.   But if so, why is it that we never notice this contrariety in our visual sensations?

936. This difficulty will disappear if the reader only bears in mind what I said about the sense of sight in the preceding article.

I there observed, that when the eye is considered as a tactile sense, that is, as a sense which immediately perceives colours, we cannot with propriety of language say that it perceives an *image*, since, viewed under this aspect, it perceives coloured little *spots* and not anything further.   Now so long as the colours perceived by the eye are considered in themselves alone, and not in so far as they are *signs*, it is of no consequence to us what position they have on our retina, for they mean nothing ; and the task of comparing them, through reflection on ourselves, with the position of our eye, must be extremely difficult if not altogether impossible.

Later on, when the spots have assumed for us the nature of images, our attention, as I also observed, is no longer detained in them.   From that time forth, what we seek by the use of our eyes is, not to know what takes place in the eyes themselves, but to know the bodies outside of us.   Hence in the same proportion as we get accustomed to direct our attention to external objects on occasion of the visual sensations, we become incapable of fixing it on the small organ in which they are and on the modification it undergoes.

937. In the second place, strong as is the sensation of light is so far as extrasubjective, the extreme minuteness of the extension it fills in so far as subjective, renders it very difficult for us correctly to measure that extension.   And as to the

position it has relatively to our own eye, advertence to it is
an impossibility.   In truth, in order to know and to advert to
the fact, that the tiny little image has, relatively to our eye,
a certain position rather than another, we must, (1) observe
the position of the coloured spot ; (2) observe and advert to
the position of the eye ; (3) compare these positions together;
(4) observe which part of the coloured spot represents one
extremity and which part the other extremity of the external
object ; (5) observe and advert that the part of the spot
representing the upper extremity, corresponds to the lower
part of the eye and *vice versâ*.   Now all these operations are
extremely difficult, nay, in all probability impossible.   Not to
be endless in this matter, I will content myself with pointing
out the difficulty of the third of the steps just named, that is
to say, the comparing of the position of the coloured spot
with that of our eye.   How do I feel the position of my eye?
By the fundamental feeling only.   And how do I feel the
position of the coloured spot?   By the acquired sensation.
Now we have seen how difficult it is to advert to the fundamental feeling.   How much more difficult, then, must it be to
advert, in it, to the relative position of the parts felt, and to
advert to it with such clearness, distinctness,[1] steadiness and
fulness of grasp as is necessary for enabling us to compare
with it the position of the acquired sensation, namely, of the
coloured spot of which I am speaking?

938. These considerations prevent my being able to agree
with those Ideologists who affirm that we in the first instance
see external things upside down, and that what sets them
right is the subsequent use of our touch.   On the contrary, I
hold that we always see them the right way up, and cannot
see them any otherwise.   I hold, moreover, that it would be
utterly impossible, even with the keenest observation on ourselves, to notice by means of the sight alone this singular
fact, that ' When we take the figure of the visual sensations as
a sign of the external bodies, the part in the sensation which,

[1] I also believe that it is quite impossible for us distinctly to advert in the fundamental feeling to the *relative* position of its parts without the aid of adventitious sensations.   Nay, can the fundamental feeling be said to have any parts clearly distinguishable ?

relatively to the position of our eye, is lowest, indicates the uppermost part of the external object; and, conversely, the part in the sensation which, relatively to the eye, is highest, indicates the lowest part of the external object seen by us.[1]

ARTICLE V.

The criterion of the figure of bodies consists in their figure as perceived by the touch.

939. The touch combined with spontaneous motion immediately perceives extension (837–875).

Hence it is by this sense that the limits of extension—I mean size and figure—are perceived.[2]

Therefore the shape of the things which is perceived by the touch joined with motion is the criterion whereby shapes presented to us by the sight must be tested.

---

[1] The erroneous notion that the eye sees objects in an inverted position, and that the touch rectifies that position, was started in modern times by Condillac and Buffon; and it is singular to find how succeeding writers copy and repeat it blindly after them. Houy (*Traité élémentaire de Physique*, vol. ii.), Fodéré (*Physiologie positive*, vol. iii.), not to mention Alagarotti and all the more recent Italian authors, have known no better than to repeat the same assertion. We must, however, except Melchior Gioja, who, in the midst of innumerable errors, makes this good observation:—
'It seems absolutely false that the sensations of touch have the power of correcting the impressions of sight. In fact, the sense of touch assures us that a stake fixed in the bottom of a clear pool, and protruding above the surface, is straight, and yet our eye sees it bent at an angle, and continues so to see it even after we have touched it again and again. So also, the touch assures us that our own countenance, as reflected in a mirror, has no existence in the empty space behind it; nevertheless the eye persists in telling us that it is there. Again, an artist who has painted a globe on his canvas, knows for certain that this globe is drawn on a perfectly level surface, and yet, in spite of that, his eye deposes that one

half or more of the globe stands out from the canvas, projecting towards the spectator.'
'Supposing the explanation produced by the above physiologists were true, namely, that the sense of touch rectifies the impressions of sight, objects ought to appear to us inverted until the touch has undeceived us; but this is not the case, as may be proved by the fact that those who have been born with cataract, on its removal see the objects not upside down but the right way up.'
'Lastly, objects ought to appear upside down to those animals which are almost entirely wanting in the sense of touch; yet they act in such a way as to justify the opinion that they see things the right way up even as we do' (*Esercizio logico sugli errori d'Ideologia e Zoologia*, p. 98, &c.).
[2] Space is not subject to change of figure for the same reason for which it is not subject to change of size. Two different figures are simply two portions of space independent of each other. One space, therefore, can never be transformed into another. Likewise, it would not be correct to say that one figure in space is changed into another. If a figure is replaced by another, the second is not a transformation of the first, but a new figure altogether.

ARTICLE VI.

Errors which the sight occasions concerning the figure and size of bodies.

940. The light serves to make us perceive bodies at a distance from us, because these bodies refract and reflect it in such a manner that its modifications maintain a constant proportion with the size, form, distance and other qualities and conditions of the bodies themselves.

But this is on the supposition that the rays of light in their passage from the bodies to our eye are not turned aside from their straight course or altered, as is the case when they encounter some fresh medium on the way, or are differently grouped together through accidental causes. Whenever this happens, the impression made by the luminous rays on our retina is no longer in accordance with that fixed ratio and proportion by which we have learnt, as by sure indications or marks, to form our judgment respecting bodies ; and therefore if we take that impression for our guide we shall be led into error. Hence such optical illusions as that of the oar which seems bent in the water, or of the mirage, or of those apparently huge masses of rock which are sometimes seen in polar regions, where the air through condensation acts as a lens, and which, on a close approach, are found to be nothing but small bits of stone ; and other similar illusions which the sense of touch discovers and corrects.

CHAPTER XIV.

ON THE EXTRASUBJECTIVE PERCEPTION OF BODIES BY MEANS OF THE FIVE SENSES CONSIDERED IN RELATION TO ONE ANOTHER.

ARTICLE I.

Different sensations are united and cause us to perceive one and the same body by all referring together to one and the same space.

941. The sensations of smell and of taste have a very confused extrasubjective perception (920), and are not therefore adapted to serve as representative signs of distant bodies. For while, on the one hand, the distinct perception of these bodies arises from the distinctness with which we perceive their size and figure, the odoriferous and saporiferous particles in striking their appropriate organs do not, on the other, maintain any law of proportion with the size and figure of the external things. Nevertheless they are of some service in this direction. Through our regularly finding, for instance, that in the presence of a certain flower a certain scent is perceived which ceases on its removal, that scent becomes associated in our mind with the odoriferous object known to us by means of the touch and the sight, and serves us therefore as an *indication* of the same. But although smell and taste are not naturally representative signs of the bodies perceived by the touch, they can artificially be converted into signs of anything as well as of any thought.

942. The same may be said of sounds ; only that sounds can be made still more serviceable by art, which skilfully disposes them into harmonious combinations, and draws from them the various languages spoken by the human family (921).

943. The visual sensations, on the contrary, as we have

seen, are already harmonically ordered and disposed by nature itself; and as a consequence they become representative signs, not indeed of all thoughts and things, because, for this, training and art are necessary, but of the external bodies perceived by the touch.

This arises from the relation which the sizes and figures of the various visual sensations have with tactile bodies and with their distances. The sizes and figures of these bodies being perfectly represented by the proportional sizes and by the figures of the said sensations, it comes to pass that, through long habit, the latter sizes and figures are no longer regarded merely as signs of the former, but are identified with and taken for them. In this way, the visual sizes and figures occupy for us the same space as the things outside of and at a distance from us. But the visual sizes and figures are depicted in various colours. Therefore these colours also are transferred outside our eye and applied to the external bodies and believed to belong to them; in other words, the bodies are regarded by us as variously coloured.

944. Thenceforth we are not content with calling the coloured spots on our retina signs of external things, or representative signs, but find it quite natural to call them *images*; as if the light when placing the colours in our eye, looked first at the bodies to do with them as an artist who, when painting the likeness of a person, seems to take from him the various tints and shades, and all the manifold details that go to make up the picture, whereas in truth they are all productions of his own.

ARTICLE II.

Of all sense-perceptions, the visual is that which most arrests our attention.

945. When we have contracted the habit of judging of distant bodies from the tints of the colours, and contracted it to such a degree that the bodies and the colours are located by us in the same space, so that we take them for one and the same thing (941–943), then our visual perception becomes

beautiful and pleasing, rapid, useful, easy, distinct, sharp [1]
and precise, and therefore much more attractive to us than
the immediate perception which we have of bodies by means
of the fundamental feeling, or of touch and motion. We
are then so taken up with the visual perception, that we
no longer give any thought to the other ways of perceiving
bodies, but act as if everything was known to us through the
sight alone. What we do not see, we seem not to know at
all, and even the perception of touch appears to us blind
and dull.

946. Nor is this an error confined to the vulgar ; philosophers also—who do not in an instant wholly dismiss their
previously contracted vulgar habits of thought—allow themselves to be so carried away by the clearness and attractiveness
of the sight, that they reduce all they have to say about the
perception and knowledge of bodies, to it alone.

This observation is not mine, but Dugald Stewart's, and
he makes it in the following passage :—

' In considering the phenomena of perception, it is natural
to suppose, that the attention of philosophers would be
directed, in the first instance, to the sense of seeing. The
variety of information and of enjoyment we receive by it ; the
rapidity with which this information and enjoyment are conveyed to us, and above all, the intercourse it enables us to
maintain with the more distant parts of the universe, cannot
fail to give it, even in the apprehension of the most careless
observer, a pre-eminence over all our other perceptive faculties.
Hence it is, that the various theories, which have been formed
to explain the operations of our senses, have a more immediate
reference to that of seeing ; and that the greater part of the
metaphysical language, concerning perception in general,
appears evidently, from its etymology, to have been suggested
by the phenomena of vision. Even when applied to this
sense, indeed, it can at most amuse the fancy, without con-
veying any precise knowledge ; but when applied to the other

[1] Sometimes the sight gives us a sensation more apt to be adverted to, or discerned than the sensation of touch. Thus a fine rose-leaf yields to the touch a sensation so slight as to be indistinguishable from that of our own fingers, but the eye discovers its presence at once.

senses, it is altogether absurd and unintelligible' (*Elements of the Philosophy of the Human Mind*, ch. i. sect. 1).

947. By applying therefore to our perceptions of external bodies generally the phraseology proper to the sense of sight, we lose ourselves in mere *metaphor* :[1] hence innumerable errors, and a multitude of questions as useless as they are insoluble, all of which vanish once we rectify our expressions, even as superstitious notions are dissipated by the light of sound religious teaching.[2]

[1] Metaphysical expressions borrowed from the sense of sight and applied to the other senses are in such universal use, and it is so difficult to keep clear of this common defect of philosophical language, that I would not dare to affirm I myself may not sometimes have stumbled into it in this very work. Here I will only call the reader's attention to a word used by Galluppi, who was certainly not unaware of the danger and impropriety of expressions of this kind. He gives the name of *intuition* to the perception of bodies made by all the senses indiscriminately (*Critica della conoscenza*, vol. ii. § 71). Now the use of the word *intuition* for explaining the immediate perception of bodies by all our senses alike, seems all the less appropriate, in as much as the eye perceives bodies, not immediately, but only through the medium of the luminous rays.

[2] This impropriety of language is abused chiefly by the Idealists. They draw one of their arguments precisely from the fact of the size of bodies changing according to distances, as may be seen in Hume.

By way of showing how old is the delusion of attributing to all the senses generally what belongs to the sight only, it may be useful to note it in Aristotle. He first tells us that size and motion are *common sensible qualities*, and then says that, with regard to these, our sensitive faculty deceives us much more than with regard to the other sensible qualities proper to each particular sense. And why? Because sizes and motions change with the change of distances. Here, therefore, the senses generally are credited with what belongs to the eye alone, which Aristotle calls the *principal sense* (L.

iii. *de Anima*). To speak truly, he ought to have said that a much more frequent error is that of attributing colours to bodies, whereas colours are only sensations in the optic nerve. But Aristotle seems not to have been aware of this, and to have himself imbibed the common error. I will take this occasion to make another remark upon the defects which, as I think, are to be found in Aristotle's analysis of our sensations. He does not appear to have always adverted to those *habitual judgments* which are continually mixed up with the sensations, but to have, as is commonly done, confounded them with the sensations themselves. Take for instance the passage where he says : 'A sense *very seldom* errs in respect of the objects proper to it.' This phrase, *very seldom*, is commonly interpreted to mean (and the context as well as the manner of speaking of the Philosopher leaves no doubt on the matter), that a sense is fallacious in respect of the *objects proper to it* when its powers are impaired, which happens very rarely in comparison with the length of time in which it is in a sound state. But here it must be observed, that the deception which takes place when a sense is not in its normal condition, does not lie in the sense itself, but in a judgment which we add thereto ; so that not even in this case does the sense deceive us in respect of its proper objects. It is only an occasion of error to our judgment, whence all errors proceed. The doctrine of S. Augustine on this point is much preferable to that of Aristotle. He says: 'Si omnes corporis sensus ita nuntiant ut afficiuntur, quid ab eis amplius exigere debeamus ignoro ' (*De Ver.* xxxiii.). 'If all the corporeal senses depose according as they are

ARTICLE III.

Do we in our sensations receive only the species of corporeal things, or do we perceive the things themselves?

948. Aristotle and the Schoolmen said, that in sensation we do not perceive the things themselves, but only their similitudes, which being impressed upon our organs, are conveyed by them to the mind.

This view respecting the similitudes or sensible species seems to me to have originated in the error I have just indicated, namely, in applying to the senses generally what belongs to the sight only.

If those philosophers had taken pains to analyse the operations of each sense, they would not have extended what is proper to the noblest and most attractive among them, to all the others, but would have spoken of each in terms appropriate to itself.

The analysis I have made above of those operations has shown, that, of all the five senses,[1] the touch is the only one which perceives bodies immediately.

But we have seen also that the four senses, of sight, hearing, smell and taste perform two very different functions. The first function proceeds from them in so far as they also are organs of touch, and it consists in giving us an immediate perception of the corpuscles which come in contact with them; although owing to the incalculable minuteness and multitude of the corpuscles themselves, the perception, however vivid, is confused. The second is of quite another character, and it arises from this, that the sensations which these special organs give us in their tactile capacity are made use of by us as *signs* for knowing the external bodies placed at a distance from us. And this second function the sense of sight, owing to its peculiar nature, performs for us much more efficiently than the three other senses.

affected, I do not know what more we can require of them' (*De Vera Relig.* xxxiii.).

[1] I say the five senses, because our first perception of a body is made with the fundamental feeling, and this perception, besides being immediate, causes us to perceive the corporeal nature more intimately than any other perception, as I have already explained.

Accordingly, the visual sensations may very properly be denominated *species*, or *visual species*, in order not to confound them with *ideas*; for the meaning of the Latin term *species*, corresponds with that of the English words view, look, aspect (Italian *vista, sguardo, aspetto*).

949. Nevertheless these *visual species* are not, as I have said, full similitudes of the bodies, for they do not present to us the body itself (a solid),[1] but one of its elements only (a surface). Moreover, as regards colours, they are, as I have also observed, a cause of deception to us by leading us into the erroneous belief that the surfaces of bodies are coloured —a belief which finds its expression in the word *images*, commonly applied to the said visual species.

950. But if the pure surface is not a full similitude of the bodies themselves, it is nevertheless, as I have also said, more than a mere arbitrary sign, there being in it a vestige and even a true, though partial resemblance of the external bodies: (1) in the perception of a corporeal *force* (first element of a body); (2) in the proportional *extension* (second element of a body); (3) in the *figure*, resembling the surface of the external body; (4) in some other tactile qualities, such as *hardness, roughness, smoothness, softness*, &c., which are all effects of the force variously distributed in extension.

Besides all this, there is between the species resembling the external body and the body itself, a very close connection established by nature, and arising from the unceasing radiation of the luminous rays from the body, as I have before explained.

---

[1] The visual perception of bodies is always completed by us through *habitual judgments*, or *associations of ideas*. When I look at a portrait what do I really see? A mere surface. But does this surface remind me only of the superficial limits of the person represented? No; in that painting I seem to see the person himself living and entire. That likeness brings up to me at once the complete idea of the person, so that I fancy myself as being in his company, and speaking to him. Now whatever is 'solid,' so to speak, in that person—his body, his soul, his learning, his manners and his virtues—is all remembered by me with a single act, is all added by me, quite unconsciously, the instant I fix my eyes on those lineaments with which I have always been accustomed to associate so many ideas. And these associations accompany the use, not of the eye only, but also of the touch; for a single touch very often causes me to think the whole solid object complete in all the qualities I know it to possess.

ARTICLE IV.

Error of Reid in excluding all sensible species in our perception of bodies.

951. Aristotle was therefore mistaken in extending to all the senses[1] the *sensible species*, which belong to the sight alone.

Reid would not admit any *sensible species* at all, and so fell into the opposite error.

Aristotle attributed to all the senses what he should have limited to the sight, namely the power of informing us concerning bodies by means of *species*; Reid attributed to all the senses what he should have limited to the touch, namely, the power of perceiving bodies immediately, without the intervention of either *species* or similitudes.

ARTICLE V.

Reid's distinction between sensation and perception.

952. Reid, then, allowed no kind of *sensible species* in the perception of bodies.

On the contrary, in describing how we come, by the aid of the senses, to know the existence of bodies, he put down *sensation* and *perception* as two things totally distinct. Now

---

[1] The impropriety of the phrase *sensible species* as applied to other than visual sensations, appears to me inexcusable. But putting this impropriety aside, there may be a true sense in both the following propositions, which seem to be diametrically opposed: 'The touch perceives bodies immediately,' and 'the touch perceives bodies through similitudes.' In fact, the first proposition is true in this sense, that the bodies act immediately on our organs; and the perception of this their immediate action on us, supplies us with that essence whereby we know them (for we only know them by their action). Therefore, the essence called *body* is perceived by us immediately. The second proposition is also true in this sense, that the action produced in us by external bodies is a modification of our own body; and this modification gives us a sensation terminating in an extension. Now in this extended sensation, we perceive the external body as in its similitude. The twofold manner of speaking applicable to the tactile perception has its reason in the duplex nature (subjective-extrasubjective) which we have found to belong to sensation. This duplex nature does not, however, exclude that constant and necessary conjunction of the two elements, whereof the sensation is the result. But though each of the two above propositions is true in its way, the second could not be applied to the perception we have of our body by means of the fundamental feeling. As thus perceived, our body is not known to us through any similitude whatever; but it may become a similitude of external bodies in the manner I have explained.

although I have already more than once touched upon this distinction of Reid, I may nevertheless examine it better in this place. Here, then, is the passage where he describes *sensation* in so far as distinguished from perception :—' When I smell a rose, there is in this operation both sensation and perception. The agreeable odour I feel, considered by itself, without relation to any external object, is merely a sensation. It affects the mind in a certain way ; and this affection of the mind may be conceived without a thought of the rose, or any other object. This sensation can be nothing else than it is felt to be. Its very essence consists in being felt ; and when it is not felt, it is not. . . . It is for this reason, that we before observed that, in sensation, there is no object distinct from that act of the mind by which it is felt' (*Essays on the Powers of the Human Mind*, Essay II. ch. xvi.).

On the other hand, he seems to speak elsewhere (Essay I. ch. ii.) as if his division of sensation from the *perception* of external objects were only a mental abstraction.

This might lead us to believe, that the division did not exist in reality, since by abstraction we in some sort divide mentally even those things which it would be a contradiction to think as really divided.[1]

[1] It seems to me that Reid is not perfectly consistent here, or at least does not explain his meaning with sufficient clearness. On the one hand, he says that *perception* is in its nature entirely different from *sensation* ; the former being the product of a *natural judgment* by which we affirm the existence of external bodies; the latter being strictly confined within the soul which feels itself modified. This naturally leads to the inference that perception and sensation are acts of two different faculties. He seems to affirm the same thing still more pointedly where he ascribes perception to a mysterious faculty belonging exclusively to the mind, and therefore totally different from the faculty of sensation. But then on the other hand he tells us, that there is no *sensation* without a *judgment* ; that in the common manner of speaking, to which he makes appeal, the term *sense* always expresses a capacity to judge ; and that philosophers did wrong in dividing sensation from judgment, and attributing them to two faculties (*Essays on the Powers of the Human Mind*, Essay VI. ch. ii.).

What particularly deserves notice is, that Reid finds philosophers in contradiction with themselves, without at the same time being able to say why they are so.

Philosophers, he observes, define the sense as a faculty which, without any judgment, gives us ideas ; and then they define judgment as the act of a faculty which compares the ideas given us by the sense. As a consequence of this (he proceeds to remark) philosophers, in order to derive ideas from the sense, are obliged to define sensation in the same way as they define judgment ; and in proof of his assertion he quotes a passage from Locke (*Essay*, &c., Book IV. c. ii.), where this author calls the eyes *judges* of colour, thus clearly crediting the sense with the faculty of judging.

But it is not so. For Reid attributes *perception* to a faculty different from that which gives us *sensations*—a mysterious *faculty* that has nothing to do with *sensitivity*. This faculty is a certain *quasi-inspiration* of nature, as he expresses it when describing the perception affirmative of the existence of the external object of which we have sensation. It seems therefore indubitable that his distinction between *sensation* and *perception* is a real one.

The observation is perfectly just; but although Reid noticed the inconsistency of these philosophers, he could not, as I have said, point out its cause. The reason of this inability was because those philosophers had not drawn a clear distinction between the nature of *sensation* and that of *intellection* or *idea*; that is, they had not observed that, whilst no idea can be formed except through a judgment, no judgment is needed for receiving a *sensation*.

They saw therefore, on the one hand, that sensation differs from judgment; but on the other, imagining that a *sensation* is more or less the same thing as an *idea*, and yet being also aware that judgments are indispensable for the formation of ideas, they, contrary to the distinction previously laid down by themselves, took to the expedient of describing sensation as though it were a judgment.

Reid thinks this contradiction can be removed by at once defining *sensation* as being itself a *judgment.*

In support of his opinion he appeals to common sense, *i.e.* to the general belief of mankind, which he considers must be inferred from the language in common use, since it is by the ordinarily spoken language that the common beliefs of men are known. Finding therefore that the words *sense, sentiment,* taken from the Latin *sentire, sententia, sensus,* are used for expressing *judgment* or *opinion,* he concludes that men generally look upon sense and judgment as one and the same thing.

But this explanation only shows, that for a man to say to himself: ' I purpose to follow common sense,' is no absolute security against error. For the general sense of mankind, like a volume written by a most wise and learned hand, requires to be read with great circumspection and discernment.

Indeed, if it be true that men generally confound sense with judgment, as Reid maintains, I should say that this ought to be termed a common error, rather than a common truth. The arguments I have adduced in proof of the distinction between the sensitive faculty and the intellectual seem to me not to leave even the shadow of a doubt on this matter (See Vol. I. *passim,* but especially No. 218, &c.). But the expression, ' The sense judges,' to be excusable, must be regarded only as a compendious way of saying that ' Sensations are followed by judgments.' Nevertheless, in my opinion, this expression is often understood too grossly by the vulgar, who have never analysed the operations of their own spirit, nor distinguished between those of sense and judgment, which are most nearly akin to one another, and always conjoined. Hence if they come to reflect on them, they do not see their difference, and fall into the error of taking them for one and the same. As regards those other manners of speaking by which we say: ' So and so is of this sentiment ;' ' I am of this sentiment,' &c., to express operations proper to the understanding, I do not see any incongruity in them ; for there is in us an intellectual sense which is the principle and source of all our intellectual operations (553) : ' Est enim sensus et mentis,' S. Augustine says (*Retract.* I. 1); but this sense must not, by any means, be confounded with the corporeal senses,

ARTICLE VI.

Galluppi makes an improvement in the philosophy of Reid.

953. In the distinction made by Reid, Galluppi noticed a defect. It was this : assuming with Reid, that we *perceive* bodies by a faculty different from that by which we receive *sensations*, and that no link whatever can be shown to exist between these two faculties, scepticism in regard of our cognitions about bodies would be inevitable. For if, when affected by sensations, we are necessitated to believe in the existence of bodies for no other reason than that nature impels us to it, ours is a blind persuasion, an isolated and arbitrary assent, a mere fact with nothing to justify it in the eyes of rational beings.

Galluppi therefore rejected Reid's real distinction between *sensation* and *perception*, and considered it a mere abstraction.[1]

According to him, the perception of bodies is included in sensation, and thus our spirit finds itself placed in immediate relation with the external bodies, *by the nature of the case* indeed, but not, as in Reid's theory, *without being able to show reason* for it.

In Galluppi's system the objective and subjective (I use his own words) are two co-relatives which in the sensation form one and the same thing. He says : ' The object of perception is a condition without which the perception could not exist. The objects of our primitive perceptions are the *concretes* (*i concreti*), *i.e.* the subjects modified. Every sensation is of its nature the perception of an external subject. The relation of the sensation to the external object is not merely the relation of causality, but also the relation of the perception to its object, a relation which is essential to perception. Moreover, it is not the relation of a representation to the thing repre-

---

[1] In his *Saggio filosofico sulla critica della Conoscenza* (vol. ii. ch. vi. § 114) Galluppi says : ' In sensation, consciousness distinguishes our internal modification from the subject felt as a thing outside of us. A multitude of subjects so felt is, therefore, the *objective* which our consciousness isolates and distinguishes from the *subjective*. And as to the modifications of external realities, they are not isolated in our consciousness from the sensation ; hence the *phenomena* (*apparenze*).'

sented. I hold, therefore, that sensation is the *intuition*[1] of the object.[2]

ARTICLE VII.

What does the author's analysis of sensation, as above explained, add to the theory of Galluppi?

954. Reid, then, held that our spirit communicates immediately with external bodies,[3] but pronounced this communication inexplicable.

Galluppi, by making a better analysis of sensation, found that the perception of bodies was contained in sensation itself. He thus did away with the difficulty which Reid had considered insuperable, namely, as to how from sensation we pass to perception.

The analysis I have attempted to make of sensation gives this result, that whilst Reid had divided the perception of bodies from sensation by too wide a gap, Galluppi fell into the opposite extreme.

955. It is quite true that between sensation and the perception of an external body there is a close connection ; but this connection arises, not from the nature of sensation or of sensitivity in general, but from the special nature of acquired sensations.

In fact, I have shown that, prior to all acquired sensations, there is in us the fundamental feeling of our own body.[4] The soul being united with a body by a wonderful bond and, so to speak, interpenetration called *life*, the vital feeling pervades

---

[1] On the word *intuition* as applied to sensation see note to No. 947.

[2] *Saggio filosofico sulla critica della Conoscenza* (vol. ii. § 71).

[3] A serious defect in Reid is that he does not see in what this immediate communication consists. I have placed it in *sensation*; he, on the contrary, speaks of intellective acts which immediately lay hold of external bodies. From this error Galluppi himself is not wholly exempt ; and this betrays the *sensism* with which his system is infected.

[4] It might be asked, ' Whether the *Ego* pure and simple contains in it a passivity,' and therefore a perception. But to reply to this question, I should have to enter upon the analysis of the *Ego* itself—an argument of a higher order than I wish to treat in this work. Suffice it to say, that even if the analysis I speak of were to show that a passivity, and therefore a perception, is included in the *Ego*, this perception would have nothing to do with the perception of external bodies, which is now the subject in discussion. My present aim is, not to demonstrate in general that 'Sensation or feeling can exist in us unaccompanied by any perception,' but to demonstrate that ' We can have a sensation or feeling unaccompanied by the perception of external bodies,'

the whole extension of the sensitive body, which I therefore term its *matter*.

Hence, whilst no external sensation can exist without the first feeling, of which it is only a modification, it would not be true to say, that the human subject (*Ego*) and its animal feeling cannot exist without some external sensation.

956. As regards the external sensation, therefore, the reader will remember how and with what limitations I have found it to be connected with the perception of bodies.

The touch, I have said, communicates immediately with external bodies.

The four senses, of sight, hearing, smell and taste, communicate immediately with the stimuli respectively proper to them in so far as they are organs of touch, that is, in so far as they come into actual contact with the various corpuscles.

The sense of sight (as also, with a certain proportion, the other three senses in the manner I have explained), although not communicating immediately with bodies at a distance from us, cause us to know them through signs or *sensible species*.

957. It cannot, however, be said that the senses, even in so far as they are tactile, and therefore in so far as they place us in immediate communication with bodies, perceive the bodies themselves fully. They only perceive some corporeal elements, and, amongst them, a force acting on us, and a superficial extension. To complete the perception of bodies, *solidity* must be added, that is, space in all its three dimensions, or certainly the possibility or expectation of other tangible surfaces revealing themselves to us according to a certain law.

Now these new surfaces within that given space are discovered and perceived by means of the touch united with motion, and thus there arises within us an *expectation* of further similar discoveries, according to the same law. In this way is the sensitive perception of external bodies completed.

958. Seeing, therefore, that the sensation of touch has not, by itself alone, a full and complete perception of bodies, but perceives only some corporeal elements, I have said, that until that perception has been completed by an association of

sundry tactile sensations, it would be more correct to call it not *perception of bodies*, but *corporeal perception.*[1]

959. In this sense, it would not be inappropriate to say that we perceive bodies by means of certain tracings or impressions which they leave in us, and which are an incipient perception of them.

960. Moreover, although this *corporeal perception* comes to us immediately from the external bodies, yet it is in us, that is, in the sensation with which we feel affected by their action. Now this our 'feeling affected by their action' is a *passivity* on our part, and a passivity which extends to the whole of the *surface* embraced by the sensation itself. To be conscious therefore, as we naturally are, of this passivity, is to be conscious, (1) that something external is acting on us, and (2) that this something is *extended* (a body). It is true, that so long as this external thing, this body, is considered as acting on us, its extension and that of our sensation are identical, and therefore there is an immediate communication between it and ourselves. But when we (even by a mere abstraction) consider it in its own self, apart from the connection it has with us through its action, we find that, in ultimate analysis, its real extension is known to us only by the extension of our sensation. Considered as so divided, our sensation becomes a *similitude* of that body, *i.e.* because it has an equal extension with it. In this sense it can be said that external bodies are known to us through the *similitudes* they leave in our senses, or in our phantasy. And this proposition is thus reconciled with the other which affirms that through our senses we communicate immediately with the external world : but it is a dangerous proposition to use unless we accompany it with some sort of comment.

---

[1] The fundamental feeling of our own body is the only means by which we feel in a complete manner a solid body, namely, our own. No external sensation, taken by itself alone, gives us so much.

CHAPTER XV.

ON THE SENSITIVE AND INTELLECTUAL PERCEPTIONS OF BODIES CONSIDERED IN RELATION TO EACH OTHER.

ARTICLE I.

Distinction of the two perceptions, sensitive and intellective.

961. Amongst modern philosophers I do not know of a single one who has not, at least sometimes, confounded the *sensitive* perception of bodies with the *intellectual.*

This induces me to believe that the seizing upon the right distinction between these two perceptions is a matter of great difficulty, and that it will therefore be useful to throw as much light upon it as possible. To this object I mean to devote the present chapter, referring also, as I go on, to the vain controversies which have been occasioned by the confusion aforesaid, and which vanish the moment that confusion is removed.

962. First of all, we must consider attentively, that the sense has always a *singular* for its term. If this principle be well kept in mind, it will enable us to ascertain exactly what belongs to the sensitive and what to the intellective perception. For it necessarily leads to the following consequence: ' Whatever in the perception of bodies is found to be in any way characterised by *universality*, must be attributed to the understanding, and not to the sense.' [1]

Now what is the intellectual perception of a body? It is that act by which we judge that a certain *object* possessed of the nature of *body* really exists. It is evident that we cannot

---

[1] This truth was known and affirmed by all antiquity. Thirteen centuries ago, Boëtius expressed it very pointedly thus: 'Universale est dum intelligitur, singulare dum sentitur' (*Sup. Porphir. Proœm. in Prædic.*); and this was only repeating what Aristotle had said nine centuries before.

make this judgment if we have not in our mind the notion of *existence*, which is universal.

963. Let us, then, restrict our attention to the purely sensitive perception, and see what there really is in it.

By the fundamental feeling we feel our own body as part of ourselves. This perception is complete, but at the same time difficult to be observed and analysed. Let us turn, then, to the touch, which is the second way in which we have sensitive perception of bodies.

The tactile sensation, as such, is subjective ; but it is also *corporeal perception*, 1st in so far as it is the term of the action exercised on us by something external to us, and 2nd in so far as it presents to us this term characterised by superficial extension.

The repeated and varied sensations of the touch, which are very soon assisted by those of the sight, become associated, and create in our sensitivity the expectation of finding, by means of motion joined with the use of force, new surfaces beneath the one already perceived. The *instinctive expectation* of cases similar in kind is a law to which the sense also is subject, as experience shows. By doing certain acts a great many times, the sense acquires a habit, an inclination, a species of instinct to repeat those acts in the expectation of similar results. This instinctive *expectation* of fresh corporeal surfaces, after the first has been removed, perfects the sensitive perception.

964. We will now see what our understanding does in order to form its own perception of bodies.

So soon as the corporeal elements hitherto described have been sensitively perceived, the understanding completes the perception in the following manner.

Every sensation we experience has two relations : one on the side of ourselves who are affected by it, and in this sense it is *passion* ; the other on the side of the principle or agent which causes it in us, and in this sense it is *action*. Thus *action* and *passion* are two words indicating one and the same thing under two different and contrary aspects.[1]

[1] See also the two long notes to n. 453 (TRANSLATORS)

Now the *sense* does not perceive the thing of which we are speaking, except as *passion* and *expectation* of new passions; the understanding alone is able to perceive it as *action*.

By so doing the understanding adds nothing to the thing, but simply considers it in an *absolute* way; whereas the sense perceives it only in a particular *respect*, in a way relative to its own self. The understanding, turning off as it were its eye from us, particular subjects, looks at things in themselves; whereas the sense never dissociates itself from the particular subject to which it belongs, namely, from us.

To conceive an action as coming from outside of us is, then, proper to the understanding. But the conception of an action includes the conception of an agent; therefore the understanding, by perceiving an action as coming from outside of us, always perceives an *agent* in so far as existing in itself, that is, it perceives a *being in action.*

The understanding does all this by means of the notion of existence which it carries with itself.

When, therefore, the understanding perceives the *agent* here spoken of, as a being distinct from ourselves and *furnished with extension*, it has the *perception of a body.*

From all this we can see that our understanding, in order to perceive a body, considers simply what is supplied to us by the senses, not, however, in a way relative to ourselves, as the sense does, but in an absolute way, objectively, by applying to it the universal notion or idea of existence.

The intellectual perception of a body is therefore the union of the intuition of a being (agent) with a sensitive perception (passion). In other words, it is a judgment whereby we for the first time pronounce as subsistent the being which our understanding sees acting on our sensitivity; it is a primitive synthesis.

965. But if this judgment is abstracted from, and the body is considered only as in a state of possibility, we have then the *pure idea* or *simple apprehension* of that body.

ARTICLE II.

Locke confounds the sensitive perception of bodies with the intellective :— objections urged against him in consequence.

966. According to Locke, our soul receives simple ideas *passively* from the impressions of external things.[1] He thus confounds with *ideas* not only *sensitive perception*, but sensation also.

All antiquity, on the contrary, had held firmly that the passive sensations are not by themselves *ideas*, but that a certain activity of the understanding is requisite in order that we may, from sensations, have ideas.[2]

[1] Locke, after teaching most distinctly that our understanding does not go beyond the ideas furnished to it by sensation and reflection, concludes thus : 'In this part the understanding is merely passive' (*Of Human Understanding*, Book II. ch. i.).

[2] That a certain activity of the understanding is indispensable in the formation of ideas, is a truth handed down to us from the remotest antiquity. Plato, besides admitting a subjective intellectual activity, thought it necessary to say that ideas existed by themselves, separately from the mind. Aristotle considered activity as inherent in the human subject ; hence his 'Acting Intellect,' *i.e.* an intellect characterised by a primitive and essential act. In the Fathers of the Church, a belief in the necessity of this activity of the understanding in order to form ideas from sensations, transpires everywhere from their expressions. Let us hear with what force S. Augustine puts it: 'Et quid illa corpora sunt quæ foris per sensus carnis adamavit, eorumque diuturna quadam familiaritate implicata est, nec secum potest introrsum tanquam in regionem incorporeæ naturæ ipsa corpora inferre, imagines eorum convolvit, et rapit factas in semetipsa de semetipsa. DAT ENIM EIS FORMANDIS QUIDDAM SUBSTANTIÆ SUÆ' (*De Trin.* X. v.).—'As the soul, allured by the charms of those corporeal objects, has become enamoured of them, and through a certain long familiarity has become enslaved to them ; so it comes to pass, that, not being able to take them into itself, because corporeal things cannot enter into the incorporeal, it elaborates their images, and having thus produced them in and from itself, carries them away with it ; for in forming these images, IT GIVES THEM SOMETHING OF ITS OWN SUBSTANCE.' In this passage we may see how large a share the great Bishop of Hippo allows to the activity of the soul in the formation of ideas. Nor must it be supposed that this truth was unknown in what are styled the dark ages ; for no one, unless his mind has been vitiated by false systems, can fail to see that in forming ideas on occasion of the sensations, our understanding evidently puts forth an activity. I will adduce a testimony from the eighth century. Let us hear how the master of Charlemagne, in describing the origin of ideas, makes use of phrases which unmistakably point to the intellectual activity : 'Nunc autem consideremus' (writes Alcuin) 'miram velocitatem animæ in formandis rebus quas percipit per carnales sensus, a quibus quasi per quosdam nuntios quicquid rerum sensibilium cognitarum vel incognitarum percipit mox in seipsa eorum ineffabili celeritate format figuras, informatasque in suæ thesauro memoriæ recondit.'—'Let us now consider the wonderful rapidity of the soul in forming the things which it perceives through the corporeal senses, from which, as by so many messengers, it perceives whatever sensible things it perceives' (not, be it well observed, *all* things, but *sensible* things), 'known or unknown, forms at once in itself, with unspeak-

967. This error of Locke was at last noticed. It was clearly seen that in order to form ideas, an operation of the understanding on the sensation is necessary. But when the nature of this operation had to be defined, modern philosophers were divided in opinion.

Laromiguière considered ideas to be a product of the meditation of the understanding on the sensations. This was a step in advance : it only remained to state precisely in what that *meditation* consisted. Laromiguière reduced it to a simple *analysis* ; and hence he defined an idea as 'A distinct sensation, a sensation evolved out of other sensations' (vol. ii. ch. i.).

Galluppi also looked upon ideas as a product of *meditation* on the sensations ; but found that Laromiguière was wrong in restricting that *meditation* to analysis. He observed that analysis cannot give us the ideas of *relation*, since these ideas, by the admission of Laromiguière himself, require a comparison, and therefore a *synthesis*. Besides, they have no external reality, and consequently are unable to act on our senses. On these grounds, Galluppi thought it necessary to

able celerity, their images and, having informed these images, lays them up in the treasury of its memory.' And a little further on, he gives the following definition of the soul : 'Anima, seu animus, est spiritus intellectualis, rationalis, SEMPER IN MOTU, semper vivens bonæ malæque voluntatis capax.' And of its activity he speaks thus : 'Nec etiam aliquis potest satis admirari, quod sensus ille vivus atque cœlestis, qui mens vel animus nuncupatur, tantæ mobilitatis est, ut ne tunc quidem, cum sopitus est, conquiescat' (*De Animæ Ratione ad Eulaliam Virginem*).— 'The soul is a spirit, intelligent, rational, ALWAYS IN MOTION, ever living, capable of willing good or evil.' . . . 'Nor again can we sufficiently admire the mobility of this living and celestial sense, called mind or soul, a mobility so great, that even when we are asleep, it is not still.' Five centuries later, S. Thomas and the rest of the Schoolmen taught the same doctrine on the necessity of an intellectual activity in order that sensible things might be perceivable by the understanding. Of this, I have elsewhere given incontrovertible proofs. And it is singular to find how S. Thomas not only denies to sensations the capacity to be of themselves perceptions of the mind, but also affirms that it is not enough for them to be *abstracted*, unless they are first *universalised* by this faculty, as is clear from the following passage :—'Formæ sensibiles, vel a sensibilibus abstractæ, non possunt agere in mentem nostram nisi quatenus per lumen intellectus agentis immateriales redduntur, et sic efficiuntur quodammodo homogeneæ intellectui possibili, in quem agunt' (*De Verit.* X. vi. ad 1).—'The sensible forms, that is, the forms abstracted from sensible things, cannot act on our mind except in so far as they are rendered immaterial by the light of the acting intellect, and thus rendered in some way homogeneous with the possible intellect whereon they act.'

We may therefore safely say that all ages have recognised this fact, that, 'For the acquisition of ideas, an activity of the understanding is necessary.'

supplement Laromiguière's analysis by *synthesis*, and wrote
thus : 'Some simple ideas are a product of the analysis of the
sensible objects, whilst others proceed from synthesis. Some
simple ideas are objective, that is, they correspond to some
realities ; others are subjective, that is, they do not correspond
to any object outside our spirit ; they are simply intuitions of
the spirit itself, originating from its synthetic faculty' (*Saggio
filosofico sulla critica della Conoscenza*, vol. iii. ch. i.).

968. This was a further step in the reconstruction of
philosophy. But did Galluppi study well the conditions under
which intellectual *analysis* and *synthesis* are alone possible ?
I think not ; and this omission caused him to miss the mark.

In fact, as I have already observed, a reflection or meditation, a synthesis or an analysis which adds nothing to our
sensations, can never produce an idea ; for it never gets
beyond the sensations themselves ; it terminates and rests in
them ; it becomes as it were individualised with them. The
intellectual operation therefore which forms ideas must be
such as to *add* to the sensations the *universality* which they
have not in themselves. Without this, we shall always remain
with pure sensations alone.

Now to *add universality* to a sensation simply means to
see it under a universal aspect, that is to say, not merely in
the individual entity which it has precisely now and here,
but first of all in that entity which, because *purely possible*,
admits of being realised at any time and in any place, and
lies therefore outside our actual perception ; in short, it means
to see that sensation in its essence, or what comes to the
same, in its idea. Such, and no other, is the kind of *meditation* necessary in order that, from sensations, ideas may be
formed. There must be in it an intellectual activity capable
of considering things, not in so far as actually existent, but
in their intrinsic nature, and as a 'possible' that can be
realised independently of any limit as to time or place. This
activity, this abstraction, this species of analysis, evidently
presupposes in us the idea of *thing* in general ; it presupposes
the knowledge 'that every sensation or sensitive perception,
everything which affects our senses has, besides its individual

existence, an essence or a possible existence.' Thus the
intuition of *possible being* is a condition, without which a
meditation capable of producing ideas from sensations is
inconceivable.

The same conclusion is arrived at by examining in particular what are the requirements of *synthesis.*   I have shown
that no comparison can be instituted between two or more
things without an antecedent *idea* with which to compare
them.   Synthesis therefore supposes in us some universal
ideas as already formed (180–187).   Had Galluppi only
asked himself the question, ' What are the conditions necessary for that meditation which from sensations forms ideas,'
I am sure that his natural perspicacity would at once have
seen the truth I am stating ; nor would he, therefore, have
committed himself to a sweeping denial of all innate ideas, or
attributed the origin of ideas to an intellectual activity vague,
wholly insufficient for the purpose assigned to it, and inexplicable.   He would thus have extricated himself from the
meshes of Sensism.

ARTICLE III.

*Reid understood better than the other philosophers the activity of the
human spirit in the formation of ideas, and yet he fell into the same
error as they.*

969. Reid understood better than the other modern philosophers the nature of that activity by which the human spirit
on occasion of sensations forms ideas.

He could clearly see the inconsistency of Locke, and
demonstrate that this writer, after representing sensitivity as a
purely passive faculty, when he comes to speak of it as the
source of ideas, associates with it a judgment, without perceiving that judgment must, according to his principles, be an
operation posterior to ideas, and consequently cannot be
their cause.

Reid therefore distinguished perception from sensation,
and said that the latter is passive and incapable of yielding
ideas, whilst the former is active and consists in a spontaneous and natural judgment which engenders in us the
persuasion that the external bodies exist.

He maintained that sensation has no similarity whatever to perception, but that perception always follows immediately upon it by an inexplicable law of nature, and that this proximity is the reason why in common discourse judgment is attributed to the sense—a manner of speaking he praises and defends.[1]

'I cannot pretend,' he says, 'to assign the reason why a word which is no term of art, which is familiar in common conversation, should have so different a meaning in philosophical writings.[2] I shall only observe, that the philosophical meaning corresponds perfectly with the account which Mr. Locke and other modern philosophers give of judgment. For if the sole province of the senses, external and internal, be to furnish the mind with the ideas about which we judge and reason, it seems to be a natural consequence, that the sole province of judgment should be to compare those ideas, and to perceive their necessary relations.'

'These two opinions seem to be so connected that one may have been the cause of the other. I apprehend, however, that if both be true, there is no room left for any knowledge or judgment, either of the real existence of contingent things, or of their contingent relations' (*Essays on the Powers of the Human Mind*, Essay VI. ch. ii.).

970. How ought Reid to have proceeded after this observation? Having perceived the *necessity of a judgment* for the formation of ideas, he should have inquired into the

[1] And yet, according to his principles, he ought, in this manner of speaking, to recognise a common error; for, to say 'the sense judges' is to confound sensation with perception; two things which he, nevertheless, takes great pains to distinguish from each other, declaring over and over again that they are entirely different in kind and dependent on principles which no power of observation is able to reduce to unity. If, therefore, the common expression cited by him attributes the two operations of sensation and perception (judgment) to the one faculty of sense, clearly the testimony to which he appeals in support of his system is all against him. So difficult is it often-times to ascertain what collective mankind think, or to know whether they think aright; nay more, whether on certain things they have any opinion at all!

[2] According to Reid, the word *sense*, as used by philosophers, means, 'A faculty which gives us ideas without any judgments;' but, as used in common discourse, it means, 'A faculty which gives us ideas together with a judgment.' This observation of Reid confirms the fundamental proposition of the present work with the authority of mankind at large, who in their way of speaking show that they believe 'A judgment of the mind to be necessary for the formation of ideas.'

conditions necessary to render that judgment possible. The analysis of judgment would have revealed to him the absolute necessity of an antècedent *universal idea.*

But whether it was that his courage failed him, or that he felt unequal to the task, or that the strong aversion which the philosophical education of his time inspired to admitting even the least intellectual element as connate with the human spirit, deterred him from an analysis which would inevitably have forced upon him that admission ; he suddenly stopped, and contented himself with saying that the judgment in question emanated from human nature itself acting under a law *of which no explanation could be given.*

Galluppi was not satisfied with language so vague, and felt convinced that the perception of bodies could not be a thing entirely different from sensation. He took therefore to examining the relation between these two facts with the object of re-uniting them if possible ; and as a result he concluded that every sensation was of its nature a perception, and that it was of the essence of perception to perceive something, namely, to have an *object.* Thus did he bring back that confusion which Reid had striven so hard to banish.

But any one who considers this matter carefully, will see that the divergence of these two able writers arose from not having understood the true distinction between *sensitive* and *intellective* perception.

Reid's attention fell on the intellective perception, and he saw that it must be something wholly different from sensation ; since it required a *judgment*—the operation of a faculty essentially active, whereas the sense considered by itself alone, is a passive faculty.

Galluppi thought of the *sensitive perception*, and saw that it is conjoined with sensation, or rather contained in it : hence he denounced as an error the division established by the Scottish philosopher.

In consequence of his mind being wholly taken up with this species of perception, Galluppi was not in a position to estimate correctly the amount of intellectual activity demanded by the formation of ideas. He could indeed see

that ideas are produced by the meditation of the understanding on the sensations; he understood better than
Laromiguière the nature of this meditation, for whilst the
latter had limited it to analysis, he demonstrated the necessity of a synthesis; but here he stopped.

Had he continued his inquiry, had he submitted to analysis the *synthesis* itself, he would have discovered that this
operation was impossible without a *judgment*: hence he
would, like Reid, have been able to appreciate the full extent
of the intellectual activity necessary for the generation of
ideas. Having thus found the necessity of a *primitive judgment*, he could easily have detected the need of a universal
idea anterior to the judgment: and in this way he would,
both, have grasped the nature of the *intellectual perception* of
bodies, and laid open the source from which alone it could be
derived.

971. The natural steps, therefore, by which philosophy
arrives at the discovery of the *idea of being present by nature
to the human spirit*, when considered, not in the chronological
order, but in that of the philosophical doctrines, are as
follows :—

Firstly. It is believed that sensations are substantially the
same as ideas (Locke).

Secondly. It is seen, that ideas depend on *meditation* on
the sensations.

Thirdly. This meditation is analysed and believed to consist in *analysis* alone (Laromiguière).

Fourthly. A deeper examination of it reveals the need of
synthesis also (Galluppi).

Fifthly. But a synthesis is impossible without a judgment;
hence that meditation must be an act of the faculty of *judgment* (Reid).

Sixthly. The analysis of this faculty shows the necessity
of antecedent universal ideas.

Seventhly. These ideas are classified and their connection
is investigated. By taking a consecutive series of them, it is
found that some have greater extension than others, and

that the less extensive can be easily derived from the more extensive.

Lastly, the consequence is drawn, that the most universal idea of all, not having any other idea above it more extensive than itself, cannot be derived from any. This, therefore, is the primal idea; and in it one sees the possibility of the judgments (No. 5) which are necessary for the formation of all other ideas.

ARTICLE IV.

Continuation.

972. What I have said of Reid shows that he was fully alive to the necessity of distinguishing sensation from the intellectual perception of bodies, but overlooked the middle term between the two, namely, the *sensitive perception*. Hence his contention that sensation and intellectual perception, although conjoined as to time, are entirely different in nature.

Nevertheless Reid, in many parts of his writings, furnishes us with unmistakable evidence that his notions of the intellectual perception and of the idea of bodies, were far from clear and distinct. This he owed to the prejudices of his day, when for a man to suppose that there could be a source of knowledge higher than acquired sensation was enough to make him an object of derision.[1]

---

[1] To see how general was the confusion of thought which followed the time of Locke, and how completely the distinction between sensations and ideas had been lost, it will suffice to observe how it became the fashion to apply the name of *Idealists* to Berkeley, Hume and their followers. These writers had deliberately set to themselves the task of reducing all human cognitions to *sensation* alone; and in support of their system they argued thus : ' The sensations are in us; therefore the external world is in us.' Hence, as they called sensations *ideas*, so they called themselves *Idealists*; and everybody gave them the same name; whereas their proper appellation should have been purely that of *Sensists*. This observation accounts also for a fact which at first sight seems a puzzle; I mean the very close affinity existing between *Idealists* and *Materialists*. When we consider that the term *Idealists* is applied here in an improper signification, and that it only means *Sensists*, the wonder ceases; for any one can see that from *Sensism* to *Materialism* the transition is very easy. In the meantime, however, that *surprise* which is generally felt at seeing philosophers who style themselves *Idealists* so very easily consorting with *Materialists*, is an involuntary testimony of the conscience of mankind, which thus deposes to its being fully aware of the difference between *ideas* and *sensations*, although philosophers seem to have forgotten it.

973. This is seen especially where, in referring to the teaching of Aristotle, he confounds the *sensible species* of this philosopher with *ideas*.

The sensible species have nothing to do with ideas. When I receive a visual sensation, I receive a sensible species of the distant body. The body which I perceive by means of that species has not touched me ; what has touched me is the light reflected therefrom. The species is, therefore, unquestionably different from the tangible body, to which through habit I refer it.

Now this *visual species* of the body is quite another thing from the *idea* I have of the body perceived.

The *idea* is essentially universal, the *species* is essentially singular.

The *idea* supplies me with the definition of the body ; the *visual species* serves me only as a *sign* of it.

To have the *idea* and the *intellectual perception* of the body, I must judge, (1) that a being *exists*; (2) that this being has modified me by *acting* on me in a mode determined by extension and other sensible qualities. In order to do this, I must, (1) feel affected by the sensible qualities ; (2) by means of the touch and of motion, perceive these qualities as proceeding not from me, but from something which acts on me from without (sensitive perception) ; (3) make a judgment to the effect that this something which so acts on me, partakes of existence. In short, intellectually to perceive a body, is to perceive it as one of the 'possibles' that has been realised, and in that form, or with those determinations which my senses present to me.

Now nothing of this is required for my having the *visual sensible species*: not the intellect (the faculty which has the intuition of being in general) ; not the judgment (the faculty which applies the idea of being in general to the singulars perceived by the sense) ; not even the sensitive perception itself. It suffices that I have the visual faculty which is common to animals, without my associating with the visual sensation any other sensation, operation or idea.

974. Possibly, Reid was misled by the metaphorical

language used by Aristotle. The Greek philosopher describes the *sensible species*, the *phantasms*, and the *intelligible species* or ideas, as being substantially one and the same thing—as little images, or εἴδωλα, which, falling in succession under the action of the three powers of *sense, imagination* and *intellect*, become gradually purified and spiritualised, like a liquid or a powder which grows more and more refined by passing through different sieves or filters, one of finer structure than the other.[1]

975. Reid, then, viewed all these affections indiscriminately as a *medium* of communication between things and ourselves, and combated them all, thus involving *sensible species, phantasms* and *ideas* in a common destruction.

Hence, also, he speaks of Plato's *ideas* in the same strain as he does of the *sensible species* of Aristotle, as if both fell under the same category, so that the arguments which told against the latter would likewise destroy the former—a destruction, which, to say the plain truth, is impossible.[2]

[1] *Essays on the Powers of the Human Mind* (Essay I. ch. i.). Dugald Stewart, a disciple of Reid, repeats the same error in his *Elements of the Philosophy of the Human Mind*, (ch. i. sec. i).

[2] (1) Reid asserts that the word *idea* has two significations, *i.e.* a philosophical and a popular one. He would wish us to discard ideas in the first, but to retain them in the second signification, the only one he thinks worthy of adoption. But is it true, that he is here in agreement with the great majority of mankind? I have already answered this question in the negative (106, &c.). What, in fact, are these two alleged significations of the word *idea*? Philosophically speaking, an *idea* is a *medium* through which we cognise external objects. Popularly speaking, an *idea* is an *act* of our mind, by which we think the objects themselves immediately. Now, how does Reid prove the existence of this second signification? Here is his argument : ' In popular language, to *have an idea* of anything is to *conceive* it. To have a distinct idea of it, is to conceive it distinctly. To have no idea of it, is not to conceive it at all. It was before observed, that *conceiving* or *apprehending* has always been considered by all men as an act or operation of the mind, and on that account has been expressed in all languages by an active verb. When therefore we use the phrase of *having ideas* in the popular sense, we ought to attend to this, that it signifies precisely the same thing which we commonly express by the active verb *conceiving* or *apprehending* ' (*Essays on the Powers of the Human Mind*, Essay I. ch. i.).

But, if he draws this consequence by observing the meaning of the phrase ' to conceive a thing,' I can draw an opposite conclusion by observing the meaning of the phrase ' to have an idea.' To *have* is precisely the same as to *possess*, and possession does not mean an *act*, but a *state*. Therefore the phrase to *have an idea* expresses nothing more than a *state* of the mind which has the idea. Now, just as I should be wrong if I were to insist on drawing from this meaning of the phrase to *have an idea*, the meaning of the phrase to *conceive a thing*; so it seems to me unreasonable to pretend that the meaning of the latter phrase shall decide the meaning of the former. I grant that the verb to *conceive* expresses an *act* or operation of

ARTICLE V.

*Do we perceive bodies through the principles of substances and of
causation ?*

976. Des Cartes said, that we know the existence of bodies
through the principle of causation ; and this opinion was em-

the mind ; but for this very reason I
deny that the two phrases mean the
same thing. Is it not true that we can
have an idea without actually conceiving,
i.e. thinking the thing to which that
idea refers? Clearly, then, the act
by which we conceive a thing is not
the same as the mere possession of the
idea of that thing. I would also observe that, so far as I am aware, the
two phrases, *to conceive a thing* and *to
have an idea*, are found current in all
languages. Now, according to Reid's
principles, this would not be the case
unless the general sense of mankind
really intended to express two different
things ; for when language constantly
marks a distinction by means of two
different words or phrases, it would be
preposterous to say that that distinction
is not really meant. Indeed it is by
this very argument that Reid, in another
place, confutes the impropriety of the
language of Hume (*Essays on the
Powers of the Human Mind*, Essay I.
ch. i.).

Is there nothing solid, then, in the
doctrine of Reid concerning the exclusion of ideas? I think there is, and I
will explain how. I admit with Reid,
that philosophers generally have erred,
not indeed in recognising a distinction
between *ideas* and the *act* which our
spirit makes when conceiving things,
but in the way in which they understood these ideas.

Reid distinguishes three things in
human thought : '(1) the thinking subject ; (2) the act which the mind makes
in thinking ; (3) the object thought or
conceived.' Following, as he says, the
common sense of mankind, he will
admit no other elements in thought but
these three. Philosophers have introduced a fourth, namely, a *medium*
between the object thought and the
thinking mind, to which medium they

have given the name of *idea* ; and this
he believes to be mere fiction (*Essay I.*
ch. i.).

It really seems that some philosophers have considered ideas as the sole
and perfect *medium* through which we
cognise real things. This is an error.
The *idea* of a thing does not, by itself,
give us the knowledge of any actual
reality. It only presents to our mind
a ' possible.' It is not, therefore, the
perfect and *entire medium* of the knowledge of real things, as S. Thomas has
observed in so many places. Something besides it is necessary in order
that we may have this knowledge. In
the case of corporeal things, there must
be the *corporeal sense*, whereby we immediately perceive the passions produced
in us by the external agents called
bodies. The *feeling* we experience of
these agents, and the *idea* joined with
that feeling, are the two elements of
our *perception* and cognition of bodies.

It would, then, be a mistaken notion
to suppose that the subsistence of bodies
becomes known to us by means of ideas
alone, as though they were *perfect
images* of those bodies. Bodies are
forces which act immediately on us, and
our sense receives this action ; but
this species of perception is not the intellectual perception of bodies. It is
we—subjects at once sentient and intelligent—who form this latter kind
of perception. Afterwards we separate
from it the *idea* (*a*), and this *idea* which
at first had for its element and matter the
experimental *feeling* of the *bodies themselves*, is what enables us to know them
in an universal or intellectual manner
(*b*).

This, I believe, is what the Schoolmen meant by saying that the *idea*
abstracts from *matter*. They meant to
say that the idea does not represent the
real and subsistent thing, that it is not

(*a*) Universalisation (TRANSLATORS).   (*b*) *I.e.* as *intelligible* or *possible* bodies (TRANSLATORS).

braced by a great many philosophers after Des Cartes, and, I speak seriously, even by so pronounced a Sensist as Destutt-Tracy.

Galluppi denied that we cognise bodies through the principle of causation; and opposed to Destutt-Tracy the following conclusive and self-evident argument: 'If external objects are cognised by means of the principle of causation, then the principle of causation is not derived from those objects' (*Saggio filosofico*, &c., L. ii. ch. i.). To this argument the French philosopher could give no reply. But I would say to Galluppi: The principle of causation cannot come from real things; it comes from the idea of being in general (569).

977. All the other arguments urged by Galluppi against the principle of causation as our means of knowing external bodies, may be reduced to the following: 'If the faculty of sense does not place us in direct communication with the external objects, the principle of causation can only create to us an external world *a priori*; and thus Idealism is inevitable.'

an adequate *image* of the real bodies, but stands in need of *sensation* in order to give us the knowledge of them. In this sense, I also admit that the idea is a kind of *image* or *similitude*, as I have explained more fully in the note to No. 107.

But I certainly do not, in any of the tactile *sensations*, recognise a *sensible species* as *really* distinct from the sensation. I say it is distinct only by the different aspect in which the *sensation* itself is considered.

These observations go to prove, that in ascertaining the opinions of philosophers, we ought to use greater diligence than was shown by Reid, lest we should attribute to them opinions which they would repudiate. Garvius, for instance, by a more careful study of the expressions of Plato, came to the conclusion that the relation established by that philosopher between ideas and external objects, was not at all that *medium* between the mind and the objects which Reid took it to be (See *Legendorum Philosophorum veterum praecepta nonnulla et exempla*).

Be this as it may, I think that on the present question Reid is right so far as this, that to call ideas a *medium* by which we know things, is a way of speaking calculated to create ambiguities. I join company with Reid in maintaining that the intellectual perception of bodies is *immediate*, that is (to use his expression), performed without the medium of any *reasoning* (*Essays on the Powers of the Human Mind*, Essay II.); because as soon as our *sense* perceives a body, the *understanding* also perceives it at once, making its first judgment upon it without anything between. The sense and the understanding are therefore two faculties which, immediately and as it were hand in hand, co-operate in the perception of bodies. The pure *idea* of body comes subsequently to the *perception*, inasmuch as in it we abstract from the actual subsistence of the body, whereas in the *perception* we think also of the *presence* and *subsistence* of the body as acting on us. In this sense, the *idea* of body is not a *medium* but an *element* of the *perception* of bodies.

This argument shows, that our author while intensely occupied with the necessity of the *sensitive* perception, forgot to observe the *intellective.*

978. I hold with him, that our spirit communicates immediately with the external world; but this implies the necessity of sensitive perception. Otherwise there would be no material to which we could apply the principle of causation ; for this principle, if left to itself alone, is sterile ; its real fecundity can be seen only by its application to particular things. But communication with the external world by sensitive perception is not as yet *intellectual perception*, in which alone the *cognition* of bodies consists.

The *sensitive perception* of bodies is immediate ;[1] it is a fact, and has therefore no need of an intellectual principle for its formation. By analysing this fact, we can very well discriminate in it, as Galluppi does, between the act of perception and its object (or rather its *term*, because, speaking properly, the *sense* has no *object*), as also the intimate and necessary connection of the one with the other.

But the *intellectual perception* of bodies is a judgment ; and a judgment requires an intellectual principle, or at least an *idea*, in other words, it requires a *universal*, which, when reduced into a proposition, takes the form of a principle. Now, this universal which enables us intellectually to perceive bodies, is the idea of existence or being in general, as has been explained throughout this work.

ARTICLE VI.

The intellectual perception was confounded with the sensitive, in respect also of the internal feeling and of the Ego.

979. Philosophers, by confounding the external sensitive perception with the intellective, mistook two facts for one.

The same confusion, the same suppression of an essential element, took place in respect of the internal sensitivity, or the feeling of our own existence. I noticed this when speaking of Malebranche (439).

---

[1] The intellectual perception also may be called *immediate* in this sense that it is formed by a first judgment.

But to make the thing still clearer, let us consider this confusion in the fundamental principle of the philosophy of Des Cartes.

'I think, therefore I exist.' Such is the corner-stone of the Cartesian edifice. But against this, there stood an objection as obvious as unanswerable. It was the following:—By saying 'I think, therefore I exist,' you evidently assume the knowledge that whatever thinks must have existence. You start therefore from the implied notion of *existence.* Consequently, before proceeding further, you are bound to account for this notion upon which the entire value of your philosophy depends.

980. If this objection had been calmly listened to, and men had put themselves on the road to which it pointed, with no other desire than to find the truth, it would have led them straight up to the principle of all philosophy, the idea of existence.

But Des Cartes made nothing of that objection, and declared instead that by the opening sentence of his philosophy, 'I think, therefore I exist,' he had not intended to announce the result of a reasoning, but a truth of immediate perception,[1] not observing that his *therefore* belied his answer.

Was not Des Cartes capable of feeling the force of the objection? Who can doubt that so powerful a thinker was capable of this and much more? But there lay in his formula a portion of truth which held him to it, so that he had not the courage to abandon it. To put the matter briefly, it was necessary to distinguish the *perception* of the EGO as a feeling, from the *intellectual perception* of the same EGO. The first was immediate and simple, given by nature; the second was also immediate, but not simple, because it supposed an universal idea, the idea of existence. Through missing this distinction, Des Cartes attributed to the intellectual perception what could only apply to the feeling. He had half the truth on his side, and his opponents had the other half; neither side was right.

981. To be convinced that Des Cartes was speaking of

[1] See his Answer to *Second Objections.*

the intellectual perception, and attributing to it what could only belong to the feeling, it is enough to observe the tenor of his language ; for language is the portraiture of ideas. 'I think' (he says), 'therefore I exist.' Could it be denied that by these words a reasoning is expressed ? What does the word *therefore* indicate but an inference ? Is *thinking* the same thing as *existing ?* Assuredly not. In our case, *thinking* is the attribute or the predicate applied to a *being*. And can we intellectually conceive a being, if we do not know what *being* in general is ? The whole of that long passage of his first meditation, where he lays down the formula, ' I think, therefore I exist,' is a continuous course of reasoning.

982. Speaking of this principle, Galluppi says : ' By that reasoning, Des Cartes simply means to say, " Our existence is a truth of such a nature that to deny it or to call it into doubt, is to confirm it " (*Saggio filosofico*, &c.). Nothing could be better said ; but to know that either by denying or by doubting our existence we confirm it, is neither more nor less than a reasoning. It is a deduction of the relation in which the act of denying or of doubting stands to *existence*. In order, therefore, to form this judgment, this synthesis, *existence* must be known separately from and antecedently to the act of denying or of doubting. If I perceived what it is "to deny" and " to doubt," and nothing more, I could not perform any intellectual operation, for in a simple perception in which all is individual, no distinction, no analysis is possible except by the aid of some universal notion or idea.' [1]

---

[1] All the arguments of Galluppi are directed to prove that the *perception of the* EGO is immediate. But I would add, that this perception may be considered either simply as a *feeling*, or as an *intellectual act*. Considered in the first way, it has not the nature of intellectual perception. To have intellectual perception of the EGO, I must make a synthesis, a judgment by which I apply the idea of *existence* [predicate] to the EGO as a *feeling* [subject], saying, *I exist*. Then it is that I have intellectual perception, because I have perceived myself not merely in relation to my particular or subjective self, but in relation to objective existence ; in other words, as belonging to the general class of *beings*. When I have this intellectual perception of myself, I have yet a third step to make, namely, to *advert* to the same perception. How am I drawn to this *advertence*, the result of the new reflection on myself ? By my attention being aroused in consequence of an unusual and vivid modification supervening in my internal activity, in a word, by my acts. Here is the proper place for the starting-point of the philosophy of Des Cartes, ' I think, therefore I exist.' The force of this proposition is equivalent to this

other : ' By making use of my thinking powers, I become *aware* that I exist.' The argument holds good with regard to *advertence*, but not with regard to simple intellectual *perception*, and still less with regard to *sensitive* perception. Indeed, philosophy could not have started from any other point. For, when is it that man begins to think philosophically? Not, certainly, while he has sensitive perceptions only ; for thus far he does not *think*. Nor yet when he has come to have intellectual perceptions, but nothing further ; for although he now *thinks*, he does not *reflect* that he thinks. This is that kind of intellectual life which most men lead. A time comes when man reflects that he thinks, and here philosophy begins. Now our mind can only set out from the state in which it actually finds itself. A man who begins to philosophise is in the state of reflection and advertence. He starts therefore from this state ; and

so did Des Cartes, when he said, ' I think, therefore I exist.' But antecedently to this state, there is that of *direct knowledge*, and that of *pure feeling*. It was therefore natural that, after Des Cartes, Locke should arise, namely, that from the examination of thought, one should go back to analyse sensation, on which thought is based. In this process, however, it was easy to miss a link in the chain, which (for many reasons which I have already indicated) is very difficult of observation and advertence ; I mean the link of our first and *direct knowledge* ; and this was, in fact, completely passed over. Des Cartes, then, set out from *reflection*, while Locke occupied himself with *sensation*. The analysis of *simple knowledge*, which stands between the two, and is the key for understanding both, was forgotten ; and this deficiency I have endeavoured to supply to the best of my ability by the present work.

CHAPTER XVI.

ON THE NATURAL DIFFERENCES BETWEEN SENSITIVELY
PERCEIVING OUR BODY AS CO-SENTIENT WITH OUR-
SELVES, AND SENSITIVELY PERCEIVING IT AS A FORCE
ACTING EXTERNALLY ON US.

ARTICLE I.

*Difference between the two principal ways of sensitively perceiving
our body, i.e. subjectively, or as co-sentient with us, and extrasubjectively, or as a force acting externally on us.*

983. Our body is felt by us with a subjective perception,
and also with an extrasubjective one, like any other body.

But though the modes of perception are two, the thing
perceived in them is one and the same. How, then, does the
one perception differ from the other? I answer :—

By sensitively perceiving our body as *external to us the
sentient subjects*,[1] we feel an *agent* ; but, by sensitively perceiving it as *sentient*, or, to speak more correctly, as *co-sentient*
with ourselves, we feel a *patient* ;[2] in other words, we, the

[1] I advisedly refrain from saying
'by perceiving our body as *object* ;' because the body is not an *object* except
in reference to the intellectual perception, which apprehends it as a *being*.
The *sensitive perception*, on the contrary, perceives only an action extraneous to the subject. Strictly speaking,
the *object* of an intellectual perception
cannot be called *active* (an *agent*) ; it
can only be designated as *present* to the
mind. It is indeed true, that in perceiving the object we put forth a certain
amount of our intellectual activity ; but
this activity does not in the least affect
the object itself. It only produces the
act by which we perceive it. On the
other hand, the object perceived, in
which we cannot produce any alteration,
and over which we have no power whatever, is what *informs* our cognition.
Hence the saying of S. Thomas : ' The
intelligible species is the formal principle of the intellectual operation, even
as the form of any agent is the principle
of the operation proper to it.'—*Species
intelligibilis principium formale est intellectualis operationis, sicut forma
cujuslibet agentis principium est pro-
priae operationis.* (Cont. Gentes, i.
xlvi.)

[2] *Feeling*, merely in so far as subjective, *i.e.* as affecting the sentient subject, is not something *done* but something *suffered*, not an *activity* but a
passivity. The same must be said of
what is *co-subject*, *i.e.* part of the sentient
subject (TRANSLATORS).

sentient subjects, feel ourselves in, and conjointly with, the body.

Action and passion are direct opposites. Therefore by those two modes we perceive the same nature indeed, but under different and contrary aspects ; in the first, as causing the sensation but not feeling it ; in the second, as feeling the sensation but not causing it.

984. These aspects are so contrary that no similarity can be found between them. Hence what we perceive in those two modes presents itself to us as two entities, two different natures. For this reason the differences are not by any means gradations within the same species, but, as I have said, they are *aspects* either of which directly excludes the other.

Nor is there question here purely of two ideas diametrically opposed to one another, *i.e.* the idea of a body as agent, and the idea of a body as patient ; but there is question of a particular action and passion such as is that of the sense. If we, the sentient subjects, consider our passion—that is, the pleasure or pain felt by us—in the external principle which causes it, we have the *agent* ; and if we consider it in ourselves who suffer it, and in whom it terminates, we have the *patient*, that is ourselves as modified by the passion.

ARTICLE II.

Has the mechanical impression made on us by external things any like-ness to the sensation which follows upon it ?

985. An external body which touches a sensitive part of our body produces in it certain movements, in other words an *impression*.

This impression is either perceivable by the sight or the touch, or inferred through reasoning. If a needle pricks my hand, I can see the puncture with my eyes, and can also lay my finger on the little wound it has made, and thus become aware of the change that has taken place in my body. But if the impression is too minute to be seen or touched, I infer it by arguing from analogy. For instance, the impression which the globules of light make in my eyes—that is to say, the

quivering of my optic nerve—is so slight and delicate, that
there is no chance of my being able to notice it by the sense
of touch.[1] So in like manner the wonderfully slight impressions produced in my nostrils, or in my palate, or in the tissue
of my acoustic nerve, by the corpuscles which severally excite
these organs, cannot be detected by the sight or the touch,
nor perhaps even by the use of the most powerful microscope.
But being cognisant of the mechanical actions of bodies, I
reasonably conclude that those most minute corpuscles act on
my eyes, nostrils, palate and ears, and must therefore produce
in them certain irritations and alterations.

The idea, therefore, which we have of a mechanical *impression* made by external bodies on our own is the same as
we have of similar impressions made on any other body ; for
example, of an imprint on wax, of a footprint on soft ground,
of a motion excited in any material substance.   These effects
fall under our touch and sight, like the changes which take
place in our body, and are followed by sensations.

986. Now I say that the *impressions* have not the slightest
resemblance to sensation considered in its subjective part ;
although, given the impressions, sensation is instantly excited.
Nay, there is between these two things a veritable opposition
or contrariety.

An imprint, a protuberance, a movement, an external
body, perceived (by the touch), is an *agent* which produces in
our organ a sensation.   The sensation on the contrary is a
passivity ; it means a *patient* (the sentient subject) feeling
sensibly affected in himself.

But *agent* is the contrary of *patient* (983).

Therefore the mechanical *impression* made on the sensitive
body, and the *sensation* in so far as subjective, are of entirely
different, nay contrary natures : each excludes the other, in
the same way that *yes* excludes *no*, and *vice versâ*.

To render this distinction more clear, let us consider the
impression made by a little ball of iron forcibly pressed down

[1] The movements made by the pupil
when struck by the light are not the
effect of the light alone, but depend also
on other physical principles, and on the
spontaneity of the soul.

into a sensitive part of our body so as to be half buried there. This painful impression will be in the form of a circular indentation equal to half the size of the ball; and in it we shall vividly feel two things: (1) the part affected by the indentation; (2) the ball which causes the affection.

Now, the feeling of the part affected, although simultaneous with and referred to the same place as the perception of the ball, is beyond all question quite different from that perception.

Suppose the part thus affected is the arm. In feeling our arm hurt we feel a *patient*; but in perceiving the ball we feel an *agent*; the two feelings are opposed and inconfusible.

The part of the arm felt is that *concave* surface which has been formed by the thrusting down of the ball; in it, therefore, a body is felt of *concave* form. The part of the ball perceived is all that *convex* surface which by its pressure violently displaces our flesh; in it, therefore, a body is felt of *convex* form.

To the *concave surface* of the arm a sensation is referred; in it, therefore, a body is felt as feeling. To the *convex surface* of the ball no sensation is referred; what is there felt is, not a body which feels, but an insensitive body which causes a feeling.

In sensation, therefore, the external body (extrasubject) and our own body (co-subject) are opposed and contrary to one another, and hence cannot by any possibility be confounded together. The sensitive perception of the external body is the sensation itself, but only in so far as that sensation is excited by an action which comes from outside of us.

We will now apply the same distinction to the *sensation* and the mechanical *impression.*

What do we mean by the word *sensation*, and what by the word *impression*?

By an *impression* we mean a thing perceived by us as an external agent; by a *sensation* we mean a thing felt by us as *sentient subjects*, felt in ourselves. Let us return to the experiment of the ball.

How do we perceive the impression (considered wholly

apart from the sensation) which the ball has made in our arm? In the same way as we perceive the ball, which is insensitive.

We look at the part which has been affected, we put our finger into the indentation. This is how we see and touch the impression made by the ball.

But do we also herein touch and see the *sensation* which we have experienced or are experiencing in consequence of that impression? Certainly not. The sensation is neither visible nor tangible; it is perceivable only by an internal feeling of our soul; it is sensible through itself.

But after we have repeatedly looked at and touched that small cavity, we say to the bystanders: 'See what an impression the action of that little ball has left in my arm.' We call what falls under our sight and touch an *impression*. Such is the value of this word. An impression is a modification which a body undergoes in the disposition of its parts, and is perceived by our sensories, principally the sight and the touch. It is not a sensation, but an external term of the sensories.

Surely, then, a mechanical *impression* made in our body has no resemblance to the tactile or visual sensation through which it is perceived! That impression can be seen and touched by others as well as by us who have received it, whilst the sensation which follows it is felt by ourselves alone.

987. And here it must be attentively observed that when we with our touch or sight perceive the impression left in our arm by the ball, new sensations arise in us, which can be analysed in the same way as we did the sensation produced in us by the action of the ball.

In fact, on touching with our finger the cavity left in the arm by the ball, we experience a feeling in which we can note two parts or elementary feelings of an opposite nature, namely:—

(1) That in the finger which touches the cavity;

(2) That of the cavity touched by the finger.

The same must be said of these two feelings as we have said of those of the arm and of the ball. We feel the finger as *co-sentient* with us, we feel the cavity as *acting on* the finger.

We feel the finger with a sensation which refers to a convex extension, we feel the cavity of our arm with a sensation which refers to a concave extension.

It is not to this cavity that we refer the sensation produced in us by touching it, but to the finger with which we touch it. The finger perceives the cavity as insensitive; and so also does the eye. In respect of the finger and of the eye, that cavity is purely the term of an external action. The finger and the eye, by touching and seeing, feel sensibly affected as parts of ourselves, the sentient subjects; the cavity feels nothing, but causes the feeling in our eye and finger.

Now that cavity is called *impression*, in so far as it falls under the sight and the external touch.

It has therefore nothing sensitive in it, but is entirely outside of the tactile or the visual sensation. It is precisely the opposite of sensation. Consequently, the *sensation* considered as subjective, and the mechanical *impression*, are as unlike each other as any two contraries can be; hence neither of them can in any way be taken as a degree or a species of the other.

ARTICLE III.

Materialism refuted.

988. All the arguments of Materialists are founded on the confusion of sensation with mechanical *impression*.

Not understanding that these two things are essentially of an opposite nature, they strive to make out some similarity between them, so as to be able to explain the first by the second, or rather in the second to find the first.

They do not reflect on the meaning attached to the words *impression, motion*, &c. All these words are extrasubjective indicating non-sensitive agents, and invented to express, not things that feel, but things external to and perceived by the senses. Thus sensation, in virtue of its very definition, is excluded from the things which these words signify.

It is therefore an abuse of language, a confusion of ideas,

---

a manifest contradiction, to pretend—as do Materialists and those who are inclined to agree with them—to explain sensation by reducing it to a *motion* in the parts of our body or to a mechanical *impression*. In order to *feel* the motion of the parts, and the *impression, sensation* is indeed required ; but *sensation*, precisely because it is sensation, needs nothing but itself, and cannot be seen, or touched, or compared to any of the things which are seen and touched.

989. Epicurus thought that our sensations consisted of certain wonderfully subtile images or forms which, issuing continually from bodies and flying about in all directions, found their way into our souls, and left in them perfect representations of the bodies themselves.

This mode of explaining sensation was only a play of the fancy, and explained nothing.

The error lay in taking what is known to us as the external term of our senses for the subjective sensation itself. Whence could Epicurus have drawn the notion of these imaginary entities, except from what we know by the senses ? They were perfect resemblances of the things which are seen and touched ; only that his fancy gave them so fine a composition that they could not be caught hold of by such gross organs as we at present possess. But sensation can be nothing of all this ; for it has no material substance to fall under our senses, to be observed with the miscroscope, or touched with an organ of greater delicacy than ours. There can be in it nothing *extrasubjective* ; it is the act itself by which the sentient subject feels, therefore the opposite of what is extrasubjectively perceived.[1]

---

[1] It seems incredible that the subjective perception of our body could ever have been confounded with the extrasubjective in so gross a manner as we find in certain Materialists, who, deluded by their imagination, suppose that they have satisfactorily explained something, when in point of fact they have only mixed up together things essentially contrary and irreconcilable. As an instance of this, take Robert Hook, who was one of the earliest members of the Royal Society of London, and frequently read papers at its *Séances.* In a lecture he gave *On Light*, and which is the seventh in his series of Lectures (I quote from Reid), he maintains that ideas are material substances. In his opinion our brain is furnished with a proper kind of matter for fabricating the ideas of each sense. The ideas of the sight, he says, are formed of a kind of matter resembling the Bologna stone or some kind of phosphorus ; the ideas of the hearing are made of some material resembling the chords of a violin, or those plates of glass which are so arranged as to take sound from the vibrations of the air ; and so of the rest. The soul may fabricate hundreds of these

H H 2

990. Aristotle described the sensations which external bodies cause in us by the simile of an impression made by a seal on soft wax, which receives in itself the form, but nothing of the matter of the seal. This simile is false and material. When we speak of the impression on the wax, we speak of a thing which we see with our eyes, and touch with our hand— therefore of a thing external to our senses. But sensation has nothing to do with this. It is not the external *agent*, but the *passion* which our sensories suffer, and which is in them, or, to speak more accurately, it is an affection of our sensitive principle. In order that the impression made on the wax might in any way resemble our sensation, it should have to feel itself; and in that case the sensation would not be explained but transferred from our flesh to the wax. There would always remain the question as to what sensation is. There would still be in the wax the *impression* and the *sensation*, the one outside of, opposed to, and incommunicable with the other, without a shadow of similarity.

991. Hume calls *sensations* by the name of *impressions*; whereupon Reid very justly observes that he ought to have stated distinctly whether by the word *impression* he meant the act of the mind, or the object of that act (*Essays on the Powers*, &c., Essay I. ch. i.). Now on this word, confusedly and improperly used, Hume builds up many sophisms.

992. Erasmus Darwin defines an idea as ' A contraction or motion or configuration of the fibres which constitute the immediate organ of sense' (*Zoonomia*, Sect. II.) [1]; and he defines sensation as ' An exertion or change of the central parts of the sensorium, or of the whole of it, beginning from one of those extreme parts of it which reside in the muscles or organs of sense' (*ibid.* Sect. V. 2). Here again the extrasubjective term of perception is confused in the grossest manner with the

ideas in a day; and as they are formed they are pushed further off from the centre of the brain where the soul resides. By this means they make a continued chain of ideas coiled up in the brain, the first of which is furthest removed from the centre or seat of the soul; while that at the other end is always at the centre, being the last idea formed.

How a sane man could abandon himself to such ravings is to me simply incomprehensible.

[1] Erasmus Darwin, like all Materialists, does not understand the true distinction between a *sensation* and an *idea*.

subjective sensation. Why were the words *contraction, motion, configuration* invented, except to signify things in which the passion of our tactile and visual organs terminates? For words signify things in so far as known to us. Sensation, on the contrary, expresses, not a term of that passion, but purely the affection of the sentient subject itself. Hence a *contraction*, a *motion*, a *configuration* can be touched and seen, at least with organs finer than ours; but is it not absurd and ridiculous to say that an *idea* is a thing which can be felt by the touch or seen by the eye, be the power of these senses ever so acute?

993. Let us take another materialist, Cabanis. The same equivocal language, the same gross confusion between the subjective and the extrasubjective, is noticeable in him all through. He does not make an *impression* wholly identical with a *sensation*; but then he says that the impression is carried to the brain, that the brain reacts, and that this reaction constitutes or completes the sensation. He sees nothing strange in establishing an analogy between the brain and the stomach, and defining the former as a *digester of thought*! And yet he is never tired of taking credit to himself for the accuracy of his philosophical expressions, for a method experimental and precise, and for mathematical-like consecutiveness in the series of his propositions.

I will therefore quote a specimen of his rigorously philosophical style: ' Dira-t-on que les mouvements organiques par lesquels s'exécutent les fonctions du cerveau nous sont inconnus? Mais l'action par laquelle les nerfs de l'estomac déterminent les opérations différentes qui constituent la digestion ; mais la manière dont ils impreignent le suc gastrique de la puissance dissolvante la plus active, ne se dérobent pas moins à nos recherches. Nos voyons les aliments tomber dans ce viscère avec les qualités qui leur sont propres ; nous les voyons sortir avec des qualités nouvelles, et nous concluons qu'il leur a véritablement fait subir cette altération. Nous voyons également les impressions arriver au cerveau par l'entremise des nerfs : elles sont alors isolées et sans cohérence. Le viscère entre en action ; il agit sur elles, et bientôt il les renvoie métamorphosées en idées, que le language de la physionomie et du geste, ou les signes de la parole et de l'écriture, manifestent au-dehors. Nous concluons avec la même certitude que le cerveau digère en quelque sorte les impressions ; qu'il fait organiquement la sécrétion de la pensée' (*Rapport du physique et du moral de l'homme*, Mémoire II.). With what assurance does this man speak ? Is it not surprising that with ideas so confused he should imagine that he sees everything as clear as daylight ?

That contemporaneously with the sensation which we are conscious of feeling, our eye perceives our external organs in a new configuration, impressions made in them, motions in a word, is unquestionably true. But the only inference that can be legitimately drawn from this fact is, that the order of the subjective modifications—that is, those which we suffer in ourselves—and the order of the extrasubjective modifications— that is, those which the action of an external body produces in our sensitive organs materially considered—though utterly dissimilar in their nature, are related to each other by a law which ought to be diligently observed and ascertained. It will therefore be very useful, while we are experiencing this or that species of sensation, to note well what motions and configurations are presented to our touch and sight in the organs affected. But since, at the same time, our sensation is a thing which cannot be externally seen or touched (and to say otherwise would be an absurdity, an unintelligible jargon), we shall always have to distinguish it from the motions and configurations exhibited to our sight and touch. Indeed these impressions exist for us and have a name solely because they are terms perceivable by our external organs of sense, there being no other faculty capable of perceiving them.

Our philosophic physician would not have fallen into so strange a confusion and cloudiness of mind if he had curbed his imagination and contented himself with taking facts for his guide, as he so emphatically professes to do. To him it seems manifest that we *see* the impressions go up through the nerves to the brain, even as we *see* the food go down into the stomach ; and that we *see* the brain returning to us these impressions changed

into ideas, judgments, &c., as we *see* the stomach sending off
the food in an altered state into the alimentary channels.
Now as to the digestive virtues of the stomachs of fowls and
other animals, as also to the various transformations which
food successively undergoes in the process of assimilation, I
am well aware of Spallanzani's manifold experiments and discoveries.   But with regard to those *brain-digested* impressions
about which Cabanis feels quite positive that we are *fully as
certain* as about the digestion of the stomach, I must confess
that I have never read or heard of any experimentalist having
attempted to demonstrate anything of the kind.   It would
indeed be extremely interesting could we, by dissecting various
animals, catch the *impressions* as they are being conveyed in
the nerve-filaments, and extract them as we do the food from
the alimentary channels, or else detect them in the brain at
different stages of *digestion*—now as ideas, now as judgments,
and now again as groups of ideas and of judgments—and thus
be able to submit them to the microscope, or take of them
any other experiment we might think fit, just as in the case
of the food.   Cabanis gives us his word that these impressions
are *seen* to enter the brain, as food is seen to enter the stomach ;
but all I can say is, that if he has seen them, neither I nor any
one else that I know of has ever had this privilege.   I wish,
however, to observe that the germ of his error is noticeable in
his expressions themselves.   Taking a most superficial view
of his subject, he assumes that all we know we know it by
means of the sight and the touch and the other senses, and
that nothing exists except what falls under our external observation.   In this supposition ideas also must, as a matter of
course, be seen with the eye, and touched with the hand ;
for we have knowledge of them.   That such is his belief we
can clearly perceive by his phraseology, which is all borrowed
from the sense of sight, and applied to sensations and ideas
no less than to the food received into the stomach.   But as
to his being totally ignorant of the other source of our cognitions—namely, *internal experience*—and his reducing everything to the external experience of the senses, the following
passage will leave no doubt in our mind :—' Nous n'avons

d'idée des objets que les phénomènes observables qu'ils nous présentent : leur nature ou leur essence ne peut être pour nous que l'ensemble de ces phénomènes' (*ibid.*).   Having thus excluded the facts of the internal feeling and of consciousness, he was inevitably thrown on the absurd and material system of *Empiricism.*   Such was the consequence of that miserably defective observation which overlooks and excludes the series of the most elevated facts which our nature contains, and on which we, subjects at once sentient and intelligent, can bestow our attention.

994. It must however be acknowledged that the distinction between the *subjective* and the *extrasubjective* is not easy to grasp.   This plainly appears from the fact that even writers of very high philosophical attainments employ, quite unconsciously and unsuspectingly, expressions which, by their inexactness, favour materialism, and thus serve this wretched and ignoble doctrine like so many little roots which keep it, as it were, so fastened to the soil that it can never be eradicated altogether.[1]

[1] Reid deserves much credit for having reprehended the use in philosophy of certain forms of expression which, by their inexactness, lead to Materialism.   For instance, to say that sensation takes place by way of an *impulse* of the nerves on the soul, is to express a supposititious and material imagination. Reid notices this in Locke.   'Mr. Locke,' he says, 'affirms very positively that the ideas of external objects are produced in our mind by impulse, that being the only way we can conceive bodies to operate in us ;' and he shows how gratuitous is this reason given by Locke.   Respecting this opinion of Locke, however, it is right to observe that he retracted it in his first letter to the Bishop of Worcester, and promised to have the obnoxious passage rectified in the next edition of his *Essay.*   But, ' either from forgetfulness in the author ' (it is Reid who speaks) ' or negligence in the printer, the passage remains in all the subsequent editions I have seen ' (*Essays on Powers of the Human Mind,* Essay II. ch. iv.).   In like manner the able Scotsman calls attention to the ambiguity likely to arise from the phrases *outside* or *inside the mind,* and others like them taken from the extrasubjective perception of bodies.   The expression *outside* and *inside the mind,* to have a correct meaning, must not be understood as relating to *place,* but only as indicating that ideas either are in the *thinking subject* or are not at all. Nevertheless, it seems to me that sometimes Dr. Reid is too severe in his censure of certain phrases which, to my thinking, are quite allowable, even when taken in a proper sense ; such, for example, as the word *representation,* applied to the mind.   It is true that this word is usually taken to signify something exhibited before our eyes in space.   But I would remark that, even if we restrict our attention to thought alone, we can, and indeed must, conceive that what our mind thinks of is *represented* to it ; for on the object of its thought the mind has no power ; it does not pervade nor become identified with that object ; the object is always distinct from and inconfusible with it ; and it appears to me that this manner in which the object is in the mind may be fittingly expressed by the word *representation,*

ARTICLE IV.

The line of demarcation between Physiology and Psychology.

995. The distinction between *sensation* and *impression*— between our subjective feeling, and what we perceive *extra-subjectively*—fixes the line of demarcation between Physiology and Psychology.

Physiology and Medicine are and can only be the product of *external observation*—namely, the observation which is made by means of the touch, the sight and the other sensories. Psychology, on the contrary, is the result of *internal observation*—namely, of all that takes place in our consciousness.

Physiology and Medicine deal with the body as an external *object* ; Psychology deals with the soul, and with the compound of soul and body in so far as it is *subject*.

Physiology investigates the natural state of our body, the different effects to which it is subject, the classification of these effects, their uniformity, or the laws according to which it operates. Now all these effects, changes, modifications, laws, to which our body is subject are simply so many *terms* of the touch, the sight, and the other senses, and so many *objects* of the understanding. In this science, therefore, the body is considered as a thing purely external and objective.

The same must be said of Medicine: it takes note of the morbous changes or modifications of the human body, and of the remedies by which it can be restored to health ; and all this by a continual use of *external observation*.

996. It is indeed true that, even in these sciences, regard must be had to what passes in our consciousness ; but this is not the scope to which they tend and in which they terminate. If they turn their attention to man's affections, or to the influence which an intense mental application has on the body, this is purely in view of ascertaining the effects produced by these things. If they take note of the effects which

&c. I am furthermore of opinion that certain expressions which apply to the sense of sight may also be applied to the understanding, not only in a metaphorical, but in a proper sense ; because these two powers, although entirely different in their nature, operate in a way analogous to each other.

the different habits of the body produce on the soul and on the intellectual faculties, this is only that they may find the way to bring the body to that sound condition which will best enable it to serve the soul. In all these investigations the Physiologist and the Physician study the body by means of external observation, and therefore purely as *object.*

The Psychologist, on the contrary, depends on another kind of observation, the internal. The facts of consciousness are the objects which engage his attention. He considers the EGO, the *Subject* ; and if he regards the body as *Object*, this is simply on account of the relation which the body has with the Subject. He does not end in that. The interior consciousness is the proper scope and subject-matter of the science he cultivates ; all other things are nothing but means or helps to it.

997. Hence we may conclude, that even if an Anatomist could with his dissecting knife succeed in laying open to the eye the minutest fibres in the body of animals, and if microscopes were invented of such magnifying power as to reveal the intimate texture of bodies in a manner incomparably more perfect than has hitherto been attained ; yet, if the interior observation of the facts of consciousness be taken away, the Psychological science would not derive any benefit from these discoveries, nor advance a single step.

ARTICLE V.

On the systems that have been propounded concerning the union of our soul with the body.

998. So long as our body is considered as it presents itself externally to the senses, its nature is entirely dissimilar from that of the soul, and therefore no possibility can be seen of the one communicating with the other.

Nay, it could be demonstrated that, speaking of our body in this sense, any sort of communication between it and the soul would be a contradiction in terms.

999. Now I must observe that it has always been the custom to consider the body under this limited aspect : hence

some philosophers of great ability, seeing the absurdity of which I speak, rejected the '*Physical-influx*' theory altogether, and took to devising other systems; among which that of *Occasional causes* by Malebranche, and that of *Pre-established harmony* by Leibnitz, are the most celebrated.

But the necessity of these systems arose simply from an incomplete observation of our body—namely, from its having been considered only partially, that is, in so far as it is out-side of us, the sentient subjects;[1] whereas it ought to have been considered as co-sentient or *co-subject* with ourselves; for the question was merely as to How the body could be, together with the soul, the subject of sensations?

1000. It was erroneously imagined that the union of the body with the soul could be conceived to be like the com-mixture of two fluids, or the binding together of two solids into one block, both of which things fall under our external experience, can be seen by the eye, touched by the hand, and sensibly experimented upon in many ways. Only it was imagined that the soul is of so subtile a nature as to escape external observation, even when aided by the use of instru-ments; but this always on the assumption that it was itself like one of the most minute visible substances, and that its union with the body was effected like those between sub-stances of this description; and consequently that it could also be observed by the senses, provided their perceptive powers were adequate to the purpose.

1001. Instead of this it should have been distinctly under-stood, that, to know what our body really is, we must not be content with the external observation, but must furthermore have recourse to the internal; and that the body thus observed is found to be very different from what it appears to the ex-ternal senses, with other properties more intimate and *essential* —properties which cause us to know it as *matter* of our fun-damental feeling, and joint cause thereof.

It was therefore necessary, setting aside all external images,

---

[1] If whatever we sensibly perceive is outside of us, how could an action which takes place *in* us be explained by that which, essentially and by the hypothesis, is outside of us?

to enter into oneself, to consult one's own consciousness, to reflect on the feeling of the *Ego*, and thence to draw the concept of that union which it was sought to explain.

Thus it was in the fundamental feeling itself that the body could have been discovered, conformably with the thought of St. Thomas ; since it is in that feeling (and consequently in the soul) that we feel that action which is characterised by a *mode* and a *term* called *extension* or *space*.

1002. In the feeling of the *Ego* there is, therefore, found the action of a force different from the *Ego*, but which the *Ego* feels, and, in feeling it, expands the feeling of its own self into an extended term.

This feeling, into which the *Ego* is drawn by a natural force (in respect of which it is passive), is a fact.   Therefore the union of our soul with the body ought to have been accepted as *a fact* certified by observation on ourselves ; as a primitive fact, a fact which is our nature itself. Had this been done, the difficulties of admitting this union could not even have been conceived ; there would no longer have been any sense in them.

ARTICLE VI.

Relation between our body considered as EXTERNAL *to us and as* CO-SUBJECT *with us.*

1003. The subjective and extrasubjective ways, then, of perceiving our body, give us two concepts of it, which are not merely different, but contrary in some way to one another— the concept of *co-subject* and the concept of *extrasubject*.

This contrariety arises solely from the limitation of the two concepts, in consequence of which limitation the one excludes the other.

Hence, when the body is considered in these two different concepts, contrary propositions are the result.

The two following may serve as examples :—*The body is in the soul*, and *The soul is in the body*.

Both these propositions are true, but they relate to the two opposite concepts of the body.

It is true that *the body is in the soul* when the body is

considered as subjective ; because in this case the body is only an *agent* operating in the soul.

It is true that *the soul is in the body* when the body is considered as extraneous to the subject, and the soul is considered in the effects which it produces in this *extrasubject*.

1004. I say in the *effects*, because if we consider a soul in its own self, it is a *Subject*, and can neither be a term of corporeal feeling, nor commensurate itself with a place.

Hence, if the intelligent soul is considered in itself (as *Subject*), and is compared to the body or the ' extended,' we have a third proposition which is also true—namely, that *the soul is not in any place* because it is *simple*.

All these distinctions serve to do away with a great number of difficult questions, which, unless we correct our phraseology and reduce it to philosophical propriety, can never be put an end to.

ARTICLE VII.

On the matter of the fundamental feeling.

1005. When treating of the fundamental feeling, and of the subjective part of sensation, which is a modification of the same, I observed that, properly speaking, we cannot say that this feeling has an *object*, but can say only that it has a *matter* wherein it terminates.

When, however, the operation of the understanding is added to that of the senses, we perceive external *objects* and give them the name of *bodies*. But, on reflection, we discover that among the bodies so perceived there is one which constitutes the *matter* of our feeling, which we therefore call *our* body.

Now, what is the difference between *object* and *matter*? This point deserves careful investigation.

1006. Our body, whether in its natural state or in its modifications, presents two aspects. In so far as felt by our fundamental feeling, it is the *matter* of this feeling ; and in so far as perceived by the special organs of sense, it is their *term* as well as their *stimulus*, and thereafter an *object* of the understanding. This is as much as to say that the *matter* of the feeling is something between the pure *subject* and the *term* of the feeling. It is not the sentient subject, for it is the thing felt ; and it is not a pure *term* of the feeling itself, for the feeling does not exist without it.

1007. The first difference, therefore, between the *matter* and the *object* of a faculty consists in this, that the object is not essential to the subsistence of the faculty, whereas the matter is a constitutive element of the faculty, so that, if we abstract from it, the faculty is no longer conceivable. Thus, without light, air, odoriferous or saporiferous particles, a man would not have the sensations of colour, sound, smell or taste ; and yet he could, for all that, be conceived as possessed of the several organs of these sensations in a sound and perfect state. Why so ? Because those stimuli are not the *matter* of the sensories, but only *terms* of their acts, and *objects* when perceived by the understanding.

1008. This difference between matter and object cannot be thoroughly grasped unless by forming a correct notion of what a *faculty* is. Be it then understood that every faculty is a *primal act*, which, given the necessary conditions, produces other acts, varied according to the variety of the conditions. Now, this primal and permanent act is called *faculty* in respect of the secondary and transient acts. Every faculty must therefore consist in a certain *activity*, kept, as it were, in a state of tension, and ever ready to issue forth into this or that act, according as occasion offers, like a cross-bow ready for discharge. With this concept of a faculty well fixed in our mind, we shall see that, even as every *secondary act* requires an external term for its production, so the faculty or *primal act*, in order to exist and to be thinkable, requires its own internal term. Again, as the faculty, unlike its operations, is something permanent, so also must its internal term be something permanent ; for the faculty and its term stand and fall together. Consequently, if we take away the term of its operation, the faculty still remains ; but if we take away its own internal term, the faculty no longer exists.

1009. Now the *matter* is precisely a permanent term, proper to certain faculties, and forming one thing with them.

But since this term conjoined with the faculties contributes to make them what they are, and cannot be conceived separate from them, it is therefore designated by the name of *matter*, and not simply by that of *term* ; this latter word being also applicable to everything in which the acts of a faculty terminate externally.

Nevertheless the character of indivisibility from the faculty does not, by itself alone, suffice to constitute the *matter* of a faculty ; because every faculty has a term, but not every faculty has a matter.

1010. The second difference, therefore, between the *object* and the *matter* of a faculty is this—that the object, as such, is neither passive nor passible ; [1] whilst the matter, as such, presents itself to our mind both as without activity in respect of the faculty, and as liable to receive modifications.

The objects of my cognitions do not act as *stimuli* on my mind, they simply reveal themselves to it by informing it. On the contrary, the impression, for example, of the external light on my eye is a sort of violent action which, besides being a term to my sensitivity, draws it out into the act of sensitive perception. And speaking in general, the objects of cognition hold, in respect of the cognitive faculties, if not an active, certainly an impassive state. They are *present to the mind*, and that is all. The terms of our practical faculties, on the other hand, hold a passive state.

Now, when the term of that *primal act* which constitutes the faculty itself is of the impassive kind, and present to the faculty in such a way that the latter is, in respect of it, simply a recipient, we then call it *object* and not merely *term*, though it is this too ; nor yet do we call it *matter*, because this word,

---

[1] It is customary to say, for example, that a bar of iron struck by a hammer is the *object* of the action of the hammer, and so of everything which a mechanical force or instrument acts upon ; and this seems to agree with the etymology of *objectum* (a thing set opposite to another). But this way of speaking proceeds from the manner in which our mind conceives these things, so that the notion of *object* is added by the mind. If we abstract from this addition, neither of the two material things *has* anything outside itself ; and if, through coming violently into collision, they should happen to break each other or to be altered in their structure, there will be mutual clashing of forces, but there will not be *objects* ; for the concept of *object*, as such, implies unchanged identity and impassibility.

as I have observed, means something passive or modifiable. And we also call it the *form* of the faculty, *i.e.* an object of such a nature that, by being permanently united with the subject, it constitutes this subject in a primal act from which many operations subsequently proceed, and which goes under the name of *faculty.*

This is why I have said elsewhere that the *idea of being in general* is the *objective form* of our intellect ; whilst, on the other hand, when speaking of our body as felt by the fundamental feeling, I have called it the *matter* of that feeling, inasmuch as 'it is a permanent term of the primal act of our sensitivity, and devoid of activity in respect of the same act considered as complete.'

1011. The *matter* of the fundamental feeling has, however, a third and most notable characteristic. Not only is it, in respect of the fundamental feeling considered as complete, a term without activity, and simply with the *capacity* to offer itself thereto as a passive term, but this capacity itself, this *passive susceptiveness*, is very imperfect. I mean that there is in the *matter* a certain *inertia* whereby it impedes its receiving that state which the activity of the feeling could impart to it ; so that the feeling itself finds a restraint put on the fulness of its action.

Nor need any one say that, since this *inertia* opposes the feeling, it must therefore be an active force in respect of the feeling. For I would first of all observe that when there is question of an action whereby the thing acted upon is raised to a better condition than belongs to it by its own nature, then the circumstance of that thing yielding itself freely to the action is not absolutely necessary to the thing itself, but belongs only to its perfection.[1] The capacity to receive improvement is an intrinsic activity ; by the reason of contraries, therefore, the incapacity to be improved is a want of that activity—seminal as it were—of that recondite virtue which, if it does not exist, cannot be developed ; hence the absence of it places an obstacle to the perfection which might be com-

---

[1] Hence the thing could be without it, because a thing can exist without having attained to perfection (TRANSLATORS).

municated to the thing. The resistance, then, which the *matter* makes to the feeling is not a true—that is to say, an active—resistance ; it is simply incapacity, *inertia*. Nor are these reflections mere abstract subtilties ; they describe the *matter* of our fundamental feeling just as it presents itself to an attentive observation. Careful observers will find that their fundamental feeling does not diffuse itself over an extension, so to speak, void, but over an extension where it meets with certain obstructions and also, if one will have it so, with certain changes and violences, according to constant laws. These laws are (1) those which constitute the relation between the sensitive body (matter of the fundamental feeling) and the external bodies ; and (2) those which constitute the relation of the same sensitive body with the *Ego*, *i.e.* the feeling we have of ourselves.

But even more than to the perfection of the sensitive body let us attend to that of the fundamental feeling. This feeling would be more perfect in the same proportion as the body were found to yield itself up more perfectly to its control. If therefore we find that when the body happens to be altered for the worse, the feeling suffers in consequence, and any one wishes to say that this fact argues the presence of a force in the body, I shall not oppose him ; but he must, on his part, admit that in this case the force is only such as to make the feeling weaker. Now the feeling and its *matter* form together only one thing, only one faculty, as I have before observed. Consequently the force here referred to is the passive and imperfect part of this faculty, not the formal and perfect part ; and it is chiefly for this reason that our body in so far as felt subjectively by us is called the *matter* of the fundamental feeling.[1]

---

[1] We must carefully distinguish between the *principle* and the *term* of an act. However difficult of conception it may be, it is nevertheless an undeniable fact that the principle of the act may be *simple*, while its term is manifold or *extended*. Hence the extension in which the sensation diffuses itself with its term does not cause the *Ego* (which is the principle that feels) to be any the less simple, as I venture to think I have incontrovertibly proved elsewhere (672–691). This fact escaped the notice of Malebranche, and it was owing to this oversight that he did not see the possibility of our body communicating with the soul. In the famous controversy he had with Arnauld, the latter had the advantage of being able to press him with the following excellent observation,

1012. But here a difficulty suggests itself. In the course of this work I have described the body as a force acting upon the soul, and causing or exciting in it the fundamental feeling. How, then, can the *matter* of the fundamental feeling, which is no other than the body itself, be described here as *passive*, and even characterised by *inertia* in respect of the action of that feeling ?

My answer is this :—

In the first place, the *matter* of the fundamental feeling is not the body with all its properties. For in its matter the fundamental feeling does not perceive the body relatively to the special sensories, except in so far as it offers itself as a passive and inert term of the same feeling. The energy, therefore, which the body may have in producing the feeling is not included in the matter itself of the feeling. The following observations may help us to understand how this can be.

1013. A being which is acted upon by a force in a given way may thereby be itself drawn into two different kinds of act : (1) an act terminating in the very force which has excited and promoted it, so that the force becomes passive in respect to the same ; (2) an act terminating outside that force. We will consider the first of these two cases.

Can I not set a force in motion in such a manner that the action into which I have drawn it will recoil on myself? For

in which, however, we see the usual confusion between sensations and ideas, or rather between sensitive and intellectual perception. Arnauld writes thus :—

'Rien ne me paraît plus étrange que de dire que les corps sont trops grossiers, pour pouvoir être vus immédiatement par notre âme. Car on aurait raison d'alléguer la grossièreté et l'imperfection des corps, s'il s'agissait de les rendre *connaissans* . . . Mais quand il s'agit seulement *d'être connu*, que peut faire à cela l'imperfection des choses matérielles?' *Connaître* est sans doute une grande perfection en ce qui connaît ; . et ainsi ce qui est dans le plus bas degré de la nature intelligente est quelque chose sans comparaison de beaucoup plus grand et plus admirable, que tout ce qu'il y a de plus accompli dans la nature corporelle. Mais *être connu* n'est qu'une simple dénomination dans l'objet connu ; et il suffit pour cela de n'être pas un pur néant. Car il n'y a que le néant qui soit incapable d'être connu : et être connaissable, pour parler ainsi, est une propriété inséparable de l'être, aussi bien que d'être *un*, d'être *vrai*, et d'être *bon* ; ou plutôt c'est la même chose que d'être *vrai* (*Des vraies et des fausses idées*, ch. x.).

Properly speaking, the difficulty of Malebranche consisted more in explaining how bodies could be *sensitively perceived* than how they could become *objects of cognition*. Nevertheless the remarks of Arnauld may also, in part, hold good in respect of the sensations of a being at once sentient and intelligent.

example, a fowling-piece will sometimes inflict a terrible injury on the hand that has pulled the trigger. But this is much more applicable to a spiritual agent, which, as we know by experience, moves by a marvellous spontaneity. To set a spiritual substance in motion, then, there is more need of an occasion than of a *cause*, since the intrinsic energy of that substance breaks forth into spontaneous acts whenever the suitable occasion and conditions are posited. Hence there may be in the body a force which draws the spirit into the act of feeling, and at the same time this act (which is itself an energy) may recoil on the body as on its necessary term. Indeed, the laws according to which the spirit is first moved to the act of feeling are unknown to us; at least they are to me. Still, there is no absurdity in conjecturing that such laws exist, and that they emanate from the nature itself of the spirit. For in all the beings of the universe which fall under our experience we uniformly find these two things: (1) that in their operations they follow certain laws; and (2) that these laws are not imposed on them arbitrarily, but flow as consequences from their nature. Applying the same remark to the spirit, it is not unreasonable to think that the energy intrinsic to the nature of this being causes it to operate whenever the proper conditions for so doing are present. Now, as the analysis of the fundamental feeling shows, a necessary condition is that the body be fittingly organised. It might be, therefore, that, given the body so disposed, its union with the spirit, and the feeling which results therefrom, should follow in virtue of a law belonging to the nature of the spirit itself.

What may be set down as certain, however, is that the body may be passive in respect of the fundamental feeling, notwithstanding that it was the first to originate and promote the same, or certainly was a necessary condition thereof. Now it is only when viewed under this aspect that the body is called *matter* of the fundamental feeling. The energy which moves the spirit to feel is the *principle* of the feeling; the body which the feeling invests is its matter as well as its term. Although, therefore, by consulting our consciousness,

we can discover that in our fundamental feeling we are passive—that is, acted upon by an external force—-nevertheless
this force cannot, as acting on us, be the *matter* of that feeling.
This may help us properly to estimate the value of the distinction which the ancients sometimes made between *matter*
and *body*.

1014. In the second place, I have to observe that, although
the body is capable of receiving in itself the energy by which
it operates on the spirit, nevertheless, ordinarily speaking, this
recondite energy is noticed less than the other qualities of
bodies, and principally their *extension* and their *inertia*.

The better to understand this fact, it will be well to recall
to mind the following propositions which I have already
demonstrated.

(1) The various ways in which we perceive bodies give us
different perceptions of them, so that the identical bodies seem
to be *different beings*.

(2) The reason of this seeming difference is (*a*) partly
because our perception of bodies is mixed up with a good deal
of the subjective element ; and as this mixture takes place in
various forms, it gives as a result various *proximate terms* to
our perception ; and (*b*) partly because by one mode of perception certain properties are discovered in a body which
remain hidden when the same body is perceived in another
mode ; hence that body seems a different being. Thus, in
perceiving an external body by means of our sensories we only
find in it certain qualities which are, so to speak, blind, and
do not perceive the aptitude which the corporeal substance has
to serve as matter of the fundamental feeling ; this aptitude
being discoverable only by means of that feeling.

(3) Hence the word *body* comes to vary its meaning,
according as our thought connects it, with what we perceive
in one mode, or with what we perceive in another.

(4) The more common meaning is taken from what we
perceive in external bodies through the five sensories, because
this kind of *perception* is easy of advertence, whereas it is only
with great difficulty that the perception effected through the
fundamental feeling, or even through the subjective adven-

titious sensations, can be *adverted to* and kept *distinctly* before the mind.[1]

By these considerations we can see the reason why the popular meaning of the word *body* does not, commonly speaking, include that recondite force by which our body acts on our spirit, and by reacting on which the spirit unites the body to itself. This reason lies in what takes place in our adventitious sensations, whence is mostly derived that idea which we express by the word *body*. Let us reflect on it for a moment.

1015. By acting on any of our organs, the external body simply produces a change or, to say it in general, a motion in the sensitive form of that organ. Given that motion, the spirit feels a new sensation. But in feeling this sensation, it does not put forth an energy altogether new. By the law which has been explained above (705, &c.), the spirit felt its body until now 'in the sensitive state in which it actually was.' This living body, through being now acted upon by the external body, has undergone a change in its sensitive state. The sensitive principle, therefore, following up its action in accordance with the same law, feels the new state of the organ affected. Clearly, there has not been here any radically new action of our body on the spirit. There has only been an action between two bodies—that is to say, an action of the external body on ours ; and that action has not been governed by any special law, but by the same mechanical, physical and chemical laws which are common to all bodies, even inanimate. The spirit therefore has not, in this fact, united itself with any new body ; no new body has acted on it ; the previous action of its own body on it has not been submitted to any new experiment. From this we see that all the action of bodies which can be perceived and noticed in our acquired sensations is purely *external*—namely, such as external bodies exercise on one another. As, then, these sensations do not contain in them that internal and permanent action which our

---

[1] It should furthermore be observed that with our external organs we perceive primary qualities and necessary to bodies, though of little use for making us understand the nature of the *corporeal principle* (855, 856).

body exercises on the spirit, so it comes to pass that the word *body* is not, generally speaking, associated with this species of action, but only with the mutual extrasubjective action of bodies conformably to mechanical, physical and chemical laws. Now the effect of this exclusion is, that the word *body* as used in ordinary discourse does not awaken in us the thought of any activity on the spirit.

1016. In the third place, it should be very attentively considered that that *activity* which we have ascribed to the body does not emanate from the nature itself of the body taken in the popular sense. This fact alone suffices to justify the common practice of not extending the meaning of the word *body* to the said activity, and particularly in connection with our spirit.

1017. To see this, let us examine the character of the action of bodies, whether on one another or on our spirit itself.

I. *Motion* is not essential to bodies ; each body receives it from without. Now, it seems quite certain that the action of external bodies on our organs is wholly due to motion. *Resistance* is nothing but the distribution of motion in the several parts of a body. *Cohesion* is simply the fulfilment of a law determining the number of parts amongst which the motion must be divided. Therefore such action as external bodies are seen to exercise on our own is an activity, not proper and essential to those bodies, but coming to them from without. Hence, in respect of this power of motion bodies are really *passive* : they simply receive and then communicate what they have received (motion).

1018. II. Let us come to the action of our body on the spirit. It seems evident that this action also is not comprised in the nature of body (extrasubjectively considered), and that therefore the body receives it from a principle external to itself. If the energy which shows itself in acting on the spirit were of the essence of a body, all bodies would necessarily have to be conceived as animate. And yet no such property as animation is included in the common concept of *body*. Although, therefore, our body *acts* on the spirit, it does not do so by an active principle intrinsic to its nature, belonging to it for the sole reason that it is a body, but by a received activity. Consequently, as regards this activity, the body is both *inert* and *passive* ; it receives and does not give.[1]

In the fourth place, the following reflection seems to me of more importance than all those I have offered until now :—

I have said that the *body*, according to the concept usually formed of it, has not, in its nature as body, the energy of acting on the spirit, but receives it. Now might not such energy come to it from the spirit itself? Have we not seen that 'It is possible for one being to excite in another an activity of such a character as to recoil precisely upon itself' (1013)? Cannot this observation, which we have applied to the action of bodies, be applied with much greater force to the action of the spirit?

1019. The study I have made of this question induces me to look upon the following as a probable result :—

I. The human spirit is bound in its action by certain conditions. One of them, for a certain species of actions, is the existence of a body constructed with a suitable organisation. So far no action is as yet requisite on the part of the body, but only a given state, which the body cannot give to itself, but must receive from without.

II. As soon as the spirit finds itself suited with a perfectly organised body, it would seem that the spirit, having now the condition necessary for performing the species of action aforesaid, acts conjointly with this body, and constitutes it in that energy which is called *life*, and through which the body acquires the ultimate properties of living bodies.

III. This energy received by the body is such as in its turn to react on the spirit, and draw it into the act of the fundamental feeling.

IV. The fundamental feeling pervades the body and makes it its *matter*—that is, its seat, its mode of being, its extension.

V. The body in this state of *matter* of the fundamental feeling retains some of its *inertia*, and, as a consequence,

---

[1] From this S. Thomas draws the demonstration that the soul is a thing different from the body (*S. I.*, lxxv. 1).

remains subject to the external action of other bodies. Hence, given a change in the *matter felt*, the fundamental feeling also undergoes a change, not indeed by reason of a new action of the *matter* upon the spirit, but because the spirit is bound to terminate its act in its matter, which is the passive term of that act.

PART VI.

CONCLUSION.

CHAPTER I.

EPILOGUE OF THE THEORY.

1020. The original faculties of the soul are two : a sense for *Particulars* and a sense for *Universals*.[1]

The sense for particulars constitutes the faculty which is more commonly called *Sensitivity*; and the sense for universals constitutes the faculty which is more commonly called *Intellect*.[2]

1021. Every faculty is a particular Primal Act, and is constituted by a term essentially inseparable from it ; which term is called *Matter* if in respect of the faculty it is *passive*, whilst it is called *Form* if in respect of the faculty it is *impas-*

---

[1] I have already explained what is to be understood by a *Universal* (No. 107, &c.). We must not suppose that any one thing can be *universal in itself*: each thing, in so far as it is, is singular and determinate. A *universal*, therefore, simply means an entity of such a nature that we can by means of it know many, in fact an indefinitely great number of, things. Consequently *universality* is nothing but a *relation* and, properly speaking, can only belong to *ideas*; for, as we have seen, it is through *ideas* that we are able to cognise an indefinite number of things, and under this aspect each *idea* is also called a *species*. It would indeed seem at first sight that there are other things besides ideas which may in this sense be called *universal*. Thus a *portrait* seems to be *universal*, because it is representative of all the persons whom it resembles. But this is a mistake. Universality does not belong to the portrait considered in its own entity, but is an addition made to it by an *idea*. It is through the *idea* of the portrait that the mind compares that portrait with the persons and finds a similarity between them and it. This similarity is not in the material portrait itself, but in that *one* idea by means of which the said comparison was made. The unity of an idea is, therefore, what constitutes the similarity possible between things (No. 177).

[2] I have reduced the faculty of the intellect to a *primal sense* (Nos. 553–558).

sive and *object*, so that its presence places the subject in that act which constitutes the faculty (1006, &c.).

The essential term of sensitivity is its *matter*; the essential term of the intellect is its *object* and *form* (1010 and 480-485).

1022. Sensitivity is either *external* or *internal.* The *external* has for its essential term the body, extended corporeal matter. The *internal* has not a term distinct from itself, and moreover it has for a distinct term the idea of *being in general* (473-479 and 630-672).

Hence the faculty of *external sensitivity* consists simply in the fundamental feeling of our own body (721-728).

The faculty of *internal sensitivity* consists in the feeling of *Ourselves* (692-720).

The faculty of the *intellect* consists in the act by which we intue *being in general* (480-485).

1023. If the *matter* of sensitivity is taken away, the *sensitive being* no longer remains. If the *form* of the intellect is taken away, this faculty ceases to exist, but there still remains the concept of a *sensitive being.* Hence *being in general* is a true object apprehended by the intellect and distinct from the sensitive being ; but the term of sensitivity is a constitutive of the sensitive being itself, and as it cannot be conceived distinct therefrom, so it cannot be entitled to the name of *object* (1010, &c., and 409-429).

1024. Intuition requires something distinct from the intueing subject, and is therefore essentially objective. Sensation, on the other hand, requires only a *matter* (449*n.* and 742-752). Hence the intellect is *a primal act of intuition* ; but sensitivity is only a *primal act of feeling.*

1025. In our fundamental feeling all these faculties exist before beginning to operate—that is, the feeling of ourselves conjointly with our body (sensitivity) and the intellect.

This innermost feeling, perfectly *one*, joins together the sensitivity and the intellect. It has moreover an energy, a spiritual insight as it were (rationality), with which it sees the relation between the two. This function constitutes the *Primitive Synthesis* (528-555).

If the energy which springs from the intimate unity of

the fundamental feeling is considered in a more general way—
that is, in so far as the *Ego* has the capability of seeing *relations* generally—then that energy is the *Reason*, and the *primitive synthesis* becomes the first *function* of this faculty (622,
and 480–482).

If that same energy is regarded purely with reference to
the virtue it has of effecting the union of a predicate with a
subject, it then takes the name of *faculty of Judgment* (338).

1026. The *primitive synthesis* consists in that judgment by
which the *Reason* acquires *Intellectual Perception.*

We do not pass to any operation whatever, unless drawn to
it by some stimulus or motor.

The *external sensitivity* is the faculty first drawn to its
operations, and its stimuli are external bodies acting on our
organs (514, &c.).

The *external sensitivity* excited by these stimuli wakes up
our consciousness to the fact that we are being subjected to a
passivity proceeding, not from our own body, but from a body
detached from us. Then it is that the new sensation, namely,
the modification of our corporeal fundamental feeling considered as the term of an external action, becomes *sensitive
perception*, whereas till then it was purely sensation and that
fundamental perception by which the soul is united with the
body (630–691).

1027. Wherefore the *first material part* of human cognitions supplied by sensitivity consists in :—

(1) The feeling by which the *Ego* perceives itself conjointly
with its body (fundamental feeling).

(2) The sensations, *i.e.* the modifications of this feeling.

(3) The sensitive perceptions of external bodies.

1028. Through the reason considering these things in
relation to *being* in general and forming *intellectual perceptions*,
these same things—in themselves purely particular affections
of our spirit—have *universality* added to them ; and hence,
under this aspect, the reason is denominated the *faculty of
Universalisation.* To this peculiar faculty belong all the
direct acts of the reason (490–500).

The *reflex acts* belong to *reflection*, which is another *function* of the reason (487–489).

1029. All the acts of our spirit in so far as it is rational, and the terms of these acts, constitute the objects of reflection. Sometimes, however, the name of *reflection* is given, though somewhat improperly, to the direct application of the understanding to the sensations (511*n*.). The objects of reflection therefore consist :—

(1) In that act by which the *Ego* has intuition of being in general.

(2) In the acts of the faculty of universalisation.

(3) In the acts of reflection, and in its terms or results.

Reflection has two operations, *Synthesis* and *Analysis*; it decomposes and it unites (490, &c.).

To *analysis* belongs the faculty of *Abstraction* (494, &c.).

1030. The external stimuli move the *external sensitivity*; the physical instincts move in the first instance the *Imagination*, and awaken the faculty of *Universalisation*.

The corporeal images awaken the faculty of dividing ideas from perceptions.

Language alone, received from society, can draw into its act the faculty of *Abstract Ideas*, and thus give to man the dominion over his own powers, the use of his *free-will* (487, &c.).

1031. Lastly, when through the abstract ideas supplied by language man has acquired the full use of his *free-will*, or the dominion over his own powers, he can set all those powers in motion, and enter freely on that road of progress wherein the various human faculties can be indefinitely developed.

CHAPTER II.

IN WHAT STATE THE AUTHOR FOUND THE DOCTRINE OF THE ORIGIN OF IDEAS.

1032. There is a *popular knowledge* and a *philosophic knowledge*. This distinction has been very accurately marked by S. Thomas.

The reader cannot fail to have noticed the relation in which this work stands to the *popular knowledge*. He must have seen that it is not, as it does not profess to be, anything more than the development of a truth which is universally known and continually alluded to in common conversation—the truth that *man has in him the light of reason*.

When occasion served, I endeavoured also to show its relation to *philosophic knowledge*. Whatever appeared to me consonant with truth in the philosophers who preceded me, I took note of it, and was glad to turn it to account. But in order to do greater justice to those writers, I will now add a few words by way of conclusion.

1033. Several of them caught a glimpse of the importance of the *idea of being in general,* and of its intimate and essential conjunction with the human mind. In modern philosophy I find that Malebranche was one of those who saw this best, as the following passage from his *Recherche de la Vérité* (Book III. ch. viii.) will show: 'La présence claire, intime, nécessaire . . . de l'être, sans restriction particulière . . . de l'être en général, à l'esprit de l'homme, agit sur lui plus fortement que la présence de tous les objets finis. Il est impossible qu'il se défasse entièrement de cette idée générale de l'être.' And what seems not a little remarkable is that this illustrious follower of Des Cartes should have perceived that to think of *being* is more essential to our mind than to think of ourselves—a truth not observed by his master, and directly opposed to the whole foundation of the Cartesian philosophy ;[1] for Malebranche subjoins : 'On peut bien être quelque temps sans penser à soi-même, mais on ne saurait, ce me semble, subsister un moment sans penser à l'être ; et dans le même temps qu'on croit ne penser à rien, on est nécessairement plein de l'idée vague et générale de l'être.'[2]

Neither was he ignorant of the objection which is so commonly made by shallow thinkers and tiros in philosophy, who, having as yet paid very little attention to what passes within themselves, are ever ready to say : 'If we were continually thinking of being we should certainly know it.' He replies to this objection precisely as I have done, in concert with all antiquity. He shows that the objection proceeds from deficient observation, and from confounding together two facts which stand quite distinct in our consciousness—namely, (1) the act of our mind, (2) the advertence to that

---

[1] Des Cartes has justly been charged with *petitio principii* in his manner of establishing the criterion of certainty (*Principles*, &c. Part I.). First he said : 'Clear perception is the criterion of certainty ;' and by means of this *criterion* he found the existence of God. And then he said : 'Clear perception might deceive me, but in the existence of God I have an infallible security of the truth of that perception, because it (the perception) comes from God, Who cannot deceive me.' It would seem incredible that a man of such marvellous abilities as Des Cartes should not have perceived the manifest vicious circle contained in this manner of reasoning. But the more evident and inevitable the error in the Cartesian system, the stronger is the proof it affords of the erroneousness of the system itself. Des Cartes saw that the perception of his subjective self stood in need of something else, in order to be authoritative, and that it did not necessarily contain infallibility in it. This support, which is undoubtedly needed by the subjective

perception, is *the idea of being*, which has essentially in it *objectivity* and *necessity*. But Des Cartes, not knowing this truth, had recourse to the idea of God, thus erring in two ways : (1) by deducing from the *perception* what was to make the perception itself valid in the eyes of reason ; which was a vicious circle ; (2) by having recourse to the idea of the *First* and *Subsistent Being*, instead of that of *common being*. This second error suggested to him his *a priori* demonstration of the existence of God, which, in the manner he presents it, is a blunder, as I have said, because it rests entirely on the ambiguity of taking being in a purely ideal form, for the Subsistent Being itself. Nevertheless the efforts and errors of Des Cartes prove the necessity of the *idea of being*, for which I contend, quite as much as his authority would have done, had be openly expressed himself to that effect.

[2] This is precisely the observation which had been made by the author of the *Itinerarium*, as we have formerly seen.

act. Here are his words, following shortly after those I have last quoted :—

' Mais parce que les choses qui nous sont fort ordinaires, et qui ne nous touchent point, ne réveillent point l'esprit avec quelque force, et ne l'obligent point à faire quelque réflexion sur elle, cette idée de l'être, quelque grande, vaste, réelle et positive qu'elle soit, nous est si familière et nous touche si peu, que nous croyons quasi ne la point voir ; que nous n'y faisons point de réflexion ; que nous jugeons ensuite qu'elle a peu de réalité, et qu'elle n'est formée que de l'assemblage confus de toutes les idées particulières ; quoiqu'au contraire ce soit dans elle seule et par elle seule que nous apercevons tous les êtres en particulier.' How near does not this man seem to discovering the clue out of the intricate labyrinth of ideas ! He has it in his hand, and does not see that he has it. Instead of saying with S. Thomas that the idea of being is a created light, he will have it to be God Himself : hence his error. Up to this point he had proceeded with a keen observation of human nature, and with a faultless logic ; now he forsakes his method, and by a stroke of the imagination cancels the immense distance which separates the creature from the Creator. But had he not said that the idea of being is a *vague* idea ? that it is the idea of *being with no particular restrictions*, that is, *indeterminate* ? of *being in general* ?[1] Now the idea of God is not vague. God is indeed infinite, but not *indeterminate*. Lastly, He is not the *being which is common* to all things, and much less *being in general*, but He is the First Being, perfectly distinct from all else, complete, outside of all genera. This distinction between universal ideal being and subsistent being is a truth preserved in the deposit of the Christian traditions which so eminent a man ought neither to have been ignorant of nor neglected.

1034. It is well known that the system of Malebranche

[1] S. Thomas and S. Bonaventure say with perfect propriety of language, that God is not the ' common being,' but the ' Supreme and Absolute Being.' It is easy to perceive that Malebranche had imbibed from his age a spirit of more or less disesteem for the authors of the Scholastic period, and, I would almost say, for all authors a little more ancient than Des Cartes, excepting S. Augustine, from whom Des Cartes also had drawn.

was forestalled in France by Père L. Thommassin.   Contemporaneously with the latter, Padre Giovenale, of Anaunia, in the Italian Tyrol, was thinking out a similar theory.   This learned Capuchin, but little known to fame,[1] published a book in Latin, wherein he propounded the very system which, under the elegant pen of Malebranche, made so much stir in the world of letters ; and I must say, for the sake of truth, that, on comparing the two works, I found that Padre Giovenale has presented the doctrine with much greater fulness and moderation.   This author shows himself duly sensible of the difficulties which I have pointed out against Malebranche, and does not pass them over.   He restricts and adapts the meaning of his expressions so as not to contradict the great tradition of Catholic truth, and proceeds on the track beaten by the Fathers, seeking continually to reconcile on this point S. Augustine with S. Thomas.

1035.   And, before all these, the Platonists who once more flourished in Tuscany under the great shadow of the Medici, had, on the lines traced out by the most ancient philosophy, risen to a clear apprehension of the importance of the idea of being.   Marsilio Ficino, who may be called the head of that school, teaches clearly that the notion of being is innate in all men ; and the reason he gives in proof of it is very noteworthy.   He says : ' All men *judge* that a certain thing does not exist at all, that another thing exists in a more imperfect way, and again another in a less imperfect way.'[2]

---

[1] The work of the Tyrolese Capuchin was printed in Augsburg under the title of *Solis intelligentiæ cui non succedit nox, lumen indeficiens ac inextinguibile illuminans omnem hominem venientem in hunc mundum*, etc., *per P. Juvenalem Anauniensem Ord. Capuccinorum. Augustæ Vindelicorum, Typis Simonis Utschneideri Reverendiss. ac Altiss. Principis et Episcopi Augustani typographi, Anno* 1686.   It is singular that Padre Giovenale died in the same year as Malebranche, 1713.   Possibly this work was the first seed of those doctrines which were subsequently developed and illustrated by the two Fathers Ercolano and Filibert, of the Reformed Franciscans.   Those who wish to know more about Padre Giovenale may refer to the *Biblioteca Tirolese* of Jacopo Tartarotti, augmented by Todeschini, Venice, 1733; also the *Memorie Storiche della Città e Territorio di Trento*, by Conte Francesco Barbacovi, vol. i.

[2] On this subject the book of Cardinal de Cusa, entitled *De Apice Theoriæ*, deserves pre-eminently to be read. Père Thommassin drew from Ficino, and quotes him in support of his opinions. Both these able men hold the following doctrine, which agrees perfectly with that which I have set forth :—' *Being* is so resplendent that there is no possibility of thinking that it is not.' 'Through being we know other things, but being is

Now the need of the idea of being in order to *judge* was precisely the way by which we, in this work, came to see the indispensable necessity of this idea as concreated with us, and antecedent to all other ideas. It is, however, to be regretted that Ficino did not undertake to develop this thought, full of fecundity though it was, and that he attached to it no more weight than to so many others of comparatively less importance. Moreover, the Platonists generally fall into that same confusion which I have noted above, between the idea of 'common being' or 'potential being,' and the idea of the 'First and most Actual Being,' thus transforming human reason into the Divine Essence.

1036. The truths of which I am speaking were not unknown to the Schoolmen, as is evidenced by the many passages I have quoted from them. It does not appear, however, that they applied themselves much to examine the *connection* of the truths which they knew ; and for this reason they did not succeed in giving to the system on the origin of ideas all that simplicity and precision of which it stood in need. Hence for many of them our *first concepts* issued from a source recondite and obscure, or which at the very most they described vaguely and in metaphorical language ; or else they declared those cognitions to be a kind of instinct. So did Dante understand the Scholastic doctrine, stating it in the following lines :—

> ' Ogni forma sustanzial, che setta
> È da materia, ed è con lei unita,
> Specifica virtude ha in sè colletta ;

known through itself ' (Thomass. *Tract. de Deo Deique propriet,* S. I. ch. xiv., art. 1). Cardinal Gerdil expressed the same opinion in his celebrated work against Locke and in defence of Malebranche. What escaped the notice of all these authors, as it seems to me, is the great distinction between *being in potentia* (idea, essence of being), and *being in act* (see 530, &c.). It is by means of this distinction that S. Thomas (*S. T.* q. II. art. 1) demonstrates that God is not among the things known through themselves. They say : ' Being cannot be conceived as devoid of being,

therefore being exists.' There is here an ambiguity in the term *being.* If by *being* you mean *ideal being,* certainly you cannot think it *except as* being, and necessarily so ; but you must not confound *ideal being* with *subsistent being.* Nevertheless the reasoning of Ficino and of P. Thommassin—which is also that of Des Cartes and S. Anselm, and of which we find traces in S. Augustine and many other ancient writers—contains a deep element of truth whereof I reserve the exposition for its proper place.

La qual senza operar non è sentita,
  Nè si dimostra mai che per effetto,
  Come per verde fronda in pianta vita :
Però, là onde vegna lo 'ntelletto
  Delle prime notizie, uom non sape,
  E de' primi appetibili l' affetto,
Che sono in voi, sì come studio in ape
  Di far lo mele : e questa prima voglia
  Merto di lode, o di biasmo non cape.' [1]

1037. And that our first concepts spring from a source without light, from a blind instinct, from a law of human nature, and nothing else, is the doctrine to which all modern philosophy has at last reduced itself, from Reid to Galluppi. For Reid refers these cognitions to a mysterious suggestion of nature ; Kant, even while going so far as to restore the use of scholastic phraseology, attributes them to certain subjective forms belonging to the same nature ; and these two opinions have been revived of late in France, where two opposite parties seem bent on deriving man's first cognitions from a single principle of blind and instinctive faith. Lastly, in Italy, Galluppi, although he has confuted with much acuteness the errors of all these writers, still retains the denomination of *subjective* for the ideas of *unity*, of *identity*, and such like, as though they issued from and owed their existence to the thinking subject himself. But, if the *first concepts* are not wholly independent of the subject, and have not an objective existence, then I do not hesitate to say that the validity of human knowledge is shaken to its very foundations, that certainty no longer exists, and that scepticism, while, on the one hand, an impossible system, becomes, on the other,

---

[1] *Purgatory*, c. xviii. Carey translates thus :—

'Spirit, substantial form, with matter join'd,
Not in confusion mix'd, hath in itself
Specific virtue of that union born,
Which is not felt except it work, nor prov'd
But through effect, as vegetable life
By the green leaf. From whence his intellect

Deduced its primal notices of things,
Man therefore knows not, or his appetites
Their first affections ; such in you, as zeal
In bees to gather honey ; at the first,
Volition, meriting nor blame nor praise.'

The simile of the bees is taken from Aristotle (*Metaphysic*, i. 10).

inevitable. Wherefore to place human knowledge and human certainty on a firm foundation, I do not see any other way than to rest the whole of our cognitions on an object which is always before us, is necessary, universal, and independent of us and of all created things ; and this is the theory of the innate idea of being which I have endeavoured to set forth in this volume.

CHAPTER III.

THE WAY BY WHICH THE STUDIOUS MAY MASTER THE THEORY EXPOUNDED ABOVE ON THE ORIGIN OF IDEAS.

1038. Nevertheless, it is not so easy to understand well the theory expounded above, nor can this be attained by a mere perusal of the present volume. It is furthermore necessary that the reader should attentively observe human nature in his own self. Unless he does this, the probability is that he will think he has perfectly mastered the theory, when in reality he has only misunderstood my opinions, and formed of them a concept wholly at variance with the truth.

For this reason, I think it will not be useless to point out here at the end an easy way, by following which any one who cares for such studies may surely arrive at a satisfactory result.

This way consists in carefully taking note of four points, on which the whole power of the student's mind should be concentrated. Let him but master thoroughly these four points, and he will find the rest of the doctrine easy of comprehension.

Nor must it be supposed that these four points are either the most difficult or the most mysterious that can be met with in the study of human nature; nevertheless they are such as will ensure one's assent to the most marvellous truths. I will explain. Men do not refuse credence to a truth of fact, even though the fact be inexplicable and mysterious, provided they have by their own steady observation made themselves perfectly sure of its existence. Now the four points I speak of are truths which, once well understood, place us in a position to be able to fix our attention even on things that are most recondite and hidden within the intelligent spirit, and to observe them in a manner which leaves no room for doubt.

1039. The four points, then, are four distinctions which may be taken as the test whereby to tell whether one has mastered the above theory of the origin of ideas or not. They are as follows :—

(1) The distinction between *sensation* and *sensitive perception* (740–748).

(2) The distinction between the simple *idea* of a thing, and the *judgment on the subsistence* of that thing (402–409).

(3) The distinction between *sensitive perception* and *intellectual perception* (961, &c.).

(4) The distinction between an *act of the spirit* and *advertence* to that act ; for example, between feeling and adverting to the feeling (548, &c.).

Now, whosoever has succeeded in fully grasping these distinctions, which are so many facts of the human spirit, and in making himself familiar with the use and application of them, has certainly comprehended, or cannot fail to comprehend, the genuine nature of the Theory I have done my best to explain in clear and simple language, without, however, forgetting that, although my words may perhaps serve to put the reader on the road to truth, they never can infuse into his mind the truth itself.

END OF THE SECOND VOLUME.

LONDON : PRINTED BY
SPOTTISWOODE AND CO., NEW-STREET SQUARE
AND PARLIAMENT STREET

www.ingramcontent.com/pod-product-compliance
Lightning Source LLC
Chambersburg PA
CBHW022129020426
42334CB00015B/819